A SHEARWATER BOOK

Kitchen Literacy

Kitchen Literacy

How We Lost Knowledge

of Where Food Comes From

and Why We Need to Get It Back

Ann Vileisis

With a new Afterword

ISLANDPRESS / Shearwater Books
Washington | Covelo | London

A Shearwater Book
Published by Island Press

Copyright © 2008 Ann Vileisis

All rights reserved under International and Pan-American
Copyright Conventions. No part of this book may be reproduced
in any form or by any means without permission in writing from
the publisher: Island Press, 1718 Connecticut Ave., NW,
Suite 300 Washington, DC 20009.

SHEARWATER BOOKS is a trademark of The Center for Resource Economics.

Library of Congress Cataloging-in-Publication data.
Vileisis, Ann.
Kitchen literacy : how we lost knowledge of where food comes from
and why we need to get it back / by Ann Vileisis.
p. cm.
Includes bibliographical references and index.
ISBN-13: 978-1-59726-144-9 (cloth : alk. paper)
ISBN-10: 1-59726-144-0 (cloth : alk. paper)
1. Cookery, American—History. 2. Food habits—United States—History.
3. Diet—United States—History. I. Title.
TX645.V55 3007
641.5973—dc22   2007025781
British Cataloguing-in-Publication data available.

The paperback edition carries the ISBN 978-1-59726-717-5

Printed on recycled, acid-free paper ✪

Design by David Bullen

Manufactured in the United States of America

10 9 8 7 6 5 4 3 2 1

To my mother, Janet Taylor,

and my grandmothers, Phyllis Fleming and Vita Vileisis,

for teaching me about the ways of the kitchen

and for nourishing my curiosity and creativity always.

CONTENTS

Know thyself.

SOCRATES

You are what you eat.

often attributed to
BRILLAT-SAVARIN

Not to know at large of things remote
From use, obscure and subtle, but to know
That which before us lies in daily life,
Is the prime wisdom.

MILTON

(Epigram in *Mrs. Lincoln's
Boston Cooking School Cookbook*, 1902)

Kitchen
Literacy

Missing Stories

Has it ever occurred to you just how odd it is that we know so little about what we eat? Each day we feast on cereal, bread, salad, soup, chicken, cheese, apples, ice cream, and more. Over the course of our lives, each of us has eaten thousands of different foods. We have tasted their saltiness and sweetness, crunched their crispness, chewed their fleshiness, swallowed them, and incorporated their nutriment into our bones. Yet despite this biologically intimate and everyday physical connection, most of us have little idea where our foods come from, who raised them, and what went into making them.

The absurdity of this situation struck me about ten years ago. The news was rife with stories about how large-scale food production harmed health and the environment: pathogens such as *Salmonella* and *E. coli* had become more prevalent in meat and eggs raised under crowded factory-farm conditions; pesticides used to grow foods were contaminating drinking water and harming the health of farmworkers and their children; agricultural chemicals were causing declines in amphibian and bird populations; the cod fishery was collapsing; and the fungicide methyl bromide, used in growing strawberries, was even linked to the erosion of the earth's ozone layer. I began to wonder, were these the berries and eggs that I bought?

As I pushed my shopping cart through the supermarket aisles, questions rose insistently in my mind: How were my eggs raised? Who grew my tomatoes? Where did my fish come from? What about the milk? The colorful boxes, cans, and jars that had long appeared familiar and comforting now looked cryptic. Each product, I realized, was the culmination of some hidden story that I — and most of my fellow shoppers — had never bothered to consider. Everything we ate had a story, but we didn't know any of them.

I was just starting to grasp that choices I made about what to buy in the supermarket had punch and bite — in real places and in real people's lives. Yet when I shopped, these matters had rarely before come to mind. A much narrower set of criteria had always guided my decisions. When picking tomatoes, for example, I'd rather unconsciously considered their appearance, firmness, price, and gratifyingly low caloric content, along with the culinary possibilities of salads or sauces. I'd never considered where the tomatoes had come from, how they were grown, and who did the work of raising them.

Now I started to wonder: Why did I consider some things but not others? Why did I *think* the way I did about my food? I began to have vague misgivings about what might be happening beyond the scope of my awareness, yet it was difficult to take responsibility when the whole supermarket system seemed to make it almost impossible for me — or for any of us — to know about the origins of our foods.

I was certainly curious about the stories behind my milk, eggs, and tomatoes, but even more, I was drawn to larger questions: How on earth did we get into the modern situation where we know so little about what we eat and yet regard it as entirely normal? How was it that basic ignorance about foods had become truly the norm in our culture, and what difference has it made?

That's what this book is about.

To FIND the answers to my questions, I looked to history. By keeping my bead on what America's home cooks have known and not known about their foods, I began to track the gulf in understanding that rapidly grew over time as distance between farms and kitchens widened.

Two hundred years ago, most Americans knew a lot more about what they ate in a direct, firsthand, rooted-in-the-earth way because most had an actual hand in growing a sizable share of their foods. As America went

H

from being a nation of farmers to being one of workers and consume
growing numbers of city dwellers had to grapple with procuring ai
cooking foods in new ways. Over the course of only a few generations, we
went from knowing particular places and specific stories behind our
foods' origins to instead knowing very little in an enormous and anonymous food system.

Those who have written about food history have dropped clues about
this cognitive shift as they've chronicled how Americans adopted new
products, new nutritional understanding, and new culinary practices in
the dynamic social context of urbanization and ethnic diversification.
And those who have written trenchant critiques of America's modern
agriculture have generally regarded the separation of consumers from
producers as a lamentable side effect of a much larger industrial transformation of America's economy, landscape, and culture.

Yet as I began to wrestle with my own food choices, what intrigued me
most was the uncharted terrain in between those other histories and
analyses. I wanted to home in on how people's thinking had changed as
the experience of eating became wholly separate from that of raising and
producing foods. How had our mental habits as shoppers, cooks, and
eaters evolved toward the out-of-sight, out-of-mind approach that I'd
recognized in myself and in others?

In seeking to understand this drift toward indifference, I found an
important clue in the work of anthropologist Claude Lévi-Strauss. In
the late 1960s, he made the perceptive suggestion that food must be just
as "good to think" in a cultural sense as it is to eat in a nutritional sense.[1]
The idea that foods must be appealing in our minds as well as in our
mouths becomes particularly illuminating when considered through
the lens of history. As foods were changed to meet the demands of
America's rapidly urbanizing society—often in ways that did not at first
appeal to many people—the mental framework we consumers used to
understand food was invariably stretched and fudged to accommodate
those changes. At the same time, what constituted a home cook's competency was also radically transformed. By investigating these shifting
frameworks—the defining and redefining of kitchen literacy that went
hand in hand with industrialization—we can better grasp how and why

the more shadowy and unappetizing context of our foods' origins was gradually whittled away from the ken of what we know about what we eat. We can also begin to discern some of the far-reaching implications of this subtle but unmistakable drift in our everyday way of thinking.

THIS HISTORY begins in a late eighteenth-century kitchen, exploring the day-to-day work of one woman who depended on a substantial body of traditional knowledge to feed her family. Martha Ballard knew specific, intimate details of the foods she cooked: the age and sex of the animal that became her roast lamb, the garden stories of her knobby potatoes, the contours of the cornfields that supplied her bread flour, and the muscle it took to transform raw ingredients into satisfying meals. Martha and most other women of her time knew where much of their food came from and how it was made.

Following the dominant urbanizing trend, this story next takes us into city markets and then grocery stores to explore how the kind of first-hand knowledge Martha possessed was upended and transformed over the course of the nineteenth century. At first, most rural transplants to the city expected to know the same things they had always known about their foods—the places, particulars, and stories of their foods' provenance. In early city markets, shoppers could still pinch a goose's webbed foot, look a fish in the eye, or talk with a farmer. But before long, the scale, complexity, and anonymity of the emerging food supply system made such awareness impossible as fewer and fewer people with more and more machines delivered food products from farther and farther away—especially after the transcontinental railroad linked the coasts in 1869.

Because the lengthening food chain was plagued by problems of adulteration, particularly in the case of factory-made foods, late nineteenth-century women did not readily welcome these new products into their kitchens. Some factory foods challenged a cook's traditional means of appraising ingredients with her senses: cans concealed their contents with tin armoring; oleomargarine with artificial coloring effectively mimicked butter. Moreover, as America's food system industrialized with the logic of mass production, the very idea of knowing where foods came from and how they were made became less appealing. As food production became more abstruse, a newly emerging mass media cut its teeth by helping to ease upper- and middle-class Americans into accepting new ways of shopping, cooking, and eating.

It took a relentless legion of admen and home economists about five decades to convince America's skeptical homemakers to adopt the new products and new ways to think and "know" about foods. Over the course of these decades, what had once constituted valued knowledge passed on from mother to daughter was rejected and deemed irrelevant, while what had first been mocked as ignorance was eventually elevated to a desirable and respected status. For example, knowing about the lives of animals that became meat had been considered essential kitchen lore until the 1880s, but then the big Chicago meatpacking plants with their tidy cuts and wrappers made this knowledge obsolete and memories of it repugnant. Before long, as the barnyard was distanced from the kitchen, ignorance about all farm animals became typical and even a matter of prestige. Through the same period, knowledge of brand names, which had seemed at first rather trivial, became the hallmark of a contemporary woman's food savvy in the new industrial age.

Eventually, by the late 1920s, a new ideal of modernity had gained powerful cachet in society and exerted new influence on what attributes were valued in foods; the uniform and hygienic trumped the flavorful and distinctive. As homemakers learned to rely more and more on advertisements and outside experts for information, they came to mistrust their own taste buds and kitchen know-how. Indifference about the origins and production of foods became a norm of urban culture, laying the groundwork for a modern food sensibility that would spread all across America in the decades that followed. Over time, the mores that trendsetting, affluent city women adopted in their kitchens influenced broader cultural ideals even for the poorest mothers of the rural South, many of whom aspired to cook, serve, and eat processed foods they couldn't afford.[2] Eventually, American shoppers of every class and gender would experience this transformation in one way or another.

Within a relatively brief period, the average distance from farm to kitchen had grown from a short walk down the garden path to a convoluted, 1,500-mile energy-guzzling journey by rail and truck. As food production became more remote and complex, consumers' fundamental literacy about foods shrunk and wizened even as a guise of new "knowledge" based on brand names and ad-attached attributes was erected. The everyday task of feeding families had once depended on the substantial knowledge of homemakers and other household helpers, but more and more, this work depended on what might well be called an unspoken covenant of ignorance between shoppers and an increasingly powerful food industry.

Ultimately, the ignorance of shoppers became as integral to the modern food system as any technology or infrastructure. The new sense of "knowing" that had been vigorously cultivated to encourage homemakers to trust experts and accept modern foods went on to shield an increasingly industrial style of food production from public scrutiny in the 1940s and 1950s.

During these critical decades, agriculture was utterly refashioned to meet industrial ideals of efficiency: small farms were consolidated into larger farms operated by fewer people with larger equipment and more petroleum; more synthetic fertilizers and pesticides were brought into use to grow high-yield monoculture crops; more wetlands were drained to bring more farmland into production; more rivers were dammed to irrigate more cropland in arid but temperate areas; and the expanding use of antibiotics permitted meat production to grow to a scale never before imagined.[3] All these changes had consequences for rural communities and landscapes nationwide—and for dinner tables, too, as hundreds of new additives and pesticide residues became routine parts of the American diet unbeknownst to those doing the cooking and eating.

Although rising interest in gourmet cooking and then widely publicized perils of the chemical age would prompt many Americans to question the modern food system in the 1960s and 1970s, through the same period, new generations grew up with paler expectations of what they could and should know about foods and cooking. As more women opted for careers and—by economic necessity—worked outside the home in the 1960s, 1970s, and 1980s, time available for learning about foods and for home cooking became constricted in many households. (Few men were helping to shoulder the work of shopping and cooking just yet.) As families more frequently consumed quick-fix convenience dinners and ate meals out at popular fast-food restaurants, indifference about foods' sources further increased. Ultimately, we have ended up in the absurd situation today that most of us, as consumers, know very little about what we eat; and, sensing a "dark side" to our foods' production, many of us don't even *want* to know.

Typically, the history of America's remarkable food system has been recounted as a singularly progressive tale. Yet for many of us, the marvel of fresh leafy lettuce in the winter nests right beside uneasiness that our children don't know milk comes from cows. This characteristic modern uneasiness about not-knowing and not-wanting-to-know our foods is just as deeply a part of our history, our personal experience, and our psyches as the triumphant ease of serving Hamburger Helper.

ANY AMERICAN history that examines how we've lost track of where our food comes from must confront a deep, almost wistful question that lurks just below the surface of our collective consciousness: Is the "where" where our food comes from "nature"? Of course, our food does ultimately come from soil, sunlight, and water, and for tens of thousands of years the human experience of procuring food—be it by hunting, gathering, or agriculture—was linked closely to knowing the ins and outs of the natural world. Today, however, beyond the supermarket, food derives not only from an obscured nature but also from behind-the-scenes tractors, gasoline, laser-leveled fields, fertilizers, irrigation ditches, pesticides, combines, migrant workers, laboratories, sanitized factories, stinking feedlots, semitrucks, and highways.

In spite of this—and perhaps because of this—the cultural idea of nature (as opposed to the soil, sunlight, and water that make up the physical environment) has become an important, if confusing, category for how many of us think about our foods, and one worth examining more closely from a historical perspective. It's not surprising that concern about the "naturalness" of foods first emerged when the food system began to industrialize. Yet over time, our cultural bearings about what "natural" means, in terms of both land and food, have gradually shifted as American society has adopted a more generally urban outlook.

Def. of "Natural"

For this reason, from behind today's shopping cart, it's difficult to imagine our food as a means of physical connection to the natural world. When we consider "connecting to nature," we are more inclined to imagine gazing at a spectacular waterfall than to consider rows of crops on a farm, let alone the frozen-foods aisle. In one of those great modern ironies, food is rarely regarded as "natural" unless it has been so labeled.

Yet each time we eat a turkey sandwich or a bowl of cereal, we are dependent on land and water — we are fixed in food chains that link us to places that are surely embedded in ecological systems. Author Michael Pollan has recently described eating as "our most profound engagement with the natural world."[4] Indeed, through food, we are irrevocably attached to the natural environment. The odd thing is that, by habit, we rarely realize this, and collectively, our lack of awareness has given us a distorted view of our place as humans within the larger world. With the supermarket nearby, we live with a detached assurance that our stomachs will always be full, even as industrial farms severely degrade soils, consume enormous amounts of fossil fuels, pollute waters with excess nitrogen and toxins, and inadvertently spur pests and microbes to alarming potencies.

Though our modern culture's estrangement from the natural world has oft been lamented from many angles, it seems important to consider afresh how losing knowledge of our foods has contributed to this rift. Through history, we can see that what we know (and don't know) about our foods has played a central role in how we perceive ourselves (and fail to perceive ourselves) in the broader context of the natural world. Understanding this dissonance becomes especially crucial as environmental consequences of large-scale food production become more evident and more troubling.

WHILE URBAN and suburban eaters have, for the most part, embraced the benefits and convenience of the modern food system and adopted its requisite habit of "looking the other way," a growing number of Americans have recently become more concerned about where and how their foods are produced. Today, interest in local and organic vegetables and meats has burgeoned into a sophisticated revolution, with organic sales growing by 20 percent each year and farmers' markets sprouting up in cities everywhere.

This revolution draws on many motivations and historical tendencies, yet central to them all has been the desire of shoppers, cooks, and eaters to better know the provenance of their foods. By knowing more, these hopeful consumers aspire to both avoid and subvert the harmful aspects of the dominant food system, and—in the process—to find better-tasting, healthier fare.

This movement of eaters remains small relative to America's mammoth food economy, but already it has become a promising force toward reforming some of the most egregious excesses of modern industrial agriculture. In the final chapters, I will discuss this emerging trend of consumers striving to bring knowledge and stories of foods back into their kitchens and lives in new ways.

Ultimately, if our market-driven society is to build a healthier food system, we as consumers will need to recognize how our everyday choices affect the larger environment and, then, to forge a new and influential role for ourselves. In an age when farms and factories of food production seem impossibly remote from our dinner plates, history can sharpen our outlook with its perspective and its ironies, and remind us of the opportunity for change.

CHAPTER 1

A Meal by Martha

In the center of a wooden table on a pewter platter sat a baked leg of lamb. One earthenware bowl held a heap of steaming, fresh green peas, while another contained sliced cucumbers, likely drizzled with vinegar. The table was plain, but the savory smell of the roast meat made mouths water and elevated this meal, like many simple meals, to a humbly exceptional status.

At the time, it was ordinary, but in retrospect, it seems utterly distinctive: everyone sitting at the table knew exactly where the foods came from. The lamb came from a nearby farm, while the green peas and cucumbers came from a garden just down a path out the kitchen door.

This particular meal was prepared and served on August 15, 1790, by Martha Ballard, who recorded it in her diary with an understated satisfaction: "had Bakt Lamb, Green Peas & Cucms [cucumbers]."[1]

Martha Ballard is one of few eighteenth-century American women who left a diary. Over the course of twenty-seven years, she made notes about her daily life in a series of small hand-sewn booklets. Best known for her work as a midwife (her career is brilliantly chronicled in Laurel Thatcher Ulrich's book *A Midwife's Tale*), she delivered over eight hundred babies, hastening at all hours—under the serene dome of starry nights or through blinding snowstorms—to aid laboring women in the area now known as Augusta, Maine.[2]

During that same period, Martha also conceived of and prepared thousands of meals for herself and her family. Her diary is filled with details of weeding and cooking, seeds and eggs, turkeys and cows, and through its pages we can begin to grasp what a woman two hundred years ago knew about the foods she cooked.

Martha's baked lamb dinner is a good place to begin. In the intimate circle of a meal, our attentions are directed to the physical and the sensuous, to aromas and flavors, to smaller scales and specific places. Through the details of dinner, we can begin to unearth a consciousness about cookery very different from our own.

In 1790, the year this lamb was served, Martha was fifty-five years old and living in a home beside the mill that her husband, Ephraim, leased. The couple had made their lives there along Bowman's Brook for five years. At this place, her oldest daughters had grown through adolescence, while her youngest son had just reached his tenth birthday. The Ballards' waterwheel powered not only a gristmill but a sawmill, one of several that formed a backbone to the budding industrial economy of the Kennebec River valley, based on felling and milling trees from northern forests and then shipping timber south to the growing city of Boston.[3] While Ephraim's mill was integral to the greater regional economy, Martha's garden was central to the family's household economy.

At the time, it was customary for women to have purview over the garden. In her diary, Martha most often referred to it as "my garden," claiming authority for what happened on the small patches of land she presided over. In 1790, Martha spent parts of sixty-one days working in her garden.[4] I imagine her moving amid rows of plants in her long, homewoven flax skirt, the billows of indigo-dyed fabric catching on cabbage leaves and her hem unavoidably sullied by garden dirt. She starts by picking bugs in her "east garden," which was nestled up against the house and situated to catch morning sunlight. Then she walks around to inspect peas tendrilling in another plot, located by the door to take advantage of an already-fenced-in space used for storing firewood in winter and thereby well mulched with "chips." After a shift of kitchen work, she might head down to pull weeds in another garden sited alongside the barn. Finally, in the late afternoon, she might find time to do some hoeing in a plot set by the brook, convenient if summer proved droughty and wilting plants required extra watering by pail.[5] It was in this plot that

Martha had planted, tended, and picked the green peas and cucumbers she served to her family on August 15.

In the case of the "bakt lamb" dinner, as with most meals, the distance that most ingredients traveled from field and barn to table was within a walk of the housewife. Because 95 percent of colonial women lived outside towns, this farm-to-table distance was typical.[6] During the summer, a housewife could walk twenty steps into her yard to gather eggs or herbs. Vegetable gardens stretched farther from the kitchen door—often covering one or two acres with squash, cabbage, turnips, string beans, and potatoes. In the early spring before the garden came ready, she might venture somewhat farther to gather wild greens for "sallets."[7]

In the course of their work, housewives like Martha walked these short distances back and forth countless times. These walks wore a woman's body, but they also drew her attention to the land and animals she tended. She knew exactly where to look for eggs laid by a furtive red hen, where wild grapevines hung from oaks, and where the muskmelons sweetened best in a warm spot against the barn. The details of the place were part of her everyday life, her work, and the meals she prepared.[8]

The lamb served for dinner in August 1790 came not from the Ballards' pastures, but from the farm of a Mr. Porter, who lived ten miles to the west.[9] The lamb came as payment for the work of Martha's eldest son. Such barter tied families together in a close web of relationships; neighbors traded help and food all the time.[10] The web of exchange served as a safety net. If hard times hit one neighbor, others had the wherewithal to help. While most families had the capability of raising nearly all of their own foods, they usually chose to grow some and to buy and trade for the rest. For example, meat other than lamb could have come just as readily from the Ballards' own pens and pastures—from animals cared for by Martha, her husband, and their children. They had a milk cow, pigs, and chickens but had not yet started a flock of sheep, probably for want of space at the mill site.[11]

When Martha noted the baked lamb dinner in her diary, she did not specify bread, but a coarse and crusty loaf likely rounded out the meal. Most often, Martha made her bread from rye and wheat—she called it "brown and flower bread"—and sometimes from corn as well.[12] Martha baked with flour milled from grain that came from fields cultivated by her husband and sons but also with wheat, corn, and rye that came from other farms as payment for milling or midwifery. In her diary, she noted with particular satisfaction baking bread from wheat grown by her husband: "I have Sifted our flower & Bakt, it makes a fine bread indead."[13] As her hands plunged into the sticky sponge of dough, as she kneaded in the wooden trough hewn by her son, as she formed loaves and set them to rise, and as she pulled the hot fragrant bread from her oven, Martha knew exactly where her flour came from.[14] The flour was not an anonymous powder. She knew the curve of the fields where the wheat grew, the hardened muscles of her husband's arms that cut it, and the coursing waters of Bowman's Brook that ground it between millstones. Her mind, hands, and palate could discern how bread made from grain grown by Mr. Ballard differed from grain grown on a farm up the Kennebec at Sevenmile Brook.[15] Whether you or I could taste a difference between these crusty loaves she baked, we can never know, but for Martha, a deep sense of place was a fundamental part of cooking and eating.

Envisioning a Foodshed

Starting with the lamb, green peas, and bread, and imagining some of the places that Martha depended on to bring this meal to her table, we become aware of a foodshed. This modern-day term refers to the area of land from which food is drawn.[16] I like to envision foodsheds from a maplike aerial perspective: the kitchen sits at the center and shaded lobes reach out across hills and swales of the landscape to encompass the areas that supply a meal's ingredients. In the case of this meal, a long lobe would reach to Mr. Porter's farm ten miles to the west; a small lobe would reach two hundred feet south to the garden patch by the brook; and a lobe for bread would reach to the northwest where the Ballards' corn and wheat fields yielded their grains. From the perspective of a seventeenth- or eighteenth-century New England cook, the notion of a meal's foodshed would have been more grounded: most ingredients were drawn from an area of less than fifty acres, much of it in view from the kitchen door.[17]

In the relatively small and familiar space of such a foodshed, the interdependence of field and kitchen was abundantly clear. A farmer had to mesh his knowledge of the place with the demands of the table. For example, to bake a typical 1,300 pounds of "rye and injun" bread each year, a housewife needed twenty-eight bushels of grain—half rye, half corn. That meant a New England farmer would have to sow two to three acres each year to provide for the family's bread and also to feed livestock through winter.[18] The very way a farm looked was shaped to a large degree by a family's appetite.

Washington Irving evocatively captured the close relationship between appetite and land in *The Legend of Sleepy Hollow,* published not long after Martha baked her lamb. When a hungry Ichabod Crane arrived on horseback at the Hudson Valley farm of his beloved Katrina's father, he saw before him a banquet. "In his devouring mind's eye he pictured to himself every roasting-pig running about with a pudding in his belly, and an apple in his mouth; the pigeons were snugly put to bed in a comfortable pie, and tucked in with a coverlet of crust; the geese were swimming in their own gravy; and the ducks pairing cosily in dishes, like snug married couples, with a decent competency of onion sauce."[19] To Crane, the landscape appeared not as the gardens, orchards, farm fields, and pastures but as a vast table set with mounds of mashed potatoes, pens of pork chops, and paddocks of pies. In his hungry imagination, the bountiful land morphed into a feast.

The scene reminds me of cartoons I watched as a child—ones in which fleeing chickens and pigs turned into giant drumsticks and pork chops in the mind's eye of a comic predator. However, Irving's metamorphosis of landscape into opulent feast was not just fantasy; in a fundamental way, it reflected preindustrial Americans' sensibility about land. Well-tended and improved land could yield a cornucopian spread and was regarded as a source of food and a sign of wealth, not just as backdrop or scenery. Envisioning and knowing a landscape as one's fount of food is far different from what most of us know and experience when driving through the countryside today.

MARTHA's baked lamb dinner is a single meal, but it could stand for many others mentioned in her diary and for thousands of others cooked by women in preindustrial America. Of the more than seventy different foods mentioned in Martha's diary, most came from local sources in a small, known foodshed; they were eaten in season, when available, or in preserved (dried, brined, or sugared) forms. The few items that came from afar tended to be those used only in small amounts, such as cinnamon and nutmeg, or the special, once-a-year Christmas-day orange.[20] Though corn bread and salt pork might substitute for dark bread and lamb, depending on regional differences in ecology, culture, and season, growing food, cooking food, and eating food connected most people in preindustrial America to familiar patches of land.[21]

Nature in Martha's Garden

As the work of procuring and cooking food tied people to the land, it linked them closely to the workings of the natural world. But could their gardens and fields be considered "natural"?

Some modern thinkers have contended that agriculture is decidedly not natural — that the innovation of agriculture ten thousand years ago began a wholesale destruction of nature. Indeed, landscapes transformed by farms no longer provide as much wild habitat and sustenance for native plants and animals. Farming disrupts communities of soil organisms, including fungi, microbes, and bacteria, and draws fertility away from the land. Farms displace forests and wetlands, usurp water from rivers, and can set loose soils that cloud streams with silt.[22]

Yet at the same time that farming changes and disrupts nature, it relies and rests upon nature's rhythms. It was this aspect of farming that was most tangible to preindustrial Americans whose lives were tied so closely to the cycles of seasons and the whims of weather. The idea that farms and gardens could be anything other than part of the natural realm was to them unthinkable.[23] By looking at the details of Martha's days, we can begin to appreciate just how much she (and other women of the time) had to set her own life within the overarching patterns of the natural world in order to produce food for her family. Consider, for example, the sheer variety and number of vegetables she grew: cabbage, beets, carrots, parsnips, French turnips, peas, cucumbers, pink radishes, greens, musk-melons, watermelons, string beans, eight varieties of shelling beans,

potatoes (including a blue variety one year), scallions, onions, pump-
kins, and squash.[24] Some of these were regular members of the garden
cast grown each year, whereas others were varieties Martha added or
experimented with as she expanded her garden and had the chance to
obtain new types of seeds. One year she noted setting four hundred
plants in her garden.[25] Many years she noted planting between fifty and
eighty cabbages — more esteemed in the 1790s than they are today — and
then storing a similar number in her root cellar in the fall.[26]

Martha also grew a variety of herbs for kitchen use. She regularly
pinched off sprigs of parsley, sage, and other herbs to freshen up meats
and probably beans. Consider the meal she noted preparing on one rainy
Sunday in May: "we Dind on a fine Legg of Cornd Pork stufft with green
herbs from our Gardin." For a surprising December roast of veal loin, she
wrote, "I gathered parsly, fresh and green, from my Gardin for to put in
my gravy."[27]

In addition, Martha grew quince, plums, apples, currants, berries,
cherries, and rhubarb — fruits that invariably showed up in the pies and
tarts she baked to sweeten winter days.[28] And she grew many medicinal
herbs for use in her midwifery work.[29]

More remarkable than the variety and number of plants is how
Martha managed to tuck them all into both the niches of her garden's
terrain and the hours and contours of her days. Raising the important
biennial beets, cabbages, carrots, and parsnips demanded vigilant attention over a two-year period. Cabbages had to be harvested each fall,
stored carefully in straw or in sand in the cellar (heads were judiciously
used through winter), and then the "stumps" had to be replanted every
spring. Nursing plants through this cycle provided a welcome flush of
early greens and, later in summer, seeds for the next generation. Each
spring, Martha planted both cabbage stumps in their second year and
new seeds to start the cycle again.[30]

Other vegetables she cultivated had different strategies for reproduction. Potatoes had to be stored safe from freezing and rot through winter
and then, in spring, cut into chunks with active "eyes" for replanting.
Peas and beans had to be planted by seed every year and did best set near

fences they could climb. For all the seeded plants, Martha had to let at least one grow out, and then gather seeds, dry them, and store them safely through the winter in little cloth bags sewn for that purpose. "I have been makeing bags and fixing my Gardin Seeds," she wrote one evening.[31] In those improbable packets of new life—some sharp and faceted, some smooth and mottled, some tiny, some coin-sized—she encountered the miraculous mundane.

When it came to planting, the most crucial cue was the last day of frost. Only after the ground thawed and the soil warmed could seeds begin to grow. Yet as soon as the ground was ready, a countdown to fall's earliest freeze began. Because timing was so critical, many farmers and gardeners looked to signals in the natural world or to particular phases of the moon to help them determine when to plant.[32] Martha was likely aware of a body of planting folklore, passed from neighbor to neighbor and spelled out in the pages of almanacs: *Frost is out of the ground when you hear the first frogs. Plant barley when elm leaves reach the size of a mouse's ear. Plant corn when oak leaves grow to the size of a squirrel's ear.* In one place, the best sowing time corresponded to the return of robins; in another, to the arrival of bobolinks.[33] Such place-specific cues were based on closely evolved relationships in the natural world that coincided with and usually indicated the end of frosts.

While natural cues and moon phases offered guidance, careful attention to day-to-day weather was often the key to a farmer's success, so even those who kept austere diaries made detailed notes about wind, rain, temperature, and storms—all of which had the potential to be devastating.[34] Many regarded the vagaries of weather as signs of God's approval or disapproval, an outlook sometimes tempered by, sometimes conjoined with, popular belief in astrology. In addition to moon charts, almanacs featured weather prediction tables based on the celestial transits of planets and stars.[35]

While awareness of nature's cycles intermingled erratically with astrology and religious beliefs, all construed the work of raising plants and animals as fitting into a larger cosmos beyond the influence of human desires. Although Martha wrote little about the whys of the world in her diary, she did occasionally offer prayers of thanks for good weather or allude to astrology, revealing her sense, too, that the world was operating on terms larger than her own.[36]

ONCE VEGETABLES were planted, Martha had to know what made them grow. She sprinkled ashes around her cabbages and brought manure from the henhouse and barnyard into her garden for fertilizer.[37] In addition, she rotated the positions of her crops, which would have also improved her soil's fertility. One year, for example, she planted cabbage and turnips in the dooryard; the next, she planted nitrogen-replenishing beans.[38]

In the weeks after sowing, days lengthened and warmed, and up through dark soil came not only the greenly sprouts of beets, parsnips, and peas but also weeds. Weeds demanded perseverance and had to be pulled—and pulled—until the desired seedlings gained clear advantage. After one spell when Martha was gone from home for a week delivering babies, she came back to find her garden overrun. "The weeds almost gained mastery," she wrote in her diary, but over the course of the next week, with diligence and muscle, she managed to wrest "mastery" back from the unwanted plants.[39] Weeding was done by hand or by hoe. Sometimes Martha's youngest son and daughters helped, or daughters did onerous housework, such as laundry, enabling Martha to tend her garden.[40]

To control insect pests, many gardeners let chickens and ducks range freely among plants during the day, or they might lay down a wilted cabbage leaf or an old shingle, and then squash all the bugs hiding under it early the next morning. Picking bugs was a job that often fell to children.[41] For bad infestations, some gardeners applied repellent concoctions made from black walnut or tobacco leaves.[42]

In the course of the twenty-seven seasons of gardening that Martha recorded in her diary, she mentioned difficulties with "worms & Buggs" only a half dozen times.[43] In those few instances when insects caused "great damage" to her young plants and bean vines, Martha tackled the problem straightforwardly by going out to her garden early in the morning, searching for the bugs, and killing them.[44] More often than not, insects were simply an expected part of the garden scene, and it was no surprise when bugs and caterpillars hitchhiked on vegetables into the kitchen. Removing them simply became the first step of cooking.[45]

Martha's description of "Buggs" was unspecific. Indeed, most farmers at the time didn't yet know about the helpful work of bees and earthworms in the garden, but some were beginning to make astute observations about complex relationships in nature. Several, for example, noticed that the same birds that nibbled newly planted seeds also ate noxious insects later in the season.[46] Almanac editor Robert Bailey Thomas recognized that even reptiles played a role. "I never suffer any of my family to kill those little innocent animals called striped snakes, for they do me much service in destroying grasshoppers, and other troublesome insects," he explained in the *Old Farmer's Almanac.* Toads too were "of essential service especially in a garden, to eat up cabbage-worms, caterpillars, & c."[47] According to Thomas, the keenest farmers appreciated the way that natural food chains worked to their benefit and attributed such help to the impeccable design of God's creation. His strong admonitions, however, implied that many farmers were not so keen and were inclined to kill the very birds and snakes that could help them.

Whichever way farmers and their wives interpreted the presence of birds, toads, and bugs in their gardens and fields, one thing is certain— everyone knew that their growing foods could be eaten by a host of other competitors. To most preindustrial Americans, the food chain was eminently tangible. Although most wolves had been killed off by the late 1700s, birds and bugs remained, continuing to make it apparent that each of nature's creatures was the favorite meal of another. As "American farmer" J. Hector Saint John de Crèvecoeur put it, "nothing exists but what has its enemy, one species pursue and live upon the other."[48] Whether farmers and gardeners were warring against bug and bird competitors or trying to live in some harmony with them, they met up face-to-beady-eyed-face in the cabbage patch.

Tales of Turkeys

As I read through Martha's diary—following along day after day as she spread manure, planted seeds, pulled weeds, noticed sprouts, and then

picked, cooked, and savored the first peas and string beans of the season
— I began to appreciate the way that she knew the complete stories of
many of her foods.[49]

Such stories become especially evident in the case of the animals that
provided the milk, eggs, and meat that her family ate — many of which
Martha and her children fed and tended each day. Consider, for example,
the turkey eaten in November 1792. It first showed up in her diary as a
large speckled egg under her "blak turkey" back in April. She had received
two turkeys the December before as payment for her midwifery work.
These two hens hatched their own clutches of eggs in May, but Martha
added seventeen more, received from a neighbor, to incubate beneath
the warm feathered body of each hen. Three weeks later, she recorded the
day when the eggs began to hatch, and then the day when the mother first
paraded her chicks in the yard. "My Black Turkey Brot out 14 Chicks," she
wrote.[50] Then through the summer, Martha made notes about the two
hen turkeys rearing their flock of forty-three young turks, all of which
strutted and wandered in the farmyard and fields, compelling her, at
times, to chase them down.[51]

By the time September came around, these same turkeys began to
appear in meals in a rather matter-of-fact way. On October 21, 1792,
Martha wrote, "killed a Turkey & Cookt it for Dinner"; then in December, "killd 2 Turkeys & Cokt one of them."[52] In her diary, Martha's words
often chronicled a seamless movement from killing to cooking in a single
sentence, echoing the seamless sequence of an afternoon's work.

Cycles of life and death were clearly part of Martha's work as a midwife, but they were also part of her work preparing meals for the family.
For the sake of food, she killed animals with the grip of her own hands,
twisting the necks of chickens and feeling their warm bodies become
limp and lifeless. She pulled feathers, cut necks, wings, and legs, and
dropped meaty parts into a kettle of boiling water to make soup to nourish her sick son.[53] The necessity of the task meant that there was no sentimental self-consciousness about the killing of animals; having meat to
cook and eat was the primary aim of raising livestock in the first place.

While hogs, sheep, chickens, and turkeys all cycled through the Ballard
household economy at various times, milk cows were the mainstay. A

good cow was the single most important animal an eighteenth-century family could own because it had the greatest potential for generating wealth by turning pasture forage into milk that would become butter and cheese, and into calves that would become meat or next-generation milkers.[54]

Although Martha's cows didn't have names per se, she referred to them by descriptive monikers, such as "thee speckled Cow" and the "Bell cow," and she made spare notes about their lives in her diary.[55] She noted when the "red cow" got lost and when the "amazingly Sweld" udder of another required tending.[56] She recorded when each cow gave birth and sometimes wrote a brief description of the new calf. Several weeks after the birth, male calves were usually butchered, and Martha noted preparing the customary spring meal of "veal's head and harslett," a dish that converted tender young lungs, brains, and eyes into a seasonal specialty.[57]

Likely it was the intimacy of milking that made cows the most familiar and favored animals. Twice a day, year-round—even through the bitter

1.1. *In rural areas and small towns, the work of milking a cow each day—shown here in an 1819 woodcut—made members of most families intimately aware of where their milk, butter, and cheese came from.*

cold of winter—someone had to sit beside the cow's warm body, and pull firmly at its teats. Only occasionally did Martha note in her diary walking to the barn early in the morning and late in the afternoon to milk the cow.[58] Given the unpredictable nature of her work as a midwife, the relentless task of milking would have been passed at times to children, to her husband, or to other household helpers.[59]

The reproductive cycles of animals' lives were yet another set of natural cycles that governed the flow of Martha's days. With the abundance of eggs in early summer came the urgency of using them in cakes or custards or preserving them in brine; with the profusion of milk after calving time came the necessity of processing it into butter and cheese.[60] Summer was the season for animals to fatten on grasses. With the onset of cold in autumn came butchering time; given the cycles of rot and spoilage, anything dead would begin to decompose unless cold or freezing temperatures could stall it. While Martha readily killed her turkeys and other fowl, the work of butchering larger animals, such as cattle, hogs, and sheep, was considered men's work and was usually orchestrated by a neighbor or by her oldest son. Martha, like most housewives, was nevertheless involved in processing and preserving the meat and offal into edibles for winter—from corned beef, tongue, and rennet, to sausage and calves-foot jelly.[61]

When a cow was butchered, Martha recorded its final weight in her diary. Some were remembered long after their deaths. One dark evening in January 1798, Martha noted making candles and using up the last tallow from a cow killed more than a year earlier.[62] The animal that had provided milk, butter, and then stew for her table also afforded the glimmering light that made it possible for her to record her memories and reflections in the waning hours of winter days. The lives of farm animals were closely interwoven with Martha's own life, and so it seems fitting that their stories became braided together in ink on the pages of her diary.

The Energy of Eating

So far, we've considered meals as centers of foodsheds, as integrations of human know-how and natural cycles, and as the culminations of stories, but the light of the cow's tallow points to another useful way of thinking about a meal—in terms of energy.

Not until the early twentieth century would home economists and efficiency experts begin to describe the human body as an "engine" and food as the "fuel" needed to keep it going. By then the science of nutrition had fleshed out the "calorie-idea" to show in a quantitative way what people had always known: you had to eat to live.[63] And it wouldn't be until the early 1960s that ecologists discerned the way that kilocalories cycled through entire ecosystems when large creatures ate smaller creatures and then ultimately became the food of the most miniscule microbes in an interdependent web of energy and life.

In the most fundamental sense, eating is the way we humans fit into this larger web: the sun provides energy to grow plants, animals eat plants, and we humans eat both plants and animals to derive our nourishment and vigor. Yet we must also expend energy to obtain food. Today, most of us work elsewhere and press buttons for cash to buy food, but in Martha's day, people expended a great deal of bodily energy raising plants and animals to eat.

Thinking about a meal as calories of energy would have been foreign to Martha, but, in a practical sense, she would have had a clear awareness of how much energy went into cooking every meal—both how much work it took and how much heat it consumed. She would have known how long it took to tend the turkeys and lambs that became her meat and how much effort it took for her husband to raise, harvest, thresh, and mill wheat. She would have known the amount of energy it took to bake bread by the armfuls of wood needed to heat her oven and by the days it took her husband and sons to fell and haul the firewood. In one entry, she described hauling logs from woodpile to hearth by the number of steps it took her: "brot a burden of wood which took 300 & 50 Steps."[64] Knowing the amount of energy used in this firsthand way led Martha and many other women to economize on both time and wood by doing all their baking work once or twice a week.

A firsthand sense of energy meant that housewives routinely used leftover food scraps in the next meal or otherwise tossed them into the dooryard to feed chickens. Many farm families kept a swill barrel near the door for accumulating kitchen wastes, which were then fed to the hogs. The swill barrel served to keep the kitchen in a closed loop with the farmyard, returning what was not used to fortify and enrich that which remained. The pervasive bearing of frugality that kept most Yankee housewives looking for ways to avoid waste and to make do was based on awareness of connections.[65]

Energy was also tangible in a more personal sense as all the physical work that went into the yearly planting, hoeing, harvesting, hauling water, milking, and churning. After long days of bustling from task to task, from attending a birth to baking an ovenful of pumpkin pies, Martha sometimes noted feelings of fatigue in her diary. In one entry, she reflected, "A womans work is Never Done as ye Song Says, and happy Shee whos Strength holds out to the End of ye [sun's] rais."[66] During the busiest times when Martha spent days working as a midwife away from her own home, she opted to purchase butter from a neighbor rather than to churn it, and to buy biscuits at the general store rather than to bake them herself. After her daughters married and started their own households, Martha enlisted young nieces to apprentice or hired daughters of neighbors to help her with the continuous demands of household work.[67] However, as she aged, the long years of joint-wearing work began to make her body ache, and Martha complained increasingly about a deep, almost sorrowful exhaustion in her diary. In one entry she wrote, "I feel fatagued but must put up with my lott."[68] Ultimately, the energy that had gone into raising food and feeding her family was drawn from the mortal energy of her own body.

Consciousness of Cookery

Starting with a dinner of "bakt lamb" and green peas, we have immersed ourselves in the garden and kitchen of an accomplished eighteenth-century woman. Considering all the expertise, muscle, time, and energy that went into Martha's meals is humbling. While I find it interesting to mull over the difference between arduous efforts required to pull together a meal back then and the relative ease of doing it today, perhaps the most telling and intriguing difference lies in the pattern of how we *think* as we plan and prepare meals.

In the modern-day configuration of supermarket and kitchen, I usually begin plotting what to cook for dinner a couple of hours ahead of time, imagining what already sits in the cupboard and in the refrigerator drawers, remembering what my husband and I have eaten recently, and factoring in what we like and how much time I have. Sometimes, an appealing plan jumps into my head immediately. Other times, I wrestle with the tiresome question and realize I'll need to run to the store to pick up a needed item. From the time I start chopping and dicing in the kitchen, with my husband's help, it usually takes us about thirty minutes to prepare a good simple meal.

I can feel inspired to prepare almost anything—an exotic dish like grilled fish with lime- jalapeño-coconut chutney—or just something quick and easy like a spinach frittata. But no matter what I decide to make, I will go to the store, gather all the ingredients, and then cook them. This is the implicit logic that most of us follow, no matter what we eat and how we like to cook; it rests squarely upon the infrastructure of our modern food system.

I have a funny little collection of lost shopping lists that tells me other cooks do the same. The first one I found fluttering in the wind, attached to a thorn on a rosebush growing in my front yard. A truly ephemeral text, it offered a code to the thought process of its anonymous author, a cook who seemed to have planned for several meals that week: frozen turkey, sour cream, eggs, wine, olives, prime rib, avocados, ham, and oranges. The tattered list included particular brand names and prices, signs of a careful, economy-conscious shopper. Another list, left accidentally on a shelf at the market, midspree, divulged a shopper with the intention of preparing a special, unfamiliar meal: ground turkey, lemon, parsley, cumin, paprika, butter, onion. Finally, the list from my bachelor neighbor, given to me unintentionally when he wrote a phone number on the other side, included frozen chicken potpies, frozen pizzas, and chocolate almond Häagen-Dazs.

All three shoppers, despite their different approaches to cooking, share the same mental framework. The thinking and shopping might happen anywhere from a week to fifteen minutes ahead of time. Now that many supermarkets are open twenty-four hours a day, one doesn't even need to plan to get there before closing time. Food is always available; all we do is pay.

Now, contrast this modern mental framework with the mindset of an eighteenth-century cook like Martha. The project of procuring food was not a sliver of experience squeezed in as quickly as possible but rather a dominant and all-encompassing focus for her and each member of her family.

Martha had to be thinking ahead of time—sometimes more than a year ahead of time—to ensure that she'd have the stores needed to cook meals for her family. To eat cabbage greens in May, she had to plant cabbage seeds the spring prior, nurture the plants through summer, carefully dig them up and bed them in the root cellar through winter, and then replant them in early spring. To eat sausage in April required feeding and fattening young animals the summer before; to eat pumpkin pie in March demanded tending to a pumpkin patch the summer before and then harvesting and drying the chunks of orange flesh to be saved through winter.

Interwoven with the firsthand knowledge of particular places and stories of plants and animals, and the day-to-day practice of fitting work into windows ordained by season, was a frank awareness that food came from the land. The earthy details of growth, frosts, rot, storms, and "buggs" made nature's larger cycles and patterns plain and made its opportunities and limitations tangible. This awareness mentally situated most preindustrial Americans in foodsheds, food chains, and myriad stories, and it spiritually situated most in a larger cosmos as well.[69] The work of raising food meant being embedded within, vulnerable to, and dependent upon the natural world.

FROM THE perspective of a single life such as Martha Ballard's, things can often seem unchanging. The ins and outs of Martha's days—hoeing, sowing, weeding, harvesting, baking, cooking, churning, milking, year after year after year—seemed an ageless continuation of what had long been the province of rural women's work. Martha passed these skills and responsibilities down to her daughters and to other young helpers who apprenticed in her household. However, in the course of Martha's life, a revolution had convulsed the colonies, and the Louisiana Purchase increased the young nation's geographic size threefold. Closer to home, the population of Augusta, Maine, had more than doubled, bringing many of the shifts that inevitably come when cities begin to grow.[70]

Some of the most significant of these historic changes would center on the task of supplying America's urban dinner tables. Over time, people's knowledge of food, their relationship with its production, and —as a consequence—their sense of connection to the natural world would all be profoundly transformed.

CHAPTER 2

To Market, to Market

The skills of good cooking were most often passed from mother to daughter in preindustrial America, but not all young women had the advantage of motherly training. An orphan, Amelia Simmons had managed to learn to bake pies and roast lambs by her own wherewithal. Ultimately she'd made her way in the world by working as a cook in various households in the Connecticut and Hudson river valleys.

Simmons's difficult path prompted her to write a book to guide other young women in the critical realm of cooking. Published in 1796, only six years after Martha Ballard served her "bakt" lamb, Amelia's *American Cookery* was the first cookbook published in America. In many ways, Amelia's recipes echoed Martha's style in the kitchen, especially in her use of local ingredients and fresh herbs paired with meats. Though cookbooks published in England had been used in the colonies during the seventeenth and eighteenth centuries, they did not take into account the different environmental conditions and therefore the different ingredients found in New England. With its *Johny cakes* made from corn and its *Pompkin pudding*, Simmons's *American Cookery* was most useful because, as she put it, her recipes were "adapted to this country."[1]

Amelia's recipes sometimes began in the garden. For fruit pies, she advised gathering pears and plums "when full grown, and just as they begin to turn." To make pickles, she recommended using "small and fresh gathered" cucumbers.[2] The "buggs" that Martha encountered in her garden, Amelia acknowledged from a kitchen perspective.[3] By her account, a cook preparing daily meals routinely encountered the snails, caterpillars, and other insects that beleaguered her plants outdoors as well as regularly witnessing the wear and tear that weather wreaked on vegetables.[4]

Similarly, some of Amelia's recipes confirmed the close familiarity that a woman who cooked could have with animals' lives. Her recipe for a *fine Syllabub from the Cow*—a frothy, sweet-cream dessert topping—directed the cook to "sweeten a quart of cyder with double refined sugar, grate nutmeg into it," and then carry the bowl right to the underside of a cow's warm body and "milk your cow into your liquor."[5] As we know from Martha's diary, a rural or small-town housewife would have known her cow's age, its disposition, and how often it had given birth. Milking and caring for the animal on a daily basis, she would have known what the cow ate and how that changed the consistency, flavor, and color of its milk through the seasons.

The Transcription of Kitchen Know-How

While *American Cookery* corroborates the intimate ties between a late eighteenth-century cook, her food, and the places and particulars that produced it, the cookbook also hints at some significant trends that were just starting to diminish housewives' firsthand knowledge of their foods and foodsheds.

Even though most meats, vegetables, and grains consumed in New England were still produced locally, markets had developed to the extent that it was common for many cooks to use some foods produced quite far away. While the great majority of ingredients Simmons recommended in her cookbook derived from local sources, some few came great distances by ship, expanding the otherwise circumscribed foodsheds of American cooks and eaters to unknown landscapes across the globe. Often expensive, these exotic ingredients, such as nutmeg, cinnamon, and citrus, were used in small amounts as flavorings.[6]

When a food came from far away, a cook could not have intimate knowledge about where and how it was made. Although many of Amelia's recipes called for prodigious amounts of sugar—"double refined" no less—she was apparently not much concerned about the circumstances that provided this sweet ingredient.[7]

Some New Englanders, however, were increasingly troubled by the dark and bitter fact of slavery hidden behind sugar's sweet countenance. By 1798, the United States was importing roughly 67 million pounds of brown sugar and 20.5 million pounds of loaf sugar, all grown, harvested, and processed by slaves in the West Indies.[8] Every March when sweet sap flowed within the trunks of New England's maple trees, Robert Bailey Thomas, that venerable editor of the *Old Farmers Almanac*, railed against buying slave-produced sugar. "Feast not on the toil, pain and misery of the wretched," he exhorted readers in 1804. To Thomas, eating West Indian sugar not only made one complicit in slavery's evil but also meant ingesting some part of those very evils.[9] Through the early nineteenth century, many self-reliant New Englanders followed Thomas's advice and used the cheaper maple sugar they could produce from trees on their own farms. But cane sugar had its sweet and easy appeal, and as its price decreased, cooks like Simmons who purchased sugar from merchants in town would become ever more common.[10]

The case of sugar arrayed in stark terms the problematic aspect of consuming distant foods, but as New England's towns and cities grew and larger urban populations inevitably required supplies from a larger foodshed, increasing numbers of shoppers would face the prospect of buying more and more foods anonymously produced in far-flung locations.

Beyond the lengthening distance between farms and city markets, *American Cookery* hints at another social shift that would play a key role in diminishing housewives' firsthand knowledge of their foods' provenance. In the well-heeled households where Amelia Simmons worked, the mistresses were *not* doing the cooking.[11] With the rise of urban affluence through the nineteenth century, it would become surprisingly common, even in middle-class households, for domestic servants rather than housewives to do the cooking—a trend that would profoundly influence women's attitudes toward knowing and working with foods.[12]

Finally, Amelia's decision to write *American Cookery*, as well as its brisk sales, indicate an inchoate hunger for knowledge about cooking. Amelia believed there were many other women like her, "who by loss of their parents, or other unfortunate circumstances" were "reduced to the necessity" of going into domestic work. This "rising generation of Females" needed a way to learn how to cook in order to earn their living.[13] The problem of young women's "ignorance" about cooking would soon become a popular topic, eventually filling the pages of dozens of cookbooks and household guides in the mid- and late nineteenth century.

While Amelia sought to share her recipes "to improve the minds of her own Sex," she did not think it necessary to include advice about procuring foods at market.[14] Simmons's publisher, however, had more foresight. Unbeknownst to Amelia, a "transcriber for the press" took it upon himself—or, more likely, herself—to tack seventeen pages of "rules and directions, how to make choice of meats, fowls, fish and vegetables" to the thirty-page cookbook.[15] Much dismayed and perturbed by the sizable preamble, Amelia apologized profusely for this "affront upon the good sense of all classes of citizens" when she had her book reprinted, without it, by another publisher a few years later.[16] She regarded it a grave insult to tell her readers something so elementary as how to choose foods, explaining that "long experience has abundantly taught those who reside in cities, and in the country, how to distinguish between good and bad, as to every article brought into market."[17]

However, the very idea that a cook might need advice about selecting foods was just becoming ripe as more women relied on purchased ingredients. In 1800, the great majority of Americans still had a hand in raising most of their own food, but the roughly 6 percent who lived in the nation's small cities—and who purchased more and more of their provender—were already beginning to confront the quandaries of the attenuating food system.[18] The transcriber of Amelia's cookbook was likely one of those city dwellers, and she (or he) aptly recognized the growing need for guidance in negotiating the urban marketplace.

In this context, the transcriber's addition, grandly identified as "DIRECTIONS for CATERING, or the procuring of the best VIANDS, FISH, &c.," can be considered prescient: it's the first written record of what specific considerations American women summoned when buying foods in town.[19] Though written as prescriptive advice, the sections about how to choose flesh, fish, poultry, roots, and vegetables are grounded in rural lore with close attention to places, particulars, animals' lives, and sensuous details.

The transcriber describes remarkably nuanced relationships between taste and particular places in her recommendations about how to choose the best fish at market; for example, "Salmon Trout" tasted best when "caught under a fall or cataract." For perch and roach, "the deeper the water from whence taken, the finer are their flavors."[20] (The first popular southern cookbook similarly distinguished the particular habitat that toothsome fishes came from; in her *Recipe for catfish*, author Mary Randolph specifically advised using "small white catfish that have been caught in deep water."[21]) These recommendations suggest that a cook could learn specifically where a fish came from and discern how its place of origin was related to its taste. The transcriber also noted the difference between the taste of shad "taken fresh and cooked immediately," and of those "thirty or forty miles from the place where caught." The fresh shad stayed firmer and was "esteemed elegant," but the distant shad had a particular "higher relished flavor to the taste."[22] Amelia's recipes for fish didn't match the transcriber's appreciation, though; she included only one recipe for dried cod, which entailed soaking and scalding for seven hours. Nevertheless, subtleties based on particular places of origin, distances, and time elapsed from catching were apparently perceptible to some who cooked and enjoyed fish.

Attention to flavor and place extended to vegetables as well. Because those who shopped at markets still often relied on gardens, the transcriber's advice about selecting vegetables was, in many cases, advice only about what varieties of seed to use and where to plant them. The richness of a potato's flavor depended on the ground where its parent plants grew, and attention to place was even more critical with cabbages. "All cabbages have a higher relish that grow on *new unmanured grounds*," the transcriber wrote, "if grown in an old town and on old gardens, they have a rankness, which at times may be perceived by the fresh air traveller."[23] To avoid smelly boiled cabbage, a cook had to begin with the soil in her garden. Peas were "the richest flavored" when picked "*carefully* from the vines as soon as the dew is off, shelled and cleaned without water, and boiled immediately." [24]

When it came to choosing meats, even if a housewife in town was no longer involved in raising animals or butchering, she still would want to know about the life of the animals that she intended to cook, serve, and eat — particularly their sex, age, diet, and work history. The transcriber advised that the females of all species of animals, birds, and fishes gave meat more tender and flavorful than the males — an observation that reflects the natural tendency of female animals to accumulate body fat. The flesh of oxen, which were used for farmwork, was less tender and juicy than that of cattle, and the best mutton was from grass-fed animals, two to three years old. [25] Age was especially important in the case of birds and could be ascertained by bill or leg color. The transcriber offered specific guidelines about the leg and bill colors of old and young pigeons, plovers, blackbirds, geese, thrashers, and larks, but as a general rule of thumb advised that "speckled rough legs denote age, while smooth legs and combs prove them young." [26] Knowing an animal's age was important because it decreed preferred methods and times for cooking; older, tougher meats were best stewed long over a low fire.

Although knowing where foods came from and how they were grown, along with specifics about animals' lives, was certainly useful when buying foods in town, the transcriber suggested that a woman's senses were her most trustworthy guide. With some foods traveling greater distances, market vendors at times used "deceits" to give them a semblance of freshness. For example, fishmongers sometimes peppered or painted the gills of saltwater fishes that were brought upriver by boat. [27] To choose a good fish, a cook needed to closely examine its gills. She had to look the animal straight in the eyes and determine whether they were cloudy or clear. To choose a fresh fowl, she had to inspect its "vent," or anus. [28] A shopper's sense of smell was critical, too, for the quality of many wild rabbits, birds, and fish could best be judged "by scent." To avoid stale partridges, the transcriber recommended "smelling at their mouths." [29] Nor were poking and prodding out of the question. To choose a good piece of oxen flesh, the transcriber advised homemakers: "dent it with your finger and it will immediately rise again; if old, it will be rough and spungy [sic], and the dent remain."[30] To figure a goose's age, a shopper could pinch the "thickness of web between the toes"; in young birds, the web was "tender and transparent," but it grew "coarser and harder with time."[31]

All these fine points a woman might use to choose foods at the market were considered mundane, and so they were rarely recorded, let alone regarded as "Knowledge" with a capital K. At a time when firsthand experience still played a larger role in most women's education than the written word, the transcriber's effort to capture everyday know-how in written form is noteworthy; it reveals how traditional, rural knowledge informed the thinking of housewives and cooks who were beginning to purchase more of their foods in town and city markets. Perched at the turn of the nineteenth century, *American Cookery* looked both backward and forward. With Amelia's recipes and the transcriber's addition, the book assembled traditional cooking know-how and also bent it to be useful in the newly emerging urban scene.

Through the nineteenth century, other cookbook writers would follow the transcriber's lead and include more and more advice about "marketing" to address the needs of increasing numbers of women who purchased their meats and vegetables in cities. (In an ironic historical twist, the term "marketing," which we now reserve for the act of persuading shoppers to buy, once referred simply and forthrightly to the act of going to market to shop.) As time went on, the books would include more admonitions about foods in the city markets. In her 1829 cookbook, *The American Frugal Housewife,* Lydia Child recommended getting butter from "honest, neat, trusty dairy people" or a "friend in the country."[32] In her 1841 cookbook, *The Good Housekeeper,* Sara Josepha Hale warned against buying city-raised pork fed on the offal of slaughterhouses.[33] In their attempt to reach readers who lived in small country towns, as well as in large cities, cookbook writers readily blended rural know-how with urban circumstances. Lydia Child matter-of-factly recommended that country women make cakes and custards with the large numbers of eggs readily available from backyard flocks, while their city cousins, who were "obliged to buy eggs," use a recipe that required only three.[34] The potentially diverse audience of cookbook users meant that a mix of rural lore and urban skepticism would continue to inform the body of food knowledge that writers included in their books.

Indeed, most cookbook writers at the time assumed that all home-makers and cooks needed to know the attributes of genuine articles of foods—directly as they came from the farm—in order to judge potentially doctored or withered variants sold in city markets. This may be the most important reason that the practical marketing advice proffered by household experts throughout the nineteenth century remained firmly rooted in rural tradition, even as the food system began to change dramatically with urbanization.

As cities grew and new market relationships between cities and hinterlands developed with advances in transportation, increasing numbers of cooks would buy their food instead of growing it, and with this change, they would know less and less about where and how their foods were raised. Over the course of the nineteenth century, traditional knowledge of the places and particulars that provided food would gradually fade, and ultimately be lost. And with it, a sensibility that recognized the farm as a source of natural bounty would be lost as well.

To Market

When Amelia published her cookbook in 1796, town and city foodsheds were largely constrained by the endurance of a horse. However, in the first three decades of the nineteenth century, new advances in transportation started a cascade of change that permitted both the growth of cities and the westward expansion of profitable farming—trends that would wholly reconfigure the relationship between America's kitchens and farms.

Canals and railroads—by extending the reach of city dwellers' appetites far into the hinterlands—enabled cities to grow on the fat of land elsewhere. The aggregation of tens of thousands of alimentary tracts packed into the small space of eastern cities set up a grand peristalsis that drew more and more foods from an ever-expanding foodshed. As early as 1820, the Erie Canal had garnered the farmlands of the Genesee and Ohio valleys into New York City's foodshed. The fertility of freshly plowed soils produced impressive yields of wheat and corn, which when shipped at low cost by canal, lowered prices for consumers. By the 1830s, mass-produced flour became the first staple food item that even frugal Yankee farmers were buying from afar instead of growing for them-selves.[35]

At the same time, as cities grew in size, some locally produced foods became less desirable. For example, in the largest cities, many people depended on poor-tasting, poor-quality milk from swill dairies where cows were fed the fermented mash left over from whiskey making. By significantly lessening transport times, speedy railroads opened the possibility of hauling clean milk from grass-fed country cows. By 1851, the Erie Railroad carried nearly eight million gallons of milk from nearby Orange County into New York City each year.[36]

By 1860, the growing demand of urban eaters had already prompted New England's traditionally self-reliant farmers to reconfigure their lands with more cash crops to supply city tables with vegetables, fruits, butter, and poultry.[37] And with more than 30,000 miles of railroad tracks fingering into the countryside, city appetites had also begun to reshape landscapes and ecologies beyond the Appalachian Mountains, where forests, prairies, and wetlands of the Midwest were transformed into bonanza grain farms and rangelands. Foodsheds formerly limited by the 150 miles a wagon might travel were extended to the 1,000 miles a train could travel in the same time. After the Civil War, the South too joined the eastern urban foodshed when former cotton plantations were con-verted to truck farms and began to supply winter vegetables and fruits to northern cities. Steamships from Charleston, Savannah, Norfolk, and Bermuda hauled tomatoes, potatoes, peas, cabbage, onions, strawber-ries, and cherries twice a week during peak harvest times.[38]

For many city dwellers, the most apparent effect of the railroad was not the possibility for new travel, but for new eats. The abundance was most dramatic in the markets of New York City, and no one knew the ins and outs of these markets better than Thomas De Voe. Apprenticed as a butcher in the late 1820s, and then working in Jefferson Market (in Green-wich Village) through the 1860s, De Voe's life and work spanned the hey-day of the open-air food markets and America's first frenzy of urban growth.[39] From his vantage point at the meat counter, De Voe made astute observations about purveying and procuring foods in the city—topics regarded by many as too banal to record. However, De Voe was no ordinary butcher. He might more aptly be described as an epicure naturalist, and it is this naturalist inclination that makes him so fascinating.

Like many men of his generation, De Voe grew up hunting and fishing. He recalled scouting the Manhattan countryside for meadowlarks in the neighborhood of Twenty-fourth Street at a time when life in the country and life in the city were not so far apart. Even as the city grew up around him and places to hunt disappeared, De Voe and his friends continued to shoot squirrels and pigeons.

De Voe expected to know many of the specific places that his meats and vegetables came from, often within walking or riding distance. It made sense that the sturgeon in the market were the same as those seen "leaping clear out of the river some eight or ten feet" by almost every ferryboat passenger crossing the Hudson in the summer.[40] Although De Voe lived in the city and likely purchased foods at the market where he worked, he still linked foods to their place of origin—a commonsense habit of mind practiced by most people with a rural background, which, in the mid-nineteenth century, still meant most Americans.

To De Voe, knowing where a food came from was essential because its taste was incontrovertibly tied to its place of origin. In some cases, he knew to the stream where the best fish had been caught; for example, the finest pickerel came from the Hudson tributary Saugerties Creek.[41] Oysters and clams were known by dozens of names depending on where they came from, such as Saddle Rocks, Mill Ponds, and the much esteemed Blue Points.[42] Each had earned a different reputation for taste, so their place-names carried particular meaning for mollusk eaters.

At the market, much of the food arrived just as if it were homegrown or hunted, replete with dirt, roots, bugs, feathers, scales, and eyeballs. To negotiate the stalls at the marketplace was to glimpse at places imagined beyond the city's edge. The mountains of potatoes, tables heaped with fatty hams, bushels of corn, and baskets of delicate tomatoes, together with strings of teal and piles of shimmering, stinking mackerel, were the way an urban eater could encounter the fruitful and creative natural world outside the city—both of farm and of wilds beyond.

Like most Americans, De Voe generally regarded what came to market as a product of nature's farms, streams, and seas. But he was particularly curious, and in the tradition of America's great naturalists he set out to investigate and record the flora and fauna of the market. His book *The Market Assistant* reads much like a natural history guidebook. Indeed, De Voe consulted several naturalist guides in order to make sure he correctly reported all species of wild birds and fishes, though he was careful to distinguish various folk names and to explain which creatures were common and which were rare.[43]

Following conventions of natural history, De Voe divided market comestibles into taxonomic categories. There were "Domestic, or tame animals" and "Wild animals," "Poultry" and "Wild Fowl and Birds," and for each he described dozens of species and varieties routinely found as food in city markets. For example, he cataloged thirty-five types of wild-fowl, including brant, mallard, bald-pate (American widgeon), and eighty-four other kinds of wild birds.[44] He inventoried the sixty-six types of fish commonly found in markets and an additional ninety-three found only occasionally. By midcentury, with the railroad's far-reaching tracks, it was not uncommon to find wild animals at the city's largest markets, such as lower Manhattan's Washington Market.

Though De Voe made taxonomic distinctions, he made no distinction between what was of nature and what one might eat. Any animal or plant—farmed, gathered, trapped, or shot—might be found as food, for someone, in the marketplace. Food was simply the part of nature that people ate.

As a butcher, De Voe clearly had a predisposition toward animals, but he also described eighty-two types of vegetables that regularly came to market, plus many varieties: fifteen distinctive potatoes, nine kinds of peas, five different cabbages, and three types of celery—each with its own attributes and flavors. In addition to the garden vegetables, the wild greens, such as dock, dandelion, lamb's lettuce, and pepper cress, which had long augmented springtime diets of country families, also showed up in city markets, as did an assortment of wild mushrooms. In the urban marketplace, a city shopper could find all of nature's bounty on display.

As a good naturalist, De Voe carefully identified and described each food, what it looked like, and where it came from. He took care to articulate the transition from animal to flesh to food that he saw in his everyday work of slaughtering and dressing meats—from sheep to mutton, from calf to veal, from pig to pork, and from ox that had worked faithfully with a farmer for years to beef ready for sale at his stand.[45] Sometimes De Voe even described the function of a particular cut in the body of its living animal source. For example, in the case of "Beeve's tongue," he explained that in "the living animal's mouth" the tongue was "very rough, being almost a compact bed of spines, which nature has furnished to draw the grass or other food into the mouth."[46] In the details of his description, De Voe recognized how the apparently purposeful design of nature persisted in animal parts even as they entered the marketplace on their way to becoming human food.

De Voe's epicurean bent and penchant for natural history drove him to a minor obsession. In much the same way that an avid birder keeps a life list of birds seen, De Voe recorded and sometimes sketched new edibles that came to market. And he sampled most everything. For each of over a hundred types of birds, he described with great nuance which were "flavorful," "delicate," "fishy," "sweet," and "esteemed," preferring, for example, the flavor of a green-winged teal to that of a blue-winged teal. For those creatures that only rarely made it to market, such as eagles or western mule deer, De Voe tracked down other eater's accounts to fill gaps in his own (baby eaglets, if you are wondering, "made very good food").[47] More than most, De Voe was a man who knew the natural world through his taste buds.

Because of his keen interest in what came to market and his work as a butcher, De Voe was acutely aware of the growing ignorance of shoppers plying the market stalls. As the city was increasingly populated by born-and-bred urbanites, fewer shoppers could draw upon knowledge gained through raising food firsthand, so they often didn't know the first thing about how to choose what to eat.

Many mistakenly thought that because eggs came in different colors, sizes, shapes, and textures, they could not all be fresh. Because these shoppers had never gathered eggs, they did not understand, as De Voe explained, that every hen had "an individual peculiarity in the form, color and size of the egg that she lays." Smooth, cream-colored eggs, rough, chalky, granulated ones, buff eggs, snow-white ones, spherical eggs, oval, pear-shaped, and "emphatically egg-shaped" chicken eggs could all be found in the market.[48] To confound matters further, guinea hen, peafowl, and duck eggs might be found among those laid by other birds. And the baskets of such myriad confusing eggs were only one category of comestible.

The lack of basic food knowledge that De Voe encountered in his dealings with market shoppers had grown, fostered by the urbanizing trend that was wholly transforming America's landscape and culture. In 1820, when New York's Washington Market was new, only three cities had populations greater than fifty thousand. With only 7.2 percent of the population living in urban areas, America was still profoundly rural.[49]

However, by the middle of the nineteenth century, the trend of young people moving to cities had picked up pace. Just as westward expansion dimmed the prospects of eastern farming, new mill-powered factories began to turn their wheels in eastern cities, offering alluring new possibilities for work. As hopeful rural migrants joined immigrants escaping poverty and war in Europe, America's cities swelled.

By 1860, when De Voe was writing his book, nearly 20 percent of Americans lived in large towns and cities. By 1880, the number would climb to nearly 30 percent, and then with another influx of immigrants, it would catapult to over 45 percent by 1910.[50] As the ratio of those farming to those not farming rapidly began to shift, the work and experience of procuring food also changed markedly.

On market days, farmers hauled livestock, fruit, eggs, butter, potatoes, and other vegetables from the proximate countryside to supply hungry eaters. Millers, bakers, fishmongers, and butchers supplied city dwellers with flour, bread, fish, and meats that the new urbanites could no longer readily furnish for themselves.

Instead of spending days outdoors working in fields and gardens, greater numbers of Americans were spending their lives working indoors in factories, offices, shops, and homes. Though some city dwellers, especially the poorest, persisted in keeping small animals and gardens in back alleys, most had to delegate the work of procuring foods to market men and the fishermen and farmers who supplied them.[51] In delegating this work, city dwellers were also relinquishing the opportunity to know their foods firsthand.

Who Did the Shopping?

Thomas De Voe described Jefferson Market as teeming with throngs of people from all walks of life, but just who were the ignorant shoppers that he bemoaned? He fondly recalled the days when discerning gentlemen had shopped with large baskets in the early morning, and then times when the "good housewife, who would not trust anybody but herself to select a fine young turkey," came to market. But increasingly, it was servants, stewards, or other unknowledgeable "go-betweens."[52] A question so simple as "who did the shopping?" leads to complicated answers and surprising implications for what Americans knew and would expect to know about the foods they were eating. It wasn't just the reach of the railroads or the abdication of cabbage growing that made it increasingly common for city dwellers to know less about their foods. New ideas about women's proper role in the emerging urban, industrial, and class-stratified society held important sway as well.

As more and more factories manufactured low-priced goods, women's traditional role in household production work was significantly diminished. To accommodate this substantial economic shift, a new domestic ideology emerged in the 1830s, particularly in towns and cities, that encouraged middle-class women to forget weaving cloth and making candles and instead to focus on being better mothers and wives. The new urban domestic vision construed men venturing into the competitive workplace to earn enough money to support the family while wives nurtured children and created a refined and peaceful haven at home.[53]

The new idealized vision of home demanded a higher standard of housekeeping in middle- and upper-class households, with greater elaboration of meals, dress, and cleanliness. The higher standard meant that —even without the work of making soap, feeding fowl, and planting potatoes—the work of child care, laundry, cooking, and cleaning was still far more than one woman could handle. Increasingly, middle-class urban women hired domestic servants to perform the tedious, physical aspects of housework and reserved the "elevated" tasks of teaching children, decorating parlors, reading books, and comforting husbands for themselves.[54]

When Amelia Simmons had fashioned her toothsome roast meats and election cakes, only the most affluent urban households hired live-in servants. However, by the 1840s, the advancing prosperity of a burgeoning new middle class of urbanites had made the hiring of "domestics" quite prevalent. In 1845, one out of four Boston families hired domestic help, the highest rate in the nation, and, before long, families in other cities followed suit. In 1860, 85 to 88 percent of households headed by professionals or managerial workers in Milwaukee hired domestics, as did over half of clerical and sales workers; even 16 percent of skilled wageworkers hired domestic help. By 1870, about one in eight families nationwide hired domestics, but the rate was much higher in cities, with their deepening disparity of wealth. A quarter of families in New York, Baltimore, and San Francisco employed live-in maids.[55]

The widespread hiring of servants in the mid-nineteenth century hinged upon a massive influx of impoverished immigrants. Between 1845 and 1860, approximately 1.5 million Irish immigrants, fleeing the misery of the potato famine, came to America.[56] With few options, many poor, unskilled Irish women and children were willing to work long hours for low wages in the households of others. Similarly, after emancipation, poor and dislocated black women also sought jobs as domestic servants.[57] It was the availability of these poor women that made it possible for the new idealized domestic vision to flourish in middle- and upper-class American homes.

In this context of increased economic and social stratification, America's rising class of "ladies" considered it most appropriate for domestics, who clearly inhabited a lower social milieu, to venture to market — with its foul stenches, flies, filth of manure left by delivery horses, and crowds of lower-class shoppers — to purchase meats and vegetables.[58]

However, as America's "ladies" readily discovered, the young immigrant girls they hired rarely had the skills and knowledge to pick foods

2.1. *In the mid- to late nineteenth century, hiring domestic help was a common way for affluent and even middle-class homemakers to cope with the burden of household work. This staged humor shot of a maid disrupting dinner suggests the scorn with which domestics—and their kitchen-related duties—were often regarded.*

well. With their previous experience of cooking and eating limited to poverty diets of boiled potatoes, many domestics had no idea how to approach the poached fishes, pigeon pies, and roasted meats they were now expected to prepare, let alone how to select eggs or pinch a goose's webbed foot to test its freshness.

The ineptitude of domestic servants was a popular if irksome topic of discussion among the women who hired them. In 1850, Elizabeth Sullivan Stuart described how she took on a "raw" Irish girl who had arrived in America only four days earlier and "did not understand the name of an article in the house."[59] One doctor explained that most girls hired as domestics "never saw a leg of mutton boiled or roasted. Several of them cannot even prepare their own dinner bacon or pork."[60] Sara Josepha Hale wrote about a new Irish servant who peeled potatoes with her fingernails.[61] Many mistresses felt compelled to adopt a missionary role in instructing these unskilled helpers about the basics of cooking.

However, the problem of servant ignorance, some realized, was compounded by the ignorance of young mistresses themselves, many of whom had stopped doing household work. In embracing new, genteel roles that elevated refined skills such as playing piano and speaking French, affluent young women were no longer learning common skills such as darning and baking. Coming of age in households where lowly domestics, not mothers, did the cooking meant that a generation of young women had grown up without learning the skills needed to run the ideal households over which they were now expected to preside.

By midcentury, the gap between what women didn't know and should know had become grist for a growing tide of domestic literature. With a respectful nostalgia for sturdy-armed grandmothers and country cousins who could wring soup from stones, reformist writers from Lydia Child and Catherine Maria Sedgwick to Sara Josepha Hale penned cautionary tales about what the loss of traditional knowledge would mean for society. If young women didn't know how to bake bread, the very health and well-being of families would be at risk.[62] Some lamented the "vanity, extravagance, and idleness" of young ladies, but most household writers tacitly recognized that maintaining femininity, respectability, and status required remaining aloof from knuckle-abrading, fingernail-dirtying work.[63] The resolution they proffered to shore up affluent women's domestic respectability was a detached, bookish approach to foods that informed the women but kept their hands free from dough, guts, and soot.

Charged with this mission, domestic writers amassed compendia of what they deemed to be essential household knowledge for ladies to learn and master. Most presumed that their readers would use the information, not to perform household tasks themselves, but rather to instruct and supervise servants more attentively. This supervisory role offered affluent women a comfortable middle ground between the toil of endless housework in an age of increasing expectations and that pernicious old vice, idleness.[64]

The approach of delegating rather than doing came to bear directly in the work of shopping. Following in the manner of Amelia Simmons's transcriber, most household writers included meticulous details about how to choose foods at market. As well-known writers and sisters Catherine Beecher and Harriet Beecher Stowe explained in their 1869 *American Women's Home,* even "those who were not themselves obliged to go to market, should have the knowledge which will enable them to direct their servants what and how to buy."[65] One woman in late nineteenth-century St. Louis executed the detached approach of knowing-but-not-doing by riding in a carriage to the central market and then sitting and waiting until her black butler brought bunches of celery and watermelons for her consideration and approval.[66]

A passage from Catherine Beecher's *Domestic Receipt Book* reveals how skin-deep knowledge could suffice even in the realm of bread baking. With no small measure of zeal, Beecher extolled the critical importance of making good bread to family life. "The last grand essential to good bread is *good care,*" she explained. "Unless the cook can be fully trusted, the mistress of the family *must* take this care upon *herself.*" At first, you might infer that Beecher was suggesting the mistress make the bread. However, reading further, you will realize that Beecher was recommending that the mistress simply *supervise* more closely: "She must, if needful, stand by and see that the bread is wet right, that the yeast is good, that the bread is put where it is warm enough, that it does not rise too long, so as to lose its sweetness (which is often the case before it begins to sour), that it is moulded aright, that the oven is at the right heat, and that it is taken out at the right time, and then that it is put in the right place and not set flat on to a greasy table, or painted shelf to imbibe a bad taste."[67] A loaf so baked by a backseat baker like Beecher must have trembled to rise.

This aloof approach toward the work of procuring and preparing foods was reflected not only in the practice of hiring domestics to market and to cook but also in the popular brownstone architecture of affluent urban homes. For much of the nineteenth century, kitchens were located in dark, airless basements, which kept the messy activities of the hired cook separate from the rest of the family. Before innovations in ventilation and cleaner fuels, the dirtiest aspect of kitchen work was the sooty, smoky job of tending to fires and coal stoves, an especially unpleasant — and insalubrious — task on hot summer days in an enclosed space. Other necessary but messy meal-preparation work, such as plucking feathers, eviscerating birds, and scrubbing dirt from carrots, was also considered unsavory. Negative associations both with the work of food preparation and also with the poor and uncomely women who did the work affixed a stigma to handling foods.[68]

As women of rising affluence navigated new expectations of gentility, they pulled behind them a significant change in Americans' food sensibility. By delegating the work of procuring and preparing foods, they were adopting a removed approach to foods and cooking. As standing by and watching — using head not hands — emerged as the preferred manner of affluent homemakers in the kitchen, what it meant to know foods moved into a more abstract realm.

In most cities, no more than a quarter of urban families configured their kitchens and conducted their cooking and shopping with mistress supervising and domestic doing the dirty work. However, the attitudes and expectations developed in these upper-echelon households by both employers and domestics (roughly one million women worked as domestics in 1870) would influence a broader sweep of the population, especially as mass-circulation magazines began to spread upper- and middle-class ideals and standards to households nationwide.[69] Negative attitudes toward working with food that developed in trendsetting households were already beginning to establish the desirability and gentility of a detached knowledge of foods.

At the same time, growing numbers of working-class housewives also faced conditions that pressed them to deal with foods and cooking in more removed ways. As cities grew, many were compelled to live far from central markets and had to rely on hucksters who brought a limited variety of foods by cart into neighborhoods. Installation of water and sewer lines that improved quality of life in middle- and upper-class neighbor-hoods did not keep pace with urban expansion in working-class neigh-borhoods, where homemakers had to carry every drop of water they used for cooking and cleaning.[70] In shabby, sooty, and cramped apart-ments with few implements, many found it difficult to cook anything but simple meals. Moreover, low wages meant that the cost of food could comprise 50 to 60 percent of a working-class family's earnings, pressing homemakers to prioritize price over all other food attributes.[71] With husbands, single women, and children working for wages in factories, the long hours of the industrial workday compelled many family members to eat at different hours or on the run, with dinner pails of bread, potatoes, and cold meat often replacing more complicated family meals.[72]

By the final decades of the nineteenth century, the domestic ideology that had stigmatized household work led to its very own unraveling. Middle-class mistresses found it increasingly difficult to find poorer women willing to do their cooking, cleaning, and shopping—especially as more opportunities for less-demeaning wagework opened up in fac-tories. In 1880, the number of households hiring servants in New York City had dropped to 19 percent; by 1900, that number would fall further to 14 percent, while nationwide the rate would plunge to 6 percent.[73]

In this context, household experts were compelled to revise their view of "marketing," and many began to recommend that ladies do their own. As Eunice Beecher (sister-in-law to the more famous Harriet and Cath-erine) explained, "A servant's judgement is seldom trustworthy, and the husband *may forget.*" Even if he did not forget, she explained, the hus-band could not be expected to "understand his wife's business as well as she does herself."[74]

Though many middle-class homemakers resumed going to market themselves, they retained a detached mien that had become culturally engrained. This was made easier by changes that had occurred in the food distribution infrastructure. As cities continued to grow, the impor-tance of the central markets diminished as smaller "daily" markets and meat shops popped up in city neighborhoods and budding suburbs. These smaller retail markets made it possible for women to avoid the crowded central markets that were becoming wholesale entrepôts, and many gave homemakers the time-saving option of ordering groceries by list (and later, by phone) and then having them delivered.[75]

More than most anyone, cooking expert Maria Parloa recognized that this detached method of marketing had its drawbacks. If anything, the growing variety and varying quality of foods coming to city markets and stores made the work of choosing foods more demanding. Well-known for her popular cooking-demonstration lectures and her regular column in *Good Housekeeping* magazine, Parloa encouraged homemakers to take a more hands-on approach and do their own shopping to obtain the best-quality foods. She explained that it was "impossible for the [sales]man who calls at your house, to remember all the little things there are in the market; more than that, he does not have the same idea that you do of what is a good quality and what an inferior."[76]

Parloa tried to dispel the stigma that had become associated with city markets. In some towns and cities, she explained, market days had the feel of "a reception" with "all classes, from a laborer's wife to the wife of a millionaire" present.[77] She also tried to soften class divisions by assuring readers that the hardened look of the German women who sold vegetables at the markets in New York and Philadelphia disclosed their lives of constant labor—in homes and fields, and at market—rather than selfishness or any lack of feeling. She encouraged her refined readers to smile, have a pleasant word, and fairly pay these hardworking women.[78]

Despite her encouragement, Parloa realized that "the majority of New England housekeepers" would "not go to the market and select their supplies" and instead had come to rely on grocery stores with delivery service.[79] In this context, flourishing women's magazines and newspapers now began to feature special "marketing" sections, which advised women in elaborate detail about which foods were available at markets so they didn't have to go themselves.[80] "Upon the amount of practical knowledge of marketing that the housekeeper has, the comfort and expense of the family are in a great measure dependent," Maria Parloa admonished, "therefore every head of household should acquire as much of this knowledge as is practicable."[81] Studying the information supplied in marketing columns became all the more important if a homemaker never went to market.

In 1796, Amelia Simmons had presumed it would be an insult to tell a woman how to choose her food; in her view, everyone knew from commonsense experience. But by the 1880s, assumptions had changed entirely. "Marketing" was now presented as a critical skill for housewives and a body of knowledge in its own right.

CHAPTER 3

Mystifying the Mundane

As the rapidly emerging national food system began to deliver its provender in new ways and new forms through the 1870s and 1880s, household experts continued to urge shoppers to learn about the particulars of their food—the places it came from, its proper season, and in the case of meats, the animals that provided it.[1] Still implicit in the marketing advice of urban food writers was the assumption that homemakers needed to know, and could know, the attributes of genuine articles of food directly as they came from the farm. As well-known cooking authority Maria Parloa emphasized, "a purchaser must be capable of judging the raw material."[2] But the traditional assumptions and expectations embedded within popular marketing advice would soon shift as the infrastructure and landscapes that provided America's food changed dramatically with industrialization. What had for ages been mundane would soon become mystified in the minds of most Americans.

Transformations in how people thought about their foods may at first seem simply a matter of adjusting to new tools and technologies—no different from a cook familiar with a woodstove beginning to use an electric stove and shifting from knowing how to choose the right logs and subtly adjust the damper to knowing how to manipulate the correct knobs or buttons. But there is more to these changes than merely mastering new techniques, for as we've seen, knowing food isn't solely the means to a meal; it also provides a fundamental means for making sense of our place in the world.

As more city dwellers knew less and less about the particularities of their food and its origins, cultural notions about place, wildness, and animals' lives would begin to shift, leading to an increasing disassociation between eating and food production and, ultimately, to a mental disengagement from nature.

Place of Origin

When the transcriber of *American Cookery* had recommended cabbage from "unmanured grounds" in 1796, it was expected that a cook or housewife could know the place where fresh foods came from—if not from a backyard plot, then from the ring of nearby farms that encircled America's towns and cities. Through much of the nineteenth century, this expectation persisted even as foodsheds expanded from places that eaters could know firsthand to places that shoppers could only imagine.

In her biweekly *Good Housekeeping* market reports, for example, Mrs. F. A. Benson took great pains to identify and distinguish for her readers precisely where food in the New York City markets came from. Beginning in 1885, she reported every two weeks on what came to market in elaborate detail. In the deep winter months, fish came from Oregon, the Penobscot River, Nova Scotia, Long Island, North Carolina, Florida, and Rhode Island. Mutton came from England, beef from Chicago, and lamb from hothouses in New Jersey. Poultry came from Long Island, upstate New York, Philadelphia, New Jersey, Rhode Island, and Vermont, while wildfowl came from the western states. Eggs came from Pennsylvania, Delaware, Ohio, Maryland, and New Jersey. Vegetables came from the Indian River in Florida, Havana, Virginia, New Jersey, and Delaware. Citrus fruits came by ship from the Mediterranean, Florida, England, Havana, and Jamaica.[3]

The traditional category of knowledge that linked foods to their place of origin was taking on new significance in the era of railroads, however. Knowing where a food came from could certainly indicate particular quality, as in the case of oysters or clams, but it could also alert a shopper to bad deals or unpleasant flavors. For example, Mrs. Benson explained that potatoes grown in the mucky soil of Florida's newly drained wetlands had to be washed before shipping, which meant Florida potatoes rotted more quickly than those grown in lighter soils.[4] And because hens on the south shore of Long Island were often fed with herring, their eggs were said to taste fishy.[5]

Knowing a food's place of origin also enabled a shopper to determine how far a fruit or fish had traveled to market. City dwellers were already coming to learn the often-direct relationship between the distance a food had traveled and its quality. Eggs from the nearest states were regarded as the best.[6] The same was true for snipe killed in New Jersey marshes, which were preferable to snipe shot "beyond Indian Territory."[7]

There were other new peculiarities to knowing places associated with foods. In the railroad era, it was no longer enough to know when a fruit or vegetable was in season, because foods from different places came into season at different times, and they didn't always arrive properly ripened. As fruits traveled longer distances over longer periods of time to market, they were more susceptible to decay, freezing, and bruising. To solve this problem, southern fruit shippers, following the practices of northern dairies and fishermen, tried first to keep their cars cooled with ice. They also customized boxcars to better carry the fragile contents.

Then much to the dismay of eaters, some growers resorted to picking fruits before they ripened. The unripe fruit that came to market by rail not only tasted awful but was regarded by some as "dangerous stuff" for the stomach.[8] To shoppers accustomed to well-ripened local fruits, the inability of the evolving market system to supply ripe-but-not-rotted fruit from distant orchards was difficult to understand. Traditional expectations of what constituted ripeness and quality were not so easily met in the railroad era food market, where middlemen deemed durability more important than sweetness.[9]

For culinary reasons, it was also important to know when certain vegetables were *not* in season, because some items, such as potatoes, turnips, onions, and cabbages, were held for months after harvest in the cold storage warehouses that were cropping up to store surplus foods in cities. Though cold storage was beginning to smooth out some of the gluts and droughts of supply, the ice-packed warehouses often delivered poor-quality, freezer-burned foods in off-seasons. Vegetables that had endured cold storage required special attention when cooking. To compensate for their strong flavor and wilted appearance, food writers recommended letting such vegetables sit in a bowl of cold water for several hours before cooking.[10]

Cold storage affected not only vegetables but poultry, eggs, and butter, so it was still useful for city homemakers to know something about the natural cycles of farm animals' reproduction and growth. For example, chickens' schedule of reproduction and metabolic capabilities for growth meant that eggs flooded the market during springtime, and "spring chickens"—the surplus males consigned to the pot—came several weeks later. A "spring chicken" purchased in November was likely a chicken that had been frozen—and, more likely than not, frozen and thawed and refrozen a number of times—in a cold storage warehouse. Such knowledge became more and more important as traditional tangible clues became useless. As Mrs. Benson explained, "it is [now] useless to pinch a frozen bird that is stiff and hard to discover if tender."[11]

With their columns in magazines and newspapers, food writers tried to construct an elaborate mental calendar and geography to help city shoppers understand precisely what food was in season, when, and from where. Presumably, by reading market columns, a homemaker could plan meals that made use of foods in season and could avoid getting overcharged or tricked into buying something spoiled. However, given the rapidly expanding scale of city foodsheds, even as food writers and household experts tried to reshape traditional knowledge to meet new market conditions, the emerging food system was changing faster than they could write.

The sheer number of place-names listed in Mrs. Benson's column indicates that the connection between foods and the actual places they came from was becoming less meaningful. Her column was crammed with simply too much information—far more than any student lesser than a De Voe could grasp. Indeed, Mrs. Benson's meticulously place-attentive market reports were discontinued in 1887 and replaced with a more general advice column. In the emerging national-scale food marketplace, the straightforward notion of place that had once rooted eaters to particular patches of land had become immaterial.

How did cold storage transform what "could" be done to food? How did profitability influence this?

The Waning of Wild Foods

Though rarely staples of American cooking, wild foods represent a uniquely American fare. In Europe, where freshwater fish and game animals had been hoarded by aristocrats who held virtually all the land, ordinary people had little chance to hunt and fish. America, with wild fish, fowl, and game, all free for the taking, had offered colonists a remarkably democratic source of sustenance. While the most commonly consumed foods were those raised on farms, fishing and hunting had provided additional meat, especially during lean spring times, and the importance of these freely available foods to the poorer members of society was well recognized in early colonial times.

By the time Amelia Simmons penned her recipes in 1796, wild foods other than fish had already become uncommon in the Northeast, and by the 1820s, it was considered newsworthy when wagons of white hares, partridges (ruffed grouse), venison, and a lone panther arrived at New York's Fulton Market.[12] Many of these animals and birds had long been extinguished from areas close to populous eastern cities when their forest and meadow habitats were converted to homes and farms. For example, grouse, which had been locally common, became rare by the 1830s, and as their price and prestige soared with scarcity, the birds were restricted to the tables of epicures.[13]

By the mid-nineteenth century, however, owing to the railroads' long reach westward, a veritable Noah's ark of wild creatures — deer, bear, sea turtles, robins, and Eskimo curlews — appeared under the roofs of New York City's markets once again and this time in greater variety and quantity than ever before. Wading birds from Florida together with antelope from western prairies, turtles from southern swamps, and bears from the north woods all found their niches in stalls of the marketplace. It was in this motley assemblage at market — not in the copse, marsh, or zoo — that many city dwellers saw such wild animals for the first time.

Because the creatures came from distant places that shoppers had no way of knowing about firsthand, middle- and upper-class homemakers relied on market vendors and newspaper and magazine columns to learn about choosing the best game, fish, and fowl. Ironically, learning about

3.1. *At Washington Market in New York, city dwellers encountered wild animals as food — not only common duck and grouse but also less common creatures, such as bears, seen here. The bounty of the markets conveyed the abundance of the natural world that existed far beyond the city.*

wild food gave city shoppers the opportunity to learn something about the workings of nature. Many wild foods came to market only at certain times, depending on migratory habits, for example. By reading market columns, one could discern that shad from rivers in Florida hit the New York markets in February, then every few weeks the catch advanced northward. By early March, shad came from Georgia's Ogeechee River, by late March, from the Potomac, Delaware, and Susquehanna rivers, by early April from the Hudson, and then by mid-April from the Connecticut River. Many agreed that the Connecticut River shad tasted best, and so marketing experts recommended that city dwellers seeking prime shad should wait until mid-April to buy.[14]

Knowledge of migratory habits could also help a shopper pick prized canvasback ducks, which were best when shot in December on the Susquehanna, Chesapeake, Potomac, or Delaware rivers, where large flocks fed on wild "celery." During other seasons, when these diving ducks presumably ate more fish, their meat tasted "objectionable." On the other hand, the flesh of wood ducks, which always ate seeds, insects, and fruits, had a flavor superior to that of fish-eating sea ducks.[15] Because what animals ate could affect the flavor of their meat, it was useful for discerning shoppers to know something about feeding habits of wildlife.

Though some wild foods were considered exotic, many had become the ingredients of traditional and classic American meals, such as oyster stew, codfish balls, and pigeon potpie. Indeed, the new railroad-induced abundance of some wild foods made them the best deals in town. The esteemed grouse, which had been decimated on Long Island, reappeared in New York markets when trains brought a glut of them from Iowa, Illinois, and Wisconsin.[16]

Even as the food system enlarged and began to change dramatically to support giant cities, wild foods still offered many urban Americans a visible and tangible reminder that foods came from a bountiful nature. Whether or not shoppers cooked and ate wild foods, the "fantastic game hooks," strings of fowl, and piles of fish and flesh at the marketplace created an impression of cornucopian plenty symbolically confirming America's legendary abundance.[17] And even for those shoppers who did not go to market themselves, marketing columns with their long, descriptive listings of wild creatures created a similar, if removed, trust in abundance.

This outlook from the city market was distorted by foreshortening, not unlike Saul Steinberg's famous view of America as seen from New York City. In the perception of most city shoppers, the market alone became the foodshed. The land, water, and human work that actually created the foodstuffs had receded far beyond the horizon—both literally and conceptually. Beyond that horizon, however, the wild abundance was rapidly diminishing

Before railroads had extended the force of city appetites out across the countryside, the ecological context of wild foods had been more plainly understood by local people in local economies. In the earliest round of environmental conflicts prompted by food production, flour-grinding mills had blocked the migration of wild Atlantic salmon and shad on many of New England's streams by the 1700s. Local fishermen and eaters had pushed for fish ladders or seasonal restrictions that allowed salmon to migrate to spawning grounds in the spring while still permitting mills to grind flour after the fall grain harvest. In local place-constrained economies, cooks, eaters, and fishermen were unwilling to trade off their fish for their bread. They wanted both and developed solutions aimed at permitting both to persist, for a while at least.[18]

By the nineteenth century, however, threats to river and estuarine fish habitats had intensified. As waterfront cities grew, so too did the amount of foul wastes dumped into rivers. At the same time, a new generation of highly capitalized factories demanded hydropower from new dams that blocked migration of fish year-round.[19]

It was at this juncture that canals, steamboats, and railroads expanded urban foodsheds and funneled distant wildlife into the kaleidoscopic displays of wild food in city markets. Now when the economic potential of factories was pitted against the ecological viability of fish, the apparently boundless presence of so many wild foods made it easier to ignore the deteriorating conditions of local supplies that remained. With so many fish coming from everywhere else, the fish of a particular local river no longer seemed critical.

Thomas De Voe explained this phenomenon from one city eater's perspective. A fisherman friend caught several eels in the Hudson River at the foot of Fifteenth Street. As usual, he took them home and fried them into a serpentine supper, but this time, after one bite, he could not eat the rest. De Voe wrote, "He supposed that the gas-works or refuse from that place cast into the river had affected them, as he found the taste much as the gas tar smelled."[20] Though De Voe and his friend had long fished in Manhattan waters, they accepted with resignation the pollution of this local food source as an unavoidable consequence of progress. Rather than rail against the gasworks, De Voe simply recommended that shoppers buy eels taken at sea.

This pattern would repeat itself again and again in the new railroad-supplied food system. When Atlantic salmon from Maine's Kennebec River became scarce, Pacific salmon all the way from the West Coast's grand Columbia were ushered in to replace them with no apparent loss in the city market. (Years later, Columbia River salmon would be replaced by Norwegian and Alaskan salmon.) Although earlier eaters could have told us about distinctions in taste and flavor between fish from various rivers, these nuances were lost in the growing scale of the marketplace. The loss of a specific river's fish and its particular flavor was accepted as a trade-off and scarcely mourned in the emerging national food system. On the land, too, growing pressures of market hunting together with habitat loss caused by expanding farmland proved too difficult for many wild creatures to withstand. When deer were exterminated in New York, the supply-shed simply moved farther west, and venison continued to come to market in season.[21]

Although game depletion followed quickly in the wake of new transportation routes, this was never apparent to shoppers in the city market. If a shopper could not find a curlew from New Jersey, she could find a curlew from Indiana. If she could find no curlews, she could find a snipe. If she could find no snipe, she could always buy a domestic chicken. The fact that wild birds and fish were known by many colloquial names in the market further obscured extirpations from shoppers' view. Instead, at the market all evidence pointed to a comforting, distant plenty that hid the possibility of any limits—the possibility that perhaps one day a shopper would not find what she wanted.[22]

And that, in some cases, is exactly what happened. In her popular 1886 *Philadelphia Cookbook,* Mrs. Sarah Rorer advised homemakers that wild pigeons tasted better than tame ones in pigeon pie, but before long, shoppers would never be able to find such wild birds at market again.[23] In the late 1700s and early 1800s, when "great flights" still occurred in the eastern states, thousands upon thousands of birds had been brought to market and sold for pennies.[24] The popular dish pigeon pie was made with five or six birds. At the outset of the nineteenth century, tamed birds were considered most toothsome, and it was customary for cooks to pull up "three feet nicely cleaned" through the middle of the top crust to show what kind of pie it was.[25]

By the mid-nineteenth century, however, the ease and speed of railroad transport had kindled the business of market hunting. The pigeons' habit of flocking in great numbers made them easy targets for the shotguns and nets of hunters. At a roost in southern Michigan, one hunter captured 648 wild pigeons with the haul of a single net in 1858.[26] Responding to steady demand, sixteen years later, at nesting spot in western Michigan, four hundred market hunters shot and shipped out 25,000 pigeons every day for five to six weeks — nearly 1 million birds in all.[27]

Both in their legendary sky-blackening flights and in large piles at the market, the passenger pigeons epitomized plenty. However, confronted with nets and guns on a whole new scale, their population plummeted from billions in the 1870s to dozens in the 1890s.[28] With scarcity, the former gustatory preference for tame, grain-fed pigeons changed, and wild birds became most prized for eating. Before long, the birds were served only on the tables of the richest, not as homely pigeon pie but as extravagant French-named dishes, such as "pigeon à la Lombardy," which featured pigeon meat simmered in wine and trimmed with sweetbreads, ham, mushrooms, and velouté sauce.[29]

When passenger pigeons arrived at such white-linened tables, unrecognizable under blankets of white sauce, those eaters who'd ordered from elegant menus had little clue that their dinner was tied to a distant and unraveling ecology.[30] Nor did shoppers seeking to follow Sarah Rorer's pigeon pie recipe grasp the connection between their cooking and the birds' demise. The increasingly complex webs of commerce hid what happened at the other end of the railroad tracks and so made it possible for city dwellers to eat a species into oblivion without even realizing it. In the case of the passenger pigeon, extinction became the ultimate consequence of eaters not paying attention to the source of their foods.

While market hunting put great pressures on populations of many wild creatures valued for eating, destruction of their habitats also played a significant role in the tragic demise of nature's wild menu. Like pigeons, oysters too were common nineteenth-century fare. Recipes for stews or pies typically called for hundreds of the bivalves. In her *Home Cookery,* Mrs. J. Chadwick recommended "enhancing" a gumbo soup with one hundred oysters as if she were suggesting a dash of salt or spice. In 1850, a record 145 million pounds of oyster meat (shells not included) were extracted from the Chesapeake Bay alone—a feast of roughly 6 pounds 6 ounces for every single American man, woman, and child.[31] Fresh oysters became the nation's first fast food, typically eaten by city workingmen, who lunched upon them by the dozen in oyster cellars that were more common in seaboard cities than McDonald's is today, prompting one culinary historian to call the 1800s "the oyster century."[32]

Near the oldest cities, local oyster beds were decimated by overharvest early on. The State of New York established some new beds in the Hudson River estuary by importing and planting southern seed oysters, but dumping of the city's burgeoning garbage and street sweepings into nearby waters threatened their survival.[33] Finally in 1886, the state passed a law to protect oyster beds from pollution and appointed the first "State Oyster Protector" to enforce it.[34]

One article in the *New York Times* explained that it was "not pleasant for the citizens of New York to feel that he [sic] is personally responsible for the continual defilement of the Sound and Lower Bay."[35] However, the role that each city dweller played in polluting nearby oyster beds with aggregated household waste and garbage was not readily apparent to most or even preventable from their individual perspectives. Moreover, it soon became evident that a chief polluter was industrial: Standard Oil Company had also been pouring its refinery waste sludge acids into waters around Bergen Point, killing oysters and fish in great numbers.[36]

As in the case of pigeons, distant supplies insulated eaters from the decline of oyster populations. When local oyster beds were exhausted in New England and New York estuaries, oysters from the Chesapeake Bay were hauled north to fill plates in their place. Esteemed "Blue Points" still showed up on the menus at fancy restaurants (and still do), though genuine Blue Points—the large, crooked, elongated, and heavy-shelled oysters that grew at Blue Point on the south shore of Long Island—had gone extinct in the 1860s. By the 1890s, what were served in restaurants and sold in market as "Blue Points" were small round oysters bearing no resemblance to their original namesakes.[37]

Such simple renaming would mask the decline of many wild foods. When prized canvasback ducks disappeared from markets and restaurants owing to the increased harvest of their eggs at northern breeding sites and to hunting pressures at their wintering grounds in Chesapeake Bay, the more common red-headed duck was substituted on city restaurant tables. When too few diamond-backed terrapins came to market to make the prized terrapin soup, southern sliders took their place. Once "the bona fide article" became scarce, one food writer explained, names were routinely "used to cover clever substitutes that only epicures could detect."[38] And indeed, when scarcity boosted prices, epicures became the only ones who could afford to eat wild game.

In America's culinary capital, where upper-crust diners reveled in Delmonico's highly civilized wild fare, the *New York Times* warned that the inevitable demise of wild animals would cause the country's menus and tables "to suffer." It was "only a matter of time," the 1891 article admonished, before the terrapin, canvasback duck, and oyster would disappear, "a misfortune to lovers of good eating."[39] But as distant sources and substitutes met their limits, and wild foods did indeed vanish from tables, few others voiced concern about the loss.[40]

As the most-prized species of birds and game animals became rare, sportsmen belatedly pushed for laws to stay their declines—primarily to allow for continued sport hunting rather than "good eating." A shopper might read about these laws in the marketing columns of *Good Housekeeping* or *Ladies' Home Journal* but not about the reasons for them. In fact, articles in women's magazines suggested that a "favored customer" might still purchase a grouse—again on the decline by the late 1880s— "in defiance of law."[41] Though the food writers bemoaned the effects that the new hunting restrictions would have on city tables, they seemed unaware of the effects those tables exerted on the natural world outside the city.

Wild foods had once been available to all people to hunt or fish, a hallmark of America's bountiful landscape and democratic society. However, as the growing human population elbowed wild animals, birds, and fish out of their habitats and consumed too many too fast in kitchens and restaurants, many creatures could not withstand the pressures. Ultimately, the abundance of wild animals and the distinctive foods they supplied were forfeited in a march of progress that promised to make new types of foods the heralds of democracy. Americans would place their faith in the ingenuity of an emerging industrial food system.

After 1911, when New York City finally closed its markets to wild game, the once common awareness that wild plants and animals could be delicious foods would become as rare as a curlew or a heath hen.[42] Not only were particular foods and flavors lost, but the very *idea* that food might come from an abundant nature—indicated by heavy strings of ducks at city markets and lengthy listings in marketing columns—was quietly forgotten.

The Abstraction of Animals' Lives

As the scale of America's food system expanded, in no case were changes in how cooks could know their food more dramatic than with meat.

Well into the 1880s, cookbook authors and other "marketing" experts presumed that shoppers could still learn a fair bit about the meat they were buying. For example, in her 1885 cookbook, Eunice Beecher still advised buying the meat of an ox for the best beef—but not just any ox: "The animal should be five or six years old before it is killed." Moreover, it was best to know how the animal was raised. By many accounts, the quality of beef was affected by how the animal that provided it was treated; if an animal was "badly fed," the beef would be "dark red, the fat skinny and tough, and in very old beef a horny substance [would] be found running through the ribs." And pork, Mrs. Beecher warned, "should never be bought except from a butcher whose honesty you are sure of and who knows where the pork was fattened."[43]

Beecher's recommendations depended on finding a trustworthy butcher who knew the animals that became the meats he sold. A butcher like Thomas De Voe knew which animals made the best meat by age, by sex, by breed, by what they were fed, sometimes by their work histories

3.2. *Through the nineteenth century, household experts advised city homemakers to rely on the expertise of a good butcher when purchasing meat. By 1911, when this butcher was photographed in Baltimore's Lexington Market, most beef came from animals slaughtered and "dressed" in Chicago and then shipped by rail to eastern markets.*

(whether or not they were draft animals), and even by their disposition. In the case of mutton, for example, because the cosset wether was a gentle breed of sheep and often "treated as a pet around the house or barnyard," he regarded its flesh as "generally in the best condition."[44]

Trained in the early part of the century, De Voe had learned the skills of butchering when most animals were still raised on a small scale by farmers. This traditional knowledge enabled him and other skilled butchers to identify how changes in the ways that animals were raised for city markets affected their meat. An animal housed "in a small dark pen, often breathing an impure atmosphere while fattening," for example, did "not produce well-flavored flesh." Though the flesh of confined animals was more tender owing to lack of muscle development, according to De Voe, animals "exercised in the free open air" and fattened on "short sweet mountain grasses ... always produce[d] flesh the sweetest, as well as of the highest flavor, and certainly the most healthy for human food."[45] In his experience, the taste of an animal's flesh reflected the quality of its life. The flesh of an animal was its life story incarnate.

However, by the late 1860s, the enlarging scale of city foodsheds was already making animal confinement increasingly common. In 1870, an estimated four million eastern city dwellers were eating beef from cattle that had been transported 1,000 to 1,200 miles by rail to the markets—all the time confined in desperately close quarters.[46] Nearly all beef coming to eastern markets followed a particular path. From the grasslands of the Great Plains, cattle were driven to railheads, hauled to Chicago, and then transported east by rail from the Union Stockyards. Cattle coming to New York City took the Erie Railroad to Jersey City, where they were slaughtered or prodded into boats and ferried to their final destination: Manhattan's abattoirs and butcher shops.

It was the trip by rail that most concerned traditional butchers and other critics of the emerging meat supply system. On their thousand-mile, four- to five-day journey to market, cattle were cramped and confined in rail cars without food or water. Agitated and frightened by the experience, many lost upwards of 120 pounds; others died.[47] Butchers could tell what the animals had been through by looking at their meat. Owing to the Erie Railroad's steep grades and sharp turns, which slammed animals against each other and the sides of the rail cars, nearly half the cattle that arrived by that line had severely bruised ribs. In the minds of reputable butchers—butchers trained in the traditional manner—this "yellow and livid" flesh was unfit for eating. Texas beef earned a particularly bad reputation because Texas cattle made the longest, most-tortured trip to market. Bruised and emaciated upon arrival in eastern slaughterhouses, their meat was often "discolored and tasteless."[48]

Cooks and eaters accustomed to associating the quality of an animal's life with the savor of its meat regarded the range-fed, railroad-hauled meat as inferior to that from animals raised on nearby farms. To ingest the meat of an animal that had endured such cruelty could surely not be tasteful or healthful. As one writer explained, there was no specific evidence that eating such meat harmed anyone; but "no physician" would say that "the flesh of a feverish, dull, and bruised animal, worried by long travel, and sore in every quarter from kicks and pounding is wholesome food."[49] Affluent homemakers who shopped at respectable butchers' shops could avoid feeding such "feverish" meats to their families. But at public markets, hundreds of travel-bruised quarters were sold at bargain prices every day to unknowing and undoubtedly the poorest shoppers. Indeed, the status and desirability of beef as a food made even the mediocre-quality meats seem salutary to those who could afford nothing else. To impoverished immigrant workers, many of whom had fled hunger in Europe, the ready availability of affordable meat—any meat— was a marvel.[50]

The problems of supplying beef to cities were becoming apparent not only to butchers and discriminating eaters but also to those involved in the supply end of the meat business. With injuries, lost weight, and deaths of cattle all adding up to significant losses in company ledger columns, it occurred to a young entrepreneur named Gustavus Swift that it would be far more efficient to transport just the meat of the cattle rather than live animals. Only 55 percent of each animal by weight was meat that a butcher could sell; the remaining hide, bones, and fat had only marginal value at eastern slaughterhouses.[51] With millions of cattle making the journey by train each year, that was a lot of waste—in both shipping costs and offal. Swift set out to rid the emerging beef-distribution system of this waste by bringing the factory approach of mass production to bear.

Mass production had already revolutionized the pork-packing industry in Cincinnati, fondly known by its boosters as Porkopolis. Customarily, salt pork had been made in small batches by local butchers and merchants who had taken hogs as payment from farm families in fall (when animals were fattest) and then slaughtered and cured them during the cold winter months. By centralizing operations amid corn-belt farms that could fatten and supply hogs year-round, the packing companies of Porkopolis were able to operate year-round factories and accommodate an unprecedented volume of animals. Workers on disassembly lines continuously butchered one hog after another in short shrift, and then chilled, cured, and packed their carcasses. The barrels of salt pork could be stored indefinitely and shipped by rail anywhere. Packing houses also generated a considerable business in by-products, such as lard, which was the staple cooking fat in the days before vegetable oils. Operating round the clock with unrivaled economies of scale, the pork packers sold cheaper pork and lard and still raked in sizable profits.

Swift could readily copy the efficient methods of the Porkopolis packers by corn-fattening and mass-slaughtering cattle year-round and by recycling wastes and offal into saleable products, but he could not copy their curing methods. Salt pork was already customary fare, but Americans liked beef fresh, not potted or salted. To tap latent demand for beef, Swift had to figure out how to transport meat fresh from Chicago's stockyards to eastern cities.[52]

Ice was already being used to usher small shipments of butter, fish, and fruit to market. With that in mind, Swift started off by purchasing ten refrigerated railroad cars specially designed to carry suspended sides of beef with ice packed in the bottom and the walls. To keep the meat cool, refrigerator cars had to be replenished with ice several times en route, so Swift constructed five intermediary icehouses. Then, ice supplies—roughly as much ice as meat to be shipped—had to be garnered from frozen northern lakes in the winter and stored for use on trains the following summer. Swift's enormous new refrigeration infrastructure combined with year-round feedlot fattening and mass-scale slaughtering of cattle overcame the age-old, seasonally imposed limits of butchering in a fundamentally new way. Operations grew, and by 1885 the Grand Trunk Railroad was hauling 292 million pounds of dressed beef to eastern markets each year.[53]

Once the Chicago-dressed beef arrived, Swift had to overcome a final obstacle more hampering than the distance, rot, and heat he'd handily overcome: customer revulsion. As his son would later explain, "No Yankee had ever been served a steak which originated more than a few miles from the stove that cooked it, no sir, not if he knew it." To cooks and eaters accustomed to having a slaughterhouse just outside every town or city, "the very idea of Chicago-dressed beef was repugnant."[54] Persuading people to buy beef that had been butchered a thousand miles away meant no less than changing the way eaters thought about freshness and about meat.

Most city shoppers had come to rely on the judgment of a local butcher. The best butchers took their responsibility quite seriously, carefully inspecting the living animals for any signs of disease or mistreatment before slaughter, as local ordinances often demanded. At first, Swift tried to piggyback upon their credibility by offering local butchers contracts to sell his Chicago-dressed beef, but many resisted. When a Swift agent approached one butcher about selling dressed beef in the Pittsburgh area, he was adamantly refused. "I sell no beef unless I see it killed," the butcher explained. Another butcher told him, "I wouldn't sell a pound of your beef if Fitchburg was starving."[55] Still others placed signs in their shop windows—"No Chicago dressed beef sold here"— and publicly denigrated it as "dead beef."[56] Butchers raised such vocal opposition to Chicago-dressed beef not only because it threatened their livelihoods but also because it threatened the body of knowledge they'd long held inviolate. To sell meat from an unknown animal, a week after it was butchered—a thousand miles away—flew in the face of everything they knew.

Swift was undeterred. To break the butchers' obstruction, he set up his own dressed-beef shops. Then, Swift told his retail agents to pre-cut the meat into appetizing pieces and arrange them in an attractive display to distinguish his product from that of butchers, who typically stored animal carcasses in a cool back room and then cut a customer's meat to order. Swift believed that shoppers would feel more assured if they could see just how good the dressed beef looked.[57]

Most important, Swift ruthlessly cut prices below his own costs of production, and it was these low prices that ultimately tempted city shoppers to try dressed beef shipped all the way from Chicago. Once they overcame their initial reluctance based on customary expectations, shoppers were sold. From the perspective of the market basket, corn-fattened Chicago-dressed beef was tastier and cheaper than meat from range-fed cattle made haggard by days of railroad hauling. Within only a

... years, most beef shoppers had made the leap. In 1888, one New York butcher explained that, in most places, slaughter of cattle by local butchers had become "a thing of the past."[58]

The monumental changes in the meatpacking industry illustrate a cycle that is worth notice, for it would happen again and again with other foods. The criteria that informed shoppers' thinking how to buy meat derived from a time when people either raised their own animals to be butchered or trusted a butcher who knew the farmers supplying his meats. Customary lore about meat quality fit preindustrial modes of supply and distribution. Through the nineteenth century, as the demand to feed city dwellers grew, existing networks of supply and distribution tried to keep pace by simply expanding into a pumped-up version of the old-fashioned system. During this transitional period, as more and more small farms sent their products from greater distances by rail to increasingly glutted and crowded city markets, food quality often declined because foods produced in traditional ways couldn't endure travel and still meet shoppers' customary expectations at the market. In the case of beef, as cattle made their epic, weight-losing, rib-banging trek to market, meat quality deteriorated. It was in response to this poor-quality meat (and other inefficiencies of the transitional period) that the new product emerged. The new Chicago-dressed meat tasted great and offered terrific value compared with the train-battered meats of the intermediate period. The timing of this change, coincident with changing generations, meant that the larger trend of change was not evident to shoppers or eaters. It was rarely possible for anyone to actually compare the new Chicago-dressed meats with local meats as they'd been procured in the pre-railroad manner. A similar story could be told for milk and butter, and eventually for tomatoes, as well.

Whatever shoppers might think—or more likely *not* think—about the industrial-scale slaughter and distribution system erected by Swift and other Chicago meatpackers, they soon had little choice but to buy dressed beef. The low-priced, factory-slaughtered meat flooded the market. For most city workers struggling to make ends meet (and for their employers who were determined to keep workers' wages low), cheap dressed beef was a welcome innovation.

Although women's magazines decidedly steered clear of the unsavory topic, several publications geared toward men featured stories in the 1880s that lauded Chicago's industrial meatpacking model with its disassembly lines and clever by-products.[59] Visitors were even invited to tour the giant packing plants to see exactly how the dressed meats were processed.

Those who took the invitation to tour the packing plants had a range of reactions. Company promotional materials spun the massive production and profits as models of industrial efficiency, and indeed, most visitors were impressed by the speed and scale of operations. At the same time, however, the speed, scale, and anonymity of the gruesome mass slaughter could be revolting to witness. Upton Sinclair would later describe the response of a typical tour group: "The men would look at each other, laughing nervously, and the women would stand with hands clenched, and the blood rushing to their faces and the tears starting in their eyes. . . . now and then a visitor wept."[60] At the small scale of a farm or local slaughterhouse, killing animals for meat had been an unpleasant but necessary task, a fact of life; at the colossal scale of the packing plants, it was deeply disturbing.

3.3. *This chart from Catherine Beecher's 1873 cookbook depicts a whole animal, situated in a meadow, as a source for the various cuts of beef a homemaker might purchase. By the end of the nineteenth century, meat charts typically depicted animals only as dotted outlines, with no eyes and not situated in a landscape.*

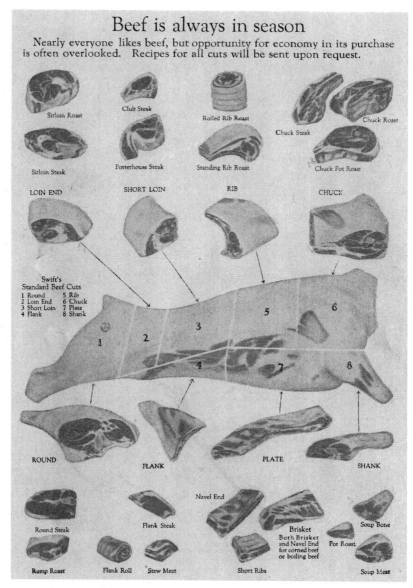

Beef is always in season

Nearly everyone likes beef, but opportunity for economy in its purchase is often overlooked. Recipes for all cuts will be sent upon request.

Sirloin Roast

Club Steak

Rolled Rib Roast

Chuck Roast

Chuck Steak

Sirloin Steak

Porterhouse Steak

Standing Rib Roast

Chuck Pot Roast

LOIN END   SHORT LOIN   RIB   CHUCK

Swift's
Standard Beef Cuts
1 Round   5 Rib
2 Loin End   6 Chuck
3 Short Loin 7 Plate
4 Flank   8 Shank

ROUND

FLANK

PLATE

SHANK

Round Steak

Flank Steak

Navel End

Brisket
Both Brisket
and Navel End
for corned beef
or boiling beef

Soup Bone

Pot Roast

Rump Roast

Flank Roll   Stew Meat

Short Ribs

Soup Meat

3.4. *By the outset of the twentieth century, after the large meatpacking firms centralized, mechanized, and standardized year-round butchering, meat charts such as this one became common; only individual cuts were depicted.*

But from the city market, a shopper couldn't hear what Sinclair would call "the hog squeal of the universe."[61] The longstanding advice of household experts—to find a reliable butcher and learn about the lives of animals that became meat—was no longer useful. In fact, it had become downright distasteful. To know about the actual lives and deaths of cattle in Chicago's stockyards would be enough to make most people pass on the pot roast.

In 1893, Maria Parloa assured *Good Housekeeping* readers that lingering prejudice against Chicago-dressed beef was no longer justified. "After years of costly experiments," she explained, "all the arrangements are now so perfect that the animal is killed while in a fresh healthy condition; the meat is thoroughly chilled and packed in refrigerator cars and brought to the market partially ripened and in better condition than if the cattle were brought in cars and killed near the markets."[62]

Parloa advised shoppers not to worry themselves anymore about "the living animal standing on its feet" but instead to study diagrams of cuts "as they are found dressed in the markets."[63] Such diagrams would be published and widely distributed by Swift and the other packing companies to inform shoppers and to promote the various available meat products.[64] The individually named cuts—rump roast, sirloin steak, brisket, chuck roast—were typically shown in rough relation to the dotted outline of an animal's body. As city dwellers purchased more and more cuts of dressed beef in packages at markets, knowledge and awareness that meat was linked to a particular animal, let alone a knoll of pasture or an expanse of grassland, was lost. In such a very short time, the warm, living, breathing animal that had made the steaks and roasts vanished with scarcely a trace from the mind's eye of America's shoppers.

CHAPTER 4

Denaturing the Senses

Through most of the nineteenth century, cooking experts had agreed that a woman's senses were her best guide when it came to choosing foods at markets. Appearance was paramount. There was "a bright look to the scales of fish freshly pulled from water never seen on those a day caught," and all their stripes and speckles looked more defined. Odor was also "an unfailing criterion." Freshly caught fish had "the clean sweet smell of celery."[1] Excellence of butter could be determined "by an acute taste and smell which discovers the 'rosy' odor and rich grassy flavor."[2] And to pick a tender chicken, a shopper had only to bend "the grizzle at the end of the breast bone" to make sure it was pliable.[3] Sight, scent, taste, and touch — these were the ways an informed shopper chose foods.

This was all well and fine for most leafy, fleshy foods stacked in city market stalls, but by the 1890s, a whole new class of manufactured products — called "made-foods" or "prepared foods" — began to enter the diets of urban middle-class eaters.[4] Following in the steps of Swift's dressed beef, these processed foods took advantage of the cheap transport afforded by railroads and the new technologies of food preservation and mass production to meet the demands of growing numbers of city eaters. Made-foods wrought a revolution in the experience of everyday living. Ultimately, they would answer the urban society's needs for cheaper, convenient, less-prone-to-spoilage, sanitary foods, whose producers were accountable for their quality and safety. But at first, these cans, cartons, and jars were subject to suspicion, scrutiny, and controversy.

Prepared foods challenged the traditional sensibilities of late nineteenth-century eaters. Having made the adjustment to relying on unknown people and distant places for the grains, vegetables, and meats they purchased, shoppers now faced a new set of mysterious technologies, substances, and processes used to deliver a newfangled class of foods to local grocery stores. Pre-made foods came into kitchens in entirely novel forms with no resemblance to their state in nature. Others appeared as if they came straight from nature but, in fact, did not. The new factory-made foods thus confounded both the senses and common sense.

The Debut of Cans

Today, canned foods seem comfortably familiar. When cut open with a few cranks of a can opener, these perfect cylinders of shiny metal readily reveal their contents. Alphabet soup, creamed corn, and SpaghettiOs were my childhood favorites. And tomato soup—its commonness emphatically iconized by painter Andy Warhol's dittoed Campbell's cans—still has a comforting taste if one ignores the sodium content now listed on its label. In the cupboards of most homes, lowly cans contain familiar flavors that millions of us have lunched and lived on. But 120 years ago, these plain tins were at the front line of a new revolution. And like most revolutionaries, they were suspect.

Now we live among so many black boxes—televisions, computers, cell phones, and microwave ovens—all of which operate in such hidden ways that one needs an advanced degree in electrical engineering to understand them. It may be difficult, then, for us to fathom living in a world where most objects in daily use made sense, where people expected that household tools and objects be transparent in their workings. But try to imagine, for it was into that world that cans made their debut.

Initially developed as a way to feed Napoleon's soldiers on their interminable Russian campaigns, canning had come to the United States by the 1820s. At first, most American canneries sold their products for ship provisions. When the California gold rush and then the Civil War boosted the demand for these "hermetically sealed foods," the nation's major canning centers in Baltimore; Portland, Maine; and Oneida, New York, expanded operations. In 1870, the U.S. census counted canneries for the first time—ninety-seven to be exact—making and filling thirty million cans annually, all by handicraft technique.[5]

As is often the case after a war, the industries that had expanded to meet wartime demand tried to maintain their business by selling to civilians. Strangely enough, the same features that had made cans ideal for carrying into enemy terrain, the storm-whipped Atlantic, and the wilds of the West made them perfect for conditions of city life, where the supply line had become similarly attenuated, with more eaters living far from farms that supplied foods.

Traditionally, rural housewives had learned to store foods by caching them in cold cellars, by smoking and curing them, or by treatment in crocks of brine or sugar, but these customary methods of food preservation were proving unsatisfactory in urban America. In new multistory apartment buildings, residents no longer had extra room to store foods through the winter, and those families lucky enough to enjoy central heating found it impossible to keep foods cool. Purveyors of canned goods set out to capitalize on these limitations. Like many factories, canneries began to incorporate mass production and mechanization techniques in the mid-1880s and stepped up output.[6]

All their benefits notwithstanding, foods sealed up in metal turned out to be a hard sell. Americans had regarded tinned oysters and potted beef as the food of explorers, fortune seekers, ocean travelers, and soldiers. Cans were fine for camp-outs, but it was quite a different matter for mother to serve them as ordinary everyday fare. How could any self-respecting homemaker let these uncanny capsules of industry encroach upon the intimacy and tradition of her family's table?

Canned foods were unlike any other that preceded them. Before cans, foods were leafy and earthy with attached greens and clinging soil. They were odorous animals with ears, eyes, and tongues. With their ragged irregularities and pungent smells, foods—even in the marketplace—were clearly of nature. Their fleshy parts had to be held in the hands to be washed, cut, or sliced. But cans—be they filled with salmon, dandelion greens, oysters, or tomatoes—had no swish or splash. As difficult to open as coconuts, cans challenged the expectations of would-be cooks and eaters with their distinctly concealing tin armor.

One canned food salesman explained this difficulty to colleagues in training. There is no business with the "seeds of destruction" so firmly planted within it as that of canned fruit and vegetables, he told them, because "you are always selling something which your customer cannot see."[7] Another canned food expert put the problem into historical perspective: "The taking of the work away from the home and away from observation, except to a comparatively few, has developed a lurking suspicion that possibly some of the material used and the care taken in preparation are not all that they should be."[8] Not being able to see, smell, or touch what was inside a can until it was home made it impossible for shoppers to determine the quality of its contents using traditional and sensuous cues.

This could lead to some unpleasant experiences. One woman found "the whole head—beak, wattles, and comb—of a rooster in a can of chicken which had been highly recommended."[9]

Even worse, poor quality could mean spoilage. Traditionally, most foods—by virtue of their animal and vegetable origins—began to decompose soon after harvest. Apples and potatoes might last for months in a cold cellar, but by late winter a housewife would likely find some putrid specimens. The natural relationship between deterioration and the passage of time had been familiar, but with cans, this connection suddenly became uncertain. There was no way to tell when a can's contents had been caught or harvested or when the can had been sealed or how well. And it was difficult for those accustomed to the usual trajectory of rot to believe that the perishable foods packed in cans would be wholesome whenever they were opened. Shelf life was a new attribute of factory-produced foods that shoppers had to learn. It mattered little if corn was canned in August 1887 or August 1889. The label on one early can aimed to make this clear by explaining its contents would "keep good any length of time."[10]

Although most cans preserved foods without spoilage, not all

succeeded. If improperly sterilized or poorly sealed, cans could swell as
their contents decayed and became sickening or even deadly. Before
1895, packers (as canned food manufacturers called themselves) believed
that the canning process depended solely on expunging air from cans.
With incomplete understanding of bacteriology, they did not yet realize
that the mysterious and seemingly random spoilage that plagued the
industry was caused when cans were not sufficiently heated to destroy
bacteria, including the lethal and can-bulging *Clostridium botulism*.
With dozens of small-scale canneries experimenting with new techniques to improve quality and reduce costs, it was not uncommon for
homemakers to encounter unsavory, if not unsafe, samples.[11]

That's what happened to poor Susan McSorley, who purchased a can
of molasses from her corner grocer. The label assured her that the sealed
can contained "absolutely pure food" that would "not ferment." However, when she took it home and tried to open it, the putrefied contents
exploded the can, "the lid was thrown aside and something shot out like
the shot of a gun and struck her full force in the left eye."[12] Seriously
injured, McSorley sued her grocer. In one of the first cases of its type, the
jury decided that the grocer was responsible. But understandably, the
grocer appealed, and the court instead found the molasses manufacturer
to be liable. In the emerging industrial-scale food chain, the retail grocer
was only the final link, so the old-fashioned covenant of trust between
seller and buyer had to be reconfigured with more formal strictures of
legal liability to reflect the new bounds of accountability.

Most spoilage problems were less explosive than McSorley's, occurring after cans were opened, partially consumed, and then left unrefrig-
erated before their contents were finished up. The fact that canned foods
would "keep good any length of time" changed, of course, as soon as the
can was opened. Household advice columns frequently warned homemakers about this crucial subtlety that they were apparently unfamiliar
with.[13]

Then there was adulteration. Buyers of food had always had to be
wary of deceptions, but the new manufactured foods — cloaked in seemingly guileful packages — made adulterations even more difficult to
detect. In the summer of 1874, one reporter for the *Chicago Times* took

canned and packaged foods purchased at leading grocery stores to a local high school chemistry teacher, whose lab analysis revealed that much of it was artificially colored and contaminated with sawdust.[14] Similar stories of adulteration appeared in big city newspapers through the last three decades of the nineteenth century, affirming the bad reputation of cans and other made-foods.[15]

Rooster heads, botulism, explosions, sawdust, and spoilage were not the only hazards of early cans. One investigation found that metals from the plating or solder that sealed cans—lead, zinc, and copper—could leach unpredictably into the contents. In 1884, the *New York Times* reported on a family that became sick from eating tomatoes; their doctor attributed the illness to the zinc chloride flux used to solder the can's lid.[16] As one household expert explained, buying canned food was "a continual lottery in which 'hope springs eternal' with succeeding purchases."[17] With all the problems encountered by those brave souls who tried cans and other "manufactured mysteries," as one contemporary food writer called them, one can only imagine the fearful rumors that spread.[18]

To gain public trust, the canning industry worked hard to improve its products. However, even when proper canning successfully halted spoilage, it created a host of other problems. The heat of the retorts overcooked and altered the texture, flavor, and appearance of canned foods in unmistakable ways. The firm flesh of salmon became soggy, and the bright colors of ripe fruits and vegetables faded into wan hues. A homemaker might be enticed by a bursting pod of emerald peas pictured on a label glued to the outside of a can, but on the inside, she was likely to find pallid globules saturated with sugar water.

Increasing competition prompted many packers to experiment with the rapidly developing science of chemistry to deliver products that seemed more like the authentic garden vegetables shoppers knew and expected. Some tried adding synthetic substances to their products to intensify colors and modify flavors. With corn, for example, the heat of canning turned the kernels a deep yellow tint that was not associated with the pearly whiteness of freshly picked ears, so packers introduced a bleach additive to emulate a more fresh-picked look. With cherries and berries, a reaction between the metal tins and acidic contents caused the fruits to turn white, so packers added coal-tar dyes to recoup the deep scarlet color.[19] Paradoxically, the more that packers strove for natural appearance, the less "natural" the foods became.

While deceptive substances added to foods, such as chalk in flour and hayseeds in jams, were clearly adulterants, the preservatives and dyes that manufacturers added were harder to categorize. They were intended to make processed foods seem more authentic and pleasing, but were these legitimate benefits, or did they too mislead shoppers into buying poor-quality foods? Many homemakers—conceiving of food factories as giant kitchens—saw no reason for manufacturers to use ingredients that a cook would not use in her own kitchen and regarded these aesthetic additives as adulterants.

In 1885, Ellen Richards, a leading figure in the nascent Home Economics movement, lamented the situation in which city homemakers increasingly found themselves: "We buy everything, and have no idea by which the articles are produced, and have no means of knowing before hand what the quality may be. . . . Relatively we are in a state of barbarous innocence, as compared with our grandmothers, about the common articles of daily use."[20]

In the 1880s, women's magazines, not yet restrained by a conflict of interest with advertisers, carefully guarded the traditional female sphere of food expertise from industrial incursion and advised their readers to be suspect of all manufactured foods. Columnists in *Good Housekeeping* recommended that readers avoid adulterated items by "buying foods as near the unmanufactured state as possible—pepper in the berry, coffee unground, honey in the comb, fruits for jellies."[21] With foods compounded in factories, the articles explained, a woman knew nothing about their actual ingredients, how they were raised and put up, or who prepared them. In the case of manufactured lard, for example, a housewife had no guarantee that "the animals that rendered it were healthy when killed."[22]

Indeed, the enormous scale of food-processing operations and the new composition and form of manufactured foods made it impossible for cooks and eaters to evaluate foods in customary ways. Like many women, home economist Christine Terhune Herrick "resolved, with a sick shudder, to live by the kindly fruits of the earth, whether animal or vegetable, when they came to [her] fresh, and to renounce canned foods and all their works."[23] In the confusion of the fast-changing urban food scene, "abstinence" from prepared foods seemed the safest rule for conscientious homemakers to follow.[24]

The Power of Labels

Artificial colors and flavors didn't have their intended effect until after a shopper bought a can, took it home, opened it, served its contents, and tasted the meat, vegetables, or fruit inside. With a populace accustomed to homemade and unbranded products, food manufacturers also had to figure out a way to make their products more appealing up front—before purchase. To do this, they relied on labels to put a familiar face on the seemingly strange new foods.

Because the contents of cans and other containers of manufactured foods were hidden, the labels were really the only thing a shopper had to go on. Images on labels often showed attractive vegetables in their just-picked state—such as larger-than-life cobs of corn or pods of peas—propped before the fields or gardens. Text on the earliest labels typically described how a product was made and assured that contents were genuine and pure. This information reflected the traditional, rural perspective of small-scale food producers but also met the customary expectations of shoppers. For example, one early label explained that the jar's contents were "prepared by straining the seeds and skins from tomatoes and evaporating the watery particles by slow heat." Thus the jar contained "about a dozen tomatoes"—something that would not be evident to a shopper looking for the first time at a small container.[25] Packer Nathan Winslow of Portland, Maine, provided loquacious detail on his canned-corn labels, which read as if he were talking directly to a shopper: "Our works are located in the country—in the very midst of our corn-fields—so that there is the least possible interval between the gathering and sealing up of the corn, and it will be easily understood that it must be far preferable to that which has been carted a long distance before it has been put up." The label continued, "In the latter case, it is usually gathered the day previous, and when it arrives at the Factory, it is necessarily in a heated and sweating condition."[26] In the decades following the Civil War, when many urban residents had grown up on rural farms, such rudimentary information appealed strongly to traditional food sensibilities.

Natural images were also pervasive on early labels, often showing up in ways unlikely to occur to the modern mind, such as the frog that appeared on a label for Brookside Sugar Corn canned in Brooklyn, Long Island (Brooklyn still had a frog-filled brook). Striding his lanky green legs before a field of corn, the frog held up a golden ear for all to examine. Apparently, gangly frogs and cornfields still seemed to be compatible and reassuring images to potential buyers of canned corn.[27]

Pictures of the places where foods came from were also featured prominently on labels. Cans of beefsteak tomatoes sold by "Anderson and Campbell" sported labels that showed their canning factory in a pleasing pastoral setting, specifically Camden County, New Jersey, "acknowledged as the best tomato lands to be found on this continent."[28] Canned-seafood labels also made much of geographic pedigree. For example, Maine's leading packers, Burnham and Morrill (now best known as the "B&M" of baked-bean fame), packed and sold cans of Machias Bay Lobsters and Cape Shore Mackerel, which showcased images of these presumably unpolluted water bodies.[29] By reading labels and sampling cans, buyers could infer that particular places had earned

4.1. *Labels on the earliest cans and boxes typically used natural motifs to attract potential buyers. This label apparently appealed to those who could still associate corn with cornfields and gangly frogs with the natural brooks that flowed nearby.*

reputations for quality and began to associate those places with their products—Maine with lobster, New Jersey with tomatoes. With such labels, places of origin were taking on a new sort of meaning in the emerging national food system: they were becoming marketing referents.

Canneries tended to use very place-specific labels because most were small operations that processed vegetables or seafood from a circumscribed farm belt or port. However, larger manufacturers, drawing from hundreds of farm producers in broader foodsheds, used their labels to draw attention to the source of their products in more general and suggestive ways. On its packages of lard, for example, Swift—already one of the nation's largest food-processing firms—used images that recapitulated the process of rendering in traditional farm style. (In the first elliptical framed image, a farmer wielding a knife entered a barnyard with several hogs. The second frame featured the portrait of a handsome hog. And in the third frame, a cauldron of lard hung suspended over a fire.[30]) By suggesting that Swift made lard the old-fashioned way, the package label kept industrial-production methods under wraps while tacitly providing the information that most shoppers expected to know.

To nineteenth-century cooks, the fact that lard came from hog fat was not only freely acknowledged but laudable. As such, early admen played with the humor of hogs being the best authorities on lard. On trade cards (similar to baseball cards)—some of the earliest promotional materials developed and distributed by food manufacturers—Swift and Co. depicted a hog schoolmarm teaching a class of hog students about the merits of its Silver Leaf Lard.[31] And N. K. Fairbanks & Company printed a whole series of amusing lard cards with porcine characters hawking their own compounded-by-factory fat. One card featured a corpulent hog king practically bursting out of his throne, holding a corn staff and wearing a crown of corns. The heading read "Sample Hog from which N.K. Fairbanks & Co.'s Lard is Made." Beneath the regal hog, the caption reads "Corn makes me King."[32] In the early promotion of mass-produced lard, conveying the quality and authenticity of its animal source was key, and what could be more authentic than a fat, handsome hog declaring that he'd feasted on corn before being rendered?

4.2. Trade cards were one of the earliest ways manufacturers promoted pre-made food products. This card played with the humor of genuine lard coming directly from a pig, making clear the connection between food and its animal source but belying increasingly industrialized means of production.

How was advertisement crucial to eroding traditional culture norm

In the realm of early trade cards, hogs were not the only anth
morphic creatures that spoke about the merit of the foods they ...
soon become. On a card promoting canned Boston Codfish Balls, a
potato and a cod walked arm-in-arm by the sea, happily canting their
fate—to become tasty fish balls.[33] Food ads with such matter-of-fact
references to their animal sources reflected the mindset of nineteenth-
century cooks and eaters, who still expected to know that animals they
ate were in good health or, in the case of farm animals, well cared for. Yet
with labels, packages, and trade cards, this expectation was increasingly
answered with a rather empty jocularity that glossed over the conditions
of animals that became food in the newly emerging industrial economy.
The humor of talking hogs and codfish—willing and happy to go to the
table in human service—belied the industrial processes that had begun
to transform animals into factory-made products on an unfathomable
scale.

When breakfast cereals first arrived on the market in the 1880s, their
manufacturers also used particular images and copy on boxes and trade
cards to assure shoppers of the quality and origin of their product's
ingredients. Because grain was graded and blended in remote elevators
long before it reached mills, cereal makers couldn't boast about any particular patch of land where their grains were grown.[34] But that didn't
stop them from evincing the origin of their grains in a more general
sense. For example, the American Breakfast Cereals Company printed a
series of trade cards featuring wheat, oat, corn, and barley plants, which
produced the grains it milled, together with images of wild, grain-loving
birds, such as quail and meadowlarks.[35] Even after adopting the portly
Quaker we all still recognize as its trademark sign of purity, the Quaker
Oats Company featured sheaves of oat plants on its oatmeal packages for
decades.[36] The pictures of birds and grain plants cloaked the packages
with a sense of authenticity that breakfast-cereal eaters today can no
longer grasp since most of us would be hard pressed to distinguish
between the oat and the wheat plants that become our loops and flakes.

From cans to lard to cereals, manufacturers used labels and trade cards
to mesh their new products with the traditional food sensibility of the last
generation of Americans who had a predominantly rural background.

4.3. *Trade cards for American Breakfast Cereals portrayed wild grassland birds as connoisseurs of grain, emphasizing the natural source of crops that became cereal products.*

The labels and cards referred to real places, plants, animals, and processes with which shoppers might still be familiar. Intended to stand in for traditional observation and knowledge, these referents nonetheless attempted to relate food items to the actual places that created them. As new manufactured foods begged questions about how and where they were made, labels and early promotional materials made an effort to supply reassuring, practical answers.

But labels and trade cards could go only so far. Confronted with frequent reports of adulteration and dangerous spoilage, new and unfamiliar modes of processing and preserving foods, synthetic colorings and flavorings, preservative chemicals, and rumors that pre-made foods caused "dyspepsia" or more serious illnesses, many city dwellers felt a sense of unease. As new types of foods were supplied by an enlarging, impersonal, and difficult-to-understand distribution system, anxieties of city shoppers, cooks, and eaters surged up like a bad case of heartburn.

The Mimicry of Margarine

While cans smartly concealed the odors and consistency of their contents, making them impossible for homemakers to check by sight or smell, another new product frustrated the senses by close imitation. Oleomargarine, the dyed-yellow fat spread, looked and tasted like butter. Initially developed in France as a cheap and durable wartime butter substitute, in the United States, oleomargarine served to transform the waste fats of the growing meat industry into a profitable product. Supplied by city abattoirs, a handful of oleo factories began operation in New York in the 1870s, processing the fat of about twelve thousand cattle each week to produce twelve million pounds of "artificial butter" each year.[37]

The industry grew substantially in 1883 when the Chicago packinghouses began to tap their own mammoth fat supplies to make oleomargarine. Beef fat removed during slaughter was washed in water, minced by machine, then pressed through a cloth to yield light yellow oleo oil. The oleo oil was mixed with deodorized lard (hog fat), salt, coloring, and sometimes milk and butter. Each firm used its own formula, and variations in supply or conditions often required adjusting recipes. For

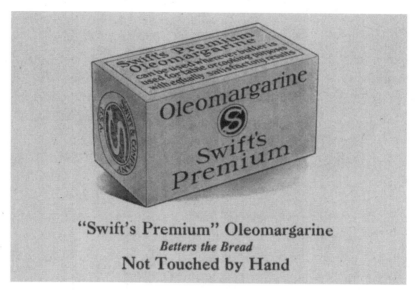

"Swift's Premium" Oleomargarine
Betters the Bread
Not Touched by Hand

4.4. *When oleomargarine first entered the market, dairy farmers were irked by ads and packaging that suggested its similarity to butter. Eventually, with growing concern about germs, cheap margarine that was "not touched by hand" would begin to appeal to shoppers.*

example, more lard was typically added during cold winter months to assure better spreadability. By 1886, Chicago packers were manufacturing thirty million pounds of butter substitutes annually.[38]

Oleo's greatest virtue—its similarity to butter—was also its chief stumbling block. Manufacturers emphasized the resemblance by packing oleo into tubs, just like those traditionally used to sell butter, and then calling it "butterine." Early oleo labels and newspaper ads often implied or directly stated a comparison with butter, using copy such as "churned especially for lovers of good butter" or "[it] betters the bread."[39] Some particularly cunning packages were labeled as "BUTTER-ine" with the "ine" in very small letters.[40] Because it looked like butter, oleo often ended up on the retail market selling as butter, but for much less.

It was this imposture that irked dairy farmers. Already beset with difficulties of an economic downturn in the 1870s, they saw oleo as a fraudulent and threatening competitor. Organizing politically, they succeeded in banning the sale and manufacture of oleo in Pennsylvania and

New York.[41] When these laws were subsequently deemed unconstitutional, the dairymen took their case to Congress.

There, in the hallowed halls of the Capitol, America's lawmakers debated the legitimacy of oleomargarine for thirteen days. Butter advocates derided margarine as a "midnight assassin" responsible for dyspepsia, disease, and death. Upon inspection with microscope, Department of Agriculture scientists had found samples of the faux butter teeming with living spores, molds, hair, bristles, and portions of tapeworms. One testified that lard used in oleo came from cholera-ridden hogs. Another testified that the strong acids and alkalis listed in margarine-making patents—presumed to deodorize stale and noxious fats—were poisonous. The chief of the Bureau of Animal Industry questioned the wisdom of introducing such "a radical change into the manufacture of an article of food which goes upon the table of every family in the land." Oleomargarine, he warned, could well produce an unexpected and "remarkable effect upon the public health."[42]

Oleo manufacturers dismissed all charges that their product was unwholesome or unhealthful and instead promoted it as an exciting scientific innovation. Their use of by-products—"all but the squeal"—meant that industrial wastes were efficiently reduced, and, manufacturers argued, hygienic conditions in their modern factories were far superior to those in milking barns and butter churns of rural America, where more than two-thirds of the nation's butter was still made.[43] As this farm butter now traveled greater and greater distances to city markets, it tended to spoil en route and often arrived in a sordid "condition closely bordering on decomposition."[44] To nine-tenths of urban buyers, one oleo advocate claimed, farm butter, "whose sole claim to superiority is that it is derived . . . through the medium of the udder," was no longer a good choice.[45] In the city, price and cleanliness were becoming more important than udder origin, and oleomargarine was certainly cheaper and more consistently sanitary than rancid farm butters.

The historic conflict between butter and margarine has been recounted as a clash between economic interests—the old-fashioned dairymen defending their turf against modern oleo manufacturers until the overwhelming efficiency of industry ultimately prevailed, giving everyone the opportunity to eat cheap, clean, factory-fabricated fat.[46] However, the deeper questions that oleomargarine posed about authenticity were not solely ruses that dairymen used to shore up their faltering butter business. Like traditional butchers who confronted trainloads of dressed beef, butter-making dairy farmers and creameries were confronting a new industrial logic that conflicted with customary practices and knowledge.

Questions about authenticity were also rife in the minds of many city eaters who found the foods in their markets and corner groceries changing in ways that were difficult to understand. One immigrant woman who ran a boardinghouse known for its good food was unequivocal about margarine when a salesman came to the door hawking the yellow spread. Unable to speak English herself, she pressed her daughter: "Tell him to save his breath because I am not buying that. Never. Never!"[47] Another working-class woman, angered by declining wages that prevented her family from affording butter, would later insist, "We don't want their oleomargarine!"[48]

According to traditional food sensibilities, good butter was the product of healthy animals and a competent farm wife or dairymaid. Oleo was no match. However, when the challenges of transportation and storage were factored into the equation of supplying hundreds of thousands of city eaters, traditional farm butter didn't fare so well. From the perspective of the city market basket, oleomargarine — made cheap with the packing giants' economies of scale — was becoming the best if not only option for working-class shoppers, whether they liked it or not.[49]

The oleo manufacturers countered most criticisms lobbed by dairy farmers, but one matter remained unresolved. They could not deny the disturbing way that oleo confounded its eaters' senses.

When food adulteration had first gained attention in Congress in 1879, Virginia representative Richard Lee Beale explained the novel situation in a telling way: "The rapid advance of chemical science has opened a wide doorway for compounding mixtures so nearly resembling nature's products that *the senses are impotent to detect the difference.*"[50]

Oleomargarine was a case in point. Wisconsin congressman Robert La Follette claimed the unctuous spread presented an entirely new sit-

uation in human history. For the very first time, human ingenuity—
"striking hands with cunning trickery"—had compounded "a substance
to counterfeit an article of food." Oleomargarine was "made to look like
something it is not; to taste and smell like something it is not; to sell like
something it is not, and so to deceive the purchaser."[51]

If oleo looked, tasted, and smelled like butter, how could an eater discern the difference? If the eyes, tongue, and nose were tricked, the very
means that a person had traditionally used to evaluate food were useless.
Without recourse to the true knowledge of their senses, eaters had no
protection against oleo's hazards or frauds. New York congressman
Lewis Beach lamented, "The four senses which God has given us . . . are
completely baffled."[52] To many, it appeared that profit-driven meatpackers and oleo manufacturers were trying to deceive and cheat city eaters
with their "greasy counterfeit."[53]

One pro-oleo scientist had testified that, chemically, oleomargarine
was precisely the same as butter, but his assertion made little sense to the
traditional mindset of those with farm experience or to those who had
always eaten butter.[54] How could the product of a Chicago factory be
equivalent to the butter crafted from cow's milk and dairymaid's effort?
The story of butter started with "sweet grasses, and the lowing herd,"
whereas the story of margarine began in reeking abattoirs.[55] This distinction between stories seemed most important to many. Even if the
oleo makers could come chemically close to butter, one senator argued,
it did not follow that the manufactured article was as wholesome as
"nature's product," which was indisputably made from the milk of
cows.[56]

One of butter's primordial characteristics was its color, "a rich, golden
buttercup hue." To the butter advocates, dyeing "dead white" oleomargarine with yellow dye was the ultimate proof of its fraudulence. They
proposed that manufacturers be required to leave oleo white or to color
it purple, green, red—*any* color other than butter's rightful yellow. But
their integrity was questioned because some creameries had already
resorted to adding yellow dye to butter.[57]

Butter's inherent golden color did, in fact, change from season to
season depending on the diet of the cows supplying the milk. It was

long-standing rural wisdom that butter was most golden and flavorful in late spring when cows feasted on verdant grass. The best butter was the deepest yellow, and this fragment of traditional aesthetic sense persisted in urban lore.

When oleo presented itself as sunny yellow "butterine" year-round, some creameries claimed they had to start adding dye during the pale butter seasons to compete. Then other dairies succumbed to keeping up appearances. Without the knowledge that linked good butter to green grass, urbanites had forgotten about seasonal variation and had come to expect the folly of ever-yellow butter.

In an oleo factory, there was no relationship between color and vernal grasses, only between color and amount of dye added. Because city shoppers associated yellowness with authenticity, a deeply tinted tub of oleo could seem more authentic than a firkin of pale winter butter. Ultimately, the faltering knowledge of urban eaters meant that even butter—long considered "nature's product"—was being shaped not only by nature but also by cultural ideas of what urban eaters mistakenly *believed* to be natural.

Eating by Eye

While the challenge of supplying city eaters was prompting changes in how foods came to market, urbanization was, at the same time, changing shoppers and their expectations of foods. Indeed, many critics saw the widespread adulteration of foods—including use of dyes and preservatives—as a clear consequence of city dwellers' ignorance of traditional knowledge.[58] It was the same problem that butcher Thomas De Voe had recognized in the 1850s and 1860s, only by the turn of the twentieth century, the number of urban shoppers had exploded.

"City-bred people, who have little knowledge of the origin and real character of food and food products, such as the country man has, and who have no childhood's acquaintance with the good things of the farm, are especially liable to suggestion," one U.S. Department of Agriculture spokesman explained. "They are governed largely by appearances in their selection of farm products and are easily deceived by the trick of a false name or a false ingredient in prepared food."[59] The *Journal of Public*

Health agreed and blamed such credulous city shoppers for actually encouraging "dishonesty in business methods by their heedless demands for the impossible in rational conditions."[60] Pearly canned corn and yellow butter year-round were just some of the impossible expectations that a new generation of city shoppers had; it was no wonder that food manufacturers were scrambling to meet their ludicrous but lucrative longings.

Harvey Wiley had also noted the growing tendency of urban Americans to "eat with the eyes," selecting articles of food primarily for their size and color rather than their flavor.[61] Of course, shoppers were accustomed to using their senses to guide their selection of food, but now, privileging the eyes alone could be delusive, if not dangerous, given the many invisible adulterants and additives. A rather rotund lover of good foods, Wiley took this threat to eating quite seriously.

Best known for his work in promoting passage of the first federal Pure Foods and Drugs Act in 1906, Wiley had launched his prominent pure-food career as chief chemist at the Department of Agriculture's Bureau of Chemistry (predecessor of the Food and Drug Administration) with an investigation of adulterants in the late 1880s. Wiley's first round of surveys confirmed that deceptive additives were indeed widespread. Not only was oleomargarine commonly sold as butter, but corn syrup was colored and sold as honey; mixtures of apple peels, hayseeds, gelatin, and corn syrup were dyed and sold as strawberry jam; pulverized nut shells were sold as spices; and concoctions of pumpkin, saccharin, and coal-tar dye were sold as ketchup.[62] Many of the foods sold in cities were not what they were purported to be. All told, Wiley estimated that at least 15 percent of America's manufactured foods were adulterated, which would have given homemakers nearly a one-in-six chance of encountering them with any given purchase.[63]

Of the intentional additives, Wiley was particularly distressed by artificial colorings. Some, such as the copper sulfate used to dye imported canned *petits pois* (small garden peas), were known to be poisonous.[64] But even those that didn't appear to harm an eater's health per se were troubling because they deceived the senses. Added colors could mislead a shopper by suggesting that a food was fresher or riper than it actually was.

To Wiley, the maraschino cherry epitomized the indignity of artificial colorings. The most common method of making them was to soak the fruits in brine and sulfurous acid until all natural color was gone. Washing away salt and acid also removed the flavorful juice, nutriment, and all other soluble portions of the cherry. According to Wiley, the product could not be "regarded in any sense as resembling even in color the natural fruit, since practically the whole of the natural fruit, except its cellular structure, has been withdrawn and artificial substances substituted in place thereof."[65] The maraschino cherry was a human fabrication of sugar, coal-tar dye, artificial cherry flavor, and almond oil.

The gaudy appearance of these cherries disturbed Wiley deeply. Although they were valued "chiefly for their supposed attractive appearance," he believed that their poor taste offset any good effect that might come from their "ornamentation." Artificial coloring would insult any discriminating eater, Wiley thought. "The very moment the consumer realizes he is eating an artificially tinted fruit . . . he becomes sensitive to the effort made to deceive him." To Wiley, artificially colored foods had "a worse taste due to the feeling of antipathy excited by their presence."[66]

The uniformity of the cherry's redness also bothered Wiley, whose food aesthetic was informed by "nature's palette," which included vegetables and fruits arrayed in varied hues.[67] According to Wiley, variegation was the norm of nature, but it was a norm increasingly unfamiliar to most urbanites, who seemed to choose their fruits based on some singular ideal of color. To meet this paragon, packers used dyes to make all varieties of fruits they received from dozens of different farms "imitate those of naturally rich color."[68] The resulting cans filled with uniformly colored contents were, as the *Journal of Public Health* put it, "beautifully colored products—but they are not foods."[69]

Poised at the brink of great changes, Wiley had a unique prospect. Like many urban Americans who had grown up on farms, he could readily look back to the traditional ways of procuring and preparing foods of his rural Indiana rearing—ways that he understood to be natural and authentic. Yet at the same time, trained as a physician and chemist, Wiley knew what the industrializing food system was dishing out in intimate biochemical detail. Even with his scientific training, Wiley followed his gut feeling that the new food-manufacturing industry with its myriad additives was "denaturing" foods—literally making them less "natural."[70] To Wiley, this was a troubling trend. Pure and wholesome foods were genuine substances naturally derived from farms by customary methods. In contrast, the new industrially prepared foods often contained little-known artificial ingredients—some that he suspected were dangerous and many that were not what they claimed to be.

What troubled Wiley was a very subtle but fundamental matter, the same one that had troubled the congressmen. Cooks and eaters had long chosen foods based on sight, smell, taste, and touch—senses that could discern a full spectrum of qualities from ripeness to rot and all sorts of distinctions in between. Now a panoply of made-foods confounded those senses. What had always been a direct, natural, sensuous relationship between eater and food seemed to be at stake.

Wiley's own discipline of chemistry stood ready to refute such phenomenological concerns by assuring eaters that the synthetically created colors and flavors were precisely the same as what nature made. As a chemist, Wiley knew firsthand how readily compound ethers could be synthesized in the lab to make, as he put it, "an approximate imitation of the natural fruit flavor." Yet his scientific knowledge of flavors' molecular building blocks did not contradict his traditional sense of the experience of taste. No matter how great a chemist's skill, he believed there would always be a "gustatory and hygienic difference between the synthetic and the natural product." And to Wiley's way of thinking, "the natural product always ha[d] the advantage of the difference."[71] Even if amyl ether and banana flavor were chemically identical molecules, they were not the same in a deeper sense. They certainly did not share the same story. And if foods of commerce could trick the eyes, nose, and tongue into actually believing these molecules were equivalent, they would rob us of our very means of relating directly to the world—through our senses. It was on this deeper level that Harvey Wiley felt troubled. And he was not the only one.

CHAPTER 5

A New Longing for Nature

In 1892, Maud Howe Elliot wrote an article in the *Ladies' Home Journal* that gave voice to an increasingly prevalent middle-class concern. City life, despite all its attractions and opportunities, had its oppressive aspects, too. To better face these problems, Elliot advised women moving to the city to carry with them all they had learned in their years of childhood and maidenhood on the farm. "You will need it in the feverish city; the memory of sky and upland, the smell of the clover, the hum of the bees, the taste of the new milk, the breath of the kine, the strength which milking and butter making have given you, the knowledge of nature's secrets: which lilac leaves out first, which oak is last stripped of its foliage . . . when blackberries are fit to make into jam."[1] Although it is hard to imagine how the memory of cow breath could be of any real help to a metropolitan woman, Elliot believed that the savor and intimate know-how of country life were grounding and therapeutic.

Her paean to rural knowledge — particularly "knowledge of nature's secrets" — reflected the growing appeal of nature and country life to those readers troubled by ills of the nation's rapidly enlarging cities. Cities were crowded, noisy, frenzied, filthy, and smoky. Among many middle-class city dwellers, there was a growing concern that urban life was somehow making them feel unsettled. And though city amenities, such as indoor plumbing and central heating, made life easier, urban living physically isolated people from the warmth of the sun, the sound of rustling leaves, and the bracing cold of night. Ease of life, it turned out, did not guarantee health, happiness, or fulfillment. Many upper- and middle-class city dwellers, struggling to conform to pressing new demands, felt gripped by urban malaise and began to look to nature as a refuge—a place apart where one might escape the frenetic pace of the city.[2]

"To those of us who work amid the artificiality of city life," writer Robert Van Court explained, "there is something irresistibly attractive in the idea of being close to the heart of nature."[3] The appeal of the natural began to permeate the life and thinking of these upper- and middle-class city dwellers who longed for contact with the natural world.[4] To satisfy their longings, many took weekend picnics under spreading oaks, spent summer vacations in the countryside, or read popular nature books by the best-selling writer John Burroughs.

The same sorts of anxieties that beset city dwellers in their physical environs were encroaching in their gastrointestinal tracts as well. Eating was one of the most visceral ways that city dwellers experienced changes of the urbanizing, industrializing society, and "dyspepsia"—the contemporary vernacular for indigestion—was becoming a frequent complaint. Because food had customarily been regarded as the fruit of nature, it is no surprise that ways city dwellers thought about nature played into ways they understood the dramatic changes in their foods, and vice versa. Indeed, the powerful and increasingly palpable polarities that ordered city dwellers' notions of country and city—nature and culture, natural and synthetic, pure and polluted—were brought to bear in the realm of eating, too.

As shoppers found they could no longer trust their senses to indicate the healthfulness of their foods, and as they realized they could no longer learn where foods came from, how they were made, or what ingredients they contained, many began to look to an ideal of nature to fill this epistemological void.

The Civility of Cookery

The notion that the "natural" could be regarded as a reassuring touchstone for city foods confronted a long-standing and deeply engrained cultural tendency to regard nature as base and crude.[5] In early America, the human place in the larger cosmos had been commonly conceptualized in terms of the Great Chain of Being, a set of metaphorical linkages — dating from classical times — that spanned from lowly plants, to animals, to humans, to angels, and ultimately to God. Nature was at the bottom, physical end of this ascending catenation. Yet in the context of the Great Chain, yeoman farmers had considered their work with the soil as a hallowed mediation bridging the corporeal earth and the heavenly realm of spirit.[6]

As cities grew and class distinctions deepened, more people began to regard work with soil not as sacred but as dirty. Farmers who could afford it hired laborers to help with the most grueling toil. In the South, where the racism and violence associated with slavery affected thinking about farm work, both blacks and whites ended up regarding farm work as backbreaking and mean.[7] In the realm of housework, both free blacks in the North and slaves in the South performed the lowliest kitchen jobs, such as plucking chickens and tending hot, sooty fires. Because such loathsome tasks had long been carried out by "vulgar" people of lowest status, Catherine Beecher explained in 1841, there was an unfortunate but persistent association between dirty work, sweat, and "vulgarity."[8]

The association of dirt with low status became even more potent in growing cities. As we've seen, when city dwellers became more affluent, many hired domestics — usually free blacks or immigrant women — to tend stove fires, shop at market, and undertake the messier parts of cooking.[9] For the majority of people struggling in the cities' lower classes, visions of prosperity meant hiring out such work to avoid getting one's hands dirty. Across the board, proximity to dirt — be it garden dirt, stove soot, or animal guts — was regarded with contempt.[10]

In this constellation of thinking, dirt hobnobbed with poverty, chaos, darkness, and savagery beyond the edges of the city, and unruly nature was guilty by association.[11] The conceptual timeline that accrued accomplishments of humanity set nature into some dark, dank past and progressed in linear rectitude, always advancing toward higher civility, refinement, and light. Nature was something to flee, and the farther

society raced from nature, the closer it would come to civilization's glow-
ing apex.

This seminal cultural story and the set of meanings it spawned had
long come to bear directly in the realm of foods. Since classical times,
when millers had ground finer, lighter flours for an upper class that
could afford to throw away much of the grain, light bread had been a
symbol of status. The vast majority of eaters had to be content with
darker breads baked from coarsely milled wheat and rye.

In America, colonists were compelled by circumstance to temporarily
abandon such hierarchical beliefs. For nearly two centuries, the type of
bread a person ate had more to do with local climate and soils than with
desire for prestige. In early New England, colonists had begrudgingly
baked "rye and injun" loaves because rye and corn grew best on their
farms; yet as America's cities grew and the limitations of local landscapes
receded, the historic high status of light breads recrudesced. With pioneer farmers growing more wheat in the West, merchant millers had to
cope with the problems of shipping flour, which could spoil when stored
for too long. The ingenious solution they devised was to "bolt" the
wheat, removing its oily and more perishable germ, and then to sell a
lighter flour that not only kept better for longer but baked up into a
whiter, and thus higher-prestige, bread. Commercial bakers began to use
the "patent flour" to make a white bread that sold in cities as a convenient
alternative to a housewife's weekly baking routine. As the commercially
produced white breads became cheaper and more available, the combination of high status and low price proved irresistible. (Though "white"
breads—not yet enriched—were far less nutritious, this was not yet generally understood.) The progression from eating dark breads to eating
light breads was regarded by many as a sign of the rising status of the
lower echelons of American society.[12]

Scorn for coarse dark foods also came into play with sugar. The
American Sugar Refining Company, which supplied most of America's
white sugar but did not control the processing of brown sugar, tapped
the deeply engrained associations of darkness and low status to its own
advantage. With promotions that featured enlarged photographs of

dark and scary-looking microbes, the company warned the public about the dangers of eating brown sugar. This pseudoscientific promotional hype was picked up and repeated in the 1901 best-selling *Boston Cook Book,* which warned readers that brown sugar was inferior owing to its tendency to become infested by "a minute insect."[13]

Even cooking itself became popularly understood in terms of the historical advance toward civility. Through the nineteenth century, as household and cookbook writers tried to stake out the critical importance of the domestic purview, many were fond of explaining to readers how cooking—that humble province of women—had elevated humanity from its formerly primitive state. As the story was typically recounted, savages had once gnawed upon raw foods and meats. It was only when people began to use fire to cook that they became civilized. Therefore, cooking was what distinguished civilized people from barbarians.[14] In 1873, Catherine Beecher included the civilizing account in her profile of bread baking. The "matter of lightness," she wrote, was "the distinctive line between savage and civilized bread." Primitive breads, made by throwing a rank mixture of flour and water into a boiling pot, required "the stomach of a wild animal or savage" to digest, unlike the light loaves produced by "all civilized modes of bread-making."[15] Although already oft-repeated, this civilizing narrative of cookery became more prevalent in the late nineteenth century with the influence of social Darwinism, with broader awareness of indigenous peoples, and with a cultural desire to endow affluent women's domestic sphere of cooking with greater respectability.[16]

Particular culinary practices and beliefs had followed from this explanatory story that made cooking a virtue of civilization. Affluent city dwellers had tended to consider domestic grain-fed fowls and pigeons more refined and desirable than wild ones through much of the nineteenth century. In frontier locales, where distancing oneself from savagery was regarded as important, the distinction between tame and wild held even deeper meaning because there lurked a long-standing belief that hunting and eating too many wild animals could make an eater degenerate to an uncivilized state. Ingesting the wildness of an animal could summon up the wildness within an eater—an early and vitalist version of the tenet "you are what you eat." As such, many believed that eating too much meat of any kind—especially undercooked meat—could make an eater aggressive.[17]

By the late 1800s, however, a certain degree of wildness was increasingly regarded as a good thing. In sharp contrast to the refined and sober personality sanctioned by genteel society, "animal spirits" referred to a certain boisterous ebullience and joie de vivre. A man who laughed too loud or played too much with his children might be said to have strong "animal spirits" and was thought to be governed more by his animal parts than by his rational parts. And this closer-to-nature vitality was measuredly admired. Mrs. E. A. Howland in her midcentury cookbook *The New England Economical Housekeeper* had recommended letting bread "ripen" before eating in order to cultivate "a greater flow of animal spirits."[18] And an 1882 breakfast cookbook recommended eating beef as the best way "to replenish animal spirits."[19]

The life of butcher Thomas De Voe, described in chapter 2, was influenced early on by his mother's belief in a similar sort of vitalism. To strengthen his "weak and shriveled" lower limbs, she brought him to a slaughterhouse three times a week and bathed his legs in a tub of warm entrails, hoping to import the animals' fleeting life force to her son's feeble muscles.[20] Whether or not the treatment fortified his legs, it undoubtedly prepared him for his life in the meat business. Clearly, ideas about nature entered nineteenth-century kitchens and lives in both physical and metaphysical ways.

For all the power and persistence of the age-old paradigm that had tucked savage nature back into a dark, dank past and set resplendent civility ahead on a pinnacle, a different way of seeing the world was gaining ground with middle- and upper-class city dwellers. People such as Maude Howe Elliot and Robert Van Court viewed nature in a more positive, elevated light, linking it to purity and authenticity, while consigning cities to a lowly coupling with artifice, dishonesty, disease, and the repugnant grime associated with germs and poverty. From their viewpoint, it was divergence from nature that was now seen as decline, and this decline was particularly evident in the food and health problems of growing cities.

While we usually regard this more positive view of the natural world as the romantic legacy of Rousseau and America's transcendentalists, its popularization at the turn of the twentieth century also coincided with troubling changes in America's food. And it may well be that greater numbers of people encountered the concept of "natural" when choosing their foods than when reading Emerson.

The worry that food was somehow diverging from nature first arose in this country in the 1830s, when the quirky but popular Christian lecturer Sylvester Graham hit his soapbox questioning commercial millers' practice of removing germ from the flour. To him, wheat was a "natural food" that "the Creator has designed for man in such a condition as is best adapted to the anatomical structure and physiological powers of the human system."[21] Tampering with wheat by bolting it disrupted God's perfect plan, threatened health, and displayed a dangerous hubris that was sure to rouse the Almighty's ire. Graham's legacy was a small legion of supporters that spread his ideas and promoted a whole-grain "Graham flour," but more important he gave voice to what would become a common idea—that traditional American food, homemade as it was eaten on farms, was the "natural" and proper food for people to eat.[22]

By comparison, city foods—more and more of which were factory-made—were distinctly not natural. By the 1880s, food writers were routinely lamenting that wilted city vegetables could not compare to corn and peas fresh picked from a country garden or that bakers' confections could not rival cookies baked from scratch with the best farm ingredients.[23] One writer protested that hard unripe fruit shipped early to market tested the natural metabolism of the body; he argued that healthful fruit could be attained only when ripening was "done upon the tree, under natural conditions."[24]

Moreover, many feared that manufactured foods, with their imperceptible synthetic ingredients, might be the culprits in city dwellers' widespread complaints of indigestion and constipation. As the science of chemistry afforded new insights into nutrition in the 1890s, Graham's midcentury spiritual concerns about bolted wheat were echoed by a growing cadre of domestic experts who feared that industrially milled "soft fine white flour" was lacking in nourishment compared to its traditionally milled, whole-grain counterpart. This was particularly troubling since the poorest families now relied heavily on bakers' white bread for a substantial part of their diet.[25]

Given these concerns, eating factory-made fare contributed to middle-class city dwellers' anxieties about the "unnaturalness" of their urban lives. When one highbrow critic lamented the anomie of urban living, he bemoaned the prevalence of "predigested" foods that were being served up to Americans by the trainload.[26] In their pappy textures and insipid tastes, these foods—several of which were actually promoted as "predigested"—exemplified the passivity of city life.[27]

Unsatisfied with the variable and often poor quality of foods they found in city markets and provision stores, those shoppers who could remember—and even those who could only imagine—longed for authentic foods, more like what they'd been accustomed to before the massive enlargement of cities had necessitated unfamiliar and unwanted changes. They yearned for the fresh and flavorful foods of the countryside—the sweet corn, rich butter, ripe peaches, homemade berry pies, and fresh spring chickens—that were, as they saw it, more natural.

The Grounding Nature of Growing Food

The appeal of authentic farm foods went far beyond a craving for familiar, good-tasting, old-fashioned comfort foods. Some had come to think about significant changes in America's urban food scene in broader sociological and psychological terms.

Raising food had long been a means of engaging directly with the natural world, and so for some the idea of city dwellers buying anonymous foods and eating out of tins and boxes signified a troubling disconnection from the land. The prospect of an increasingly urban society losing its rudimentary knowledge of the natural world seemed an entirely new and fearsome possibility. Some warned that physical distance from nature would lead to psychological divergence from nature, with untold effect. America's children—the largest generation ever to be raised chiefly in cities—would be most at risk.

The man who did most to investigate this concern was pioneering child psychologist, education reformer, and country-life enthusiast G. Stanley Hall. Born in 1844, Hall's own childhood was wholesomely rooted on a farm in Massachusetts. From this experience, he developed a strong conviction that the countryside, with its frogs to catch and trees to climb, was "the best educational environment . . . ever realized in history."[28] Hall's nostalgic enthusiasm converged with the broader cultural tendency for city dwellers to idealize country life as a corrective counterweight for the nation's growing urban ills.[29]

As early as 1880, Hall tested two hundred middle-class Boston firstgraders to determine their knowledge and awareness of nature and country matters, and he discovered an alarming ignorance of the most basic lore. Nearly 90 percent of the children had no understanding of a wheat field; 75 percent had no concept of seasons; and more than 60 percent had no concept of a beehive, a crow, a robin, or a bluebird, or of planting seeds or growing beans, potatoes, strawberries, blueberries, blackberries, or corn. According to Hall, city children inhabited a world in which meat was dug from the ground, potatoes were picked from trees, butter was wrung from buttercups or butterflies, and oats grew on oaks. Even among the 80 percent of children who did know milk came from cows, some were confused. Having learned solely from picture books, they believed that cows were the same size as mice. In his conclusions, Hall speculated that the largest cities might well produce the least smart children, and so he recommended that urban parents take kids for frequent visits to the country in order to advance their psychological development and boost their intelligence.[30]

In retrospect, it is easy to see that Hall's convictions shaped both his experiments and his conclusions. Though his prejudiced linking of intelligence to knowledge of country lore now seems preposterous, his evidence that city kids didn't know much about nature, food, or the farms where it was produced was convincing. And he was not alone in his concern that it might be psychologically detrimental for city children to inhabit such an apparently incomprehensible and disconsolate world.

By the turn of the twentieth century, education reformers lamented that as many as three-fourths of the children in some urban schools had never seen the countryside surrounding the city.[31] And the poorest

children, compelled to work long hours in factories, were even less likely
to have seen farms or natural areas beyond the city's edge. To many edu-
cators, this fundamental gap in the city child's knowledge of life's basic
workings was horrifying. "To allow a child to grow up without planting a
seed or rearing a plant," educator Clifton Hodge claimed, "is a crime
against civilized society." He feared that such ignorant, ungrounded
children would become "hoodlums and tramps."[32] Others worried that
an ignorant populace would be easily cozened into eating less-than-
wholesome foods thus permitting the already-perceived decline in
urban food quality to continue. According to Hodge, as cities grew and
modern life tended "to drift away from nature into artificialities of every
sort," teaching children about nature became "all the more necessary."[33]
A popular turn-of-the-century Nature-Study movement tried to do just
this, often by teaching city children about the origins of their foods.

Nature-Study programs typically included lessons about turnips and

5.1. *At the outset of the twentieth century, reformers became concerned that city
children might grow up not knowing where their food came from. A popular
Nature-Study movement aimed to remedy this shortcoming of modern life.
School gardens such as this one in New York City provided thousands of children
with the opportunity to grow vegetables from seeds.*

chickens alongside tales of wise old owls and sturdy oaks, though one curriculum designed specifically for New York City's poorest schools was based entirely on the study of fruits and vegetables—the cheapest and most easily obtained specimens of nature in the city.[34] Some children planted seeds in school gardens. As one teacher explained, growing plants was "a revelation and intense joy to city-bred children whose nature instinct had been starved."[35] In 1897, more than twenty-six thousand students raised plants in Nature-Study programs in New York State alone.[36] To those teaching Nature-Study classes, it was no contradiction to teach city children about farms in order to teach them about nature. The two were still regarded as closely related: how humans ate was clearly and meaningfully linked to how nature worked.[37]

While school vegetable gardens helped to teach city kids about nature's wonders, things became more complicated when it came time to teach about farm animals. The doyenne of Nature Study, Anna Botsford Comstock, explained how teaching about animals often put teachers in a difficult, if not "dangerous," position of discussing life and death with students. Typically, Nature-Study curricula had the goals of imparting curiosity and respect for life. This was easy when discussing wrens and beavers but posed "a dilemma from which there is no logical way out" when the discussion turned to farm animals. Because we lived, as Comstock wrote, "in a world where lamb chop, beefsteak and roast chicken are articles of ordinary diet . . . where every meal is based upon the death of some creature," the increasingly uncomfortable relationship between death and eating would be hard to avoid in city classrooms. If a teacher put too much emphasis on the sacredness of life, the children would soon begin to question "whether it be right to slay the lamb or the chicken for their own food," and might no longer want to eat meat.[38]

Comstock offered specific techniques to avoid this nettlesome topic. Teachers should treat death as a natural circumstance common to all, emphasize the perspective of the eater rather than the one who gets eaten, and focus on the idea that each creature is entitled to a meal when it is hungry. If Nature-Study teachers carefully followed these guidelines, city children could benefit from knowledge of cute animals and the workings of wild nature—and eat their meat, too.

Comstock's practical and well-meaning approach—to hide farm animals and the processes that brought them to the table as meat—not only was germane in city schoolrooms but reflected a new modus vivendi that was becoming common in grocery stores and kitchens as well.

Living in cities—far from farms, meadows, woods, droughts, and storms—compelled urban Americans to assume a fundamentally different relationship with the natural world. And in their view from afar, they fancied an idealized, leafy-bowered nature that was therapeutic and grounding, not one that included the dirt, fecundity, and death that was part of everyday life on America's farms.[39] As America's urban culture gained ascendancy, this was the new understanding of nature that would take hold and influence how city dwellers, suburbanites—and eventually even rural people—considered their canned and boxed foods and meats.

The Unseemliness of Stewed Songbirds

Russian immigrant Mary Antin remembered her first meal in America in the 1890s for its odd novelty: "My father produced several kinds of food, ready to eat, without any cooking, from little tin cans that had printing all over them."[40] But after that first meal—with the family happily reunited—Mary's mother took charge of the kitchen once again, and the Antins were soon eating the familiar food of their Eastern European heritage: potatoes, onions, cabbage, rye bread, and salted fish. The Antins' experience could stand for that of hundreds of thousands of immigrants, who, for reasons of low income as well as identity, eschewed many of America's newest foods and found ways to keep themselves supplied with more traditional fare.[41]

In clinging to their distinct, traditional foodways, America's immigrants interjected into the story of how we've lost knowledge of our foods a temporary countering force. From 1880 to 1920, nearly twenty-five million individuals, many fleeing hunger, came from Ireland, Italy, Russia, Germany, and several other nations to America to live—and to eat—better.[42] While low prices of America's mass-produced breads and meats enabled immigrants to eat far better than they had in their countries of origin, many persisted in finding ways to grow their own foods and to raise or hunt animals for meats. In this, they joined rural Americans in helping to preserve traditional firsthand ways of knowing many foods.

Perhaps more than any other group, Italian immigrants brought with them a strong heritage of appreciating fresh, flavorful foods. The first wave came from poor rural areas of southern Italy, where many had labored as farmworkers, or *contadini,* but few had owned land to raise their own foods.[43] As such, they strongly associated the prospect of having land to grow foods with eating well and with prestige. In America, the desire for cheap, familiar ingredients and the status of eating high-quality foods encouraged them to grow and produce their own, even in cities.[44]

In Brooklyn, Italian immigrants often grew enormous backyard gardens, bursting with tomatoes, peppers, basil, zucchini, and broccoli (usually started from seeds carried across the Atlantic). Some kept goats, chickens, and even an occasional pig in tenement kitchens and basements. They gathered dandelion greens in vacant lots. Many tapped their rural skills and started truck farms to supply other immigrant workers with fresh vegetables.[45]

In smaller industrial cities, such as those in Pennsylvania's mining districts, Italian men were able to head to surrounding farms and woods after a day of work to hunt for small game— including rabbits, groundhogs, and songbirds—to provide meat for the table, as was their custom in rural Italy. In particular, songbirds—stewed with tomatoes—were a traditional Italian delicacy.[46] However, hunting for songbirds conflicted with an American sensibility about birds that had been gaining ground for decades to culminate in a powerful bird-conservation movement at the turn of the twentieth century.[47]

Concern for birds had come first from farmers and agricultural reformers, who recognized their worth in eating pests in gardens and fields, but, before long, support for birds came from other spheres as well.[48] In 1841, Sarah Josepha Hale, influential editor of *Godey's Lady's Book* magazine, had written that it was "a sin against feeling to destroy a singing bird," especially one so "innocent and gentle" as the robin. "Any one who kills a robin to eat," she wrote, "ought to have it hung round his neck as the albatross was around the 'Ancient Mariner.'"[49] In 1863, Thomas De Voe had encouraged shoppers to avoid buying insect-eating songbirds so as not "to encourage the destruction of a single life that would be more useful to the economy of nature than its dead body for the table."[50] As a hunter himself, De Voe was less stringent than Hale when it came to robins, which he considered "fat and delicate eating" in September and October. Nevertheless, he recommended that shoppers avoid buying robins in spring months when the birds were pairing off and preparing to nest.[51]

Privileging songbirds and exempting them from the plate had to do not only with their role in eating pests but also with the prevalent explanatory story of civilization. In that story, songbirds were thought to hold a special place because, with their melodies, they'd given people the first example of music, which with human genius and embellishment had become a principal hallmark of high culture. As affluent Americans identified more and more with refined civility, they increasingly regarded hunting for songbirds, or even indifference toward bird conservation, as a sign of crudeness. As Iowa congressman John Lacey, a wildlife champion, explained, "The man or the woman who does not love birds should be classed with the person who has no love for music — fit only for treasons, stratagems, and spoils."[52]

By the turn of the twentieth century, hunting for songbirds put Italian immigrants in direct conflict with America's early bird conservationists, who had realized that bird populations were falling at a dangerously fast pace. Decades of market hunting, aided and abetted by railroads bringing boxcar loads of ducks, geese, shorebirds, and songbirds to city markets, had decimated avian populations, reducing some species to double-digit numbers. The loss of breeding and feeding habitat caused by expansion of farmland — also to supply urban demands for food — had contributed as well. In response, many states adopted game laws that restricted hunting to limited seasons. However, those who shot birds for dinner — hunters taking "potshots" at the end of a day's work — did not generally abide such laws.

Because Italian immigrants were known to hunt songbirds without regard for the new rules, they were singled out as a threat to birds.

William Hornaday, president of the New York Zoological Society and well-known advocate for wildlife, warned in *Our Vanishing Wildlife*, "Let every state and province in America look out sharply for the bird-killing foreigner; for sooner or later, he will surely attack your wildlife."[53] The matter of hunting songbirds out of season set upon a backdrop of more widespread hostilities directed toward Italians, who at that time occupied the lowest rung on the social ladder.

Just as important, Italian immigrants with an appetite for stewed songbirds landed in America at a historic juncture when ideas about where food came from and what one should know about it were very much in flux. Increasingly, many city dwellers considered it fine to eat animals raised specifically to be eaten but found it questionable to eat animals considered "wildlife."

In what might be characterized as a preindustrial view held by immigrant pot-hunters, all of nature was regarded as a source of food; wild birds and wildlife were fair game for dinner. However, middle- and upper-class city dwellers were coming to see nature as therapeutic and aesthetic; increasingly, they regarded hunting wild birds and animals to eat meat as wanton destruction of nature. This urban perspective was not solely a matter of refined aesthetic ideology; it derived from a growing conservation ethic that arose to preserve America's wildlife in the face of insupportable hunting pressures and dramatic habitat losses, occasioned as more and more wetlands, forests, and grasslands were converted into farms.

Nevertheless, the ability of affluent urban Americans to reconceptualize nature as source of solace rather than as source of food depended fundamentally on the industrializing food system, which hid, by both circumstance and design, its places of provenance and particulars of production. Paradoxically, this detached, ex-food-chain view would enable scientists who studied wild birds and animals to see the natural world in more ecological and less anthropocentric ways; however, at the same time, it would also encourage agricultural scientists and business leaders to see farmlands solely as industrial food factories, where any vestige of nature was best extinguished for the sake of efficiency and control. As a result, small farms that had once been readily considered part of nature's realm were increasingly consolidated and transformed into large monocultural acreages that best served food manufacturers and wholesalers seeking to meet the demands of city markets. Vast bonanza wheat farms, horizon-to-horizon cornfields, and immense orchards in the West would become models for America's newly emerging industrial agriculture.

In the case of Italians hunting songbirds, as game wardens began to enforce game laws more strictly, and ultimately as immigrants became acculturated and more prosperous, they adopted America's hunting restrictions and increasingly bought their meat at markets. However, many Italians, Germans, and other immigrants continued hunting in season for rabbits and squirrels through the first half of the twentieth century, and some took up the American sport of deer hunting.

Hunting for recreation by well-heeled sportsmen had never come under the criticism that pot-hunting did. In fact, early wildlife conservation efforts stemmed in large measure from those sportsmen who wanted to preserve opportunities to hunt in the rapidly urbanizing society. They regarded maintaining physical vigor in the face of sedentary city life as critical; recreational sport hunting in wild hinterlands fed that vigor.[54]

Ultimately, America's increasingly urban culture would embrace the fresh tomatoes, broccoli, garlic, spaghetti, and pizza of its Italian citizens' traditional cuisine, but wild songbirds with their melodic trills would never find a place in the nation's kitchens.

The All-Natural Body

Another way that many middle-class city dwellers considered ideas of nature in the unsteady context of urban life had to do more directly with their bodies. Facing more hectic but sedentary lifestyles and new types of foods, they seemed to be losing touch with what they should "naturally" eat and were becoming unhealthy as a result.

Cooks and eaters had long looked to nature to understand their health and eating habits. In these terms, nature was not just outside the city; it permeated the body as well. Indeed, the belief that the human body was divinely designed and calibrated for natural conditions was a foundation of natural theology.[55] When Enlightenment thinking took hold in late eighteenth-century America, earlier beliefs that poor health was a direct sign of God's wrath gave way to a new view that good health was what people should naturally have. Because the human body was considered God's creation, many believed that God had purposefully connected the enjoyment of eating with the physiological requirements of sustenance. As one writer explained, "heaven has formed us to the general taste of all its gifts."[56] Appetite was a natural instinct designed to govern what and how much a person should eat. However, the perfect calibration of appetite could be thwarted by an individual's impiety, inclination to vice or gluttony, or, increasingly, by conditions of the urban lifestyle.

As early as 1820, English physician James Johnson's book about the "influence of civic [city] life, sedentary habits, and intellectual refinement on human health and happiness" was published in Philadelphia. Johnson's assessment of London's ills offered a cautionary tale for Americans beginning to confront the problems of large cities. Johnson was already making the case that city dwellers ate too many of the wrong foods for their inactive indoor lives. Because their digestive tracts were constantly "stimulated," they became fat and dim-witted. Moreover, they became pimply because the body had constantly to rid itself of surplus nutriment by way of unsightly skin eruptions and inflammations. "Let us look around us in this great luxurious metropolis," he wrote, "and we shall not find one in ten, whose digestive organs are in a natural and healthy condition. The tint of the eye and countenance, the feel of the skin, the state of the tongue, the stomach, the bile, and the various evacuations, offer to the experienced and discerning physician the most incontestible[sic] proofs of the position here advanced."[57] Eating in a city could have profound repercussions for health and appearance.

The tendency to regard human health in terms of nature was not solely a matter of natural theology or Johnson's brand of physiology. It was rooted also in humoral health, a pervasive 2,000-year-old philosophy that anthropologist Eugene Anderson has called "the most widely influential belief system in the world."[58] In full form, humoral theory posited that illness was caused by four factors, or humors—heat, cold, dryness, and dampness—that occurred in a person's environment, temperament, and foods. To attain health, an individual needed to balance the body's most pronounced humor, usually by eating foods that exhibited the opposite traits. For example, if one's body was too "hot," then one needed to consume more "cooling" vegetables and fruits.

The four humors broadly informed thinking about foods. In her 1841 cookbook, Sarah Josepha Hale explained how good housewives had to know the "natural constitution" of each eater in the family in order to provide him or her with healthful sustenance. A cook had to adapt foods to the "age, constitution, state of health, and mode of life" of each individual.[59] It would be in poor taste to feed a phlegmatic old husband nothing but the animal foods that perpetuated constipation.

As Hale further explained, a housewife had to adapt meals not only to the natural constitution of the eaters but also to the proper season and to climate. A measure of geographic determinism became part of the equation, too. Because pepper and ginger were "productions of hot climates," they were most appropriately used in "the hot season."[60] And though an all-fat, all-meat diet was appropriate for Eskimos who lived in the coldest climes, it was not appropriate for white-collar workers living in heated brownstones. Through the nineteenth century, both natural theology and humoral theory combined to create a rather elaborate sensibility about the relationships between nature and food, body and spirit.

These general concepts gained fresh currency toward the end of the nineteenth century when more and more eaters grappled with the new realities of living and eating in cities. With so many new foods and choices, the question, "What is the proper food of man?" as Hale had phrased it, became pressing. With widespread warnings about city conditions disrupting natural health, many city dwellers worried that they weren't eating right for the particular demands of urban lifestyles.

A "natural" approach to eating had reached a small crescendo with the Grahamites in the mid-1800s, but by the end of the century, general advice about eating in accordance with nature was appearing regularly in mainstream magazines and cookbooks.[61] In their columns, household experts routinely drew upon tenets of natural theology and humoral theory when they wrote about what to cook. For example, several articles explained that blue-collar factory workers and white-collar "brain workers" living in cities needed to eat differently than farmers and lumberjacks did. Office workers were advised to avoid heavy fats entirely, for they had a tendency to "dull the brain."[62] In 1893, Maria Parloa more specifically advised *Good Housekeeping* readers to use pork "sparingly, particularly where the employment of the members of the family keeps them indoors."[63]

The affable Sarah Tyson Rorer, who'd earned her reputation at the Philadelphia Cooking School and through popular cooking demonstration tours, was fast becoming the most renowned and beloved cooking expert of her time.[64] According to Mrs. Rorer, as she was known, the biggest health problem was that urbanites had lost track of what "nature" had meant for them to eat. The unfortunate result was that they often ate far too much for their own good. "Nature intended that our food should be not only well blended but also taken in small quantities," she told *Ladies' Home Journal* readers. [65] Her own hefty figure attested that she knew firsthand the problem of overeating.[66] The headaches and "bilious conditions," indigestion and constipation that troubled so many, she explained, could be traced directly to eating out of step with nature's plan.[67]

Medical experts concurred. One doctor explained that the natural urge of appetite "so necessary for our existence—especially in early times" had now "to meet with sudden modifications resulting from the complexity of modern life." City life disrupted the body's natural and healthful instincts with "unnecessary and artificial stimulation" that resulted in "unnatural desires for food."[68] Such unnatural eating could be dangerous. Overfed women, it was feared, could become barren.[69]

To remedy pervasive urban afflictions, Mrs. Rorer advised her readers to eat in a more natural way, according to season, climate, and temperature. In the winter, she recommended "eating animal fats in large quantities, to support the heat of the body and keep up the vital power," a guidance that may have been well warranted given the limited heating in many city apartment buildings. In "the heated term" of summer, she recommended living on "fruits, nuts and succulent vegetables, with good macaroni, skimmed milk cheese (Parmesan), and such vegetable fats as olive oil"—again advice well warranted in a time when ice boxes were not yet universal.[70] Another writer explained how, in hot seasons, nature provided cooling vegetables that contained "a large percentage of water"—just what the human body needed and craved at that time of year.[71] With the increasing prevalence of cheap beef from Chicago's packers, many food writers agreed that city dwellers ate too much meat for good health. Rorer admonished her readers to eat less of it in order "to be natural and consistent with Nature's plans."[72] If a homemaker failed to heed "nature's hints," she, her husband, and family would surely suffer from indigestion, or worse.[73]

As it was with problems of city noise, filth, and nerve-frazzling bustle, so it was with city food: the best antidote was natural. City dwellers were urged to look at what they ate as a way to keep in balance and in touch with nature. If city foods failed to nourish and sate, and if urban overeating provoked stomachaches and weakened the nerves, then natural foods and natural eating would strengthen the body and set it aright.

Those city dwellers who longed for contact with the natural world could read Burroughs or picnic in the countryside. But increasingly, they were persuaded that they could make their contact with nature through the manufactured foods they bought and ate. This was the message of a new industry called advertising.

Allure of the Natural

Good advertising cleverly imitates one of nature's very own strategies. In nature, a ripe red berry attracts an eater, who, by consuming the sweet crimson flesh, will serve to disperse seeds. In advertising, a boldly promoted, colorfully packaged product similarly attracts the attention of an eater, who by purchasing it, will contribute to the profits of the manufacturer. In both cases, the eater's hunger is satisfied, but the intent of the attractor may remain hidden.

The aim of the advertiser remained particularly obscured at the start of the twentieth century when print advertising was new, and shoppers were learning to judge the medium at the same time they were learning to judge the new manufactured foods.

By 1900, straightforward labels and promotional trade cards were giving way to more sophisticated advertisements in the flourishing new mass-media realm. That year, more than 3,500 magazines enjoyed circulation of 65 million copies per issue distributed to a population of roughly 78 million people.[74] *Ladies' Home Journal* alone reached 1 million readers.[75] As circulation climbed, so too did the number of food ads. Between 1871 and 1900, the number of food and beverage ads in the highbrow monthly *Century* rose from a mere 3 pages to 169 pages annually. Small ads that had once clustered in the back pages—not unlike today's classifieds—were blown up, done up, and now peppered entire magazines with their spicy enticements.[76] In some cases, magazine ads were cleverly cloaked in the same format as articles, making it difficult to discern editorial opinion from promotional puff.

The expansion of ads reflected significant changes in the way that food was being distributed. While manufacturers had made strides in efficiency and boosted output, the burgeoning supply of food products often hit bottlenecks or gluts in the still old-fashioned and fragmented distribution system. To avoid delays that might result in costly spoilage or staleness, many firms took larger roles in promoting and distributing their own products on a national scale. The old system, which had been governed by regional wholesalers who assembled the products of small-scale producers and sold them to retail grocers, slowly gave way to a new one dominated by large-scale manufacturers supplying retail grocers directly.[77]

As paths of food distribution changed, the ways that information about food was shared changed, too. In the old system, shoppers had learned about food choices by talking with their butchers and grocers. In the new system, manufacturers informed customers directly about the advantages of their products with increasing numbers of ads, and homemakers began to rely on these ads to fill the gaps in their knowledge about new types of foods.[78]

Earlier labels had explained the places and particulars of how products were actually made, but expanding operations meant that most large-scale manufacturers—even canneries—were drawing their supplies from a wide array of places and could no longer assure the actual origin of a particular product.[79] Moreover, innovations in food processing technology—both chemical and mechanical—meant that specific descriptions of how foods were manufactured were less meaningful and less appealing to homemakers. It soon became clear to those in the advertising trade that supplying traditional information was no longer the best way to lead shoppers to a purchase.

Like many professions at the turn of the twentieth century, advertising was becoming refined by a more analytical approach. Since its advent, advertising had held a certain mystique even among its own practitioners. By what formula did it work its wonders of creating demand? University of Chicago psychologist Walter Dill Scott was the first to study how the cryptic medium actually worked, and he offered admen tips about how to make food products more appealing to shoppers.[80]

For one, food ads operated not by imparting information but by evoking emotion. According to Scott, homemakers rarely read the full text of labels and ads, but they were heavily influenced by the appearance of packages. Visual cues—even more than a product's flavor—were paramount in a consumer's choice about what foods to buy.[81] For this reason, he recommended that food labels and ads should not focus on informative details but rather should strive to "enshrine the product with favorable sentiment." For most modern urbanites, Scott explained with cocksure personal experience, appetite had become "more a matter of sentiment and imagination than for our rural ancestors."[82]

For some foods, the most effective selling sentiment might well be pastoral. The image of a country cow could best sell butter, cheese, and even oleomargarine, but so too could the image of a refreshing waterfall or a child's smiling face. New generations of shoppers growing up in the city were less knowledgeable about what foods looked like and where they came from, so traditional associations that had been the stock-in-trade of early labels and promotions carried less meaning for modern shoppers.

In fact, some traditional associations were becoming problematic. Scott chastised one second-rate ad that depicted grasshoppers dancing around the outside of an oatmeal box. Although the cereal manufacturer intended to show how its modern cardboard container kept troublesome insects out (a problem quite familiar to rural homemakers), in

Scott's opinion, the oats and sickening bugs would be "firmly united" in any urban eater's mind.[83]

Ads and labels that depicted animals on packages or cans selling meat were particularly troubling. "It is disgusting to think of eating the flesh of dead cows, hogs, and sheep," Scott wrote. Because squeamish born-and-bred city dwellers were no longer accustomed to associating meats with their animal origins, he advised that advertising copy should refer only to cuts of meat and not to parts of animals' bodies. And instead of picturing the animals that furnished the meat, ads should depict only appetizing dishes made with prepared meats "in a way that jars as little as possible against our refined and cultivated natures." As Scott explained, urbanites had become so "cultured" that they liked "to have meats garnished so they cease[d] to be flesh."[84] By attaching a pleasing sentiment to products, ads could help with this garnishment.

In addition to making foods seem appealing, Scott explained that ads worked best by making products seem familiar. When a homemaker entered a grocery store, she often encountered a bewildering array of shelf upon shelf of cans and packages behind the counter. Out of this display, she would choose the products that caught her eye—those that appealed with a familiar image or especially those that she had already seen in newspaper and magazine ads. And so it was ahead of time, through ads, Scott believed, that admen could "mold" a homemaker's ideas about what foods to buy.[85]

Following Scott's insights, admen shifted their goal from providing information to wooing buyers with the pleasing and familiar.[86] By tapping deeply held emotions and attaching potent sentiments to manufactured foods, admen set out to whet the appetites of millions of eaters for the new types of edibles. In response to shoppers' misgivings and anxieties about factory foods, admen called upon nature and used its allure to offer harried housewives the perfect antidote for urban malaise.

A modest ad for "Wheatlets" cereal in *Ladies' Home Journal* in May 1897 was one of the first to include the word "natural" as part of its appeal. Before that, some household experts had distinguished "made-foods" from those in an "unmanufactured state," but apparently it hadn't occurred to anyone to call factory-made foods "natural" just yet. However, as anxieties about city foods became increasingly understood in terms of divergence from nature, the "natural" pitch rapidly grew in popularity. Ten years later, roughly 13 percent of food ads in *Ladies' Home Journal* used the words "nature" or "natural" to appeal to potential customers. In one 1907 issue, 23 percent of food ads made use of a "natural" hook.[87]

The natural pitch took many different forms and was used to promote many foods, but admen embellished it to its greatest flourish in the promotion of boxed breakfast cereals. The cereal Egg-O-See, for example, forthrightly proclaimed "Back to Nature" as its motto. In line with Sarah Rorer's advice, copy from one typical ad advised eaters to "Keep in step with Nature" by laying off heavy meats "when spring sunshine and birds announce the warmer days" and instead "tempting the fussy appetite with Egg-O-See."[88]

Ads for Pettijohn's Flaked Breakfast Food responded more squarely to city dwellers' longing for direct contact with physical nature. A mother bear and adorable cubs appeared on every package and in every ad in some clever outdoorsy motif: camping in the woods, building snowmen, and—even more cleverly—watching a night sky starred with the constellation Ursa Major.[89] In a series of 1902 newspaper ads, Pettijohn's promised to salve city dwellers' nerves by giving an "outdoor feeling" to busy "indoor people . . . who take little exercise." One ad claimed that Pettijohn's could boost an eater's "animal spirits," summoning a traditional notion and suggesting primal vigor as remedy for modern urban faintness. Another ad went so far as to suggest that eating Pettijohn's cereal could bring "a feeling that the walk to and from the office, or the train, isn't so long and uninteresting—it makes the heels a little lighter and faster—makes you look at the sky once in a while,—and fill your lungs a little deeper."[90]

While Pettijohn's eaters were plied with camp-outs and black bears, those who filled their bowls with Shredded Wheat were treated to an even more elaborate array of natural motifs. The decorously named Natural Foods Company pulled out all stops in promoting the naturalness of its Shredded Wheat cereal. In its giveaway cookbooks and prevalent ads, eaters encountered images and copy that elevated the pitch of the natural to an art form.

Most ads started with the popular premise that wheat had been divinely designed as the perfect food for the human body.[91] The proposition made sense to nineteenth-century metaphoric thinkers because, as the ads claimed, rudimentary chemical analysis had shown that grains of wheat contained fats and proteins in the same proportions as the makeup of the human body. This "vital truth" was explicated with evangelical fervor in a Shredded Wheat promotional cookbook, four million copies of which had been printed and distributed by 1902.[92] It was a matter of natural law: when the body was "nourished in natural proportion" by such a perfect and "naturally organized food" as Shredded Wheat, "natural conditions" followed.[93] And natural conditions—a.k.a. regular bowel movements—were what anxious and constipated city eaters craved. To compete with products made from increasingly common white or bolted flours, ads for Shredded Wheat aggressively drove home the same message in dozens of newspapers: to have good health, a body needed natural food, and Shredded Wheat—made from whole-grain wheat—was it.[94] One 1903 ad admonished, "Mothers, do you not know that children crave natural food until you pervert their taste by the use of unnatural food?" The ad further warned: "unnatural food develops unnatural and therefore wrong propensities and desires in children."[95]

Although the nature where the wheat was grown rarely appeared in Shredded Wheat ads, wheat fields were occasionally shown. One ad of this sort depicted the image of a looking glass held up beside a field of wheat and, paraphrasing Shakespeare, claimed that the cereal held a "mirror up to nature." The mirror reflected not waves of grain but instead a comely, Shredded Wheat biscuit.[96]

Far more often than with wheat fields, the Natural Foods Company associated its cereal with that romantic icon of natural beauty and power, Niagara Falls. Shredded Wheat boxes featured a trademarked image of Niagara, which helped to reconcile the fact that this most-perfect natural food was actually made in a factory. Promotional materials often mentioned or showed the Shredded Wheat biscuit-baking

5.2. *Depicting a Shredded Wheat Biscuit as the "reflection" of a wheat field, this newspaper ad indicates one of the ways turn-of-century promoters used the idea of nature to ease anxieties of urban eaters. Ultimately, Shredded Wheat adopted the romantic icon of Niagara Falls as its main advertising motif.*

factory—called a "conservatory"—located in its beautiful setting right beside the falls. With 844 large glass windows, the conservatory was filled with healthful sunshine and always kept squeaky clean. The image of the luminous factory and falls was more than just a pleasing juxtaposition because the Niagara River did in fact power the biscuit ovens. As one factory-tour pamphlet explained, it was a "happy dispensation of fate that a portion of power generated by the scenic wonder of Niagara should be dedicated to the health and happiness of the human family through the manufacture of the most perfect food that was ever devised for the nourishment of man."[97] Powered by Niagara and flooded with sunlight, the Shredded Wheat conservatory seemed far more "natural" than other food factories. No other manufacturer could imply that the vigor of the nation's greatest waterfall was imparted directly into its cereal.

Ironically, Shredded Wheat was so factory-spun in its form—unlike anything in nature except perhaps a bird's nest—it became the target of countless jokes. *Life* magazine printed one about an old lady who lost her whiskbroom and afterward discovered she'd served it for breakfast as a bowl of Shredded Wheat.[98] Nevertheless, the powerful association with nature proffered by ads must have overcome the cereal's strawlike texture for the many eaters who consumed the two million Shredded Wheat biscuits baked every day.[99]

THERE HAD been no need to call food "natural" until a phalanx of what seemed to be unnatural foods arose. While insisting on the "naturalness" of their own products, food manufacturers that used the natural pitch in ads underscored the increasingly "unnatural" and synthetic state of many other factory-made foods.[100] Yet because foods such as Shredded Wheat and its old cousin Triscuits (didn't you always suspect the two were somehow related?) were themselves made in a factory—albeit a naturalized "conservatory"—the ads also began to legitimate a new though rather muddy definition of natural food. In preindustrial America, any food from the farm had been natural, but in the brave new world of mass-produced factory foods, only those labeled as "natural" seemed to fit the bill.

Nature in this light became an oddly multivalent concept. Quite often in ads, "natural" referred to the way the body's digestive tract was ideally intended to work. Other times, nature referred to scenic parklands and waterfalls. And still other ads referred to a pastoral nature, though only rarely did a country motif correspond to the land where the food was actually grown. In the world of ads, these various meanings of nature conflated and migrated to a distinctly more sentimental realm, where factory-made foods *could* be natural and—far from being culpable—now offered the perfect antidote for urban ills. With city shoppers farther from the work and farms that created their foods, the meaning of nature was becoming more malleable and prone to abstraction. Though some food ads, particularly those for canned vegetables and dairy products, continued to refer to agricultural landscapes in a pastoral light, many emphasized the more symbolic values of nature.

For example, some ads using the natural pitch went beyond agreeable associations to touch a philosophical nerve. While most companies simply promoted the therapeutic aspects of their natural foods, a few companies began to emphasize one-upmanship, contending that their products "improved on nature." Ads for Karo Corn Syrup, for example, identified the company as "rival of the bee," and explained that its syrup resulted when "man went to nature, even as the bee does, but with better equipment."[101] The theme of improving on nature would become increasingly common in ads for manufactured foods, but in the first decade of the twentieth century, such blatant hubris was still open to rebuke. Ads for Pettijohn's and Shredded Wheat took the opposite tack and instead called particular attention to their products' humility. Pettijohn's claimed that, unlike other "ready to eat fad foods," its cereal was genuine, humble "whole wheat not altered in an attempt to improve on nature." Shredded Wheat ads plainly asserted in large boldface capitals: "MAN CANNOT IMPROVE NATURE."[102]

Transcending mere pleasantries, a dialogue about the grand existential question so pressing in the face of the rapidly urbanizing culture—what was the place of people in nature?—occurred in so mundane a venue as newspaper food ads. Presumably, consumers of the various cereals and syrups would choose one product over the other not only for reasons of price and taste but in part because the ads' philosophic message matched their own outlook about humanity's hubris or humility.

Stopping short of such full-blown natural pitches, several manufacturers simply attached natural cues to their products. Seasonal change, for example, was used to sell everything from macaroni to Jell-O.[103] The prospect of June strawberries on top made early summer a good reason to buy cornflakes. And the opening of oyster season—the run of "R" months (September through April)—became a good reason to buy National Biscuit Company's Oysterette crackers.[104] In the lives of city food buyers, such natural cues and attendant cycles were already becoming less meaningful, but their presence in ads imparted a new type of meaning to shoppers. Buying factory-made products in season somehow moved them closer to the natural end of the new food spectrum and enabled shoppers to remain in step with nature's rhythms.

Some manufacturers implied that their mass-produced foods could substitute as a kind of virtual-reality equivalent for foods procured in more direct ways. For example, newspaper ads suggested that having pantry shelves "planted" with Morey's Solitaire brand canned corn, peas, and tomatoes was just like having "a kitchen garden all winter."[105] And Dillon and Douglas Company ads told newspaper readers that they knew "so well the quality of eggs" packed under their Blue Ribbon brand "that it almost amounts to a personal acquaintance with the hens that lay them."[106] Crown Sea Foods suggested that using its canned fish was just like picking your own fish seaside. "Would you like to go down to the shore as the boats come in and pick out for tomorrow's breakfast some nice, plump mackerel, still dripping with salt water?" the ad asked.[107] (Was the bit about salt water intended to ennoble the canned fish's salty packing brine, I wonder?) By offering more comfortable and familiar ways to think about using modern factory-made products, these metaphoric ads tried to reassure shoppers anxious about the mysteries of their foods' origins.

Yet ads using all these natural pitches went far beyond the gratifying implication that nature was indeed the ultimate source of the foods they promoted. The ads directed urban homemakers to consider how readily factory products might solve their problems and absolve their anxieties. Simply by buying and eating Shredded Wheat, a nervous body could be restored to its natural state of health. Simply by using Morey's canned corn, Blue Ribbon eggs, or Crown's mackerel, a homemaker could avoid the far more time-consuming if not impossible city garden, henhouse, or walk to the fish market, let alone seashore — and still expect to serve her family comparably wholesome foods. Ads were beginning to teach homemakers that using brand-name, factory-manufactured food products could be a warranted surrogate for knowledge and experience that had once been as familiar, important, and direct as knowing the hens that laid your eggs. Before long, ads would successfully instruct homemakers to no longer expect to know about the actual nature of foods, but instead to accept their sentiment as a new pseudoknowledge.

While many city shoppers were clearly drawn to the notion of buying and eating foods associated with nature, the nature claimed by the ads was no longer the nature that created the foods. Indeed, the nature claimed by many ads was associated with food products *only* by the ads' attachment. This is clearly a case of what French sociologist Henri Lefebvre has called "the decline of the referentials," or the tendency of words under the influence of capitalism to become severed from meaningful associations.[108] Increasingly, food ads helped shoppers become accustomed to new definitions of words such as "fresh" and "natural," definitions that could well be considered opposite of their traditional meanings.[109] The new definitions better served the needs of the emerging industrial food system, which could not supply foods that matched customary meanings and expectations. And they better met shoppers' desires, albeit with pretense.

Although many shoppers in the first decades of the twentieth century may have longed for foods that were more natural in a traditional sense, what they ended up getting were factory foods simply spun as natural in a new, urban sense. The changing ways that city dwellers saw themselves and their foods in relation to the natural world would further enable cooks and eaters to relinquish customary expectations about knowing the places and particulars of their foods.

The prevalent desire of affluent urbanites to be "close to the heart of nature," moreover, would fuel the suburbanization that began to swallow up farm belts that had encircled America's cities through most of the nineteenth century.[110] In the new view, such farms became less valued for the fresh foods they could supply and more highly valued for the suburban neighborhoods—sans chickens but replete with new naturalistic landscaping—they could provide. Paradoxically, city dwellers' desires to be close to nature would contribute to the emerging urban reality of eating foods from farther and farther away produced by more and more arcane methods of industry.

CHAPTER 6

Rise of the Modern Food Sensibility

On April 23, 1903, twelve young men sat down to dinner. The meal was not just ordinary fare but part of a grand experiment. Served up along with the ample roast beef, mashed potatoes, string beans, bread, and butter were capsules of the widely used preservative borax. The scientist conducting the experiment was none other than Dr. Harvey Wiley of the U.S. Bureau of Chemistry, and the men doing the eating were fast becoming known as the Poison Squad.[1] Accompanied by its dose of preservative and presided over by a scientist, the roast beef dinner could well serve as a symbol of the emerging twentieth-century meal.

As food manufacturers strove to meet growing demands of city eaters and at the same time to cut spoilage and reduce costs, many had turned to a brand-new line of preservative substances—solutions of formaldehyde and salicylic acid with trade names such as "Freezene" and "Preservaline."[2]

Though artificial colors troubled Wiley (as seen in chapter 4), it was these preservatives that riled him most. He feared they would mask the natural signs of decomposition that had traditionally signified danger to cooks and eaters. By hiding putrid odors, such preservative chemicals, he thought, could rob "nature of her means of protecting us from danger" and lure unwitting eaters to ingest rotten foods.[3]

While Wiley's first round of investigations in the 1890s had documented the widespread use of adulterants, this second and more cele-brated round examined the safety of intentional additives flooding the food supply. Many manufacturers claimed that preservatives were absolutely necessary for large-scale food production and did no harm to humans, but they had no studies to back their claims.

When the press reported in 1898 that tons of rotten canned meat—its fetid odor masked by the common preservative boracic acid—had been fed to American troops in Cuba, leaving soldiers too sick to fight, Congress finally agreed to fund Wiley's study of preservative safety.[4]

Following a research method that prudence would never allow today, he set up a series of experiments to test preservatives on human eaters. Healthy young men volunteered for a year to follow a strict regimen of diet, including the potentially harmful substances under investigation. A clever reporter dubbed Wiley's volunteers the "Poison Squad," and with growing interest in the issue of pure foods, the experiments became a media sensation.[5]

Squad members took their meals together and provided Wiley with their excretions for analysis. Wiley kept tabs on all that went in and all that came out. He wanted to know what happened to the preservatives being tested—were they retained in the body or excreted? By analyzing urine, sweat, feces, and occasionally blood, he was able to track roughly the fate of the substances tested in the body. Wiley increased the dosages over the course of fifteen to twenty days until his human guinea pigs began to suffer from headaches and stomach distress.

The most commonly used preservatives, borax and boracic acid, were the first to be tested in 1903 and 1904. Although Wiley found no notable effects from low dosages over a short period, Poison Squad members did have trouble at high doses of 2.5 grams per day. The most pronounced symptoms were burning sensations in the throat and esophagus, pains in the stomach, and dizziness.[6] Most Americans would be exposed to no more than one-quarter gram of borax a day if they ate manufactured foods, but Wiley was concerned that over the long term, even a low daily dose would burden the kidneys.[7]

Although the Poison Squad was not assembled for purposes of pub-licity, its eating in the public interest did much to build support for a "pure food" law that Wiley advocated. Newspapers and women's magazines, which had warned readers about the dangers of adulteration, now enlisted urban middle-class homemakers in the "pure foods" cause. Strong support also came from rural areas, where farmers were enraged that the wholesome foods they raised and sent to market often ended up adulterated by manufacturers before reaching shoppers.[8] By political inclination, Wiley had little use for government regulation, but he believed that people had a right to know what substances were hidden in

6.1. *Deeply concerned about the ways that industrialization was changing foods, Dr. Harvey Wiley conducted influential studies on food adulteration and additives. His research and leadership at the Bureau of Chemistry (predecessor of the Food and Drug Administration) led to passage of the first Pure Food and Drug Act in 1906.*

the foods they purchased.[9] As the Poison Squad experiments continued, pure food bills passed the House twice but failed in the Senate, crushed by influential manufacturers who groused at having to list additives on food labels.[10] In the public eye, Dr. Wiley became a beloved hero fighting companies that refused to divulge their imperceptible ingredients to shoppers.

Eventually, business support for the legislation gained ground as some of the largest, most reputable manufacturers began to recognize how a pure food law could work to their advantage. The expanding scope of markets meant that it was becoming a nuisance for national-scale businesses to deal with different states' particular labeling requirements and ingredient prohibitions. A federal law with a single set of regulations would make it not only easier for large firms to sell products nationally but also more difficult for small factories serving local and regional markets to compete.[11] In addition, some business leaders recognized that widespread adulteration had made shoppers skeptical of *all* the cans and bottles on grocers' shelves. Only by building shoppers' trust could big food firms stamp out suspicion and tap the larger markets they needed to absorb their ever growing, high-volume output.[12]

Congressional support for the Pure Foods Law was reaching a critical mass when publication of Upton Sinclair's *The Jungle,* with its revolting descriptions of conditions in Chicago's meatpacking plants, gave the bill the final jolt it needed to pass. Responding to the urgency of public outcry, President Theodore Roosevelt signed the Pure Food and Drug Act of 1906 and the nation's first federal meat inspection bill into law on the same day.[13]

Almost immediately, labels and ads began to sport official-looking seals declaring that products were "made in accordance with the Pure Food and Drug Act." In fact, many shoppers came to learn about the new law through the mounting presence of such seals, labels, and ads. In 1896, 14 percent of food ads in the *Ladies' Home Journal* had referred to "pure" foods; a decade later in 1907, 45 percent of food ads referred to "pure" foods or to the newly enacted "Pure Foods Law" as part of their pitch.[14] Many of these ads, placed by large-scale national manufacturers, instructed shoppers to trust the new security promised by the federal law.

Passage of the Pure Foods Law belied a controversy stirring over its enforcement. Most food manufacturers opposed restrictions on the additive sodium benzoate, also known as benzoate of soda, but Poison Squad experiments had convinced Harvey Wiley that the substance should be banned. His most earnest supporter in the food industry, Henry J. Heinz, backed him by drumming up consumer pressure with pointed ads.

A successful manufacturer of canned soups, beans, vegetables, pickles, and—of course—ketchup, Heinz had invested substantially in scientific research, machinery, and sanitation practices that made it possible to successfully bottle his tomato condiment without preservatives. As such, Wiley and Heinz agreed that processors who used benzoate of soda did so only to cut corners on cleanliness, costs, and quality. If ketchup could be made without benzoate, then why add the stuff at all? Heinz didn't volunteer to share his proprietary methods, but he aggressively turned public concern for pure foods into a selling point for his own preservative-free products.[15]

Heinz ads had typically promoted ketchup with images of gardens and tomatoes, but at the height of the preservative controversy, the company launched an ad campaign that invoked governmental authority to impress upon consumers the danger of using ketchups made with benzoate. Featuring frightening quotations from federal reports (penned by Wiley), a series of newspaper ads in 1909 warned about the threats that the preservative posed to health. One declared, "The United States Government Says: 'Benzoate of Soda (in foods) is highly objectionable and produces a very serious disturbance of the metabolic functions, attended with injury to digestion and health."[16] Such extravagant scorn must have surely given ketchup buyers pause. "Good Ketchup Needs No Drugs" another ad warned, belittling benzoate as a "drug" that permitted unsanitary handling, loose manufacturing methods, and use of inferior raw materials—"the kind of food you would not care to eat if you could see it made and what it is made of."[17] Heinz ketchup ads made no bones about lumping preservatives together with poor quality.

The Pure Food and Drug Act had required that preservatives be listed on a product's label, so Heinz ads instructed consumers to examine all ketchup labels carefully: "This labeling is always obscure and in fine type. You will need to look closely for the statement 'contains one tenth of one per cent of Benzoate of Soda.'"[18] Sure enough, if a shopper followed Heinz's advice and read labels, she would find that dozens of brands of ketchup crowding market shelves were the kind preserved with benzoate of soda.[19] Being able to see neither the benzoate nor the tomatoes that went into making various ketchups, most homemakers probably felt compelled to trust the Heinz ads.

However, the governmental authority referred to in these ads was not as monolithic as it may have seemed to shoppers. Behind the scenes, sodium benzoate had even the experts embroiled.

Although the sodium benzoate in ketchup was chemically synthesized from the coal-tar derivative toluene for express use as a preservative, sodium benzoate was also found to occur naturally in cranberries.[20] Chemists could now show that the substance in cranberries was exactly the same as the synthetic version derived from coal tar, confusing what had always seemed a commonsense distinction between things made by nature and things made by humans. Somewhere between ketchup and cranberry sauce, the distinction between natural and man-made became vague and subject to political and ontological debate. At the very moment when the difference between natural and artificial seemed so pressing in the theater of urbanizing culture, the science of chemistry challenged traditional categories that had long ordered understanding of the physical world as well.

The cranberry conundrum suddenly made it trickier to use nature as a yardstick to measure industrially manufactured foods. One proponent contended that the long human experience of eating cranberries without harm provided more convincing evidence about benzoate than Wiley's brief dinner-table trials. In congressional hearings, one ketchup bottler invoked natural theology in favor of benzoate. "It seems to me that if the Lord Almighty put it there [in cranberries]," he testified, "the manufacturer ought to be able to use it."[21]

Wiley did not shrink. Poison Squad experiments had him thoroughly convinced that sodium benzoate was harmful.[22] When he indicated his intention to move forward with a benzoate ban, though, a group of food manufacturers went over his head and protested directly to the president. Roosevelt, who'd been put off by Wiley's scorn for his favorite sweetener, saccharin, appointed an independent board of academic scientists to study the issue. After conducting their own metabolic studies on young medical students, they disagreed with Wiley and concluded that the impact of the small amount of sodium benzoate used in ketchup would be "very trifling" to consumers. Furthermore, they contended, the threat of food poisoning from spoilage in haphazardly enlarging city food systems was a far more serious threat to public health than a little benzoate.[23]

Though detractors criticized him for blocking the wheels of progress, Wiley harrumphed that progress did not result from adding poisons to preserve foods that should have gone "to the hog pen." He would stick to the natural and normal food of man: "'food' prepared by the Creator and modified by the cook," not by the factory.[24] Wiley held fast to his natural yardstick—a standard that had proven trustworthy in the days before rapid growth dramatically transformed the nation's landscape and food system.

Now with the meaning of "natural" thoroughly befuddled, new standards were up for negotiation. And with the establishment of the Pure Food and Drug Act, there was now a political forum for that negotiation. While the law restricted the most harmful adulterants and additives, at the same time, it established standards that would permanently sanction use of artificial colorings, flavorings, and preservatives as ordinary parts of the American diet.[25]

Though Heinz ultimately captured the market with his additive-free ketchup, sodium benzoate and other preservatives went on to become fundamental building blocks of the modern food system in which the challenge of supplying cities with plentiful, cheap, unspoiled foods made their services necessary. Labels listed preservatives and other additives in proverbial small print, but widespread concerns about food safety began to wane after passage of the federal law.

Historians have debated whether the Pure Food and Drugs Act of 1906 was passed primarily for idealistic aims of protecting public health or for the benefit of big food businesses.[26] The law effectively eliminated countless small and regional food producers that could not meet its sanitary production standards, which were based on large-scale specifications. It arguably set into motion the trend toward food-industry consolidation that would snowball to enormous proportions through the twentieth century.

What's most interesting to consider in our story, however, is how the law influenced shoppers' ways of thinking and knowing about their foods. Just as it was becoming more difficult for shoppers to learn and know about the groceries they were buying, the federal pure food law—limited and underfunded as it was—helped give homemakers a welcome sense of security about manufactured products.

Because shoppers could not evaluate additives by traditional means, they had to rely increasingly on product labels and ads, many of which allayed concerns by encouraging shoppers to trust government regulations to protect them. Doubts about adulterants, additives, and the credibility of manufacturers were soon minimized by confidence in progressive pure food regulations. The Pure Food and Drug Act pushed large-scale manufacturers to become more conscientious, eliminated fly-by-night operations, and thereby succeeded in making factory-processed foods safer and better in quality. At the same time, the new law also made it easier for homemakers to relinquish—with a sigh of relief—the expectation of having to worry about the source and ingredients of their foods in the increasingly enigmatic and anonymous marketplace.

After the turn of the twentieth century, as more homemakers accepted the norm of knowing less about where their foods came from and how they were made, their attention would be turned toward new ways of knowing foods. In the decades that followed, promotions devised by advertising experts and the advice offered by home economists would direct homemakers' attention to brand names, to new concepts of quality, to entirely new scientific understanding of hygiene and nutrition, and to other novel ways of thinking about foods. During this crucial period, responsibility and authority for knowing foods would steadily migrate from the ken of the homemaker to the province of experts in distant laboratories, government offices, and corporate headquarters.

Bolstering Brand Names and Promoting Packages

In 1901, a cartoon in the *Chicago Daily News* poked fun at factory foods and their commercially inspired monikers. It pictured "Thanksgiving Day of the Future" as a feast of boxed foods with names like "Spudette," "Turkine," and "Cran-Cran."[27] Though this grim prospect might have made readers begrudgingly chuckle, no one could dispute that brand names were indeed becoming useful for choosing foods, especially as the decade advanced and more factory-made products entered the marketplace.

Although homemakers had at first been unaccustomed to buying branded and packaged foods, they soon learned to use brand names as a shorthand way to identify a quality product and to associate it with a particular company. Presumably, no reputable food company would put its name on a poor-quality product if it wanted to stay in business. Artemas Ward, editor of a leading grocery trade journal, regarded shoppers' desire to know where foods "come from, and who is responsible for their condition and character" as the driving force behind the rapid rise of branded, packaged foods.[28] In a marketplace where poor- and variable-quality bulk foods were all too common, brand names served shoppers by enabling them to discriminate between one jam that tasted too much like aspirin, another that tasted too sweet, and yet another that suited the family's taste buds just right. Because branded packaged foods could increasingly be bought on the assumption that they would always be of the same standard quality, brand names could save a shopper time and disappointment.[29]

Brand names also served the interest of food companies by helping labels and ads to attach sentiments to products more readily. For example, "Quaker" in a word conveyed honesty, integrity, and tradition. As competition increased between firms producing similar food products, branding permitted companies to compete by appealing to shoppers with distinctive ad campaigns while avoiding the profit-draining practice of price-cutting.

Although promotions for brand-name products could encourage homemakers to try manufactured foods, the true test came at the table.

As one magazine writer explained, she knew she'd finally found a reputable brand when her family was pleased with a can of peas she served. She "naturally demanded this brand again, and it served as an introduction to other vegetables of the same make."[30] In this very way, in countless the kitchens, knowledge of brand names gradually supplanted other types of traditional and sensory knowledge that homemakers had once relied on.

At the same time brand names were becoming more familiar, the packages displaying them became more advantageous in their own right as new understanding of germs came to light. By the turn of the century, the science of bacteriology had identified foods as a significant vector for germborne diseases. The urban food supply came under the increasing scrutiny of new public health departments, and women's magazines that had railed against adulterants, additives, and short-weight packages now warned about germs, too. Readers were pressed to consider the many ways their bread or milk could become contaminated by "paws" or "perspiration" en route to market.[31] Milk, for example, could be tainted by filth on a cow's udder, germs on a milker's hands, and through any number of other encounters on its grimy path to city markets in uncovered, unsanitary milk pails, ultimately to be served up with unsterilized dippers. (Contaminated milk, in fact, had led to high infant mortality rates, especially among the poor.) At any time, foods could be touched or coughed upon by heedless handlers. Fresh fruits and vegetables in open piles at corner grocery markets could also invite bacteria-laden dust and fly excreta.[32] By all accounts, the invisible pathogens were everywhere. When homemakers learned that contaminated foods could bring disease into their homes, the packages that had before seemed to be deceitful guises suddenly became protective jackets that heroically shielded foods on their foul trip from factory to kitchen.

As awareness about the relationship between germs and disease grew, cleanliness became the paramount selling point of packaged foods. In many ads, manufacturers emphasized the exemplary hygiene of their workers. The H. J. Heinz Company boasted that its "workpeople" wore clean uniforms and that their hands were "under the constant care of manicurists employed by the company."[33] Armour's boasted that its bacon was sealed into jars "by light fingered girls," implying not only that its workers' fingers were clean but also—in that time of ethnic frictions and rife bigotry—that swarthy immigrants or African Americans were not employed.[34] Before long, many firms went one further: extolling new machinery that manufactured food products without any human hands. "No hands" would soon become the pinnacle of product desirability in cities, where poor sanitation coupled with paranoia had led to concern that poor workers' hands teemed with germs.[35] Although the notion of human hands doing the work of food preparation may have once suggested human care, with the large scale of modern food manufacturing, the thought of anonymous hands touching food was now considered repugnant. More and more, ads began to emphasize that food products were "sterilized" and "always uniform" as prime selling points.[36]

In this context, the old-fashioned Yankee inclination toward thrift, which had impelled many homemakers to buy cheap bulk goods, made way for a more modern appreciation of packaged brand-name foods.[37] With protective packages, housewives could purchase the security of knowing their food was untainted by dust, flies, or germy human hands, while the brand names printed on them assured standard quality.

The new shorthand knowledge that developed around the brand name soon became just as critical for the well-being of an urban family negotiating the urban food scene as traditional lore had been for rural families. In an exposé about bacteria-laden ketchup sold with sand and decomposed tomatoes, one home economist admonished, "There is no excuse for the alert housewife who buys these filthy catsups, for there are standard brands on the market whose name guarantees their quality."[38] Another household expert would later describe the practice of asking for brand names as "the first great step out of the wilderness of ignorant purchasing" because homemakers could make choices themselves based on information in ads.[39] Within a very short time, the knowledge of the brand name reigned preeminent. By 1920, marketing studies would show that a majority of city food shoppers routinely asked for branded packaged foods.[40]

The Home Economists' Twist

If the appeal of brand-name foods didn't grab shoppers straightaway, a rising group of household experts — the home economists — would help further to persuade homemakers of their merits through the first decades of the twentieth century.

A previous generation of household experts had gained credibility in the 1880s when city homemakers confronted adulteration and other early quandaries of the newly emerging industrial food system. In magazine articles, they'd warned against manufactured foods and offered useful advice to fill growing gaps in urban homemakers' kitchen know-how. In their view, "ignorance" about traditional ways was a critical weakness among city homemakers, who — unable to recognize genuine articles and true quality — were victimized by guile because they didn't know any better.

But increasingly, as the servant shortage intensified and the quality of manufactured foods improved, as urban culture gained ascendancy and feminist convictions strengthened, a rising generation of experts who called themselves "home economists" began to see the situation quite differently. Less impeded by the hindrance of traditional mores and drawn to the excitement of scientific progress, they began to regard manufactured foods as the vanguard of society's advancement, saving women time and giving them freedom to pursue other goals. In this new light, "ignorance" of modern and scientific ways was homemakers' biggest problem.[41] With the rise of Home Economics, the very idea of what constituted female acumen and homemaker know-how would be turned on end.

Leading home economist Ellen Richards personified the change in thinking. Remember, it was she who in the 1880s had lamented not knowing where any of her foods came from or how they were made. But by 1900, she envisioned a modern kitchen, stocked with prepared foods and connected by pneumatic tube to a supply station that could send baked goods in just ten minutes. Instead of spending hours chopping vegetables and meats for soup, a homemaker could heat the contents of a can, order a loaf of bakers' bread, and then read a book in her spare time.[42]

Despite the appeal of leisure, Richards knew that many people would find the very idea of "bread made by the yard, and pies by the hundred" objectionable. Most considered food to be a personal matter and the idea of eating en masse to be distasteful. "Each family has a weakness for the flavor produced by its own kitchen bacteria," she sarcastically acknowledged, "but that is a prejudice due to lack of education."[43] This was where her newly minted profession, Home Economics, came in. Ultimately, with their expertise and authority, home economists would teach young homemakers to appreciate the superior cleanliness and standards that only food manufacturers with their scientific methods and skilled staffs could provide.[44]

Home economists did not start out promoting the use of manufactured foods. Paralleling Richards's early career, the young discipline grew from roots in laboratory science. Richards was the first woman to study chemistry at M.I.T., where owing to stereotypical expectations about gender roles, she was compelled to direct her scholarship toward domestic matters, such as detection of food adulterants and the mysteries of bread leavening. The ambitious Richards soon opened a chemistry lab for women, where she trained female students in principles of a new discipline she called "domestic science," which was officially renamed as the field of Home Economics—Dewey decimal designation and all—in 1899.[45]

Richards and her students worked hard to gain stature in a society that refused to confer women professional respect. They spearheaded the opening of university Home-Ec departments, the development of grammar-school and high-school curricula, and eventually the establishment of a federal Bureau of Home Economics—all with the idealistic goal of bringing ordinary homes into line with the modern industrial standards.[46] Making every effort to distinguish themselves from earlier household experts who'd taught what they considered to be mere cookery, the home economists promoted a distinctly scientific approach in the kitchen. Through countless articles in popular women's magazines, they spread their ideas and techniques to households nationwide.

6.2. *By the beginning of the twentieth century, many American schoolgirls were learning how to choose and cook foods in Home Economics classes. The microscope on the table indicates the scientific orientation of instruction.*

To assist middle-class homemakers beleaguered by the lack of domestic help, for example, they recommended methods to streamline and simplify household chores. Inspired by Frederick Taylor's emerging science of efficiency, they advised homemakers to minimize unneeded motions by shrinking and redesigning their kitchens, to plan weekly menus ahead of time, to use standardized measuring cups, and to embrace new labor-saving devices, such as electric stoves and dishwashers.[47] Not only could using the new machinery save homemakers effort, it could give them a new kind of mastery and confidence. As one Home-Ec writer explained in 1896, "One feels a peg higher in the scale of intelligence for using even a dishwashing machine."[48]

Home economists also brought the budding fields of bacteriology and nutrition to bear in the kitchen. Bacteriology had revealed the ways that hidden germs coupled with ill-informed food preparation could lead to sickness, and so in place of customary methods that kept foods safe from spoilage, home economists taught homemakers that cooking now required knowing the precise temperatures and times for killing bacteria and fungal spores. They recommended that the housewife wear a bleached apron, disinfect all cooking utensils with boiling water, use an icebox, paint her kitchen white, and keep it as clean as a laboratory.[49] Nutritional science had shown that serving solely the pies and meats that everyone liked best could lead to malnourishment, and so instead of teaching students to cook dishes sanctioned by culinary tradition and what was in season at market, home economists began to instruct young homemakers to make menus based on foods' nutritional composition. They recommended using newly published tables to "compute" proteins, fats, carbohydrates, and calories in every meal to ensure that family members consumed the correct proportions of each.[50]

Despite their aspirations toward scientific precision, the home economists' understanding of nutrition was far from complete (vitamins and micronutrients had yet to be discovered). As author Laura Shapiro has explained, "they admired the way fats and sugars packed a large number of calories into a small amount of food," an interpretation that favored cheap, high-calorie foods, such as candy, at the expense of vegetables and fruits.[51] Before long, scientific understanding deepened, and home economists made every effort to correct their misinterpretations, but the idea that it was prudent to eat cheap, high-calorie foods remained stuck in popular thought until after World War I.[52]

Regardless of such devilish details, through their teaching about proteins, fats, and calories, home economists helped to popularize an entirely new lexicon of food know-how and, along with it, a new understanding of the human body.[53] By 1920, with the rising popularity of automobiles, it was just a short step to construe food as fuel and bodies as cars. As home economists began to teach young women about the importance of "keeping their own machinery fit," this new metaphoric complex would supplant the older, more organic self-concept of the human body as a system to be carefully balanced against a standard of nature.[54] With more homemakers thinking about foods in terms of calories and fuel, American bodies were figuratively and literally transformed into embodiments of the industrial age.[55]

While home economists focused their teachings on efficiency, expertise, and scientific methods, they gave little attention to the way foods tasted. In the smug words of one, food was "for strengthening [peoples'] bodies not for the gratification of their palates."[56] Although cooking special meals might well have been a way that mothers could show love or derive a sense of pride, many home economists considered it a waste of a woman's valuable time to spend hours preparing elaborate dishes that a family would gulp down in fifteen minutes. For their own good, homemakers had to be taught to put the principles of scientific cookery before their own tastes and customary ways in the kitchen.

The new knowledge proffered by the home economists was distinct from traditional homemakers' know-how in that it referred primarily to a realm that couldn't be seen or sensed firsthand. This gave home economists tremendous authority. With their lofty expertise, they claimed that they were in a far better position to teach cooking than were mothers, who had only tradition as guide.[57] In magazine articles and classrooms, home economists hammered away at homemakers' old-fashioned skills in the kitchen, pinning the blame for everything—from alcoholic husbands and striking steelworkers to sickly, underachieving children—on ignorant cooks' poorly prepared and nutritionally insufficient meals.[58] Given all the various new invisibilities to consider—preservatives, germs, calories, proteins, carbohydrates (and by the 1920s, vitamins)—a homemaker could no longer rely on her own experience, her own senses, or even her own mother. Increasingly, she felt compelled to consider what the experts recommended.[59]

Although scientific cookery began with attention to nutrition and hygiene in home kitchens, its principles increasingly pointed to the merits of manufactured products. As home economists advanced new hygienic criteria for food selection, they often lauded the uniformity, sterility, and efficiency of factory-made foods. One article about cheese, for example, asked readers to "remember the great diversity in taste, structure, and composition which was so noticeable in the old farmhouse cheeses," but then to "appreciate the greater uniformity in the factory product" and the efficient way it was manufactured.[60] In praising the hallmark attributes of factory-made foods—uniformity, sterility, and efficiency—home economists echoed core pitches of advertising and thereby helped to define and establish these traits as most desirable.

Home economists' inclination to praise manufacturers' products stemmed not only from a shared vision about the merits of scientific cookery but also from the fact that food manufacturers had started to employ legions of graduates from university Home-Ec departments.[61] As mass production tended to downgrade taste standards for foods, manufacturers increasingly relied on home economists' advice columns, curricula, and classes to back up their ads and help define changes in quality as improvements.

Despite their determined efforts, home economists met with continued resistance from many veteran homemakers, including a number who remained particularly leery of canned foods. To overcome this stubborn distrust, home economist Christine Terhune Herrick took a personal tack in 1913 when she shared with *Women's Home Companion* readers the story of how her own "prejudice" against canned foods finally "vanished." With a long docket of professional Home Economics credentials, Herrick's outlook was clearly modern, but she must have sensed the need to express some fellow feeling for her readers, many of whom—living in smaller towns and rural areas—were still wary of new ways.[62]

In her heart-to-heart column, Herrick began by explaining how she'd skeptically tried canned foods and always found them poor in taste and quality. Even more troubling was the indigestion that she and her family suffered after eating them.[63] As such, Herrick had resolved to avoid canned foods, though periodically she had a "fall from grace" during the late spring "pinch time" after she'd already exhausted all the tricks she knew for turnips and cabbages. On those rare occasions she did use canned foods, she gave them great attention, emptying the vegetables three hours ahead of time, turning them into a bowl to let them air, and finally dressing them in any way she could think of that "might remove the curse of the can."[64]

Eventually, though, after many years, some deft grocer convinced Herrick to try yet another can, and this time, the peas inside tasted fairly good. After sampling more vegetables of the same brand, Herrick realized that her prejudice was no longer justified. Canned foods tasted better and were cheaper than they'd ever been before. Improved sanitary, nickel-plated cans had eliminated the old problems of spoilage and leaching metals, she explained. Mechanized production meant perfect cleanliness because no human hands ever touched the foods entering cans. And finally, owing to the Pure Food and Drug Law, Herrick continued, "The day has gone by when an unscrupulous man could put up rotten vegetables or fruits and cover the flavor by the addition of a chemical."[65]

The improved taste of canned foods was a boon to city homemakers in particular. Because only hours elapsed between picking and canning, Herrick explained, canned vegetables actually tasted better than ones that had lain wilting in the market for a day or two. Women who lived in the country—"to whose table vegetables come direct with no appreciable interval between picking and cooking"—she wrote, were the lucky few; city housekeepers were stuck depending on the corner grocery for their "so-called fresh vegetables." Even during the bountiful late summer months, Herrick lamented, her greengrocer tried to press "withered and yellow" vegetables upon her, claiming that they were "perfectly fresh. They just came in yesterday morning."[66] Increasingly, urban middle-class homemakers, confronted with the choice between wilted or canned, would agree and opt for canned.

Yet the most stalwart homemakers remained unconvinced. One Croatian immigrant living in a small industrial city in Iowa recalled how she and her foreign-born friends made disparaging remarks about all the American women who bought canned goods rather than putting up their own vegetables for the winter.[67] High costs and the poor quality of city foods together with the potency of tradition impelled many families, especially those of immigrants and workers in smaller cities, to persist in planting vegetable gardens.

Home efficiency expert Martha Bruère ridiculed such gardening as time consuming and old-fashioned. With readily available canned vegetables, she insisted, women could be spending their time on more important matters. "Might we not have been producing noble works of literature instead of rigging up canvas to protect the carrots from the sun?" she impatiently asked her *Good Housekeeping* readers in 1913. "Who knows if a 'bestseller' may not have been lost to the world while we picked off the parsley worms by hand and drowned them in the sprinkling can?"[68]

To Bruère, who clearly valued literature over lettuce and parsing over parsley, it was inconceivable that the ignoble work of raising foods in a garden could have meaning and value beyond the money spent and the time evaporated in its care. Women never accounted for all their time when they calculated cost savings from growing food, she explained in her article "Scientific Marketing." Readers should "come out of the pleasant dream that it is an economy for every man to be his own truck farmer," she advised, and instead "take the opiate of wholesale buying."[69]

Bruère's choice of the word "opiate" is telling. Ultimately, accepting factory-made foods would require a certain suspension of beliefs and customs. Homemakers would have to abandon their reservations and relinquish their traditional expectations about flavors, textures, and cooking practices in favor of the cleaner, more uniform, easier to prepare, factory-manufactured foods.

Home economists' confident articles made this suspension of old ways easier. In place of customary ways of learning about foods and cooking, they suggested new ways: by taking classes, by consulting with nutrition tables and menu plans, by reading ads and magazine articles to keep up to date about the latest products, and by learning brand names.[70] In using terms such as calorie, protein, and carbohydrate, they promoted an entirely new and more abstract way of thinking about what to eat. In promoting the values of uniformity, cleanliness, and efficiency over taste and tradition, home economists also helped to construct a wholly new aesthetic of food quality.

Ultimately, it would be the next generation of homemakers who would embrace the new approach to cooking. Home economists' views of what constituted quality and apposite knowledge of foods influenced millions of girls coming of age and taking public high-school Home-Ec classes in the first decades of the twentieth century.[71] It was these young women who would face the challenge of building their lives amid fast-shifting economic and social currents through World War I and beyond.

With the pool of available domestic help shrinking still further in the 1910s and 1920s and greater numbers of middle-class women left to run households on their own, customary methods of food preparation were simply becoming too time consuming. A study of sixty "comfortable" New York families from 1912 to 1914 revealed that the housewives in these homes spent an average of fifty-six hours a week — eight full hours a day — on housework, probably about half of which was devoted to cooking.[72] As new opportunities for education, leisure, and employment outside the home began to open for young middle-class women, heavy housework loads left them little time to pursue other interests and goals. As historian Harvey Levenstein has explained, most women wanted to get off the hook of housework, so "something had to give."[73] The easiest solution for both overworked homemakers and aspiring food manufacturers was to shift expectations and redefine what constituted "good food."

In time, the generation that had clung to its traditional outlook would pass, and as young, up-and-coming homemakers took control of their own kitchens, they would learn to do so in a modern style.

Not-So-Contented Cows

At the turn of the century, advertising experts had aptly recognized that homemakers could have irreconcilable desires — for foods that were not only pure and natural but also readily available without toil or sweat; for foods both fresh from the countryside but also safe and hygienic. In the haphazardly emerging urban food system, with meats, milk, butter, and vegetables traveling great distances, it was often impossible to meet all such contradictory desires at once.

Ads had a particular faculty for dealing with such contradictions. If innovations in transportation, refrigeration, and packaging couldn't yet deliver foods fresh from the countryside, ads could paper over this impossibility with their potent suggestions. By attaching pleasing notions and pastoral images, ads could make a manufactured food seem to be at once natural and modern. Yet in their project of enshrining products with pleasing sentiment, ads also had the tremendous potential to deceive.

While most shoppers were growing accustomed to learning about their foods through ads, that beloved thorn Harvey Wiley was troubled by the guise of information that so many ads proffered. Resigning from his federal post after the sodium benzoate hullabaloo, Dr. Wiley continued his crusade for pure foods through a popular column in *Good Housekeeping*. A stickler for authenticity, Wiley unmasked the various ways food ads could dupe shoppers. Even in apparently upright magazines, he explained (with a wink, no doubt), ads were not always truthful.[74]

The ads Wiley found most disturbing were those touting Carnation brand evaporated milk. With the agreeable slogan we still know today, "the milk of contented cows," the ads typically depicted happy Holsteins in a pleasing pastoral setting. Carnation had started as a small company near Seattle, where the cows may well have once grazed in verdant pastures interlaced by sparkling streams and backed by the snow-capped mountains that showed up in the ads.[75] But by 1911, the small regional firm was growing into a national one, manufacturing canned milk at four factories in Washington State, two in Oregon, three in Wisconsin, and one in Illinois.[76]

When Wiley went to the Pacific Coast in the summer of 1913 looking for Carnation's "pedigreed herds" that drank from "pure mountain streams," he found that the company owned no contented cows of their own. Instead, the condensary he visited was supplied by two hundred dairy farmers who, as far as Wiley could tell, hauled their milk with no particular attention to sanitation. When he visited one nearby farm, he saw cows "so plastered with manure . . . so upholstered with filth" that he could "hardly tell their color."[77] Performing a far more careful investigation than any consumer could, Wiley determined that the cows yoked for Carnation's mass milk production were as sorry a lot as any. Moreover, he discovered that milk for midwestern markets was not made by cows in pristine Pacific Coast pastures, as ads throughout the central states boasted, but rather supplied by local cows and condensaries.[78]

In Wiley's estimation, it was "unethical, deceptive, and false" for Carnation to advertise that its milk came "from tuberculin tested cows, kept under sanitary conditions, and remaining in a state of contentment

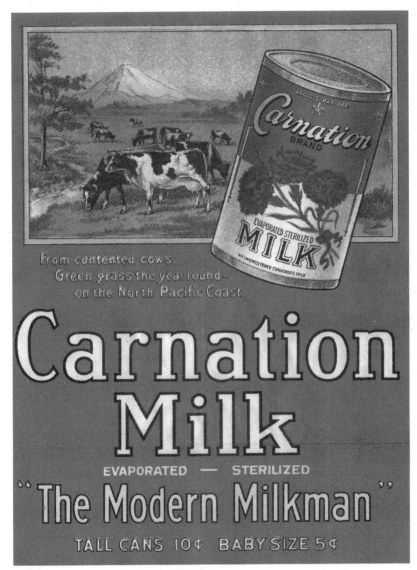

6.3. *Harvey Wiley was concerned about the literal accuracy of ads such as this one, which showed cows grazing in verdant pastures of the Pacific Northwest. When he visited suppliers in 1913, Wiley found that the canned product was being produced with milk from dairy farms less idyllic than those pictured and in several areas around the country.*

in perennial pastures," when he'd seen firsthand that it came from animals "housed in dark, ill-smelling rooms, covered often with filth, and milked without sanitary precautions."[79]

The possibility that brand-name milk dressed in neat little red-and-white cans was not exactly what it claimed to be had the potential to open a broader chasm of doubt. If Carnation ads presented half-truths, then what about other ads? Indeed, Wiley suggested that many well-known packaged and bottled foods were "fraudulent in the sense that they are not what they are represented to be."[80] However, Wiley's concerns for accuracy were becoming submerged in a rising sea of popular culture comprised of countless promotional images and messages.

Ads were beginning to exert their own powerful authority by responding attentively to shoppers' deepest anxieties and wishful thoughts. Concerned by recurrent news that their milk came from sore-covered, TB-infested animals, city shoppers yearned to give their children milk that came from clean, healthy cows pastured in the countryside.[81] Carnation's country images, ads, and slogan handily allayed shoppers' fears and promised the desired product in an affordable, sanitary can, which, when opened, reliably contained clean and wholesome milk. Most shoppers would sooner hope and believe the reassuring ads were true than fear they were not. And aside from Wiley's prodding, most had no reason to doubt the veracity of ads.

Buyers of food products were becoming buyers of meanings— meanings that could well be meaningless. As information in ads supplanted traditional knowledge, it did so with knowledge of an insubstantial sort—a knowledge that sometimes resided in the ambiguous realm of fantasy and falsehood. Through time, as consumers were exposed to more and more ads, they would eventually develop a subtle cynicism, an unspoken awareness that some of the information in ads was factually accurate and some was merely suggestive.[82] As knowing actual stories of foods came to seem less important in our predominantly urban society, the literal accuracy that was so important to Wiley would be all but abandoned. Today we don't give the accuracy of the Carnation "contented cow" slogan a second thought. We know it's just an ad. Shoppers who may have wanted to know about the source of their milk and other foods were themselves becoming contented to accept the gloss of the ads with their slogans and images.[83] Firsthand knowledge of gardening and cooking had once connected cooks and eaters to the nature of particular places, but the new knowledge of foods proffered by advertisements would connect shoppers to only a surreal web of commerce and fancy.

The Appeal of the Modern

If Harvey Wiley was troubled by ads' guile in 1913, his concern must have multiplied as advertising proliferated in the years that followed. When America entered World War I in 1917, the federal government tapped the advertising industry to aid with propaganda efforts and also to promote voluntary food conservation programs. In addition, a wartime policy that made advertising tax-exempt encouraged many manufacturers to invest in and experiment with new promotional campaigns. As a result, between 1914 and 1919, the money spent on ads doubled from $682 million to $1.4 billion, and would double again by 1929 to nearly $3 billion, swelling magazines and newspapers, and accustoming people, as one ad expert put it, to the notion that "any surface and every surface, and all approaches through the senses" were appropriate venues for advertising.[84] After the war, the ad industry took off with new stature and confidence that it could, as the trade journal *Printers' Ink* explained, "sway minds of whole populations."[85]

Wiley had hoped that the wartime experience of "victory" gardening and "making do" in kitchens might remind America's homemakers of the "wholesomeness" of foods "simple and as near to nature as possible" and usher in an era of cooking with less-processed foods.[86] Instead, the war's "meatless" and "wheatless" days seemed to spring-load the opposite reaction.

During the war, with high prices and shortages, America's large urban populations confronted the specter of food insecurity for the first time. The limits of the nation's farms, which were directed to grow extra food for war-ravaged Europe, seemed apparent in urban America, where high prices and shortages raised frustration, ire, and even food riots in some cities.[87] Middle-class anxieties about changes in foods and gouging by middlemen, which had been prevalent before the war, were replaced by anxieties about everyone simply getting enough to eat or getting the types of foods families wanted to eat, such as beef, wheat, and sugar. In this context, the emerging idea of modernizing America's farms and food with a scientific and industrial approach offered a compelling promise: cheap and reliably abundant foods, as only factories could produce.

Tired of feeling gloomy and deprived by wartime shortages and sacrifices, upper- and middle-class urban Americans welcomed the delayed but abundant postwar prosperity that buoyed the economy and enlivened the culture through the "roaring" 1920s. They viewed new films and listened to new jazz music. Young women sported new-style clothing and adopted less-restrictive gender roles. Encouraged by mushrooming ads and installment-buying plans, men and women purchased a wide array of new manufactured goods, including cars, radios, and electric refrigerators and stoves. With freer cultural attitudes and greater material comforts, urban Americans embraced a more optimistic attitude about life—a modern approach. It was in this context that manufactured foods finally came to seem more agreeable, and advertising made the crucial pitch.

Despite persistent promotional efforts to make factory foods seem familiar, clean, safe, and pleasing, food manufacturers, like home economists, had remained frustrated by lingering popular prejudice against some of their products—particularly canned foods and margarine.[88] Admen had tried to sell factory foods using a modern slant before and during the war, but their prime strategy had been to denigrate and discredit traditional methods, and their success had been limited. For example, a 1910 ad for Van Camp's Pork and Beans contrasted the difficult, old-fashioned way of preparing beans with the new and easy way of serving them from a can. A modern housewife might as well spin her own linen and weave her own carpets as make her own baked beans for dinner, the ad chided. A 1917 ad for Purity margarine reminded its readers that people had once been fearful about using telephones, implying that skepticism about margarine was similarly misguided and outdated.[89]

During the war, however, advertising experts realized that their ads needed to do more than merely assure homemakers that the new foods were wholesome and acceptable; they needed to make products more intrinsically appealing. Adopting a new strategy, advertisers seized upon the repute of technology and science to cast manufactured foods as highly modern and, once and for all, as highly desirable.

Some ads in this vein suggested that it was impossible for women to make modern foods at home. One cereal ad told homemakers, "if you could roll each separate bit [of corn], thin and ribbony, under *40 tons* of pressure—then, 'most any one could make his own Post Toasties."[90] Without powerful machinery and the intelligence of science and industry, a homemaker couldn't expect to produce anything as magnificent as Toasties for breakfast.

More and more, ads referred to the same "scientific cookery" that home economists had promoted in their articles about cleanliness and efficiency in the kitchen, but they took it further, insinuating that modern factory-made foods were superior to home-made. For example, a 1920 ad for Van Camp's Pork and Beans featured the company's "scientific cooks"—two "college-trained" men in lab coats presiding over an array of test tubes and glass flasks. They had spent four years and $100,000 to perfect the special, proprietary recipe, a heady endeavor that no homemaker could hope to emulate. The copy explained that the Van Camp's factory prepared beans "as homes can't bake them," making them easier to digest, which presumably meant less flatulent—another feat unattainable by the housewife.[91]

Ads of this sort gave the very modernity of food products a powerful appeal, but they also conveyed a subtext: that ordinary people had a declining ability to make judgments in the face of mounting technological sophistication. Advertisers recognized a collective "inferiority complex" and exploited it in their ads, reinforcing homemakers' fears about their own inadequacies by glorifying the role of experts.[92] As such, the sheer prevalence of modern-motif ads made it seem a "given" that homemakers should relinquish customary expectations and yield their judgment to scientific experts.[93]

Yet in continually reiterating the theme of industrial superiority, ads came close to mocking homemakers and fanning the feelings of indignity that were becoming a more commonplace aspect of life with the rise of populous cities and mass culture.[94] To counter any hint of discomfiture, advertisers realized they had to offer homemakers a way to feel competent, too. They did so by putting forth a new form of proficiency: if a homemaker learned to rely on what experts recommended in ads—essentially absorbing and drawing upon the finest of what authorities had to offer—she could experience a new sort of mastery by simply choosing the suggested modern product.[95]

In promoting the desirability of modern foods, ads were also beginning to subtly advance a key precept in the modern kitchen approach—convenience. Few ads in the early 1920s actually emphasized "convenience" because the idea of a woman choosing leisure over cooking for her husband and children was still an uneasy one. For most middle-class homemakers, the majority of whom did not work outside the home, esteem and feelings of self-worth were closely linked to preparing meals for the family at home. Many were still wondering—especially those in smaller towns—if it was socially acceptable, or downright lazy, to serve modern foods.[96]

While ads still trod gingerly in this uncomfortable arena, home economists' articles in popular women's magazines helped to build a feeling that "every woman" was now choosing modern products. Through the 1920s, articles assured homemakers that modern foods were so effective in reducing the amount of effort needed to prepare meals that women could spend less time in the kitchen and still create essentially the same results as before. "Every day sees some ingenious new wrinkle devised to lessen labor," raved one typical article in *Ladies' Home Journal*. "You don't have to clean up tea grounds; tea comes in individual bags, made possible by new packaging machinery. . . . You don't have to prepare the morning grapefruit any more: if you wish you can get all the meat of the grapefruit in cans or glass containers ready for the hurried commuter's breakfast. . . . Ten years ago, every woman made her own mayonnaise. Now almost every woman buys it in a jar."[97]

One important way that advertisers surreptitiously promoted convenience was with a new kind of triangulation that turned attention away from the attributes of modern foods and toward the satisfactions they provided.[98] Increasingly, ads sold not a can of spaghetti or box of cereal per se, but rather a happy husband, smart and healthy children, and elevated social status.

Consider a Cream of Wheat ad that *Ladies' Home Journal* readers encountered when they opened the magazine's front cover in September 1929. The ad featured an image of young Livingston Ludlow Biddle III, scion of the wealthy Biddles of Philadelphia, seated on a shiny new tricycle. The ad's copy described the lavish care and attention this privileged boy received, including twice daily "feedings" of Cream of Wheat, part of a diet expressly prescribed for him by "famous specialists."[99] The pitch included no inkling of the product's origin—no sheaves of wheat or pastoral fields—and no description of the product's taste or appearance, save for its brand name and a small cereal box in the lower right-hand corner of the page. Instead, the ad focused entirely on the suggestion that a mother could gain competence and prestige by choosing for her child the same breakfast chosen by world-renowned experts and served by the rich. The ad sold feelings of competency and esteem; convenience came along unmentioned.

Through the 1920s, food ads that had formerly been sited in pastures and factories, and then in laboratories, moved decisively into elegant upper-middle-class living rooms and dining rooms. With this move came the subtle implication that food products should be considered primarily in relation to the homemaker's sphere of concern: the home and well-being of family members.

Ads of this sort ushered in a new trend of offering their readers less factual and more suggestive information about their foods, effectively wrapping products "in the tissue of a dream" as one ad expert described the strategy.[100] Stripping foods of the contexts in which they were created, these ads effectively focused consumers' attention entirely on the personal and emotional contexts of how food products were consumed.

As ads instructed food buyers to turn their attention inward, the already eroding commonsense habit of thinking about foods in relation to where they came from was dramatically redirected and refocused. Indeed, as bleary-eyed millions awoke each morning to eat their bowls of Cream of Wheat or Toasties, what mattered most were the simple pleasures of warm mush or of cool crunches that occurred in each and every breakfast nook, spiced with suggestions of salubrity and satisfaction. A modern habit of consuming food products as a means of self-fulfillment was taking hold.

Nature Transcended

As the appeal of the modern and a concomitant focusing inward on family prevailed in advertising, the natural pitch, with its images of waterfalls, wheat fields, and frogs, all but disappeared in the 1920s.[101] The impulse to eliminate nature from ads was not complete—after all, it would be difficult to recast vegetables and fruits as wholly factory-made. In the new modern vision, nature could remain, but only if carefully corralled and subjugated.[102] Not surprisingly, the few food ads that persisted in using natural motifs reflected this emerging modern outlook.

If there's a single ad that captures the way that nature fit into the modern food sensibility, it's one that the California Packing Corporation used as part of an aggressive ad campaign to launch its new Del Monte brand fruits and vegetables. In 1919, the full-page color ads designed by the New York advertising firm H. K. McCann began to appear in the *Saturday Evening Post, Woman's Home Companion, Good Housekeeping, McCall's,* and other popular magazines.[103]

In a sensuous water-colored style that was the vogue, the ad depicted a handsome genie shrouded in a turban and other hanging raiment, rising up from a Del Monte can like an exotic apparition summoned from Aladdin's lamp. Only this muscular genie served up a platter of luscious fruits born of an idealized pastoral landscape beyond. It seemed that everything in this scene spilled forth from the can. "The days of magic are gone," the copy declared, "but its genie still lives in the spirit of modern science and industry."[104] Though elevating the modern had generally meant eradicating the old-fashioned and metaphysical from the kitchen, this ad sought to soften the images of test tubes and white-coated scientists by imparting some of the potency of the old order along with the

6.4. *In this 1919 Del Monte ad, the agricultural landscape recedes into a dreamy background, and human ingenuity—in the form of a can—becomes predominant, paralleling modern shoppers' diminishing awareness of the places their foods come from. Through the 1920s and 1930s, ads would increasingly direct shoppers' attention away from food production and toward food consumption.*

luster of the modern. The ad explained the new sorcery: "The DEL MONTE can is a magic container that annihilates distance and merges all seasons into one long fruitful summer."[105]

The message was unequivocal: In earlier times, Mother Nature had merited the reputation of providing over and over again. Her unending abundance was considered miraculous in its own right. But in the modern order, it was no longer dazzling enough merely to provide a yearly harvest. Annihilating distance, merging all seasons, and accumulating all harvests, it was the technology of the human can that now deserved reverence and awe.

Behind the genie lay an Eden-like farmscape, and listed in the ad's copy were the names of many places where Del Monte's fruits grew, from California and Oregon to Hawaii. The magic of the can was, in fact, the same industrial logic of specialization that had already transformed America's factories, reshaped traditional foods, and was increasingly reconfiguring America's farms into specialized production districts. As applied to farming, the key concept of industrial logic was to grow crops in places best suited to their optimal cultivation and then to efficiently funnel the resulting cascade of meats, grains, vegetables, and fruits from hundreds of farms, thousands of miles away, via railroads and magic cans, to the tables of city eaters. Rather than relying on individual farmers to figure out the best places to grow particular crops on their own nearby farms, it was regarded as more efficient for emerging agribusiness to consider the whole of America's countryside as garden and breadbasket to cities. Such big-picture, modern thinking demanded that shoppers adopt a new sensibility about foods.

Countering the traditional idea that eating locally, in season, and in step with nature was best for health and taste, the Del Monte ads now suggested that it was preferable to eat from a can those fruits and vegetables grown in the places best suited to their cultivation. Of course, cans' magic was most potent in northern climes during winter. Another ad focused directly on that point: "Right now, while Nature is sleeping under its cold mantle of snow—when all fresh foods are scarce and expensive—Del Monte brings the warm touch of summer to keep your menu appetizing and healthful."[106] In the mind's eye of homemakers hunkered down in Minnesota or upstate New York, such ads conjured visions of legendary California sunshine warming the golden skins of oranges, peaches, and pears, and made the prospect of eating from a national-scale foodshed eminently appealing.[107]

As ad campaigns proceeded to convince eastern shoppers that both canned and fresh fruit and fish traveling thousands of miles from the West Coast were now superior even in spring and summertime to the fruit and fish from nearby New York and New England, these faraway foods became hallmarks of sophistication, prestige, and the new modernity. Buying and cooking foods from distant, premier places became a way for ordinary homemakers to express themselves as modern and cosmopolitan. Local foods became lowly, parochial, and passé.

Abundant fields and farms were now accessible to shoppers mainly through the refractive prism of suggestive images and imagination. The means of production were no longer evident but were belied by appealing and novel magic. The hard work of growing food—ads made it seem —had been transcended by the miracle of technology and science.[108]

In a removed way, the complex modern food web of distant fields, processing factories, and railroad lines was increasingly admired in newspapers and women's magazines. In 1919, renowned New York City pianist Olga Samaroff, who proudly described herself "as totally devoid of all practical knowledge concerning domestic affairs as a newborn babe," told *Ladies' Home Journal* readers about a dreamy revelation. One day when she wandered into the kitchen to scold her cook, the piles of food assembled on the counter suddenly captivated her attention. "Here from all ends of the earth are gathered the elements which give us life and strength and health," Samaroff exclaimed. "These elements are prepared in ways, which represent the development of great industries, the backbone of national prosperity. Here are the fruits of sunny California. There grain from the great fields of the West or perhaps even from Australia . . . and various meats conjure up visions of great ranches in Texas. There is no end to the appeal to the imagination when one once begins to think about the contents of the kitchen in that light."[109]

To this mistress, who "viewed all raw meat with the deepest disgust" and didn't know lamb from beef in a butcher's shop, it was now fabulous and fashionable to imagine Texas ranches and far-off, fanciful factories. Samaroff's self-disclosures reveal that, to her mind, ignorance about the nitty-gritty was, in fact, a kind of virtue.[110] To Samaroff, eating globally meant ingesting prestige and sophistication associated with the grandeur of modern human ingenuity and industry. Wonderment at the grandness of fantastical food sources now fed her hunger for meaning.

IN THE FIRST decades of the twentieth century—just as it was becoming increasingly difficult for homemakers to know what they'd previously expected to know about foods—a new suite of experts stepped in and set new guideposts for what was important for people to know. First, in the face of widespread adulteration and increased anonymity of the emerging national food system, Harvey Wiley and the passage of the Pure Food Law of 1906 established a new authority for science and government. Then, as selling food became bigger business, advertising gained greater influence. By defining brand names as the single most important thing to know about foods, ads helped make more complex, customary expectations about what to know seem less relevant. Working hand in hand with manufacturers and advertisements, home economists also encouraged homemakers to adopt new ways of knowing foods by promoting scientific cookery and modern, manufactured food products. As these government officials, manufacturers, advertisers, and home economists all took larger roles in the modern food system, their expertise and authority grew. At the same time, homemakers' expertise and role in knowing foods continually shrunk.

By 1920, when America made its watershed demographic shift from being predominantly rural to being predominantly urban, a modern food sensibility had gained ascendancy in popular culture and was already starting to make inroads to small towns and rural areas. Ways of thinking about foods that had seemed so odd and newfangled to the last rural generation had become totally commonplace to the first largely urban generation. The brand names, which had at first seemed rather novel, were now utterly familiar. The cans and boxes, which had at first seemed so troublesome, were finally making it normal and ordinary to eat distant, anonymous, out-of-season foods. Even more, what had once been considered intelligence about foods was now considered ignorance, and what had once been considered ignorance was now considered savvy. The new ways of knowing foods were fundamentally reshaping America's culinary imagination and transforming middle-class attitudes toward cooking and eating.

In creating the ads and articles that made up the popular culture of the 1900s and 1910s, food manufacturers along with their advertisers and home economists had ostensibly constructed a new body of shopping knowledge to replace old-fashioned marketing lore and to match the new range of available food products. However, by promoting steadfast trust in its scientific experts and in government authority, the modern food industry had also fostered a detached, leave-it-to-us approach to foods—an approach that would be hard to call knowledge any more. Increasingly, the enterprise of feeding modern America depended not only on cultivating farms and fields but also on cultivating the ignorance of shoppers.

CHAPTER 7

The Covenant of Ignorance

On September 11, 1916, when 487 people showed up to shop at the first Piggly Wiggly grocery store in Memphis, Tennessee, few likely grasped that they were participating in what would turn out to be a portentous event in the history of everyday American life. At the market's entrance, each shopper pushed through a turnstile, and then walked—basket on arm—past rows of groceries, picking and choosing from nearly six hundred different products neatly arrayed on the shelves, each marked with a price tag.[1] At the end of the maze of aisles, shoppers came to a checkout stand, paid in cash, and then carried their groceries home. Familiar as it now seems, no one had ever shopped in this way before.

As America's first cash-and-carry grocery store, Piggly Wiggly was a progenitor of our modern supermarket. Following its lead, thousands of cash-and-carry chain stores opened in cities nationwide through the decade of the 1920s, further changing the experience of how most city dwellers and, increasingly, suburbanites procured food.[2] As chain stores and then supermarkets evolved, shoppers would face a whole new generation of products dependent on a plethora of new though veiled production methods. With these new products and methods would come new and unexpected challenges for how consumers could know their foods.

New Food Chains: The Rise of Supermarket Shopping

Before World War I, most urban grocery stores had been small, specialized, independent neighborhood markets with clerks who provided

7.1. *Through the 1920s, the Piggly Wiggly stores that opened in locations nationwide pioneered the "self-service" grocery shopping that would come to characterize all of America's supermarkets. Rather than place an order by phone, shoppers passed through aisles, picking and choosing from hundreds of products and then paying at a checkout counter.*

service. A shopper brought in a list and asked for products behind the counter, or phoned in her order. Typically, no cash changed hands; a clerk recorded the transaction in a ledger book, leaving the balance to be paid later. The groceries were then delivered directly to the shopper's home.

In the early 1910s, however, high city food prices had prompted many to look for ways to cut costs. Entrepreneurs had already applied ideals of industrial efficiency to food production in factories, but distribution—how a box of cereal from Michigan or an orange from California got to a grocery store in Brooklyn, New York—remained a haphazard, and costly, endeavor.

Railroads had lowered costs for hauling freight over long distances, but a disproportionate expense was tacked on at the last and most convoluted stage of a food's journey to market. When a box of California oranges arrived at the rail station in New York, for example, it had to be unloaded, reloaded, and hauled to a central fruit wholesale market. There it was unloaded and auctioned to a buyer who had to reload it and haul it to a neighborhood market, via horse and buggy, where it was unloaded again and finally unpacked. Ultimately, the travel-worn oranges ended up piled in neat pyramids on storefront tables. But shepherding thousands of boxes of fruits, vegetables, and other items to retail markets throughout the city required hundreds of workers, and all those workers—disparagingly known as middlemen—had to be paid, which added to the cost of food.

To reduce costs, chain stores started to do their own wholesaling. For example, A&P, which had started selling tea and coffee as the Great Atlantic and Pacific Tea Company in the 1870s, had expanded into a grocery chain with hundreds of retail outlets in several cities by 1915. An A&P buying agent could negotiate to purchase fifty boxes of oranges at a reduced price for all the chain's markets in a city, and then deliver them in company trucks (which were replacing horse-drawn wagons by the early 1910s) to each store, along with other bargained-for fruits and dry goods. A&P stores could then offer lower prices as well as a greater variety and quality of items than those offered by the independent grocers, who were stuck buying single boxes at the wholesale auction.[3]

To lower costs further, the A&P chain stores also eliminated store credit, a relict of the once seasonal nature of rural incomes that persisted at many independent markets, especially those in working-class neighborhoods where immigrants still struggled to gain footing. Then after the war, more chain stores cut clerk service and home delivery, introducing the cash-and-carry method pioneered by Piggly Wiggly.[4]

The cash-and-carry stores were intended primarily to reduce company overhead costs, but as it turned out, enabling women to shop independently also fit well with the tenor of the 1920s. This was the era of the flapper girl, or the "jazz type," when many young women, especially city dwellers, were enjoying opportunities to vote, to work clerical and professional jobs, and even to smoke in public for the first time. Some marketing experts described the modern woman by how she cooked: "the can-opener type."[5] Still, many homemakers, accustomed to ordering their foods, had to be coaxed to try out the new-style stores.

In *Good Housekeeping* magazine, ads for Piggly Wiggly stores in the 1920s promoted the new mode of shopping as an expression of modern female independence. "Only yesterday her mother depended almost wholly on the advice of salesmen when she bought food-stuffs," one ad explained, but not "the woman of today! So self-reliant in all her shopping." The woman pictured shopping in the ads was clad in a tailored coat and cloche hat, with hand on hip. "Armed with New Knowledge" and "so sure of her new skill," this woman took to her new role of supermarket shopping with zest.[6] No longer were there clerks who tried to persuade her to buy one brand over another. A woman had time to pick up colorful packages, hold them in her hands, compare one with another, consider the plainly marked prices, and make her own choice—based on "amazing knowledge" she'd obtained herself from ads, articles, and experience. Indeed, Piggly Wiggly stores presented the "New Method of Household Buying" as a "nation-wide movement sponsored by modern women."[7]

That the "new knowledge" women were using was carefully sculpted to serve the commercial intent of manufacturers and advertisers was of little concern. In fact, it added to the experience, for the new method of shopping was transcending its most tangible purpose of accruing provender. Now, not only would a woman buy foods based solely on what she needed in a nutritive sense, but she would also be drawn to products by their novelty and by promotionally infused meanings. As the supermarket ads suggested, the new method of shopping could in itself be a pleasurable opportunity to express one's individuality in the set of choices made, giving potent new meaning to "you are what you eat."[8]

Not only was the supermarket changing the experience and meaning of procuring foods, but it was also fundamentally redefining women's role in society. In the efficiency-driven industrial economy, specialization was the key, and, as many saw it, modern women's specialty was to be shopping.

Christine Frederick was unabashed about women's new role in the

7.2. Portraying supermarket shopping as an expression of modern female independence, this 1928 ad reveals one way that a new and modern approach to foods was promoted.

emerging economy. Frederick had studied with Walter Dill Scott, the University of Chicago advertising psychologist. Then, instead of following the contemporary trend of educated women to work in Home Economics, Frederick carved out her own niche as a home-efficiency expert. Following the work of industrial-efficiency guru Frederick Taylor, she'd pioneered time and motion studies of household tasks, and then shared her results as a contributor to *Ladies' Home Journal* and other women's magazines in the 1910s. It was when she drew upon her advertising and business background as well as her household research that Frederick found her platform.[9]

Living at the cusp of changing times, she became a formidable proponent of modernizing the home and housework while, at the same time, maintaining women's traditional role within it. Frederick envisioned housewives raising their own status and the quality of home life by relying more heavily on the expertise of business and industry. In terms of cooking, this meant buying the manufactured food products that increasingly crowded market shelves. To advance her vision, Frederick made a career as self-appointed liaison between America's housewives and manufacturers of food and household products.

Published in 1929, her opus *Selling Mrs. Consumer* promised to help manufacturers promote their products by revealing what women really wanted.[10] Ostensibly, "Mrs. Consumer" was the "everywoman" of modern America, but Frederick emphasized the prosperous middle-class housewife whose heart and mind admen yearned to know.

Frederick's primary aim was to convince manufacturers of women's power as shoppers in the emerging economy of "consumptionism," as she called it.[11] In the booming 1920s, Frederick explained, one billion dollars per week had passed through the hands of Mrs. Consumer. As shoppers, women made 80 to 90 percent of the spending decisions in each family.[12] Women were the new engine of the modern economy — an engine that could be profitably stoked with the proper approach. Although Frederick had disavowed the suffragist cause, she championed the collective economic force of women as shoppers, encouraging women "to vote" with their pocketbooks.[13]

7.3. *Best known for promoting consumerism in her 1929 book* Selling Mrs. Consumer, *Christine Frederick identified the modern shopper's predicament of too much information to evaluate. She recommended that homemakers learn brand names and leave the rest to food manufacturers.*

While Frederick is best remembered for promoting "consumption-ism," it is her straightforward description of the burden of knowing in the modern marketplace that is most interesting in this story of how we've known our foods.

As we've seen, home economists had encouraged women to learn a critical new expertise of invisibilities. To the germs and calories of the 1910s, they'd added vitamins, which had come to be better understood by the 1920s. And while many home economists had found work advancing modern products, many also had a sincere interest in education and regarded the pursuit of more knowledge as the best means to improve women's lives.[14]

Frederick had a more pragmatic view of what it meant for women "to know" in the modern age. Supermarkets offered so many products and presented so many choices that it had become impossible to make thoroughly informed decisions. Frederick claimed that a woman might buy 20,000 to 80,000 separate kinds of items over the course of a five-year period. To know about them all would require an encyclopedic knowledge—too much for any homemaker to cope with.[15]

In Frederick's estimation, a homemaker didn't really *need* to know about germs or vitamins in-depth or firsthand. She didn't need to know the chemistry of the ingredients, or even what all the ingredients were. All a housewife needed was enough information to direct her attention to the right types of products.[16] Then she could trust the expertise of manufacturers to make sure that there were sufficient vitamins in foods (an emerging concern) and that proper packaging precluded contamination.

Indeed, this was one of the little secrets about women that Frederick divulged. Mrs. Consumer, quite simply, did not want to be "bothered" with the additional task of knowing. "We consumers simply do not care to waste time on the great mass of technical data about household goods," she explained. Even if a woman could acquaint herself "intimately" with all the "relative virtues of Borden's or Horlick's malted milk," Frederick continued, she would "doubtless still be in a quandary as to which to buy."[17] There were now too many attributes to factor into purchases—not only ingredients and quality, but also price, service, convenience, availability, size, and "even such a strange factor as social prestige."[18] According to Frederick, the public was "willing to pay generously for being saved even the bother of thinking overmuch about its purchases."[19]

Because the mass of knowledge that could be learned about foods was now far more than anyone could handle, Frederick's solution to the quandary of the supermarket shelves was simply for shoppers to trust manufacturer's brand names, based on what they learned from ads — plus their own experience trying new products. And this, Frederick believed, women were uniquely suited to do with their practical and "native intelligence." If a new product was good, a homemaker would buy it again. Her repeated purchases would provide sufficient incentive for manufacturers to maintain quality.

Like many who wrote about domestic affairs at the time, Frederick was ambivalent about whether the women wielding spending power were "intelligent" or "ignorant." When Frederick lauded Mrs. Consumer's "native intelligence," she implied an inherent intuition rather than a learned aptitude. At other times, she scorned shoppers for being too "ignorant" even to read labels.[20] She praised women for striking up a "closer *entente cordiale* . . . with industry and trade . . . than has ever before been known in the history of trading," but then conceded that it was "largely unconscious."[21]

In this unconscious relationship between women and industry, advertising was the pied piper. Although Frederick wrote that Mrs. Consumer did "not like to visualize herself as an automaton told what to do by advertising," she explained that, in reality, women "inhale advertising as we breathe in air."[22] Through "the enlightened efforts of high-class manufacturers," she continued, the modern woman had "developed a 'consumer acceptance' spirit, — a readiness to follow where she is led."[23]

Undeterred by contradictions, Frederick performed a marketer's magic, linking pliability with power and shopping prowess with intelligence. Though the Great Depression would temporarily suppress the continued economic growth that she promised, Frederick's conflation of women's intelligence with grocery-shopping acumen would be carefully heeded by promoters of new foods when affluent times returned.

THE STOCK market crash of 1929 ended the exuberant prosperity of the twenties. During the next three years, unemployment rates soared while wages plummeted, but through the Depression—even as more families struggled to put food on the table—the supermarket business innovated and flourished.

While chain stores had pioneered centralized wholesaling in the 1910s and then promoted cash-and-carry shopping in the 1920s, it was the next generation of markets—the first real "supermarkets"—that made the formula soar by advancing a new strategy of high-volume, low-margin retailing. In the 1930s, these new supermarkets set out to beat the chains at their own game.[24]

To do a high-volume business, supermarkets needed to sell lots of products to lots of people, and so they needed lots of space to array their goods and plenty of parking to accommodate shoppers driving from miles away. (Through the 1920s, cars and trucks had begun to revolutionize the geography of everyday life as the number of Americans owning cars had climbed from eight million to twenty-three million.[25]) To draw shoppers from a broad territory, supermarkets had to offer prices low enough to make the trip seem worthwhile. In Brooklyn, supermarket pioneer Michael "King" Cullen did just this when he set up in an old warehouse in 1930 and advertised his bargain prices widely in New York newspapers. Cullen perfected what would become the supermarketers' primary strategy: high-profile advertising of "loss leaders," brand-name groceries sold at cost in order to attract shoppers in droves. He sold 30 percent of his goods as loss leaders and all the rest at a slight 1 or 2 percent markup. As long as lots of customers came and each picked up a few items in addition to the seductive loss leaders, Cullen would profit. To coax housewives to break allegiances with their local grocers and to drive as much as twenty miles to shop, Cullen and other entrepreneurs used theatrical advertising. Full-page newspaper ads declared in thick black capital letters: "ROCK BOTTOM PRICES CRUSH COMPETITORS." One supermarket expert regarded the success of such theatrics as evidence of just how readily women shoppers could be "herded from one store to another by bargains—by ballyhoo."[26] And the pleasant surprise

for supermarket entrepreneurs was that the cheap prices of the supermarket actually encouraged tight-pursed shoppers to spend more.[27]

The charm of the supermarket was that it seemed to give everybody
what they wanted. By selling so much, entrepreneurs like Cullen made a
fabulous profit despite the low margin. Shoppers struggling to make
ends meet during the Depression found cheap and varied foods. And
manufacturers profited from the high-volume sales where their brand-
name products were featured. The combination of magazine ads placed
by manufacturers, which emphasized quality, and local newspaper ads
placed by supermarkets, which emphasized cheap prices, gave shoppers
a satisfied sense that they were getting the best for less.

In 1934, there were still only ninety-four supermarkets in U.S. cities.
By 1936, that number had shot up to twelve hundred and would continue
to climb rapidly.[28] With many urban households spending up to 50 percent of their incomes on food during the Depression, bargains in the
shopping cart took on greater importance, and the frugality toward
foods that had long been part of America's culture was rekindled. In its
traditional form, frugality had entailed saving scraps and using up bits
and pieces to make stews and soups. In its new supermarket cast, thrift
meant shopping for the best deals—even if it meant driving to another
town to get them.

While low prices were the key to supermarkets' success, especially
through the 1930s, it was the plentiful array of products that remained
the most reassuring and exciting aspect of supermarket shopping.

Christine Frederick had identified the difficulty of knowing about
foods at the dawn of the supermarket era in the 1920s. Through the next
decades, with the proliferation of more products, this difficulty would
become so numbingly complex as to prompt one later critic to coin the
term "stupormarket."[29] Most urban middle-class shoppers avoided the
stupor by following Frederick's guidance—to simply learn brand names
and stick with them.

Ostensibly, city shoppers never actually chose to know less about
where foods came from and how they were raised, but the importance of
knowing stories about foods' origins had been overshadowed by other,
more pressing matters as America urbanized, industrialized, and grew.

In the face of urban squalor and increased understanding of germs at the turn of the century, shoppers had chosen hygienic and prepackaged foods. As the supply of servants shrank, homemakers more openly considered laborsaving methods, products, and appliances that eliminated unseemly work. In the wake of World War I–induced scarcity, city dwellers yearned for the security promised by a modern food system. Through the twenties, more young women tried factory-made foods as they experimented with new gender roles and work options. During the Great Depression, many homemakers were compelled to buy the cheapest foods to assure they could feed their families. Through it all, as generation followed generation, shoppers had come to trust familiar brand names, such as Quaker and Carnation, in the same way that acquaintances over the course of many years come to feel like old friends.

From the aisles of amply supplied supermarkets, industrial logic— with manufacturers specializing in knowing about foods and women specializing in shopping—made good sense. Frederick's vision of housewives with more leisure and more power was bold and promising, but she saw only part of the equation. In suggesting that housewives leave the knowing to others, Frederick was tacitly promoting a deliberate ignorance about foods.

In fact, the modern food system was coming to depend on an unspoken agreement between the food industry and unwitting shoppers—a silent accord that might best be called a covenant of ignorance. Frederick aptly articulated this covenant as the unconscious *"entente cordiale."* Food manufacturers did not want to be pestered by careful scrutiny of their ever-changing production methods. Through innovation and efficiencies of vertical integration, they had cut waste, boosted profits, and delivered a wide variety of modern, hygienic food products to supermarket shelves. And housewives did not want to be bothered with knowing details; it was precisely the unknowing aspect of the emerging food system that reduced time in both shopping and cooking and also helped recast cooking as desirable work for women of all classes. In short, knowing less seemed to offer women more.

The covenant of ignorance seemed to serve those on both sides of America's day-to-day food transactions: producers didn't have to explain, and consumers didn't feel the need to ask. Supermarkets made it easy with their array of colorfully boxed products and prominent price tags. Shoppers found it harder than ever to know about how their foods were produced but easier than ever to buy foods on the basis of brand names and cost.

Just as shoppers had been seduced by loss leaders at the supermarket, they were tempted by the most appealing attributes of modern foods, and ultimately they would end up with more in their carts than they bargained for. At the same time as it was becoming utterly acceptable, ordinary, and desirable to not know much about where foods came from and how they were produced, new technologies were entering the scene that America's shoppers may well have been advised to know about.

100 Million Guinea Pigs

Most city dwellers followed pianist Olga Samaroff (see chapter 6) in the habit of imagining that bread came from amber grain fields, meat came from rolling Texas ranches, and pears came from sun-drenched California orchards, but the white powder that showed up on a shipment of pears in Boston in 1919 pointed to another, less sanguine reality. Not only were western fruits drenched with sun, but increasingly they were drenched with lead arsenate.

Pesticides were not new. Farmers had long used homemade concoctions of black walnut hulls, lye, and nicotine to cope with insect infestations. But when farms and orchards expanded to meet the demand of growing urban appetites in the late nineteenth century, the large contiguous food crops became vast banquets attracting insects on a whole new scale. In California, growers had invested in a massive infrastructure of irrigation canals to support monoculture cultivation of high-value fruits and vegetables. Large orchard districts, watered by ditches and clustered around rail stops, soon become the norm. But fruit growers hadn't anticipated the cast of exotic insects—hidden in the roots and tucked under leaves of imported fruit stocks—that would show up to feast. As early as 1885, a full-scale invasion of pests, including coddling moths, blister mites, and peach tree borers, had hit the state's large orchards.[30] To control the invasion, desperate fruit growers turned to "economic poisons," and spraying lead arsenate soon became the favored method for coping with the troubling exotic insects.

Initially, many growers had reservations about using arsenic—a known poison—on foods, but their desperation overcame their qualms, especially as the agricultural press allayed concerns. As one farm journal explained, arsenic is surely dangerous "as a sharpe axe is, and needs to be handled with care, but it should be no more tabooed on this account than the axe."[31] Before long, Pacific state agricultural agencies were requiring all orchardists to spray their fruit in order to check the spread of pests.[32] Extension agents advised farmers to use the minimum doses needed to kill pests and reduce losses, but many saturated rather than sprayed their fruit, hoping to eliminate losses completely.[33]

Although lead arsenate came into wide use at the time when Harvey Wiley was crusading against food adulterants, he'd paid little attention to spray residues. Unlike additives whose prime purpose he saw as deception, Wiley recognized spray residues as an unavoidable side effect of modern fruit growing, and he seemed to have more trust in farmers than in food-processing companies.[34] From the start, he'd focused Bureau of Chemistry attention on guileful adulterants rather than on small amounts of chemicals that might remain on what he considered wholesome, natural fruits. Though scientists and physicians were beginning to raise questions about the hazards of arsenical compounds, which as colorful dyes had permeated most households in the form of wallpaper, playing cards, children's toys, soaps, candles, candies, and even common medicines, the residues of arsenic on apples and pears escaped notice.[35]

And so it was that fruit growers' use of lead arsenate sprays grew without scrutiny until 1919, when that box of pears shipped from the West Coast showed up in Boston, where local public health officials promptly confiscated it. The pears were "heavily spotted" with white powder, which upon laboratory analysis proved to be a distressingly high concentration of arsenic. Boston health officials began a program to inspect all pears and apples in city markets and reported the incident to the Bureau of Chemistry, the agency ostensibly responsible for protecting eaters from adulterated foods under the Pure Food and Drug Act.[36]

The 1906 law had indeed directed the agency to protect consumers from injurious adulterants in foods, but it had been unclear about what constituted injury and gave no authority to set specific tolerance levels for harmful substances. These limitations were particularly apparent in the case of spray residues. Although toxicologists warned that lead and arsenic might cause chronic health problems, it was legally difficult to relate small amounts of residues on fruits to actual cases of injury because lead and arsenic rarely caused acute illness.

Bureau of Chemistry officials had reservations about the hazards of lead arsenate, but they were also fearful about the political repercussions of raising alarm.[37] The bureau's parent agency, the U.S. Department of Agriculture (USDA), had been promoting the use of arsenic pesticides for decades and was devoted to boosting the economic interest of farmers. This created an intra-agency conflict of interest that undermined the bureau's food-safety mandate. Bureau officials were also sympathetic to western growers, who'd dutifully followed agricultural spray laws believing the sprays were entirely safe. To address the intractable problem, the Bureau of Chemistry started a program to educate western fruit and vegetable growers about residue hazards, advising them to spray more judiciously and, if necessary, to wash produce after harvest. Bureau leaders were confident that fruit growers would voluntarily lower residues and appreciate the agency's discretion in avoiding public panic.[38]

However, most fruit growers resisted the notion that lead arsenate presented any health hazards and stepped up their spraying to combat increasingly robust pests.[39] In 1920 and 1921, Boston health officials again made seizures of western apples and pears bearing heavy arsenic residues.[40] Through the 1920s as use of lead arsenate became more widespread, health inspectors in several states, including Pennsylvania, New Jersey, and Florida, seized more and more shipments of apples, celery, and other vegetables with excessive residues. In Los Angeles, several illnesses were directly attributed to the elevated levels of arsenic on cabbages, but through the efforts of local commerce agencies, these incidents were generally kept out of the press.[41]

The stakes were higher in 1925 when a British family fell ill with severe arsenic poisoning after eating apples shipped from America. An inspection program instituted to screen American apples throughout England turned up alarming numbers of fruit with high levels of arsenic. Within the year, over nine hundred articles, editorials, and cartoons in the British press lambasted American fruit and stirred up such public outrage that a full-blown apple embargo was averted only by high-level diplomacy. (This apple clash in many ways presaged the more recent European response to genetically engineered foods from America.) Recognizing that news of poisonous apples would be detrimental to domestic sales, Bureau of Chemistry officials worked with the apple industry to maintain secrecy in the United States and to quietly develop an export inspection program to ensure that apples shipped to England were safe. While fruit bearing arsenic residues four times that allowed in England continued to be sold in the United States, Bureau of Chemistry officials remained hopeful that the close call of public exposure would finally convince fruit and vegetable growers to voluntarily lower arsenic residues.[42]

It didn't. Between 1919 and 1929, the amount of insecticides used in the United States grew from 11.5 million pounds to 29 million pounds, and seizures of excessively sprayed produce burgeoned.[43] The bureau had succeeded in keeping the elevated spray residues a secret but not in reducing their prevalence.

By the 1930s, doctors were increasingly able to pinpoint actual cases of acute poisoning—some lethal—that could be attributed only to over-sprayed produce.[44] Moreover, medical concerns about the effects of long-term exposure to poisons and toxic metals continued to grow. Doctors began to present evidence that even small amounts of lead and arsenic on food products might cause "eczema, keratosis, peripheral neuritis, disturbances of vision, and neurological symptoms hitherto obscure."[45] One article in the *Journal of the American Medical Association* linked a number of cases of pediatric eczema to arsenic in mothers' breast milk.[46] A Columbia University dermatology professor wrote a review article on "chronic arsenical poisoning" in which he came up with typical breakfast, lunch, and dinner menus, purchased food at local markets, and had average portions analyzed for arsenic content. He determined that the total amount ingested from one day's meals could be more than ten times the maximum dose a physician would prescribe for medicinal purposes.[47]

Although evidence about chronic hazards of lead, arsenic, and spray residues accumulated in medical and toxicological literature, the information still remained too technical and inaccessible to provoke public concern, until Frederick Schlink and Arthur Kallett's *100,000,000 Guinea Pigs* was published in 1933.[48] Schlink was an engineer and physicist who'd become outraged in the 1920s by the wild claims of advertisements for products, some of which—especially nonprescription drugs —were actually hazardous. To his mind, the consumer was an "Alice in Wonderland" being prodded "to jump through the hoops of the advertiser—dosing himself with dangerous nostrums, brushing his teeth with chalk and [buying] scent and soap at fabulous prices."[49] Schlink realized that scientific analysis could readily determine the composition and efficacy of commercial products and that consumers, informed with such scientific information, could better judge the merits of misleadingly advertised products. With this in mind, Schlink organized a consumers' club, conducted studies on products, and then sent out a regular newsletter with his evaluations. By 1933—despite the Depression—his list of subscribers had grown from 1,000 to 45,000.[50]

In *100,000,000 Guinea Pigs*, Schlink and Kallett (also an engineer) exposed weaknesses of the federal Pure Food and Drug Act and denounced the Food and Drug Administration (FDA), which had superseded the Bureau of Chemistry in 1927, for permitting too many harmful foods, drugs, and cosmetics to come to market. While they directed their greatest censure toward nonprescription drugs, Schlink and Kallet devoted an entire chapter to lead-arsenate spray residues, explaining the prevalence of their use—by the early 1930s, up to one-half pound per person per year—and providing medical toxicological evidence of their harm.[51] "What business loss," they asked, "is equivalent in the Administration's [FDA's] arithmetic to the poisoning of hundreds of thousands of citizens, from babyhood to old age, with arsenic spray residue?"[52] Schlink and Kallet concluded that America's 100 million citizens were "all guinea pigs, and any scoundrel who takes it into his head to enter the drug or food business can experiment on us."[53] The only solution was for every "guinea pig" to stand up and demand that a stronger consumer protection law be passed. They enjoined readers to let their voices be heard "in protest against the indifference, ignorance, and avarice responsible for the uncontrolled adulteration and misrepresentation of foods, drugs, and cosmetics."[54] The book's sensational tone drew criticism but also a great deal of attention.

The guinea-pig authors pointedly questioned the FDA's policy of secrecy: "The Government has acknowledged the hazards of excessive consumption of arsenic residues; it has permitted residues large enough to constitute a serious health hazard, yet we cannot find that it has uttered one word of warning to the public, or even so much as suggested mildly that apples and pears be peeled before they are eaten."[55] After publication of *100,000,000 Guinea Pigs* and a suite of similar books, including *40,000,000 Guinea Pig Children,* the FDA began to receive letters from more and more concerned consumers.[56]

With public pressure mounting and medical evidence building about the chronic hazards of lead and arsenic, New Deal political leaders were receptive to remedying shortcomings of the thirty-year-old Pure Food and Drugs Act. However, with stiff opposition from industry and agriculture, it ultimately took a disaster to solidify broad enough political support to pass a new law.

In 1937, a Tennessee company began marketing a liquid form of the new drug sulfanilamide to treat streptococcal infections, but company chemists had neglected to test the toxicity of the liquid solvent used in their product. Before the FDA identified the problem and tracked down unsold poisonous doses, more than a hundred people, mostly children, had been killed. Because existing drug laws did not expressly prohibit the inclusion of toxic ingredients in medicines, the FDA had no legal recourse to punish the product's manufacturer.[57] With this weakness tragically underscored, Congress was moved to pass the Food, Drug, and Cosmetic Act of 1938, which included a provision that required drug manufacturers to test toxicity and report findings to the FDA before a new drug could be sold. However, lawmakers included no similar provisions for pesticides or for food additives.[58]

The updated law did give FDA legal authority to enforce a tolerance level for lead-arsenate spray residues, but hearings to determine specifically what that tolerance level should be were delayed. Then, as America was drawn into World War II, the matter was put off indefinitely. When the war ended in 1945, a flood of new insecticides, developed for wartime use, rapidly entered the market and readily superseded lead arsenate. One of these had the éclat of a war hero, but its dangers were far less clear.[59]

The Secrets of DDT

DDT had been widely used to protect American troops from perilous insect-borne diseases, such as typhus and malaria. Although government scientists who'd first studied its toxicity on animals found "startling" effects, military researchers had reasoned that using DDT during extreme wartime conditions was merited. Soldiers would be exposed only briefly through dustings of their clothing and would be spared probable death from more serious diseases that had taken so many lives during World War I.[60] DDT's success at reducing human deaths during the war was celebrated in the press as a miracle. Hundreds of articles commended this "wonder insecticide" that killed harmful insects while being "harmless to humans."[61]

Within months of the war's end, chemical manufacturers that had produced stockpiles of DDT for military use started to sell hundreds of DDT products for home and farm use.[62] Ads for the new products drew on DDT's heroic war stature, unabashedly lauding it as the "atomic bomb of the insect world."[63]

Magazine articles and ads encouraged housewives to spray it in their kitchens to eradicate houseflies and mosquitoes.[64] Even food processors used DDT to fumigate the insides of cracker and cookie boxes to keep potential pests out.[65] Before the war, homemakers had still expected to remove any bugs that might remain hidden amid cabbage leaves and cauliflower heads in the kitchen. But during and after World War II, ads and articles demonizing insects and praising DDT promoted a new, entirely bug-free aesthetic in foods.[66]

DDT was also promoted widely to farmers. Government agricultural researchers had studied ways to adapt DDT for farm use during the war, so USDA extension agents were ready with recommendations on how to use it in production of milk, apples, oranges, cotton, and many other crops as soon as the war ended.[67] After years of disputing the chronic health hazards of lead arsenate, fruit and vegetable growers welcomed what seemed to be a safer pesticide to kill pests in their orchards and fields. Between 1945 and 1950, annual pesticide production jumped threefold to over three hundred million pounds.[68] War pilots began new careers as crop dusters showering DDT—often mixed with other new insecticides including lindane, toxaphene, and parathion—across farm- and rangelands. In 1950, more than 150 different "pesticide chemical mixtures" were broadcast by aircraft across 1.9 million acres in California.[69] In 1952, nearly 3.5 million acres of California farmland were sprayed at a rate of one to three pounds per acre.[70] In a few short years, the scope of pesticide use had taken a quantum leap.

However, as DDT inundated the market for both home and farm use, FDA researchers had serious reservations. Questions raised before and during the war about the chemical's chronic toxicity continued to haunt them, and postwar research only confirmed earlier findings that DDT could accumulate in body fat and then be passed on in milk.[71] In the late 1940s, scientists found that DDT sprayed in dairy barns—even when animals were not present during spraying—showed up in milk, prompting the FDA and USDA to issue a joint warning admonishing farmers not to use the pesticide around cows.[72] By 1950, FDA scientists found that DDT was showing up in the body fat of people not occupationally associated with pesticide use; seventy-five fat samples from the general population revealed an average concentration of 5.3 parts per million of DDT.[73]

With so little known about DDT's chronic toxicity, FDA scientists had thought it premature to permit unrestricted sale of the pesticide for civilian use, but they'd had no authority to keep DDT off the market.[74] Based on the Food, Drug, and Cosmetic Act of 1938, the agency was able only to adopt provisional tolerance levels for DDT residues on foods based on tests that lasted only a few months, too brief a period to take measure of the pesticide's long-term health effects.[75]

Although there were in-house discussions among government

scientists in various agencies about DDT's chronic toxicity, a policy of keeping quiet was discreetly adopted. Rather than treat the possible danger of pesticide residues as a serious public health concern, officials at the USDA, with its orientation toward supporting the growing agribusiness sector, regarded the dangers of pesticides foremost as a potential public relations disaster.[76] In a repeat of their handling of lead-arsenate risks, they opted to keep consumers in the dark and convinced the FDA to go along with them. [77] Those in the know could only hope that safer pesticides would be developed before any major safety crisis erupted.

By the early 1950s, however, questions began to surface in the public arena, especially as rural residents encountered dangers of the new pesticides firsthand. There were stories of farmworkers seriously sickened and of livestock dying when wind blew into barns after crops were sprayed. In the wake of storms, hundreds of fish came floating belly-up as pesticides ran from fields into rivers, and sportsmen found whole coveys of quail dead. Some farmers complained of rashes on their hands; DDT in contact with wet skin was particularly irritating.[78] The USDA was typically quick to refute such stories, blaming problems on improper use and asking public health agencies to issue official assurances that pesticides posed no health hazard.[79]

Nevertheless, growing concern prompted Congress to convene hearings in late 1950. Under the chairmanship of Representative James Delaney (D-NY), the House Select Committee to Investigate the Use of Chemicals in Food Products heard expert testimony, and the safety of DDT and other new pesticides was sharply debated.

On one side, scientists from the FDA and universities argued that more research was needed to show that new pesticides were safe for general prolonged use and that a stronger law was needed to prevent the possibility of a serious public health crisis. FDA commissioner Paul Dunbar explained that use of DDT during the war had been "a reasonably calculated military risk" because the "risk of poisoning was less serious than the risk of exposure" to typhus and malaria, but he argued that other standards should govern its use in a civilian context, where people might take in small amounts, day after day, over long periods of time.[80] Other scientists raised the possibility that DDT caused cancer based on animal studies. Food manufacturers also had concerns about new residues showing up on fruits and vegetables, some of which generated off-flavors in their products.[81] Baby-food manufacturers testified about the difficulty they faced in finding ingredients without residues and complained that new insecticides had been marketed "before adequate information was available on the acute or chronic toxicity of the chemicals involved."[82]

On the other side, farm organizations joined by chemical manufacturers testified that existing laws were already adequate to protect public health. USDA officials backed them up, pointing to health studies that showed those who worked in apple orchards applying DDT—individuals exposed to higher-than-normal concentrations of the chemical—apparently suffered no ill effects. A representative from the International Apple Association called the push for new pesticide legislation as a "grab for power which is to be secured under the whip of hysteria."[83]

But there was no hysteria. In fact, the Delaney pesticide hearings generated surprisingly little coverage in the popular press and little concern from consumers. The general presumption—born of wartime propaganda—that DDT and other new chemicals were entirely safe remained in force. Most considered pesticide use the business of farmers—a matter to be hammered out in the realm of production. And many believed that pesticide issues were too complex and technical for the general public to grasp. Finally, the pesticide-manufacturing industry, the USDA, and the FDA strove to minimize publicity.[84] All these factors conspired to keep the topic out of the public spotlight.

Despite vigorous protests from the chemical manufacturers, Congress took action in 1954 and passed the Miller Amendment to the 1938 Food, Drug, and Cosmetic Act, which required pesticide manufacturers to provide data up front showing that residues left on foods would pose no risk to public health.[85] However, the new law did little to curb the rapidly increasing use of insecticides, fungicides, and herbicides in agriculture. By the early 1960s, U.S. companies were manufacturing over 782 million pounds of 100 types of pesticides each year, with over 30,000 formulas registered for sale; by the late '60s, farmers would annually purchase over a billion pounds of 900 types of pesticides, sold in thousands of different preparations.[86]

Paradoxically, the steady rise in use of pesticides was related as much to their failure as to their success. Shortly after DDT came into widespread use, evidence surfaced that the popular pesticide killed not just damaging insects but also beneficial ones, such as bees that pollinated crops and predators that kept pests in check. As such, after only a few years, there was often an unanticipated resurgence of troubling pests in fields sprayed with DDT. The common solution was to spray higher concentrations more frequently, which eventually had a second consequence: resistance. Typically, after being exposed to broad-spectrum toxins, a small number of insects was hardy enough to survive and reproduce, leaving a new generation of "superbugs" to ravage fields. Entomologists had observed this phenomenon as early as 1946, and by the early 1950s, farm extension agents were reporting widespread resistance of insects to DDT.[87]

Although pests developed resistance over a short period, most farmers, extension agents, and USDA researchers never stopped to question the strategy of undertaking an ongoing "arms race" with insects—one that required continuous and ever-increasing pesticide use. Department of Agriculture leaders, thoroughly seduced by the vision of farms run like factories, had aggressively encouraged farmers to adopt their goal of modern, insect-free, industrial-scale fields. Meanwhile, the technological optimism and the financial interest of agricultural chemical industries kept the focus on finding new and improved insecticides rather than questioning problems caused by existing ones. As early as 1946, American chemical companies had begun to produce and market a new class of pesticides—organophosphates, such as parathion and TEPP—modeled after poison nerve gasses used in German concentration camps. Promoters described them as a means to "restore a balance in nature" disturbed by the organochlorine DDT.[88]

The agricultural chemical companies had figured out how to insert themselves profitably into the farm-to-plate food chain, and supplying a new stream of insecticides made their role indispensable. Despite resurgence and resistance, production of DDT kept pace with other pesticides, growing from 37.9 million pounds in 1953 to over 124.5 million pounds in 1959.[89]

As pesticide use became more widespread through the decade of the 1950s, risks became more apparent to researchers. By 1955, when the FDA scientists tested milk samples throughout the country, they found "the presence of toxic residues in 62 percent of the milks."[90] USDA studies were also showing the presence of elevated residues in meats. Moreover, in just five years, the average level of DDT residues in body fat tissues of Americans had practically tripled to 15.6 parts per million.[91] The FDA and USDA decided not to publicize the results of their in-house research but rather made every effort to keep concerns about increasing pesticide residues in foods to a small circle of scientists and officials within government agencies and the food trade.[92]

As the modern food system had emerged, consumers' not knowing about the places and particulars of their foods had been an artifact of distance, culture, and infrastructure. But in the wake of World War II, as hundreds of new pesticides came into widespread use on food crops for the first time, there was deliberate and calculated secrecy.

In the new food chain, only a few public health experts knew about the bioaccumulation and toxicity of the pesticides used so profligately, and they chose to remain quiet. In the modern age, farmers had come to trust the authority of government and business experts to lead them in the right direction, much as shoppers had come to trust the authority of government and business experts to supply them with wholesome foods. As the distance between farms and kitchens had grown, and connections between those who grew food and those who ate it were severed, methods of food production had increasingly come to reflect the priorities and outlook of those producing, processing, and selling foods rather than those buying, cooking, and eating them.

With widespread use of persistent pesticides in the postwar era, the matter of knowing foods was ratcheted to a whole new level of complexity. Not only were consumers unaware of pesticides' problematic presence, but even experts charged with oversight were bewildered. Despite mounting evidence that agricultural chemicals might be harmful, no one fully understood the long-term effects of pesticides in human

bodies or in the environment. Few grasped the risks involved as persistent pesticides were applied in one place — such as a dairy barn — but then
showed up unexpectedly in another — such as in the body tissues of
people who lived nowhere near farms. Few grasped the risks entailed as
pesticides migrated through food chains, betokening a new and insidi-
ous way in which agriculture was beginning to affect the environment.
And with little public awareness, there was little interest in erecting a
means of further study or oversight — especially in the 1950s, when the
guiding principle of government was laissez-faire, and the interests of
prosperous and powerful industries were at stake.

Pesticides were just one of several innovations and petroleum-
dependent technological breakthroughs that contributed to wholly
changing the face of America's agriculture in the years following World
War II. Synthetic fertilizers together with new high-yield hybrid seeds
and bigger farm machinery enabled growers to substantially increase
harvests of field crops (corn, in particular), despite substantial reduc-
tions in harvested acreage. As a result, fewer, larger farms delivered cheap
corn to market at lower prices, giving animal production a boost. At the
same time, larger feedlots and poultry houses were made possible by
antibiotics that prevented crowded animals from getting sick and that
also spurred growth. By 1960, American farmers were feeding 1.2 billion
pounds of antibiotics to livestock and poultry, with implications for bacterial resistance that were only beginning to be understood; and the size
of animal operations would only continue to expand.[93] These and other
innovations delivered a clear benefit at the supermarket — mostly in the
form of less-expensive food, but changes in methods of food production
were not apparent to consumers. Although cooks may have been
appalled by conditions in crowded animal factories or concerned about
hormones and antibiotics used to boost growth rates, they welcomed
cheaper meats in their kitchens. Even though consumers would not
likely have chosen to ingest toxic residues — even in small amounts —
with their dinners, they did embrace the new bug- and blemish-free aesthetic of fresh vegetables and fruits.

As residues of pesticides — on vegetables, in meat, and in milk —
surreptitiously made their way to supermarkets and dinner tables,

knowing food was no longer something that a homemaker could expect to do herself at the supermarket or in the kitchen, as once had been construed by writers of household handbooks and magazine columns. Kitchen literacy had evolved from being a matter governed by an individual's senses, common sense, and tradition, to one governed by outside experts representing an alliance of commerce, science, and government. By the 1950s, the prospect of knowing food was becoming so complicated as to demand a larger role for public policy—with all its committees, lobbyists, and specialists in fields as divergent as food chemistry, entomology, nutrition, and toxicology.

These epistemological complexities were not yet grasped by most consumers. Through the 1950s, most people would remain unaware of the suite of issues that the Delaney Committee had regarded as a stream of synthetic chemicals—pesticides, additives, (and fertilizers)—rapidly entering America's food supply without oversight. Their attentions were directed elsewhere.

For Convenience Sake

In the same way that wartime exigency laid the groundwork for quick acceptance of DDT, it also created a set of circumstances that would foster shoppers' acceptance of a new generation of modern convenience foods. Though packaged, canned, and processed foods had gained measured popularity during the 1920s, it wasn't until World War II that these products finally made inroads into a broader swathe of American kitchens.

With tens of thousands of soldiers shipped overseas, millions of civilians moved to cities to take jobs in factories directed toward the war effort. The number of women in the workforce increased by 50 percent, and by 1945 more than one-third of all women were employed.[94] In this chaotic context, new ways of shopping, cooking, and eating became central features of life on the home front.

To prioritize high-value foods for soldiers and to prevent the shortages that had occurred during World War I, the U.S. government instituted a coupon-based rationing program for meat, sugar, butter, and canned foods.[95] Though most homemakers felt it was their patriotic duty to sacrifice usual standards during the war, many remained reluctant to use foods their families were unaccustomed to eating.[96]

In the fall of 1942, the U.S. Department of Agriculture convened a group of women's magazine publishers to enlist their help in persuading homemakers to follow wartime rationing recommendations. The publisher of *Woman's Day* expressed "no doubt that magazines should be able to help in the important job of changing the food preferences of American women to conform to the rapidly changing supplies."[97] Soon the magazines were filled with articles and recipes that focused on the virtues of making do with nonrationed ingredients, such as new frozen vegetables, beans, organ meats, and baking mixes.

In addition, the U.S. government once again struck up a mutually beneficial wartime relationship with the advertising industry. In exchange for its services to the government, the agencies again received a Treasury Department ruling that made all advertising tax-exempt during the war. Many food-manufacturing companies took advantage of this deduction to stoke recognition of their brand names even as their factories were retooled and temporarily diverted to supply the war effort.[98]

During these years, General Mills's well-known fictional cooking expert Betty Crocker took to the airwaves with her radio show *Our Nation's Rations* and gently assured homemakers that pre-made mixes offered a good way to bake special desserts without using up ration "points" for sugar and eggs. With canned foods strictly rationed so metals could be used for war needs, frozen-food manufacturers took advantage of the opportunity to persuade homemakers to try new "frosted" vegetables, fish, and meats as well.[99]

This was all in the interest of national security. However, as the war pressed on, food companies used the subsidized ads to chart a new course for postwar commerce, promising homemakers a dazzling assortment of new products when rationing restrictions were lifted.[100] Responding to the deprivation that many felt as a consequence of rationing, the wartime ads strove to rouse a potent sense of anticipation for the modern wonders of the "Machine Food Age" that would arrive in kitchens as soon as the war was over.[101]

During the war, limited supplies had compelled the food industry to innovate. To make more efficient use of materials, food technologists figured out how to reclaim calcium from eggshells and how to manufacture soups from ingredients formerly reserved for cattle feed, such as soybeans and brewer's yeast. They'd also devised new methods in processing and packaging as they strove to provide GIs with lightweight, easy-to-prepare foods, such as dehydrated mashed potatoes and whole meals sealed in airtight pouches and tins.[102] All geared up at war's end, the food industry eagerly set out to sell their new high-tech food products to civilian markets. Between 1940 and 1950, the number of food ads in women's magazines nearly doubled.[103] Before the war, there had been roughly 1,000 processed-food products on the market; after the war, 4,000 to 5,000 new products, including frozen orange juice, fish sticks, and Spam, vied for space on supermarket shelves.[104]

With so many products, the supermarkets established before the war now expanded, multiplied, and flourished anew. As more families moved to swelling suburbs, a new pattern of life became possible for a growing middle class with pent-up yearnings for comfort and ease after years of economic depression and wartime privation. To help foot the bill for new houses, second cars, televisions, and appliances—including the newly necessary home freezer—many women who'd started working during the war stayed in the workforce. In 1950, eight million wives—roughly one in four—had a job outside the home.[105] By 1953, working women—both single and married—numbered over eighteen million, and the numbers would continue to grow.[106] With less time, fatter pocketbooks, more storage space, and the new possibilities of buying packaged foods with longer shelf lives, women could shop less often, filling up station wagons with a week's worth of groceries at a time. Discerning these social patterns, the food industry was wildly optimistic about its new convenience products, expecting they would be especially popular with working women who had less time to cook.

No product better epitomized the food industry's vision for food in the '50s than the frozen dinner. A pinnacle of technological achievement, the complete frozen entrée—turkey, mashed potatoes, and vegetable—embedded in its crimped aluminum tray was introduced to supermarket shoppers in 1952. All a homemaker had to do—as the package directed—

was "heat and serve." After the meal was consumed, there weren't even dishes to clean. Despite the promise of ease, it wasn't until two years later when the Omaha-based Swanson Company cleverly tied their pre-made dinners to that other '50s technological marvel—the television—that sales skyrocketed. With thirteen million frozen "TV dinners" being popped into America's ovens, an editorial in the trade journal *Quick Frozen Foods* proclaimed, "the day of the complete meal has dawned for good." After years of resistance, the editorial explained, the public was now "'conditioned' to prepared foods. . . . It is no longer thought odd to make a meal of a precooked item such as fish sticks, chicken or meat pies, chow mein, ravioli, and similar items. The gap has been bridged. . . . The field is open!"[107]

From the perspective of the food industry, the most important aspect of the new high-tech foods, such as TV dinners and frozen fish sticks, was that they were "labor-saving."[108] One meat-industry trade journal touted "convenience" as a "magic word . . . the 'open sesame' to the feminine shopper's pocketbook."[109] As they saw it, for women with jobs outside the home, figuring out how to squeeze in the work of cooking meals after a day of work in a factory, shop, or office had become especially tricky. According to industry estimates, in 1927 the average woman had spent five to six hours per day preparing meals for her family; but in the '50s, a food industry spokesman proudly declared that a housewife relying on convenience foods could fix her family's daily meals in ninety minutes or less.[110]

With complete frozen entrées, those in the food industry earnestly believed they had created the answer to every housewife's dream—less work fixing meals. In countless articles in trade journals, magazines, and newspapers, they excitedly crowed about their successful infiltration of America's kitchens. However, according to culinary historian Laura Shapiro, their claims may have been premature. Though articles and ads in popular culture everywhere proclaimed that "women weren't cooking, they didn't want to cook, they had no time to cook," Shapiro found that many women continued to resist giving up cooking.[111] In 1954, when the *Boston Globe* ran a headline asking "Is Home Cooking on the Way Out?" the paper received a surge of skeptical letters from upset homemakers. In a follow-up story, the editor quoted from just a few: "Just how much more do packaged foods cost?" one asked. "How does packaged food assure a healthier family?" another questioned rhetorically.[112]

To many homemakers, the images and messages in the popular culture rubbed the wrong way, perhaps because they were at odds with what most women were actually doing in their kitchens. Although wartime rationing had compelled most homemakers to try new frozen products and packaged mixes as substitutes for more familiar foods they cooked from scratch, after the war, most resumed cooking as usual. Several studies through the 1950s confirmed that—despite the food industry's assertions to the contrary—the great majority of women did have sufficient time to cook.[113] Modern appliances and the availability of easier-to-use staple ingredients, such as plucked chickens, ground beef, and trimmed fresh vegetables, had made cooking meals from scratch an easier proposition than ever before. Moreover, additional studies indicated that most women found cooking to be their favorite aspect of housework. When pressed for time, most women chose to cook ahead of time or to prepare simpler meals; only 11 percent reported turning to convenience products, which were widely considered to be expensive.[114] Studies showed that even women who worked outside the home did not use convenience products any more frequently than full-time homemakers did.[115] In short, almost no one adopted the food industry's vision of modern cookery—serving pre-made meals on a regular basis.

Although the earlier generation of "modern" products—canned soups and bakers' bread, in particular—had over the course of decades become accepted and familiar staples in most kitchens by the 1950s, their acceptance did not secure blanket approval for a newer generation of pre-made food products. That's because there still lingered a persistent stigma attached to the very idea of "laborsaving."[116] It wasn't that busy women didn't appreciate shortcuts in the kitchen, but rather that cooking still carried a great deal of emotional freight and significance in most women's lives. To most—whether they worked outside the home or not —cooking meant more than serving meals: it meant nurturing a family. The thought of skimping in the kitchen went straight to the heart of a collective soul-searching that troubled many women in the 1950s as they tried to balance the new possibility of work outside the home with traditional expectations about their domestic roles. One well-known marketing study revealed that homemakers thought very poorly of other women who opted to use quick-fix foods to save time.[117]

In essence, the new convenience foods created a paradox. The very way that these products claimed to help women—by saving work in the kitchen—took away the gratification that came with work in the kitchen. But the paradox went deeper. Eliminating the need to know about ingredients and cooking were key elements of convenience—but certainly not part of its appeal. In fact, the intimation embedded in all the magazine articles and ads about convenience foods—that housewives' kitchen know-how was unimportant—threatened to compromise a woman's integrity. Most homemakers still thought they should know *something*.

Frustrated food marketers tried to take advantage of this paradox by picking up where Christine Frederick and earlier advertisers left off— by heavily promoting a new "smarts" about cooking. To reach the 1.7 million female students enrolled in Home Economics classes, food-manufacturing firms began to offer free teaching materials to Home-Ec teachers who confronted the dilemma of how to teach cooking in the face of new products that seemed to make many kitchen skills obsolete. The instructional materials emphasized the benefits of using ready-made foods and encouraged classroom-cooking activities based on recipes that combined pre-made foods.[118]

The new food "smarts" were also spread through the pages of newspapers, magazines, and cookbooks. Local food editors were particularly fond of including recipes supplied by manufacturers that recommended mixing and matching pre-made products to whip up new concoctions with mushroom soups, biscuit mix, and cans of deviled ham. One manufacturer's recipe suggested stuffing the entire contents of a frozen dinner into pie shells or parboiled peppers.[119] Floating adrift from culinary tradition, America's 1950s cuisine became like a game built around assembling parts from various boxes, jars, and cans.

The influential *New York Times* food department, aiming to chart a course between those "epicurean snobs" who still derided canned foods and those who embraced all quick foods, explained to readers that it had decided to "take the middle road" with "respect to prepared foods." The editor recommended that homemakers deal with each food "intelligently and imaginatively," for example, by adding cinnamon or grated cheese to ready-made bread mix.[120] But other publications were unabashedly claiming to take the high road to convenience. *Good Housekeeping* had long since abandoned its traditionalist inclinations and now advised "novice cooks" that "the bride who takes advantage of canned and frozen foods, packaged mixes too, need not apologize. She's smart."[121]

There is no one who promoted this promise of pseudoexpertise in the kitchen with as much zeal and conviction as Poppy Cannon, a popular TV personality, magazine columnist, and author of *The Can-Opener Cook Book*. "At one time, a badge of shame, hallmark of the lazy lady and the careless wife," she wrote, "today the can-opener is fast becoming a magic wand." Cannon flaunted her easily earned kitchen mastery: "armed with a can-opener, I can become the artist-cook, the master, the creative chef. . . . It is easy to cook like a gourmet though you are only a beginner." She continued, "in this miraculous age it is quite possible— and it's fun—to be a 'chef' even before you can really cook."[122] Cannon's embrace of canned soups as "gourmet" sauces gave can-opener cooking a "cachet of style" that was appealing in the '50s as middle-class women aspired to achieve a new standard of gracious living.[123] In her cookbook for young brides, Cannon included an alphabet and advised young cooks, "'I' stands for Intelligence. Don't check your brains at the door."[124] As both a career woman and a mother, Cannon believed that her mode of cooking was opening the way for other bright young women to blend good cooking and sophisticated style with fulfilling work.

Through the decade of the 1950s, a legion of ads, articles, and books followed Cannon's lead and focused on creating a new and favorable image—attractive, modern, glamorous, and sharp—for the kind of woman who used convenience foods. To boost homemakers' status, convenience products were extolled as foods "with built-in maid service." One article described how a top Hollywood secretary, after a long day of work, prepared an "appetizing" meal for fourteen guests, in which "every bite" had been not only "washed, but peeled, shelled, precooked, mixed, and apportioned by 'factory maids' long before it reached her hands." It was as if a "horde of servants" had slaved in the kitchen, but she was the one who received the "burst of praise" for her "home-cooked" meal.[125] Instead of being selfish or lazy, women who used the modern foods were glamorous; they were of the class that had smartly ascended above the drudgery of kitchen work. By association, the very concept of convenience was recast in a favorable light.

By end of the 1950s, women's magazines featured the new foods not only in splashy ads that were taking up more and more space, but in columns devoted specifically to "new foods." Here food writers unreservedly promoted "the pleasures of convenience foods" and enshrined familiarity with the miraculous new foods as the new kitchen literacy.[126] When asked in one such article, "What is left for the kitchen?" a top Campbell's soup executive genially explained that there was still "lots of room for imagination" in the serving of prepared foods. "The ingenious housewife can enhance" her canned soups "with croutons, whipped cream," or any of "her own special added ingredients."[127] In their kitchen work, women were encouraged to take conscious pride in modernity and delight in discovering and experimenting with the new products. In this way, their status could be elevated from mere cook to intelligent, imaginative, and even "ingenious" participant in cutting-edge technology.[128]

While the rising use of convenience foods was heralded as a "revolution" of smart women embracing new technologies in the pages of newspapers and magazines, many who worked behind the scenes in the food industry saw things differently. With sales failing to meet expectations, they turned to the field of psychology to understand why homemakers were not adopting convenience foods as readily as expected. In contrast to the "smart" women portrayed in ads and magazine articles, new psychological research on consumer motivations was revealing that many shoppers were fearful, guilt-wracked, and malleable. And these findings were readily brought to bear in the realm of food marketing.[129]

Facing lackluster sales of its cake mixes, General Mills hired a team of psychologists in the early 1950s to study why. During the war, in response to egg scarcity, food technologists had developed mixes with synthetic emulsifiers.[130] Though cake-mix packages clearly instructed "Do not add milk, just add water," many homemakers insisted on adding milk or extra eggs to make a richer cake. When the cake turned out poorly, they blamed the mix and didn't buy the product again. Based on interviews with hundreds of housewives, researchers at the Institute for Motivational Research, headed by Dr. Ernest Dichter, concluded that women didn't follow instructions because they experienced baking a cake as an emotional "act of love," so the richer, the better. The researchers theorized that big, rich cakes symbolized femininity, fecundity, and maternal abundance and thereby served as substitutes for deep-seated needs and psychological gratifications not otherwise met.[131]

Because cakes carried so much meaning in homes, the motivational researchers recognized that the boxed cake mixes were in a particularly difficult position. More than other convenience foods, cake mix elicited feelings of guilt and inadequacy in those who used them because many women believed that using mixes was a sign of poor homemaking. Moreover, the psychologists reported that housewives consistently described baking cakes as one of their most pleasurable tasks; as such, it was an area where many women were less concerned about saving time. The quick, boxed mixes, by their very nature, threatened to deprive homemakers of both an enjoyable creative outlet and a traditional source of praise and self-esteem.

At the same time, making a good cake from scratch could be difficult. Living isolated in the suburbs, without nearby mothers to consult, many young wives simply didn't know how to bake the cakes that were expected of them, and they were afraid to bake a flop. Here was where boxed mixes could offer much needed help — and tap a huge market — if only marketers could break through the guilt. Dichter concluded that the key to profiting from cake mixes lay in understanding housewives' "fear of failure."[132]

To negotiate the labyrinth of the female psyche, Dr. Dichter advised General Mills to focus on success rather than ease in its ads and to always leave something for the housewife to do.[133] Even by simply adding an egg to ready-made mix, a homemaker could have the satisfaction that she was contributing more of herself to the cake. Sure enough, after the mixes and instructions were changed to require the addition of one fresh egg, the popularity of the mixes grew. In 1950, less than a quarter of all cakes baked in homes had been made from mixes. By 1957, half—approximately 5.5 million cakes—were made from mixes.[134] Rather than risk baking from scratch, young homemakers began to trust the scientifically developed mixes to make a perfect cake every time.[135] As young homemakers bought more cake mixes and other ready-made foods, they learned to depend on food manufacturers to buffer their waning skills in the kitchen. Between 1949 and 1955, per capita consumption of convenience foods rose from seventeen pounds to forty-five pounds.[136]

An optimistic and certainly common way to think about the food industry's successful promotion of convenience foods is to consider how these foods ultimately helped to liberate women from restrictive gender roles and patriarchal expectations that had kept them in the kitchen. All the promotional articles and ads worked hand in hand to help shift social norms to accommodate the new economic reality of women working jobs outside the home, some by choice, some out of economic necessity. Perhaps more than the foods themselves, the new cultural context of convenience cooking gave women the opportunity to move more freely in new directions, to earn their own money, and to choose how to spend their time.

However, the way that books, articles, and ads promoted knowledge of convenience foods as "smart" cut another way, too. Eventually, the promotions that strove to redefine women's "smartness" about food as the opening of tin cans, the stirring of ready-made mixes, and the sprinkling of croutons, succeeded. Many young women came to believe that cooking was onerous unless ready-made products were on hand.[137] The very meaning of intelligence was reconfigured to support the new products and their high profitability. Yet in this new universe of meaning, actual knowledge of foods and cooking know-how was significantly diminished.

Despite the reformulation of women's food "smarts" in the realm of popular culture—and perhaps because of it—motivational researchers found that diminished knowledge of foods actually left women fearful and unconfident when shopping for groceries. For example, social

psychologist James Vicary found that young wives preferred anonymous supermarkets to small grocery stores precisely because they could
better hide their ignorance about foods from clerks. Another study by
the Jewel Tea Company indicated that fear was especially common when
a homemaker encountered the butcher in the meat department because
she knew so little about meat.[138]

Homemakers' diffidence was soon exploited by marketers who
observed that the large generation of children growing up in the 1950s—
the baby boomers—was ripe for cultivation as consumers. In 1955, a
third of America's population was under age fifteen. Some companies,
such as Continental Baking with its balloon promotions for Wonder
Bread, had been targeting children since the 1920s, but the practice took
on new focus and energy with a powerful new medium at the ad industry's disposal: television.

As the number of homes with TV soared from four million to forty-
six million during the 1950s, more and more families gathered around
to view novel programming—and ads—each night.[139] As one Kellogg's executive boasted to the *Wall Street Journal,* "With television,
we can almost sell children our product before they can talk."[140] Food-
marketing experts realized that children who went to the supermarket
with their mothers actually had an inordinate sway over what she picked
out. A study in Philadelphia showed that over 77 percent of mothers
bought at least one item at a child's suggestion, and nearly two-thirds of
the "decision makers" were toddlers, between two and six years old.[141] "In
the old days," the Kellogg's official explained, "children ate what their
mothers bought; now the kids tell their mothers what to buy."[142] By 1958,
total expenditures for advertising of food and grocery products (exclud-
ing soft drinks, candy, and alcohol) on television had topped $240 mil-
lion. In 1960, roughly $40 million was spent on TV advertising of break-
fast cereals alone.[143]

As young mothers chose what foods to buy, they now had to contend
with determined five-year-olds whose brand-name preferences were
based on cute animal mascots and cereal box prizes. With seductive television ads, baby boomers were thus hooked early on to the meanings,
flavors, and textures of the modern cuisine of processed foods, and with

marketers targeting children directly, mothers' food know-how was further marginalized.

In 1960, the Grocery Manufacturers of America proudly reported that young people were developing eating habits and product preferences quite different from those of their parents. This they described as "evidence of their intellectual independence."[144]

By the end of the 1950s, the number of processed foods competing for space on supermarket shelves had skyrocketed to eight thousand, and sales of manufactured foods reached a record $55 billion.[145] By 1960, a USDA study showed that homemakers were spending fourteen cents of every dollar on convenience foods, up from seven cents per dollar five years earlier.[146] Although recalcitrant homemakers had rejected the food industry's vision of serving pre-made dinners, the trend toward increased use of convenience products in day-to-day cooking was unmistakable. Through the 1950s, the number of women working outside the home had expanded to over twenty million.[147] As *Time* magazine concluded in 1959, "For such women, processed foods are indispensable; there is no other way."[148]

Hidden on Supermarket Shelves

While a homemaker may have been "smart" in saving time and "ingenious" in sprinkling croutons, she was clearly in the dark about the additives used to bring the modern feast to her family table. Metaphors of maids belied the new chemicals—many developed during the war—that were being added to foods in an unprecedented stream to accomplish the magic of convenience. By 1947, manufacturers were using more than four hundred chemical additives to bring the thousands of new food products to supermarket shelves, and the number was rapidly increasing.[149]

While trumpeting the marvel of "new foods" to their readers, women's magazines neglected to mention growing concern about these additives making their way into foods with little scrutiny. As with pesticide residues, most in the food industry considered additive use a technical matter beyond the comprehension of homemakers. If any problems became apparent, they believed that food technology experts could readily remedy them. However, a few close calls brought the issue to the attention of the FDA and then to Congress in 1950.

Through the '40s, there had been several episodes where food additives presumed to be safe had turned out to be unsafe. For example, thiourea was a substance patented to prevent the browning of cut apples, peaches, and pears exposed to the air. Though several published reports from the laboratories of its manufacturer had established its safety in terms of acute toxicity, independent drug researchers at Johns Hopkins found thiourea had a depressing effect on the thyroid. Further studies verified this finding. In the meantime, the product continued to be used for treating cut fruit. In 1946, the FDA seized a shipment of frozen peaches that had been treated with excessive amounts of thiourea and reportedly caused illness. Portions of the peaches fed to lab rats killed them overnight, leading agency scientists to conclude that even in small concentrations, the substance could be poisonous and unpredictable.[150] Then researchers at the University of Wisconsin determined that nitrogen trichloride (trade name Agene), a gas that had been used for twenty-five years to bleach 90 percent of America's white flour, caused severe neurological effects in cats, dogs, and monkeys. Animals fed a diet of "agenized" flour developed symptoms like those of epilepsy and went into seizure-like "running fits."[151] Though human bread-eaters had not developed such troubles, the fact that several mammalian species suffered such acute effects made medical researchers worry about the possibility that Agene could cause chronic neurological disorders in people. These concerns prompted the FDA to discontinue use of the gas in flour processing.[152]

A similar story can be told for Dulcin, a sweetener used for decades with no apparent drawbacks. But when FDA scientists finally got around to studying its chronic effects in 1947, they determined that rats fed even minute quantities on a day-to-day basis failed to grow to full size, suffered from blood abnormalities, and developed liver tumors.[153]

Thiourea, Agene, and Dulcin were just three of the hundreds of new additives used in food processing, but the fact that even a handful of additives posed health hazards raised the possibility that others—already hidden in foods on supermarket shelves—could be unsafe as well.

In response to these concerns, the Delaney Committee—convened in 1950, as we've seen, to investigate the flood of chemicals coming into use in food production—devoted considerable attention to food additives, and the numbers were formidable. According to the FDA, 704 chemical substances were routinely used in food processing. Of these, 428 were "probably safe as normally used," but the other 276 were either known to be unsafe or had not yet been adequately investigated.[154] Most of the substances had come onto the market only within the previous few years, overwhelming the agency's capacity to evaluate them.

The Delaney Committee's additive hearings centered on a new class of "softeners" or emulsifiers that were added to bread to keep loaves softer for longer. Made in part from petroleum and in part from fatty acids derived from edible and inedible fats, ten million pounds were already being added to the six billion loaves of bread baked commercially each year. Since shoppers often judged the freshness of bread with a little squeeze, these additives made bread saleable for a longer period.

The commercial baking industry did not want to give up its ability to use inexpensive ingredients that added what they regarded as legitimate value. A small amount of emulsifier prevented bread from going stale and thereby allowed production at a larger scale with less risk of waste. The clear benefit to shoppers was cheaper bread that didn't go stale.[155] Moreover, most American consumers had already come to expect and prefer light, squishy bread with a long shelf life.

Health experts, however, raised concerns about the safety of emulsifiers, portions of which were not derived from "biological" sources. Some pointed out that the cheap additives were already taking the place of more nutritive but expensive ingredients, such as eggs and milk—without consumers even knowing they were being nutritionally short-changed.[156] And it was this unknowing—in terms of declining nutrition and of safety—that most disturbed the few consumer representatives who testified.

Dr. Faith Fenton, representing the American Home Economics Association, contended that consumers were "entitled to know what has been added to their food and beverages and in what amounts."[157] Indeed, the 1938 Food, Drug, and Cosmetic Act had required that all ingredients be listed on a product's label in a way that could be understood "by the ordinary individual under customary conditions of purchase and use."[158] However, common foods, such as bread, became exempt from such labeling once the FDA established a generalized standard recipe. And as the agency had become more accepting of a legitimate role for chemical additives, more of them were being added to common food products— unbeknownst to consumers.[159] Mrs. Leslie Wright, of the General Federation of Women's Clubs, contended that, in the very least, nonnutritive ingredients should not be added to foods unless they had first been certified by the FDA as harmless.[160] However, it was Anna Kelton Wiley, widow of the late Dr. Harvey Wiley and a food activist in her own right, who put the matter into the most personal terms. She explained to members of Congress how "startling" it would be for "a woman consumer buying bread for her family, thinking she is giving her children wholesome bread and rolls made from wheat, milk, shortening, and eggs" to find out "that it is all a hoax and she is really giving her children a synthetic material manufactured from petroleum and coal tar."[161]

When the consumer advocates talked about wanting to know what was in the bread they purchased, they expressed a commonsense notion of knowing foods, based on what they could readily perceive and already understood to be wholesome. In contrast, those in the bread-manufacturing industry emphasized the efficacy and specific benefits of the emulsifiers. They made no distinctions between ingredients that were customary and those devised by chemists. Their notion of knowing foods was based on the idea that science alone could define and solve problems with uncontested solutions and that only those individuals experienced and well versed in scientific method had the mental capacity to analyze situations without bias. As such, they tended to dismiss those who brought forth evidence based on personal experience or values.[162]

Although additives, such as emulsifiers, didn't present the far-reaching ecological repercussions that pesticides did, the debate over emulsifier use exemplified a widening difference between how consumers and food scientists perceived foods. While absolute safety seemed a practical and prudent goal to consumer advocates, food scientists contended that science could never prove absolute safety, only that no evidence had yet been uncovered to prove harm. In a 1954 editorial in the prestigious journal *Science,* biochemist C. N. Frey, who specialized in the intricacies of bread dough, urged a "proper perspective" with regard to "chemical technology in food production," recommending that society "go forward . . . guided by the best minds and the best information that science has made available."[163]

While food-industry promoters had publicly extolled women's intelligence and smarts in choosing modern foods, behind the scenes in their private dialogues, many believed that homemakers didn't have the reasoning capability to understand what was happening to their foods and why the arcane mix of chemical additives was in their best interest. As one spokesman from *Good Housekeeping* explained to an audience of food technologists, "The consumer's lack of analytical facilities and her faith in those who supply her food make it imperative that the manufacturer bear the bulk of the burden of insuring safe, wholesome food, prepared in clean plants and with sound research behind the complete safety of any processes or any added ingredients." He continued, "Since her facilities for investigation are practically non-existent in her busy life," and she is "helpless in protecting herself," she must rest her case with those who supply her.[164]

Yet the Delaney Committee hearings made evident that no one—neither industry nor government—was adequately assessing the safety of additives on homemakers' behalf. Food manufacturers could introduce any substance as long as it had not been proven acutely injurious. And while additive manufacturers typically evaluated their products for severe, short-term effects, they rarely tested for chronic health effects, which might come only after eating a product regularly over a number of years. The FDA, with its limited authority and resources, had no way to assess the long-term hazards of the hundreds of new additives that were now coming into the food supply each year.

Although the Delaney Committee considered substances that most Americans were ingesting every day, the issue of additive use was generally regarded as a technical matter for insiders. As had been the case when the committee considered pesticides, the additive hearings attracted relatively little public attention.[165] FDA officials were genuinely concerned about the safety of some additives, but they didn't want to frighten consumers unnecessarily and were inclined by habit to work in partnership with industry. Food industry leaders believed their products were safe, yet they had good reason to suspect they'd have public relations problems if homemakers became aware of the many processing agents that went into modern foods.

After hearing testimony from government officials, industry researchers, and just a handful of consumer representatives, the Delaney Committee recommended that an amendment similar to the 1938 drug law and the 1954 Miller pesticide amendment — requiring manufacturers to show evidence of their products' safety beforehand — be passed for food additives. But the chemical industry objected strongly, and bills were repeatedly thwarted. In response, the FDA during the first term of President Dwight Eisenhower took a backseat on the issue and parroted industry claims that additives were already adequately tested. FDA commissioner Charles Crawford pointed to the lack of an "elixir sulfanilamide disaster in the food industry" as evidence of "conscientiousness" about additives and did not support new legislation.[166]

However, through the 1950s, more stories surfaced about food additives considered safe but then later implicated in chronic health effects. Coumarin, a widely used flavoring agent, was discovered to cause liver damage in animals.[167] Then the FDA's own studies of coloring agents revealed that some food dyes approved back in Harvey Wiley's era weren't so safe after all. In one incident, children at a Christmas party were made sick by eating popcorn colored with Red No. 32. Ultimately, this and two other dyes routinely used to make the skins of oranges more appealing to shoppers were decertified.[168]

By the end of the decade, with evidence coming to light about the possible carcinogenicity of food additives and of hormones increasingly used in meat production, the FDA, under leadership of a new director, changed its tune and began to advocate more actively for a new food-additive amendment.[169] However, it wasn't until 1958, when the City of New York drafted a municipal code banning the sale of meat from hormone-treated animals, that the chemical- and food-manufacturing industries reversed their opposition to the proposed legislation. Fearing a tangle of red tape resulting from different state and local regulations, the industries begrudgingly opted to support a uniform federal law.[170]

With momentum building for the new law, the *Ladies' Home Journal* broke its conspicuous silence and finally brought the additive issue to the attention of its readers in 1958 when it published a short editorial urging Congress to pass the food-additive measure. "There is no law that additives to food must be tested and found safe before they are included in foods and sold," the editors wrote. "The *Journal* . . . does maintain that the American people must not be used like experimental animals."[171] The strongly worded letter echoed the verve of 1930s guinea-pig literature but was tucked in between flashy features and ubiquitous ads for additive-packed convenience foods.

Later that year, Congress finally passed the Food Additive Law, requiring manufacturers to test for both acute and chronic health effects of new additives before adding them to food products.[172] But at the same time, it also grandfathered in substances already used in foods by allowing the FDA to establish a list of almost one thousand chemicals Generally Recognized As Safe (GRAS). Congressman Delaney claimed that more than a third of these additives lacked satisfactory data to prove their safety, but in the compromises of lawmaking, the GRAS list stood.[173] Additive use in foods would continue to increase from the roughly 400 million pounds used in 1955 to about 1.06 billion pounds, or 5 pounds per capita, in 1970.[174]

Delaney, though, was adamant about exacting another compromise, a controversial provision that came to be known as the "Delaney anti-cancer clause." It prohibited the addition of any substance known "to induce cancer in when ingested by man or animal" to foods.[175] Because scientists did not fully understand the causes of cancer and could not specify doses at which additives might be carcinogenic, Delaney reasoned that the zero-tolerance law would be prudent. Aware of the extraordinary pressures put on the FDA to set higher tolerances for carcinogenic pesticides to appease farmers and the USDA, Delaney resolved to insulate the agency from similar pressures from the food-chemical industry. The Delaney Clause would later prove increasingly contentious as it became scientifically feasible to detect carcinogens in units of parts per billion, and eventually, parts per trillion. But as Delaney had intended, the clause gave the FDA considerable new muscle to protect public health at a time of scientific ambiguity.[176]

Determined to take no chances with cancer-causing agents, the FDA's first definitive action was to pull contaminated cranberries off the market in the weeks before Thanksgiving 1959. Inspectors had found residues of the weed-killer aminotriazole, a substance known to cause tumors in laboratory animals, on the berries.[177] A few months later, the agency also banned the use of diethylstilbestrol (DES), an estrogenic hormone widely used to caponize poultry and known to be carcinogenic. Studies had shown that sufficient DES residues persisted in chicken meat to warrant a possible health threat to eaters.[178] After the FDA's initial announcements, the popular press, echoing sentiments of the affected businesses, featured experts who disparaged both the cranberry recall and the DES ban. They suggested that the stridency of the FDA—not the toxicity of residues or hormones—was the real problem.[179] But out of sixteen hundred letters the agency received, consumers supported the recall twenty to one. As a letter from one housewife explained, "I think that contamination of the cranberry crop is like the quip—no such thing as a little pregnant."[180]

As the early 1960s brought more headlines intimating the perils of the modern chemical age, the cranberry recall came to be seen as one of many incidents that portended an uncertain if not ominous future. Radioactive strontium-90 began to show up in milk and then in babies' teeth after nuclear tests. In 1962, FDA researcher Frances Kelsey just barely prevented the U.S. marketing of thalidomide, a popular tranquilizer in Europe and Canada that had caused gross fetal deformities when taken by mothers early in pregnancy.[181] And shortly thereafter, the *New Yorker* began to publish the shocking articles about the prevalence of pesticides in the environment that would become Rachel Carson's groundbreaking book *Silent Spring*. As the press tracked these stories in newspapers and on TV, it became more apparent that scientists with different expertise and different roles had conflicting opinions about the risks and safety of substances such as pesticide residues, food additives, and hormones, and the expectation of a singular, uncontested expert knowledge began to shatter. The food industry's promises of safety started to look more clearly like self-serving platitudes and began to kindle a popular perception that consumers of foods were powerless to protect themselves from invisible toxins in this chemical age.[182]

The strategy that the food industry had taken—what it considered to be a rather chivalrous bearing of the consumers' "burden" of knowing— had for decades insulated it from public scrutiny. But now this strategy was beginning to backfire. Food industry leaders had counted on the public to unquestioningly follow their lead down the plentiful aisles of modern supermarkets, to fill carts with winter tomatoes, plump chickens, TV dinners, and Velveeta, but they hadn't anticipated just how unsettling it could be for some shoppers to not know what was in their foods—especially as intimations of troubling contaminants become apparent.

Through the decades of the '50s and '60s, millions of consumers purchased, cooked, and ate thousands of new food products that turned up on supermarket shelves, but for all the convenience and apparently growing choices, by the late 1960s, many would end up feeling uneasy.

Shoppers had been relieved of the burden of knowing in the way that Christine Frederick had advocated at the outset of the supermarket era, but they had unwittingly taken on new "burdens." Although it was not reported in the popular press, in the mid-1960s, the mean storage level of DDT and its breakdown product DDE in body fat of Americans was measured at 12.6 parts per million, and scientists determined that people worldwide carried these substances in their blood on a regular basis.[183] The FDA would later report that pesticide residues in table-ready American foods peaked in the '60s and early '70s.[184] In 2003—even after DDT had been banned for over thirty years in the United States—a

U.S. Centers for Disease Control study would reveal that 99 percent of Americans still carried what has now come to be called a "body burden" of DDT and DDE in their tissues.[185]

The covenant of ignorance had shielded shoppers from knowing unsavory details about their foods; it also shielded food producers from public scrutiny. In the widening space between shopping cart and factory farm, new technologies and industrial approaches to food and farming had taken hold. But in the same space, new ideas for reform, reconfiguration, and responsibility had also begun to take root and grow.

CHAPTER 8

Kitchen Countertrends

In the late 1960s, a new Stop & Shop supermarket was constructed on the site of the "town farm" where my grandfather, as a boy in the 1920s, had walked with pail in hand to buy milk for his family. The grassy expanse of pasture that had managed to persist at the edge of the small industrial city of Naugatuck, Connecticut—known best for its rubber factories and Naugahide—was paved over with a large asphalt parking lot to accommodate shoppers and twenty thousand square feet of aisles and shelves.[1] This was the supermarket where my grandmother took me shopping for groceries when I was a child.

The replacement of the farm with that supermarket was emblematic of the grand transformation of the food system that had been taking place over the course of eight decades. It reflected enormous changes in how society regarded land; in the early 1960s, new suburbs overtook farms as still more people came to see land as more valuable for home-sites than for its ability to supply milk, meat, eggs, fruit, or vegetables. It reflected changes in how people spent time, with more and more—including growing numbers of women—working for wages and salaries in urban and suburban communities. It reflected myriad innovations in food and farm technology and the opening of interstate highways that made it easier and cheaper for more foods to travel by refrigerated trucks from farms in temperate latitudes, not only to the largest cities but to smaller towns as well. And the replacement of the farm with a super-market also reflected, as we've seen, an enormous change in the very experience of how we could know our foods. On the same site where my grandfather found grazing cows and filled his pail, I ferreted out my favorite Fruit Loops cereal with the colorful Toucan Sam on its box and bought milk in an unmemorable paperboard carton.

Yet even as supermarkets flourished in the early '60s, it was becoming apparent to a small but growing number of people that leaving the matter of knowing foods solely to experts and admen was a flawed strategy. Several lines of concern emerged from different groups and for a range of reasons—all, however, derived from a brooding sense that foods were being tampered with behind the scenes, largely for the expedience and profit of businesses that supplied them.

By the mid-1950s, some epicurean critics had begun to complain about the deteriorating taste of foods. In 1954 *Atlantic* writer Philip Wylie lamented that "science had spoiled" his supper. In particular, he critiqued the tendency of agricultural researchers to develop "'improved' strains of things for every purpose but eating." Of new peas bred to ripen all at once to expedite mechanical picking, Wylie asked, "What matter if such peas taste like boiled paper wads?"[2] Even Poppy Cannon, who despite her affinity for convenience cooking aspired to the gourmet set, lamented the "dreadful" taste of tomatoes, which were picked green and then ripened with the use of ethylene gas—a by-product of oil refineries.[3] Even in season, supermarket tomatoes tasted poor because wholesalers preferred to do business with large-scale, year-round suppliers rather than with the few remaining local growers whose farms hadn't yet been supplanted by expanding suburbs.[4]

Countering the mediocrity of America's heavily promoted, pre-made food cuisine and the insipid flavors of foods bred to industrial shipping standards, a gourmet food movement arose that looked to the renowned haute cuisine of France for inspiration. Through the late 1950s and early 1960s, a torrent of cookbooks flooded the market, and subscriptions to the magazine *Gourmet* rose 300 percent as the affluent and upwardly mobile took new interest in entertaining dinner guests with modish recipes from Europe.[5] In its American form, "gourmet" cuisine often featured menus with rich, expensive—if not pretentious—ingredients, such as pâté, foie gras, caviar, and filet mignon. The most successful

proponent of such cooking was Julia Child. Child had become enam-
ored with French food when she lived in postwar Paris with her diplomat
husband and decided to study at the Cordon Bleu cooking school.
Cooking did not come easily to her, but she turned this limitation into an
asset, writing a bestseller, *Mastering the Art of French Cooking*, which
made kitchen techniques accessible and appealing to American cooks of
all aptitudes. Child's influence increased when in 1963 she became host
of the public television cooking program *The French Chef*, which
became enormously popular.[6]

Overturning the widely promoted notion that cooking from scratch
was drudgery, Child, along with a cadre of other chefs and cookbook
authors, led America's aspiring home cooks to discover the "joy of cooking."[7] Focusing on mastery of skills, such as soufflé and omelet preparation, and on the cultural context of ingredients, such as which wine from
which region of France went best with which dish, the gourmet set promoted a knowledge of cookery that elevated the prestige of the cook.
However, as they whipped up rich sauces with whisks in copper bowls,
they raised no question that *petits pois à la Française* and *Salmon Archi-
duc* could be adequately replicated using frozen peas and canned salmon
found in American supermarkets.[8]

Beyond the matter of taste, some people disliked the perceived homogeneity of pre-made foods, reflecting a broader dissatisfaction with
suburban life captured by contemporary books such as David Riesman's
Lonely Crowd, William Whyte's *Organization Man*, and, then, Betty Frie-
dan's *Feminine Mystique*. By 1964, consumer motivation researcher
Ernest Dichter—the one who'd counseled General Mills to leave homemakers an egg to add—warned the food industry that shoppers "had
developed a strong tendency to seek something other than a mass product for millions of identical customers."[9] The appeal of uniformity had
met its limit; Americans didn't like to feel that they were indistinguish-
able mouths feeding at the end of some Orwellian food-dispensing
machine. Dichter suggested that food companies respond to shoppers'
new "psychological demand" with "distinctive packages and unusual
flavors that will convince buyers they have found something beyond
run-of-the-mill fare."[10]

Such marketing tactics may have satisfied many shoppers who were buying more and more mass-produced foods, but by the mid-1960s, another rising group was eschewing modern foods on deep ideological grounds. The young adults who embraced the 1960s counterculture movement regarded the homogeneity of manufactured foods and the rise of additive and pesticide use as political and ecological matters. In their rebellion against the materialism of the country's dominant culture, the counterculture rebelled against industrially produced foods, too. Cheap, simple, and natural became their credo; Frances Moore Lappé's *Diet for a Small Planet* became their lodestar; and beans, brown rice, and granola became their manna.

With the counterculture, the ideal of the natural, which had been excised from the food scene for decades, came back in force as a standard for thinking about what we eat. Warren Belasco, who has written insightfully about this chapter of food history in *Appetite for Change*, described how "natural" encompassed many of the counterculture's oppositional ideas: wholeness in contrast to tampering, authenticity in contrast to artificiality, purity in contrast to poison, variation in contrast to uniformity, and preindustrial in contrast to modern. Inverting notions of spoilage, counterculture eaters even rejected the ideal of sterility that the food industry had so painstakingly attached to processed foods. Instead, they embraced the microbes that made the nuanced flavors and textures of yogurt, miso, and tempeh, and the strong cheeses that stood in sharp contrast with pasteurized, plastic-wrapped, processed-cheese products.[11]

Much as it had for urban eaters at the turn of the twentieth century, the ideal of the "natural" implied a whole range of metaphoric meaning —all of it centering on a yearning for something better that seemed to be kept out of reach by a corrupt industrial food system. Yet the counterculture concept of "natural" also drew heavily from the emerging science of ecology. With its focus on the interconnectedness of life, ecology offered apt metaphors that led counterculturists to question the way that eating foods contaminated with toxins could "violate" the "inner ecology" of the human body.[12]

Awareness of ecological principles went beyond metaphor to provoke concern about the ways that industrial methods of food production could harm the environment. In the wake of *Silent Spring*'s 1962 publication, newspapers through the '60s and early '70s carried hundreds of stories confirming that DDT and other pesticides caused fish kills; polluted rivers, estuaries, and groundwater; impaired reproduction of eagles, seabirds, and songbirds; and increasingly showed up in foods and in the tissues, blood, and milk of human bodies.[13]

To evade the dubious juggernaut of processed and pesticide-laden products that lined supermarket shelves, some counterculturists took it upon themselves to procure the more natural foods they desired. A small but dedicated group headed "back to the land" to farm, joining a small but stalwart group of traditional farmers who'd all along shunned industrial methods and their expensive chemical inputs.

Concern about the industrial approach to agriculture can be traced back to the nineteenth century, when farmers worried about "mining" the fertility of their own soil to feed distant city dwellers. Consideration for soil broadened in the wake of the Dust Bowl disaster with the work of the U.S. Soil Conservation Service, which advocated soil conservation measures on erosion-prone farms.[14] Also in the 1930s, Sir Albert Howard, an Englishman considered by many to be the father of organic farming, promoted use of farm-derived composts and healthy humus. He scorned the commercially produced synthetic nitrogen fertilizers that had become increasingly available after World War I, regarding them as expensive for farmers and deleterious to soil.[15] Howard's writings inspired Jerome Rodale, who began experimenting with organic methods on his Pennsylvania farm in the 1940s. Rodale's research would become the basis for the family magazine, *Organic Gardening and Farming,* which provided technical information for back-to-the-land farmers of the 1960s and 1970s.[16]

Following a mix of ecological, agrarian ideals that put soil health first and political ideals that prioritized self-sufficiency and independence from industrial-capitalist dominion, "back-to-the-landers" formed more than thirty-five hundred farm-based utopian communes between 1965 and 1970, and still others started farming as yeoman smallholders.[17] Sobering failures befell many of the would-be farmers who tried to grow food with no experience to draw on.[18] But others gradually developed skills and then distribution networks to sell their organically grown cantaloupes, tomatoes, and string beans to others who sought foods without pesticides. Those farmers who succeeded built the foundation for a significant legacy — an alternative organic agriculture.

In the meantime, concerns that had been quietly raised in the inner circles of business and government by the Delaney hearings of the 1950s sailed into the open with the questioning spirit of the 1960s when another small but influential group took on the industrial food system in the halls of the nation's Capitol. Following in the tradition of Harvey Wiley and Frederick Schlink, a new generation of consumer advocates worked through the 1960s and into the 1970s. Ralph Nader, who'd won regard for exposing the poor safety record of the Chevy Corvair, moved on to the deceptive transformation of hot dogs. He found that new additives had camouflaged a 33 percent increase in frankfurters' fat content, a trend that cut costs for manufacturers but robbed unwitting eaters of protein and added inches to their midriffs to boot.[19] And hot dogs were just one of many types of processed foods that seemed to be changing in ways unknown to consumers.

In the late 1960s, Nader organized groups of students to study, document, and publicize how industry had co-opted federal regulatory agencies at the public's expense. In 1970, his study group published *The Chemical Feast,* a trenchant indictment of the FDA's handling of additives and pesticide residues. The book documented several instances in which regulators had concealed concerns about the safety of additives from consumers, despite mounting evidence about hazards.[20]

In 1971, Nader's "Raiders" were joined by microbiologist Michael Jacobson, who started the Center for Science in the Public Interest, a group that would become instrumental in advocating for consumers' right to know about their foods. The new consumerist critics brought economic, scientific, and legal analysis to bear. They questioned the public health effects of steadily increasing amounts of additives, fat, salt, and sugar in processed foods, and of hormones used in meat production. They pushed for accurate, nutrition-based labeling and argued against television advertising that targeted young children.[21]

Concurrent with consumer advocates' work, stories about hidden troubles of the food system continued to surface in the news through the early '70s. A spate of books, all distributed by major publishers, exposed the power of big business over what Americans ate, including Jim Hightower's *Eat Your Heart Out: How Food Profiteers Victimize the Consumer* (1975) and a best-selling exposé by former FDA scientist Jacqueline Verrett, *Eating May Be Hazardous to Your Health* (1974). The message of the books was furthered by television documentaries, such as one aired on ABC in 1973 that revealed arsenic was used to promote chicken growth in Alabama's vertically integrated chicken farms.[22]

Under increasing public scrutiny and political pressure, and with the benefit of advances in analytic science that permitted detection of carcinogenic ingredients at lower levels, the FDA was compelled to "go public" on a number of additives already in wide use. In 1969, the FDA had banned MSG in baby foods after tests indicated probable brain damage in baby animals. Then the agency issued a warning about cyclamates after two studies found that the artificial sweeteners caused cancer in laboratory animals. Both substances had been on the GRAS (Generally Regarded As Safe) list of ingredients.[23] In the early 1970s, the FDA banned several food colorings and issued warnings about mercury in canned tuna and diethylstilbestrol (DES), a growth hormone still used widely in beef production.[24] In addition, the General Accounting Office (GAO) issued several reports about the disturbing and unsanitary conditions in factory farms that produced the nation's poultry and about the residues of antibiotics and pesticides that ended up in chicken meat, even as it was served on the table.[25]

Each warning produced a barrage of news coverage that further revealed the sharply divergent views of experts in government and in industry. Since most consumers had grown accustomed to trusting scientific experts to protect the food supply, seeing the experts so thoroughly embroiled created an overall impression of confusion and distrust, leading many to believe that "everything caused cancer."[26] Consumers were left to judge the merits of conflicting arguments themselves. Surveys in the late 1970s found that shoppers ranked pesticide residues and additives as their top two food concerns, and that, as a

8.1. *By the 1980s, despite the convenience and year-round variety afforded by the modern food system, many consumers felt that they faced poor choices at the supermarket.*

result, nearly 30 percent had stopped purchasing or cut back on some food items. In one poll, consumers ranked food additives second only to cigarettes in their oncogenicity but then conceded they didn't personally have enough information to decide about cancer risks.[27]

While the food production and distribution system had evolved to match an industrial model, with consumers leaving decisions to producers, more and more news stories accumulated to suggest that this way of divvying up the burden of knowing wasn't necessarily serving the public interest. Beyond the exposés about water pollution and pesticide spills, the energy crisis of the '70s — with its attendant spike in food costs — made it apparent the modern food system was completely dependent on petroleum in the form of synthetic fertilizers, pesticides, and tractor fuel, in addition to energy required for processing and transport. Scientists calculated that the modern food system — for all its apparent efficiency and convenience—actually required between five and ten calories of fossil fuel to produce one calorie of nutritional energy.[28]

Even as serious concerns were raised and not addressed, most consumers had little choice but to continue their grocery shopping as usual. What could an individual shopper do about the fact that pesticides killed fish, that chickens were jammed into cages, or that agriculture used too much oil? Through the 1950s most American shoppers' lack of awareness about their foods may have been characterized by a naïve "I don't know," but by the mid-1970s, with more prevalent news of toxic pesticide residues and repugnant animal factories, it had become an anxious and resigned "I don't *want* to know."

While the majority of shoppers responded with indifference or steely denial, for some, the press of bad news made the simple day-to-day work of grocery shopping for a family more fraught and the issues surrounding food production ever more urgent. These shoppers looked for more secure footholds from which to make decisions about their foods.

The Persistence of the Natural

As consumers struggled to make sense of the confusion regarding the risks of additives and pesticide residues, the appeal of the natural ideal expanded beyond the ranks of the counterculture. Astute advertisers wasted no time picking up on consumers' disquiet and crafted new pitches that offered those who were concerned about chemicals in foods a soothing safe haven in new products. Following the lead of small companies that supplied popular food cooperatives, some large food corporations began to label and advertise a number of their products as "additive-free," and "all-natural."[29] In the wake of Earth Day, for example, Dannon in the early '70s offered an ad for its yogurt designed to appeal specifically to young environmentally inclined shoppers. "Read the fine print on the back of some yogurt packages," it instructed. "You may find some strange contents. Chemicals with unpronounceable names. Artificial flavoring. Artificial sweeteners. Things nature never intended for your ecology."[30] Making a direct parallel between pollution of an eater's "internal environment" and pollution of the broader natural environment, the Dannon ad reflected the potent conflation of the cultural idea of the natural—natural as pure and unprocessed—with the physical natural environment—nature as the body and also as natural rivers and landscapes, which were increasingly polluted by human industry.

Even while food industry advertisers found "natural" to be a successful pitch in the early '70s, nothing rankled food industry technologists more than this popular cultural ideal, which they regarded as old-fashioned, scientifically indefensible, and untrustworthy.[31] Since Harvey Wiley's indictment of benzoate, they'd had to defend against this potent but ambiguous abstraction. To the food scientists' way of thinking, everything—including pesticides and additives—was natural because everything in the universe was comprised of atoms listed on the periodic table. As such, everything was also made up of chemicals. To underscore their point, food technologists were fond of spouting a list of arcane-sounding chemicals and then revealing that the abstruse lingo was simply the scientific name for some common substance that most people would consider perfectly "natural," such as milk, sugar, or apple juice. Another favorite rhetorical slam dunk was to point out that all educated people knew "organic" meant any substance containing carbon atoms—as in "organic chemistry"—and had nothing to do with pesticides or soil health as back-to-the-land farmers would have it.[32]

However, the food technologists' semantic defense offended common sense. As Warren Belasco explained, "If everything was natural, then nothing was artificial—and this just did not seem right to those who, while perhaps rusty in high school chemistry, felt sure that only *some* things were natural, and moreover, that some chemicals *were* dangerous."[33] Yet the serious issues of who should control which chemicals and for whose benefit and at what costs remained muddied as an increasingly oppositional discourse centered on refuting the natural ideal—the notion that "natural" meant better.[34]

Though food industry defenders tried to shun the cultural meanings of "natural," they often slipped into the same inconsistencies they accused their ideological opponents of. When they claimed that all chemicals were natural, they couldn't resist adding that synthetically produced chemicals were superior to their natural counterparts.[35]

Moreover, they often drew upon oppositional historic narratives to argue that nature was not a source of bounty, as the counterculture would have it, but rather a meager provider and a place of starvation — not a source of pure foods, but rather of foods filled with dangerous microbes and toxins. By their account, nature was a realm of intense competition. Only with cutting-edge technology could humankind stay on top.[36]

In response to the unexpected force of their critics, food and agriculture industry leaders adopted a siege mentality. Flatly asserting the safety of all properly used pesticides and additives, they tried to push things back to how they were in the 1950s, when industry enjoyed uncontested authority and American shoppers could more easily be wowed by new, high-tech food products. They called on top experts in government agencies (FDA and USDA) and academia (often in university departments funded by industry) to issue statements about the safety of the food system, and then spread their message by supplying magazines, newspapers, and classroom teachers with a flurry of materials designed to diffuse the counterculture and consumerist critiques.[37]

Echoing marketers' past efforts to constrict concern about food solely to the arena of personal experience, they tried to focus public attention on the small risk that minute amounts of additives, hormones, and pesticide residues posed to individual consumers, thereby deflecting attention from broader concerns about cumulative effects, the environment, and the health of farmworkers (whose onerous working conditions had been widely publicized by Cesar Chavez in the late '60s and early '70s).[38] By construing risks so narrowly, the corporate spokesmen built a case that made risks seem trivial.

Another of their chief strategies was to disparage those who raised questions, calling them "communists," "quacks," and "faddists" to lump them together with individuals of an earlier time who'd hawked untested drugs and advocated oddball diets. Claiming high moral ground, industry leaders dismissed the questioners as self-centered whiners complaining about miniscule amounts of pesticide residues when millions of people in the world suffered on the verge of starvation.[39] Undeterred by American agriculture's chronic overproduction that had driven thousands of farmers out of business nor by Lappé's arguments that food distribution constraints — not supply — were the root cause of world hunger, they advanced their project of using more chemical technology to grow, process, and export more and more food as the only ethical course.[40] In regard to alternative approaches to agriculture, they dismissed organic farming as "doing nothing" rather than as careful labor-intensive attention to a diverse array of crops. This highly charged all-or-nothing discourse worked its way to the highest levels of government when, in 1971, Richard Nixon's secretary of agriculture Earl Butz proclaimed, "Before we go back to organic agriculture in this country, somebody must decide which 50 million Americans we are going to let starve."[41] Butz's hyperbolic statement was widely repeated in the press and must have given pause to many who might have wondered about the concerns critics raised.

However, food and agriculture industry defenders — in their frustration at the ahistoric view of younger eaters who were apparently ignorant about the malnutrition, food poisoning, and onerous housework that their forebears had proudly vanquished — failed to grasp the legitimacy and importance of new questions now being raised by large-scale agricultural operations. In narrowly focusing their enmity on the cultural idea of the natural, they turned a blind eye to the ecological consequences of treating land as a factory and the biology of the human body as separate from the biology of the rest of the earth.

Despite their greater financial resources and political acumen, food industry defenders watched with impatient frustration as the ideal of the "natural" continued to grow in popularity with consumers, paradoxically aided and abetted by the industry's own marketing departments, which were more attuned to what consumers wanted.[42] In 1974, an industry survey revealed that 42 percent of shoppers agreed that "natural foods are better"; by 1978, the number had climbed to 62 percent.[43]

In response to food industry concerns that additive-free, natural products might prompt shoppers to question the safety of standard brand-name foods on supermarket shelves, the Federal Trade Commission (FTC) in 1974 considered banning use of the term "natural" in marketing altogether. According to the FTC, consumers were unable to understand what the term actually meant.[44] Indeed, "natural" bore no relation to pesticide residues and seemed instead to refer primarily to a lack of additives and the number of steps involved in food processing, attributes that consumers weren't particularly adept at discerning.[45]

Despite confusion about what the word actually meant, one reason that "natural" became so popular was precisely because it seemed to offer individuals a straightforward means for understanding increasingly abstruse food choices. While food industry defenders took great pains to explain that additives, hormones, antibiotics, and pesticide residues in parts per million posed risks that were very small to individual consumers and that studies conducted on rats didn't necessarily apply to human health, most shoppers, of course, weren't prepared to evaluate such details after decades of being encouraged to ignore matters of food production. In making quick decisions at the supermarket, many were more inclined to take a commonsense approach: why buy a highly processed food with additives that might or might not be dangerous if there was an alternative labeled "natural" sitting beside it on the shelf? A shopper didn't really need to know more.

Ultimately, the FTC opted not to ban the term "natural," and by the end of the 1970s, more than one-third of shoppers reported buying products labeled as "natural" on a routine basis. But the prevalent use of the word in marketing, of course, did not mean that the food industry was responding substantively to consumer concerns about pesticides or overprocessed foods.[46]

In 1980, *Consumer Reports,* the popular publication of Consumers Union, revealed ways that food promoters played on shoppers' desires with suggestive but disingenuous labeling. Boxes of Life Cinnamon Flavor High-Protein Cereal boasted the word "nature" four times and "natural" once, but the ingredients listed included preservatives and artificial color. The "natural" of Pillsbury's "Natural Chocolate Flavored Chocolate Chip Cookies" referred only to the "chocolate-flavored" and not to the cookies themselves, which contained additives and other artificial flavorings. Quaker's "100% natural" cereal had no preservatives but contained 24 percent sugar. Anheuser-Busch's "Natural" Light Beer had many additives.[47] Clearly, foods labeled "natural" were not necessarily more healthful.

That same year, the FTC came up with standards that more specifically defined "natural" as "minimally processed," but they were never adopted owing to political interventions.[48] Moreover, the commission rarely policed deceptive labels and ads during the Reagan era.[49] In 1984, when Kraft used "natural" to describe the archetypal processed food Velveeta as "a blend of natural cheeses," Michael Jacobson's *Nutrition Action* newsletter concluded that "natural" had become utterly "meaningless."[50]

The potent cultural ideal of "natural" had been appropriated by corporate food marketers, but the reality that what we eat is linked to the broader natural world was about to become more discernible in new and far-reaching ways.

Burgers and Rain Forests

In the mid-1980s, scientists and environmentalists identified deforestation in tropical latitudes as a crucial problem. Rain forests housed nearly 50 percent of the world's living species, making them among the richest biological systems on Earth. Moreover, scientists were coming to understand how rain forests helped to moderate global climate by locking up a significant amount of carbon. Yet these valuable forests were being leveled at the alarming rate of fifty to a hundred acres per minute, primarily to create more rangeland to produce beef for export.[51] Even worse, without replenishment from falling leaves and moisture supplied by the living forest, the newly deforested lands dried out, eroded, and became infertile in only a few years' time. Then, still more rain forests were slashed and burned to make way for more cattle.

Environmentalists seeking a way to slow this destructive, climate-altering cycle of deforestation recognized that the push for more grazing land in Latin America was driven in large part by U.S. eaters' ravenous appetite for hamburgers. Fast-food restaurants had skyrocketed in popularity through the '60s and '70s, offering families a cheap, convenient, and kid-friendly alternative to cooking. By 1980s, McDonald's alone was serving five billion burgers per year.[52] The only way to change the economics of deforestation, activists realized, was to address the root cause of high hamburger demand: they had to enlist consumers' help and make them see that modest daily decisions to buy a cheap burger were ultimately connected to clear-cutting rain forests in Costa Rica.

In 1986, rainforest activists launched a highly publicized effort to boycott the fast-food emporium Burger King.[53] They staged colorful protests, with giant papier-mâché cows being fed rainforest leaves and defecating Styrofoam Whoppers, and they stirred thousands of people to write letters to the company's CEO. Sales dropped by a whopping 12 percent. According to Rainforest Action Network president Randall Hayes, "It took 18 months of lunchtime demos outside Burger Kings around the country before the company cancelled a $35 million contract for rainforest beef with Costa Rica."[54]

The Burger King boycott was successful, compelling other major fast-food restaurants to develop policies for purchasing their beef from sources that did not rely on cutover rain forest for pasture. It also triggered much broader public consciousness about the plight of rain forests and about the impacts of Northern Hemisphere inhabitants' consumption (of not only beef but also coffee and bananas) on people and environments of the Southern Hemisphere, instilling new awareness about the connection between eating and place.[55] In addition, the boycott gave environmentalists a powerful tool to tackle another controversial ecological problem resulting from food production.

In the early 1980s, it had become apparent that commercial tuna fishing was inadvertently killing thousands and thousands of dolphins, mammals known for their high degree of sentience. Both species were being trapped in fishers' nets, but tuna could also be caught using special nets that allowed for the release of trapped dolphins. Though political leaders were trying to make headway with regulatory efforts to require the special nets, they were stalled by the intricacies of international politics. Most notably, Mexico balked at giving dolphins protection because of higher costs that might accrue for Mexican fishers.[56] American environmentalists joined Humane Society activists in starting a boycott campaign to target the Heinz Corporation, which from its roots advocating pure foods had grown into an enormous conglomerate selling hundreds of popular products, including Star-Kist brand canned tuna with its well-known mascot, Charlie — the slovenly but loveable cartoon tuna who never managed to meet Star-Kist quality standards.[57]

By the late '80s, the boycott had spread, with schoolchildren writing letters, refusing to eat tuna, and, in some high schools, even organizing cafeteria tuna bans.[58] These efforts were complemented by an aggressive public-interest advertising campaign featuring full-page ads in major newspapers.[59] Internal marketing studies indicated that about one-half of consumers were willing to pay a little more to protect dolphins.[60] No longer able to ignore the issue, in 1990, Heinz announced a policy to buy tuna only from fishers who used methods that reduced dolphin mortality. Their decision, in turn, triggered all of the other major tuna processors to do the same in order to compete with Heinz.[61]

The boycotts made it clear that consumers could exercise influence. And if *not* buying a certain product could make a difference, it was only a small step to realize that choosing to *buy* certain types of products might also make a difference.

A Purposeful Palate

Through the 1960s, '70s, and '80s, the cultural gulfs between gourmets, back-to-the land organic farmers, co-op shoppers, consumer activists, and environmentalists remained too great for many to recognize the common questioning of the modern food industry that all groups engaged in for different reasons of taste, class, ideology, health, ecology, and public safety. But in the retrospect of history, we can see the genius of the crowd, with each of the different groups bringing various truths to bear and exerting a chaotic but indisputable influence. While politics, science, and ethics all cast their light, ultimately it would be the delicious alchemy of cooking that would give credence to a new approach.

No one individual better embodies how several of the countertrends began to converge than Alice Waters. Like Julia Child, Waters had spent time in France as a student and had fallen in love with the tongue-zapping flavors of fresh foods. But coming of age as a Berkeley student in the 1960s, she also identified with the inspired ideals of the counterculture — though not its dull brown-rice-and-beans fare. Like the gourmets, Waters appreciated the pleasures of cooking and eating well, but she knew the tired foods that showed up in American supermarkets simply could not compare with the fresh-picked ingredients available to cooks at markets in Europe, where small-scale truck farms persisted. By Waters's account, "No cook, however creative and capable, [could] produce a dish of a quality any higher than that of the raw ingredients."[62] Rather than make do, Waters attempted to replicate the style of cooking she'd learned about in France. Soon her passion for creating savory meals for her radical friends evolved into opening a restaurant in Berkeley in 1971—Chez Panisse, named for a fictional Marseilles fisherman who exemplified savoir vivre.

Waters asked friends to grow herbs and sent kitchen staff to forage for fresh ingredients. At first, they bartered with local vegetable gardeners, picked watercress from streams, gathered fennel from roadsides and blackberries from beside railroad tracks. The seasonal ingredients they brought back sparked talented Chez Panisse chefs to cook creative meals in the culinary tradition of the French countryside. Before long, Waters established a network of small-scale growers who could supply high-quality ingredients to her restaurant, which soon developed a superb reputation.[63]

Within a few years, Waters's restaurant shifted emphasis from French-inspired fare to menus showcasing fresh ingredients of northern California, including native wines. California cuisine, which in loose terms meant lightly cooked fresh foods with little garnishment, grew in popularity through the late 1970s and early 1980s as fern-clad restaurants nationwide began to feature spinach salads, avocados, artichokes, and grilled meats. The fresher, lighter fare appealed to taste buds and also to the growing health consciousness of Americans struggling to shed extra pounds gained in an age of abundant fast and processed foods.[64]

While Waters's use of fresh ingredients inspired imitation nationwide, her goals at Chez Panisse grew more refined. Her concept of fresh went beyond the postindustrial, nothing canned, nothing frozen, and no preservatives, to mean—quite literally—just-picked.[65] To promote her culinary approach more broadly, Waters forged relationships between farmers and other chefs throughout northern California to create a regional supply network. Through her dealings with farmers, she gradually developed an appreciation for organically raised foodstuffs, including eggs and meats. By the mid-1980s, Waters penchant for excellent-quality fresh and seasonal vegetables had grown into a broader awareness that simple choices made in her kitchen could positively influence not only the dining experience and well-being of her patrons but also what happened on farms and their environs throughout the region. In 1993, when Waters entertained President Bill Clinton at Chez Panisse, she'd managed to elevate the vision of relinking farms and tables to the headiest circles.[66]

The trajectory of Waters's career — from maverick to trendsetter — reveals her remarkable achievement in linking a sophisticated, appealing approach to food with the hands-in-the-dirt social activism needed to supply it. Her success was also a measure of the hard work and diligence of many other people — farmers, entrepreneurs, chefs, activists, and consumers — whose less-recognized efforts around the country all began to coalesce in the 1990s to exert an unexpected counterinfluence on the industrial food system.

Turning Attention Back to Farms

While the mainstream food industry had long since adopted the marketing strategy of diverting consumers' attention away from the realm of food production, organic farmers and an emerging band of organic product entrepreneurs took the opposite tack. By focusing attention back onto the places and particular methods of food production, they sought to differentiate their products, and in the 1990s their strategy began to pay off.

Since the early 1970s, small-scale farmers in California and in pockets elsewhere had been at work advancing and refining their organic methods. Recognizing early on the need to distinguish their organically grown foods, farmers had established independent certification agencies in several states to enforce common standards.[67] They'd worked to create outlets for their organic produce by organizing farmers' markets and by linking up with urban restaurants and food cooperatives.

"Co-ops" had become common in many cities and college towns

during the early 1970s, with members pooling funds to buy direct from wholesalers and organic farms. By 1979, five to ten thousand of these organizations — many with their own stores — had become established nationwide, grossing more than $500 million per year.[68]

The profitable co-op market attracted "hip entrepreneurs" who developed food products designed to appeal to shoppers seeking less-processed or organically grown foods (the same broad cultural trends that made convenience foods more desirable in the '60s and '70s also made the promise of organic convenience foods more desirable as well).[69] As hip food companies guaranteed purchase of more organic ingredients for their products, including canned tomatoes, soy milk, and tofu, they encouraged more farmers to commit to organic cultivation. In the late 1980s, organic acreage in California quadrupled in just two years.[70]

By the early 1990s, organic food had become more desirable to consumers, particularly on the West Coast, for its dual association with both healthfulness and good taste. Some organic farms grew to the scale hitherto occupied only by industrial producers. For example, the popularity of specialty lettuce mixes propelled one small farm, started by a couple of UC–Santa Cruz grads in 1984, to become Earthbound Farms, a large firm that grows organic lettuces and other vegetables on twenty-five thousand acres throughout California. In the mid-1990s, the company gained nationwide placement for its bagged lettuces in mainstream supermarkets such as Costco and Albertsons.[71] In addition, new types of chain specialty stores, such as Whole Foods and Wild Oats, sprouted up in more and more cities nationwide, catering to both epicurean and health-conscious shoppers. With rising demand for organic foods, firms that specialized in wholesaling and distributing these products took on a larger role in developing an organic food industry. Through the 1990s, organic foods became the fastest-growing sector in the entire food industry, swelling 20 percent per year.[72]

The popularity of organic foods was nurtured along by some key social trends as well as recurrent bad news about the industrial food system, which made the organic alternative look more and more attractive. Through the 1980s, for example, public awareness of connections between diet and health had increased as foods high in sodium, fat, and cholesterol were implicated in boosting blood pressure, weight gain, heart disease, strokes, and diabetes. Risk of cardiac disease from a poor diet, it turned out, was far clearer than risk of cancer from additives and pesticide residues, and so attention to diet became the mainstay of new "lifestyle" advice aimed at improving public health. The new dietary recommendations to cut salt and fat reflected new medical understanding but also fit the antiregulatory temper of the Reagan era, turning the focus away from corporate accountability and government oversight and instead directing it toward individual responsibility.[73] As the hopeful idea that individuals could exert greater control over their personal health by getting more exercise and eating the right kinds of foods gained credence, more shoppers looked for products labeled "low sodium" and "lite," which in the '80s supplanted the previously popular "natural" and "additive-free."[74]

With the link between diet and health more firmly established, however, more people became alert to issues of toxins in foods, which — after a mid-1980s hiatus — began to appear frequently in the news again with the Alar scare in 1989. Although residue from this foliar spray widely used in apple production did not itself cause cancer, after exposed to heat in processing, one of its metabolites was found to induce malignant tumors in laboratory animals. These metabolites were concentrated in processed foods, such as applesauce and juice. When the television program *60 Minutes* reported on the federal government's nearly decade-long delay in taking action, it sparked a dramatic controversy that rekindled concern about the lack of regulatory oversight regarding agricultural chemicals and propelled a host of new consumers toward organic foods.[75]

Following that, in the early '90s, a National Academy of Sciences report confirmed that pesticide residues on foods posed a greater threat to children than had been previously understood. Regulatory tolerance levels were typically rationalized from the perspective of adult bodies and dietary patterns. However, children's smaller and still-growing bodies were much more vulnerable to harm from toxins, and children tended to eat a far narrower range of foods, including some specifically known to carry residues, which further increased susceptibility.[76]

In addition, growing knowledge about the fate of pesticides in the environment affirmed that these chemicals were polluting surface and groundwater—and therefore drinking water—on a scale that had not yet been realized. In 1995, a water quality study estimated that fourteen million Americans were drinking water contaminated by herbicides that had migrated from farm fields to surface and groundwater supplies.[77] This was an exposure pathway that hadn't been accounted for in regulating pesticides.

Surprisingly, despite high public concern about the human health risks associated with pesticide exposure, very few studies examined the issue, owing to the scientific impossibility of isolating factors of cause and effect in individuals exposed to many chemicals through many pathways through an entire lifetime. However, some effects of pesticides on human health were becoming better known, in part as a result of epidemiological studies of farmworkers. Encountering pesticides in their work through physical contact and inhalation and at home through contaminated drinking water and food residues, the nation's roughly two million farmworkers faced a greater risk of pesticide exposure than any other segment of the population. According to 1992 government estimates, farmworkers suffered up to three hundred thousand acute illnesses and injuries from pesticide poisoning each year, and though limited data were available, studies also showed a disturbing pattern of evidence regarding long-term effects of pesticide exposure.[78] Farmworkers experienced greater incidence of multiple myeloma and cancers of the mouth, pharynx, lung, liver, stomach, prostate, and testis.[79] Children of farmworkers also showed greater incidence of birth defects.[80] While government risk analysis had long focused primarily on carcinogenicity (as a legacy of the 1958 Delaney Clause), more evidence for other types of human health risks, including neurologic disorders, endocrine disruption, and decreased sperm counts, continued to mount in the '90s.[81]

Closer to home for most consumers, in 1993, milk produced by cows treated with the genetically engineered growth hormone rBGH (recombinant bovine growth hormone) came onto the market. The hormone was a boon to dairy producers because it boosted a cow's daily milk production by as much as 25 percent. Although the FDA reported that rBGH was not detectable in milk itself, many consumers who were aware of the change remained wary. Critics pointed to studies that showed rBGH produced higher levels of a naturally occurring protein that had been linked with breast cancer.[82] Because there was no way to know whether or not milk was derived from cows treated with the growth hormone, more consumers turned to buying organic milk, exercising what sociologist E. Melanie DuPuie has called a "Not In My Body" or NIMB response.[83] By the mid-1990s, organic milk sales grew to $30 million annually, contributing to the swelling popularity of organic foods.[84]

All these developments coincided with broader social trends of the generally prosperous '90s. After affluent, young urbanites encountered organic foods at high-end restaurants, they sought them out for use at home. Many of them were also new parents who had become particularly attuned to food safety issues regarding children. In addition, an upsurge of environmental awareness led more of these shoppers to consider their purchase of organic foods as a means of taking action in the face of industry and government heel-dragging regarding a whole suite of environmental and related social problems associated with agriculture.[85]

Then in 2000, unbeknownst to American shoppers, a preponderance of new genetically engineered foods rapidly flooded the marketplace. The ability to "engineer" genes was based on a revolution in genetic understanding that had been building since the 1950s. Unlike classical plant breeding, which relied on cross breeding and selection to foster development of desired traits in crops, genetic engineering took genes from one organism and physically inserted them into another— sometimes creating combinations as unexpected and controversial as a tomato with a flounder gene.

In the early '90s, the first genetically engineered (GE) food to hit the market had been a tomato with an extended shelf life. The GE tomato flopped but succeeded in establishing a precedent of minimal regulatory oversight for other genetically engineered crops being developed for broader diffusion, including herbicide-resistant corn, soybeans, and canola, along with a corn engineered to express genes from the bacterium *Bacillus thuringiensis*, which produced its own insecticide Bt.[86]

These GE crops were purportedly intended to decrease pesticide use, which had been rising for decades as pests developed greater resistance to the pesticides being applied to fields. But many questions remained unanswered about detrimental effects that the engineered crops' genes could have when broadcast uncontrollably into the environment via windblown pollen. For example, genes conferring herbicide resistance, if crossed with those of wild plants or weeds, could lead to development of "superweeds." And genes that incited production of Bt within plant tissues had the potential to spur more-resistant pests and to harm beneficial insects. Moreover, many critics found it hard to believe that crops designed specifically for use in conjunction with proprietary herbicides, such as Monsanto's Roundup, would actually reduce herbicide usage. With regard to human health, critics charged that genetic engineering could introduce unexpected allergens into foods and that antibiotic-resistant genes used in the genetic engineering process might induce antibiotic resistance in eaters, especially children.[87]

Nevertheless, more than sixty million acres of farmland in the United States were planted in GE corn and soybean crops by 1999. The following year, newspapers reported that more than two-thirds of food in America's supermarkets—mostly convenience foods—contained genetically engineered ingredients even though this was stated nowhere on food labels. In 2000, more than a hundred million acres of farmland were planted in GE crops.[88] As news reports made clear that it was difficult for consumers to avoid eating genetically engineered foods, the number of shoppers buying organic foods continued to rise. As one indicator, between 1998 and 2006, the number of Whole Foods Markets—featuring organic foods in convenient supermarket form—doubled.[89]

Around the same time, America's meat production system came under greater scrutiny after a 1996 outbreak of mad cow disease (bovine spongiform encephalopathy, or BSE) in Great Britain. The brain-wasting disease in cattle, linked to a rare brain-wasting disease in humans, was caused when the naturally herbivorous cows were fed ground-up animal carcasses, including central nervous system tissues infected with indestructible disease proteins.[90] As details came to light, many Americans were disturbed to learn that burgers and hot dogs in the United States included meat from cattle that had routinely been fed animal remains, including central nervous system tissue, fat, and blood from other bovines, as well as dead pet dogs and cats, and also litter shoveled from chicken factories, which included dead birds, feathers, and feces.[91]

Consumer organizations charged that in massive-scale feedlots and slaughterhouses, it was becoming difficult to keep fecal material and nervous system tissues from contaminating meat—a concern not only for BSE but also for other troublesome bacteria that were causing higher incidence of foodborne illness. In 2002, the USDA recalled nineteen million pounds of beef and over twenty-seven million pounds of poultry—the largest food recalls in U.S. history—owing to concerns about the dangerous bacteria *Listeria*.[92] Despite assurances from USDA officials that American meat was safe, and a major overhaul of cattle feed rules in 1997, mad cow disease was subsequently found in the United States in 2003.[93] Meat sales didn't generally suffer, but organic meat sales jumped 78 percent.[94]

Just as troubling as problems of disease and bacterial illness, the trend toward larger-scale animal factories and feedlots in the '90s was creating larger-scale waste and pollution problems. The country's cattle, pig, and chicken feedlots—some containing hundreds of thousands of animals—produced 291 billion pounds of manure a day. In the rural communities where these factory farm operations were located, the sickening stench and air pollution caused respiratory health problems for local residents.[95] In the case of pig farms, the waste was typically stored in sewage lagoons—open pits that sometimes spilled over into rivers, causing massive fish kills and contaminating drinking water sources.[96]

In his wildly popular 2001 book *Fast Food Nation*, Eric Schlosser documented many of these problems associated with the meat industry as it supplied the fast-food industry, and also exposed the egregious conditions faced by low-paid, largely migrant workers in packing plants. Schlosser's work distressingly echoed the alarm that Upton Sinclair had sounded about Chicago's meatpacking plants a hundred years earlier.[97]

IN A FUNDAMENTAL sense, commercial success of organic foods in the 1990s and since has rested largely on the fact that more shoppers started to ask questions: Is my food safe and healthful? Where does my food come from? What are the consequences of my food choices? These questions often arose in direct response to troubling news, but more and more, as organic food production and distribution expanded, organic food companies capitalized on consumer restiveness and launched marketing campaigns aimed at turning shoppers' attention to the merits of organic farms.

In the early 1990s, because their marketing budgets were small, organic companies depended on their packages and other point-of-sale promotions to distinguish their products. Consider, for example, the promotional strategy of Organic Valley cooperative, which was started in 1988 by a small group of Wisconsin dairy farmers struggling to keep their farms as milk prices dropped lower and lower owing to competition from factory-farm operations that confined animals and used hormones and antibiotics to boost production. The co-op stuck with pasture and then worked to sell its milk for a higher and fairer price by making connections between its farmers and consumers. Using the sides of its milk cartons to carry personal statements from individual farmers to shoppers, the co-op was able to convey its commitment to avoiding growth hormones, to paying farmers fairly, to keeping cows on pasture, and to avoiding water pollution.[98] In effect, the pitch sold consumers a sentiment — a wholesome sense of connection to the people, animals, and places that produced the milk. And part of that sentiment was the opportunity to support a form of agriculture that was substantively less damaging to rural communities and to the environment. By 2004, owing to the popularity of its organic milk and cheeses, the Organic Valley cooperative had grown to include nearly seven hundred farms and was distributing milk nationwide.[99] Given its success at marketing organic milk, the cooperative expanded in 2004 to include Midwest soybean farmers and began to sell soy milk as well.[100]

With the aid of Internet technology, the cooperative took its approach of connecting consumers with farmers to a new level. A targeted ad campaign promised that the co-op could tell consumers *exactly* where their soy milk came from. A shopper anywhere in America could go to the Organic Valley Coop Web site, punch in the number crimped into the top of a carton of soy milk, and see photographs of the farm where the soybeans were grown, accompanied by the farmer's photo and personal statement. In this way, the cooperative offered modern consumers a new way to know about the source of their food—and with it, provided a sense of trust and transparency rare in the modern food system—albeit still ironically removed in cyberspace.[101]

In some ways, the new packages' pastoral images of cows and country-sides were not unlike those used a hundred years earlier to convey nostal-gic sentiment. Indeed, some companies used their packaging to offer lyrical language and depict bucolic scenes that belied much larger-scale —even industrial-scale—operations. Author Michael Pollan inter-viewed a Whole Foods Market consultant who described how the seduc-tive promotions gave shoppers a feeling that by buying organic, they were "engaging in authentic experiences" and imaginatively enacting a "return to a utopian past with the positive aspects of modernity intact."[102] Moreover, with many Americans feeling gloomy about the prospects for politics and environmental protection in the first decade of the new century, buying organic foods could, in the words of another organic foods marketing expert, make a shopper "feel good" and that they were "doing the right thing."[103]

At the same time organic food ads serve up satisfying sentiments, though, they also nudge shoppers to ask important questions—some quite sophisticated and specific—about the places and particulars of their foods. Organic Valley cooperative's advertising functions in an unexpectedly subversive way. Its dominant hortatory message, "come and look closely at who and how and what," instructs consumers to expect to know specific stories about their foods. While many shoppers will be satisfied by pleasing images of cows on their milk cartons, others —after reading labels and ads—may take their questioning further, ultimately advocating a new standard that can make it difficult for busi-nesses to hide objectionable practices. For example, when Organic Valley's corporate competitor, Horizon Organic, opened a massive dairy operation in the arid West, where cows were fed organic grain and hay but not given regular access to pasture, some organic shoppers were already primed to make specific distinctions about the subtleties of organic milk production. In 2005, they sent more than five thousand letters to the USDA to protest regulatory standards that permitted milk from cows that didn't have regular access to pasture to be sold as "organic." Consumer input together with testimony from pasture-based dairy farmers pressed the National Organic Standards Board to tighten its regulatory definition in this regard, though the USDA has failed to take action.[104]

Distinguishing between milk from cows fed organic grains in crowded feed lots and milk from cows grazed on pasture is just one of many complications that arose as food companies hastened to meet the continually rising demand for organic foods. Not surprisingly, ambiguities of this type generated unexpected conflict about what exactly "organic" should mean.

ALTHOUGH those who had started the organic "movement" in the 1960s and 1970s had envisioned creating a decentralized food system of co-op markets supplied by nearby farms, the organic system — perhaps predictably, given the habits, patterns, and infrastructures of modern, market-driven life — began to develop in ways that mimicked the dominant food distribution system with large supermarkets, middlemen wholesalers setting prices for farmers, industrial-scale production of processed products, large advertising budgets, and nationwide distribution from big farms in California.

As the popularity and profitability of organic foods grew, the holistic approach that small-scale farmers had practiced as "organic" gradually gave way to a somewhat sparer regulatory meaning for "organic" that could be applied to farms geared up for larger-scale production. This migration of meaning had begun in the late 1980s when some pioneering organic growers and processing firms expanded and became heavily invested in interstate trade. They recognized that, in the absence of oversight, rising demand coupled with low supply increased the risk of fraud, which could undermine consumers' willingness to pay more for organic food. Moreover, they feared the word "organic" could be rendered meaningless if appropriated by big corporate food conglomerates, as had already occurred with "natural."[105]

To head off these problems, organic growers lobbied for two significant laws — both passed in 1990 — one in California and one in Congress. The California Organic Foods Act defined "organic" in specific regulatory terms and included enforcement provisions.[106] On a national level, the Organic Food Production Act, which passed as part of the 1990 farm bill, called for creation of an independent National Organic Standards Board (NOSB) made up of organic growers and processors to define organic practices for a federal labeling program. However, implementation was delayed for nearly a decade owing to disagreement between NOSB representatives and the USDA, which continued to retain an allegiance to agribusiness and a deep resistance to many principles of organic agriculture.[107]

In 1997, this conflict came to a controversial head when the USDA rejected NOSB recommendations and instead proposed rules that would have allowed use of genetically engineered crop plants, sewage sludge, and irradiation in the production of organic foods. This proposal — so at odds with what shoppers sought when buying organic foods — unleashed an unprecedented response. More than a quarter million people sent comments to the USDA — more consumers than the agency had ever heard from before — contending that organic production rules needed to account for their concerns, not just those of agribusinesses trying to elbow into the profitable organic food market.[108]

Ultimately, the most contentious provisions were removed when the USDA finalized its organic standards in 2002. Nonetheless, small-scale farmers remained critical because the new standards still permitted large farms that used many industrial methods to attach the "organic" label to their products. Because the new standard focused primarily on what materials were allowed or disallowed, it tended to advance a watered-down approach to organic farming that emphasized substitution of less harmful inputs. For example, it was possible to apply Chilean nitrate — a fertilizer mined and shipped from the Southern Hemisphere — rather than to use agronomic practices, such as cover crops and mixed planting, to maintain fertility. Substitution was most common on industrial-scale farms that had converted to organic to capture market demand rather than on smaller farms that had grown up from within the idealistic grassroots organic movement. As more and more foods labeled "organic" have appeared at lower prices in supermarkets, small-scale growers have recognized that large "industrial-organic" farms could undermine the integrity of the "organic" label and put their liveli-hoods at risk.

Large-scale organic growers and processors have argued that the new definition encourages more farms to shift to less harmful, low-input practices, which will ultimately lead to less synthetic fertilizer and pesti-cide use and to greater availability and affordability of organic foods for more shoppers. For example, Earthbound Farms alone claims to have withdrawn 7 million pounds of synthetic fertilizers and 225,759 pounds of chemical pesticides from use annually.[109] Overall, certified organic farmland in the United States grew by 400 percent, from under one mil-lion to over four million acres (including range- and cropland) between 1995 and 2005.[110]

As corporate food conglomerates have bought up many profitable organic companies and organic foods has become a $13.8 billion in-dustry, organic agriculture has undeniably become subject to powerful economic forces that propel prices downward and compel growers to cut corners.[111] Predicting an inevitable shrinking of the organic price premium, agricultural economist Julie Guthman has even questioned whether organic farms—particularly those in California's high-rent agricultural districts—can be economically viable in the long term.[112] This is an economic challenge that remains to be addressed. Ironically, consumers' desires for foods that are both organic and cheap could squeeze many small organic farms out of production.

Yet with demand for different types of organic products—from baby lettuces to rice and pasta, from apples to frozen chicken nuggets, it seems that there could certainly be a place for different types of organic agriculture—to supply supermarkets, food processing companies, co-ops, restaurants, local customers at farmers' markets or farm stands, and off-season shoppers in northern climes. Moreover, as we've seen, the advertising muscle of big organic producers may play a vital, if self-interested, role in shifting cultural ideas about what consumers think is important to know about foods, which could benefit small-scale growers, too. A shopper might start out buying a bag of organic lettuce at Costco, or a frozen organic lasagna entrée at Whole Foods Market, and then end up heading to a local farmers' market to track down organic cantaloupes and string beans, too. Marketing studies indicate that consumers buy organic foods primarily for reasons of health and nutrition. But after buying more organic foods over time, their motivations widen to include concern about the environment and helping small farmers as well.[113]

Regardless of whether consumers buy food from small growers or industrial-scale organic operations, it is clear that a growing number of people are now seeking new and meaningful answers to a question long neglected in the kitchens of America: Where does my food come from? With new possibilities for our shopping carts, we are beginning to learn that tracking down answers need not be unsavory. Indeed, more consumers seeking more answers may be the key to pushing our agriculture and our food system in important new directions. At this point, about 30 percent of shoppers (in a broad range of income classes) buy some organic products on a regular basis, representing a small but respectable 2.5 percent of all food sales in America.[114] Whether or not organic agriculture will continue to flourish in its diversity and provide alternative models to the dominant industrial mode of agriculture depends on whether these consumers will continue to support it — not only by buying organic foods at supermarkets, but also by seeking out local, small-scale growers.[115] And whether or not organic agriculture will become more than a niche depends on whether more consumers will consider it worth paying extra to know that their food has been produced without harmful pesticides, with no added hormones, and in ways that do less harm to the environment.

Returning Stories
to the Modern Kitchen

Since the late 1990s, when I first started work on this book, the opportunities for us to know more about the places and particulars of our foods have grown dramatically. The number of farmers' markets in America has exploded, and most regular supermarkets have expanded their offerings of organic foods to include milk, produce, eggs, meat, cereals, and even familiar brand-name convenience items. More and more stores specialize in organic foods, and some have even taken to identifying the place of origin of their meat, fish, and produce. The New Seasons Market chain in Portland, Oregon, for example, highlights local products with yellow shelf tags and, by generating demand for local foods, has helped to spark a regional revival of farms.[1]

As the desire of many eaters to know more about their foods has become better understood by marketers, new products have proliferated. A shopper today might need to decide between a costly organic or cheaper nonorganic block of cheese, between apples grown locally or those grown organically in New Zealand, between "natural" eggs from hens raised outside of cages or eggs from hens fed particular diets, between free-trade coffee and bird-friendly coffee, between dolphin-safe tuna and grass-fed beef. Vitamins, calories, trans fats, sodium, antioxidants, fiber, and other food components may need to be considered as well. Such accounting of costs, ethics, and health—not to mention a measure of wariness to discount promotional spin—can be perplexing, especially when all you want to do is pick up something quick for dinner.[2]

At times, 1920s home efficiency expert Christine Frederick's view that it is too much of a "bother" to know about our foods may ring true. After all, how can we as busy urban and suburban—and even many rural—consumers *really* assess what is going on at the other end of the food chain when we know so little about the details and challenges of producing food?

This question goes to the heart of a matter that we've wrestled with ever since America urbanized and the food system developed in ways that made foods abstruse—geographically, biochemically, and politically. In one sense, knowledge about foods has deepened and advanced enormously as experts have learned more and more, yet in another, popular knowledge about foods has become superficial as the great majority of us have come to depend on the unsteady grounds of advertising to know about what we eat. Procuring food has become much easier, but knowing about our foods has become much harder, especially as more and more of them come from distant lands.

One hundred years ago, facing challenges of life in growing cities far from the farm, many people found solace in foods labeled "natural." Whatever the reality, "natural" symbolized purity, authenticity, and quality, and thereby helped to assuage a nostalgic longing for seemingly simpler times. Over the past century, we've become a far more urban society still, far more disengaged in our everyday lives from nature, and yet ever more aware and anxious about the profound ways we are changing the natural world. Today, the "organic" idea similarly assuages us with satisfying sentiments that promise not only to "reconnect" each of us to our source of sustenance but also to transform our identities—from being individuals who "cause problems" to those helping to find solutions. Some cynics have suggested that, in this way, the organic ideal—as spun up in marketing—could merely salve our anxieties with a sense of false consciousness, lulling our attention from matters that demand political attention. It's certainly easier to feel good about buying a box of delicious organic lettuce than to write a letter to a senator or to go to a public meeting about pollution caused by feedlots or bacteria showing up in foods. Indeed, if consumers are fooled into buying a box of eggs labeled "natural harvest" that shows a rustic barn set into a bucolic scene when they believe they are supporting a small farm that prioritizes humane treatment of their birds, not only are they wasting their money, but they are wasting an opportunity—an opportunity that we all have at this moment in history to nudge our food system in a new direction.

Despite the parallels between the appeal of natural foods one hundred years ago and of organic foods today, there are some important differences. Through public policy, we've given "organic" a certifiable definition; it carries substantial meaning in its link to real practices on farms, in contrast to the more malleable and imaginative meanings that have been and continue to be attached to the cultural idea of "natural." Moreover, "voting with one's pocket book"—to borrow another of Christine Frederick's phrases—is not merely a way to feel good, but it is a way that individuals can exert at least some influence, especially in the face of unresponsive politics. What we are seeing today with the local and organic foods movement can be considered an experiment in how we might exercise effective social consciousness in a mass-market-driven society. As ironic as it may sound, expressing preferences in how we shop for food might well be a way for an urban society to practice a land ethic.

What is needed for this experiment to succeed is the development of a new kitchen literacy that encompasses awareness that what we eat is linked to real people and real places. It must include a practical understanding of how to decipher the full range of information offered up on food labels—from organic certification, to disingenuous strategies some companies may use to "green up" a standard product. But it must also encompass a broader understanding of how our culture and our politics affect the people and land that supply our food.

Culturally, we are just beginning to reconsider how our consumption is connected to a broader context of consequences. Yet through practical choices available today, many of us can start to learn a new type of kitchen literacy that aims to make the food system more transparent.

Foremost, we can buy organic food and know with reasonable certainty that its production has not involved the use of toxic pesticides.[3] By buying organic, consumers can take a proactive, source-reduction approach, dangling the carrot of market demand to encourage farmers to reduce overall use of pesticides, an estimated 1.2 billion pounds of which continue to be applied in the United States each year.[4] USDA organic standards also prohibit the use of most synthetic fertilizers, all antibiotics, genetic engineering, irradiation, and sewage sludge.[5] In modern supermarket format, the organic label offers consumers a short-hand way to know their foods come from farms that follow organic methods.

Beyond buying store products labeled as organic, shoppers can go further by tracking down producers directly. Urban cooks aspiring to know more about their foods can shop at farmers' markets, which doubled in number between 1994 and 2004, and then grew another 18 percent to 4,385 in 2006.[6] Most growers at farmers' markets are happy to talk about their particular methods of farming. Some have limited their pesticide use with integrated pest management techniques; some farmers have restored wetlands and riverfronts on their land for birds and wildlife. Some grow organically, while others, ironically, have dropped their official "organic" certification owing to the costly paperwork federal regulation now requires. Instead, they rely on a relationship of trust built directly with their customers, week after week, year after year. One such farmer in California adopted his own term, "Tairwa," a play on the French *terroir*—meaning taste of place—to mark his thorough approach to farming.[7] Buying food directly from these growers gives them a fairer return for their work and good stewardship, which benefits us all. Moreover, supporting the work of local farmers reduces the amount of oil consumed in transportation, and it reinforces the long-term food security afforded by having farms close to where people live. Finally, buying locally produced foods reminds us of our reliance on land and compels us to confront more directly the consequences of our human lives; it's easier to ignore the externalities of pesticides and feed-lots if they are far away and imposing their effects on other places and other people.

Shopping at a farmers' market is certainly less convenient than

E.1. *In recent years, the number of farmers' markets has skyrocketed as more shoppers have discovered the satisfaction of buying fresh foods directly from local producers.*

shopping at a supermarket. You have to go at the appointed time and won't find everything you've become accustomed to picking up year-round. But many people regard the adventure of tracking down fresh and unusual foods — in season and from a tangible food chain — to be a satisfying reward. In fact, it just might change the way you look at the everyday world. Friends who regularly shop at a farmers' market in Washington, D.C., have confided that they've developed a new aesthetic sensibility about what foods are appealing; they now tend to pick apples with blemishes, reasoning that these less-than-perfect-looking fruits are probably less-sprayed. Inspired by novel combinations governed by seasonal abundance, they find themselves pressed to cook creative dishes that might include streaked eggplants, tender pea shoots, or crenulated Italian kale.

Beyond farmers' markets, food-conscious city dwellers and suburbanites can opt to join subscription farms, known as CSAs (Community Supported Agriculture), which have become popular in and around many large cities, including San Francisco, Chicago, and New York. In this system, a shopper cast lots with a farmer — or a cooperative group of farms—signing up and paying ahead of time for a subscription to the farm's harvest. As the growing season advances, each week members receive a box filled with vegetables and sometimes cheese, flowers, honey, or eggs that the farm raises. The box often contains a newsletter about what is happening on the farm and recipes for less-familiar seasonal vegetables, such as rainbow chard and beets. Often the farm will host an open house or workdays for members. One Chicago-area CSA promises its subscribers "over 100 varieties of vegetables, fruits, and herbs" during a twenty-week harvest season, plus an opportunity "to connect" to "the land, and those who tend the soil."[8]

Friends in San Francisco and Sacramento who subscribe to CSA farms rave about the interesting foods they've received in their box—crinkled cress, strawberry daikon, and yellow carrots—and report renewed interest in cooking. They find the cost to be quite reasonable, though they realize they may need to weather an occasional poor growing season with their farm. By participating in a CSA, consumers can begin to appreciate more closely the hard work and smarts that go into raising food and enjoy the assurance of a more tangible and personally accountable food system. Some may begin to realize that their expectation of supermarket bargains doesn't match the actual work and worth of growing foods and stewarding land well.

In addition to buying organic foods and dealing directly with farmers whenever possible, consumers can pay greater attention to government policies that affect food and agriculture. Such policies govern—among other things—how pesticides are regulated, how water quality is protected, which crops are subsidized, whether funding is available to restore wildlife habitat on farms, how foods are labeled, and how public health is factored into food regulations. Three federal agencies generally oversee the intersecting realms of health, agriculture, and environment. The USDA administers federal farm policies, inspects meat-processing plants, and oversees organic regulations. The EPA is responsible for regulating pesticides and water quality. The FDA is responsible for enforcing rules about additives, residues, foodborne illness, accurate nutritional labeling, and health claims. In addition, the FTC oversees matters pertaining to honesty and accuracy in advertising.

E.2. *Industrial monoculture farms that stretch across California's Central, Salinas, and Imperial valleys provide much of America's produce year-round, but diversion of water for irrigation and heavy use of toxic pesticides are only some of the unaccounted environmental costs. Many strawberry farms, for example, have persisted in using methyl bromide, a broad-spectrum fumigant implicated in eroding the earth's ozone layer.*

While the workings of these agencies may seem remote, a number of nonprofit organizations monitor their activities on behalf of citizens. The Center for Science in the Public Interest, Union of Concerned Scientists, Consumers Union, and Cornucopia Institute are just a few that focus on nutrition, public health, and labeling issues. Other public-interest groups focus on the environmental aspects of agriculture. Waterkeeper Alliance, for example, has worked to strengthen federal laws governing pollution from large-scale pork feedlots, while Natural Resources Defense Council has worked on pesticides. With a focus on farm policy, American Farmland Trust has worked to stem the conversion of prime farmlands into suburban sprawl, a critical piece in assuring that farms can persist near urban populations. Environmental Working Group has aimed to tackle subsidies that encourage damaging farm practices. These and other watchdog groups play key roles in assur-

E.3. *This small organic farm in Washington State is one of many that now supply farmers' markets and CSAs with fresh, local foods, produced without pesticides, in ways that foster soil fertility.*

ing that federal agencies provide adequate oversight and in pushing for legislative reforms.

Outside of Washington, D.C., other groups are working to develop more sustainable food systems on a regional basis, such as Ecotrust in the Pacific Northwest and Land Stewardship Project in the upper Midwest. Still other groups, such as Green Guerillas in New York City, have worked to promote community gardens on vacant lots in inner-city neighborhoods, some otherwise underserved by supermarkets.

Today, through our choices as consumers, through engagement in public policy, and by supporting community-based efforts, we have many opportunities to push our food system in hopeful new directions.

FINALLY, modern cooks might start gardens of their own. *The Square-Foot Gardener,* a classic book designed to guarantee beginners' success, advises novices to begin with two square feet of garden per family member in a small patch of yard or even on a patio. A garden can entail any level of commitment, from simply growing salad greens and herbs to orchestrating an array of flavorful vegetables. At the most basic level, gardening shows us what it takes to raise food, from the work of shoveling earth and pulling weeds to the joy of watching seeds grow into plants with frilly leaves. Even more, gardening offers the distinct personal satisfaction of knowing the whole story of food that you raise, gather, cook, and eat.

I've had the good fortune to try my hand at gardening as I worked on this book. I was a novice, but when we bought our house in a small town on Oregon's coast, I inherited a backyard garden that had been tended by a talented woman (whose name coincidentally was Martha). When we moved in, it was harvest time, and potatoes, pole beans, and green chard were ready to eat. Through the winter in our temperate maritime climate, bunches of parsley, followed by mustard greens and leafy kales, appeared as welcome surprises. By the time the seed catalog arrived in February, I was ready to jump in and plan my own garden.

It took time—time that I'd never before slotted into my food-preparation routine. And it took some money—but not much—for seeds and for city water. It has required that I become acquainted with the needs of worms and the competing appetite of slugs. It's pushed me to befriend neighbors who own animals and are willing to share their manure, which I've come to realize is more valuable than I'd ever imagined. The garden has also been a source of tremendous interest and delight. My husband and I have eaten from it nearly every day for the past three years. Salads with all sorts of flavorful greens and deeply colored potatoes have become our favorites.

The garden does not supply us with protein, fat, or grains. I have no delusions about my dependence on the larger food system, which backs me up if storms or hungry deer thwart my efforts. I am perhaps more awed by that system than ever before, but whenever I see the white semi-trucks roll into town to supply our local grocery stores, I remain troubled by a nagging awareness that much of my food depends on distant, unknowable farms and cheap petroleum.

Gradually, we are all learning that what we do in our everyday lives—including the choices we make about what we eat—has profound effects on the natural world. As ecologist Barry Commoner reminded us, "there is no such thing as a free lunch." Everything we humans do to live uses up resources and exacts environmental costs. But, as it turns out, some lunches cost less than others do. As consumers, we've become supremely skilled at ferreting out bargains in the shopping cart that presumably afford us more money to spend as we wish—on more goods or more services that save us time. But now, we need to learn how to "bargain" in a new sense; we need to economize on the larger, lesser-known costs of our foods—in order to afford a healthier environment for the future, for us all. With more and more people beginning to grasp the critical relationship between food, health, agriculture, and the environment, there seems to be good reason for hope.

ONE AFTERNOON early in my gardening project, I clipped a bunch of sage leaves and brought them back into my kitchen, planning to prepare a simple pasta with sage butter, fava beans, Italian kale, and grated Asiago. As soon as I placed the sprigs of sage on the cutting board to cleave their fuzzy leaves from their woody stems, a dozen tiny spiders ran out in all directions. At first, the spiders jarred against my lifelong expectation that there should be nothing alive in, on, or anywhere near my foods. But with a deep breath, a newly learned sensibility took hold and calmed me. Arachnids scurrying across my counter signified that the sage was so fresh that the spiders hadn't even had time to jump off. This is what it meant to eat food that grows and lives in my garden—herbs and vegetables that become food and home not only for me, but for other creatures as well.

I did my best to corral the tiny creatures and carry them outside, and sure enough, when I crouched beside the sage plant, I noticed how clusters of sage leaves provided perfect umbrellas of shelter for many spiders that presumably helped to control pests in my garden. Of course, I readily learned to gently shake spiders out of the sage before bringing it indoors.

But having spiders in my kitchen reminded me that my foodshed is always a part of a larger whole—whether I know the details or not. At the other end of my food chain, wherever it may be—there are always spiders, worms, birds, rivers, and people.

The sage was but one storied ingredient carried in from the garden. The kale, planted last spring, was somewhat haggard having braved an aphid outbreak in July and then several brisk storms in November. The favas I'd planted the previous October. In early spring, white flowers with inky black spots blossomed and then morphed into sturdy pods with hearty beans I harvested in May, shelled, and then stored in my freezer. The cheese I bought from the local food store. Its label noted that it came from Wisconsin, though I could discern nothing more about the land or the cows that supplied milk to make the sharp block. The butter came from a farm in northern California that has pioneered quality organic production at a medium scale, using cow manure that would otherwise pollute Tomales Bay to power the equipment that processes cheese, yogurt, milk, and butter. As modern cooks, of course, we can never know everything about our food, but on this particular evening, all the ingredients and their stories came together in a deeply satisfying way.

It's a long and complicated path from Martha Ballard's kitchen to mine, or to yours. Our industrialized food system has grown under a covenant of ignorance—with consumers not asking and producers not telling. As the stories of our foods ceased to be told, we lost track of where and how they were produced; and as we lost knowledge about our foods, we lost awareness of how eating fits our human selves into the broader natural world. But today, with new interest, new understanding, and new stories, we have the chance to rediscover some of that knowledge and awareness, and with it, we just might find a way to live better on Earth and, finally, to eat well.

Toward a New Kitchen Literacy

On Friday afternoons, I prop open my front gate. John from Valley Flora Farm unloads fifteen blue tubs filled with fresh produce, and we carry them into the yard. Others arrive and start removing lids to see what's inside this week. There are exclamations as people hold up improbably architectural heads of Romanesco cauliflower and stout boles of brussels sprouts. There is laughter when someone finds a two-legged carrot. People talk, swapping stories about how they prepared last week's fennel bulbs or buttercup squash. This year, I'm splitting a "harvest share" with a friend to supplement my own garden's bounty. We divide up turnips, squash, and onions and imagine the meals we might cook.

My backyard is a drop-off spot for the Valley Flora CSA. Run by two sisters and their mom, the small farm lies in a coastal valley just fourteen miles to the north. Abby and her mom, Betsy, have been growing baby greens and vegetables for a decade. After learning to farm with draft horses, sister Zoë brought more land into cultivation a few years ago. Now, in addition to supplying several restaurants and markets, they deliver food to one hundred happy families in three towns. I rarely see them because they're always tending the farm, but as I unload my share of beautiful, delicious veggies from the tub each week, I think of them and their lovely fields, of their hard work, ingenuity, and hopeful vision. And I am deeply grateful. My food system is no longer as anonymous as it once was when the cryptic supermarket was my only source of sustenance.

My neighbors and I are not the only ones who have taken the plunge into eating more local foods. In the two years since *Kitchen Literacy* was first published, the number of farmers' markets has continued to rise, and to meet consumer demand more small farms have cropped up, with more than twenty thousand farms now in organic production.[1] Millions more Americans have begun growing their own food, too. According to the National Gardening Association, in 2009 alone, there was a 19 percent increase in home vegetable gardening.[2] There are also more school and community gardens. So many people have experimented with eating locally in recent years that the term *locavore* was added to the *Oxford Dictionary* in 2007 and to *Webster's* in 2009.[3] Despite a serious recession, the local, organic, and slow foods movements have continued to thrive. An organic garden has even taken root on the White House lawn.

As author of a book that looks at the historical roots of these exciting trends, I'm gratified to find so many people thinking and talking about food. Everyone seems able to find their own family's story as a thread in the history that I've recounted in *Kitchen Literacy*, whether they grew up eating fresh eggs on a farm or eating boxed macaroni and cheese in a city or suburb. In the course of giving talks and meeting readers, I've enjoyed hearing how people make sense of their own personal food genealogies. One woman told me she grew up on a farm (in now suburbanized southern California) but never realized how well her family ate until she moved away for college. After years of aching for a vegetable garden of her own, she'd only recently found a place to plant and was now reveling in fresh tomatoes and basil. A Salvadoran immigrant told me that he loves living in America but sorely missed the fresh meats that he can eat when he visits home. "I can't describe how it tastes different, but it does." Several men and women expressed regret that they'd never learned to cook. Now, they yearned to learn basic kitchen skills so they could enjoy the fruits of their farmers' markets more fully.

Beyond hearing the personal food stories that connect us all to history, I've felt inspired to discover what people are doing now to build a better food system for the future. One teacher who started a school garden told me about his kids' enthusiasm for making and eating salads from lettuces and other vegetables they'd grown from seed. A young mother told me about sharing a herd of goats with a group of families— each family taking one day of responsibility per week; the children love the goats and fresh milk, and the parents have experimented with making cheese. One man increased his self-reliance and culinary skills by growing twenty-five cabbages and figuring out how to make sauerkraut from scratch. I learned about a troupe of urban food activists harvesting fruit from unpicked yard trees—keeping a bag, giving a share to tree owners, and then taking the rest to local food banks. A group of fishermen in Maine, following a CSA model, is now selling shares of its catch to consumers. Creativity, enthusiasm, and possibilities abound as more people become interested in trying and supporting new ways of procuring food all across the nation. I like to think of these new stories as ingredients for the next course of history—one that is now being created with each unfolding day.

As never before, I've come to feel the importance of history: it allows us to understand how we got to where we are today, yet it also enables us to gain perspective on where we need to head in the future. *Kitchen Literacy* reveals how America's modern food system developed and evolved to meet the needs—and exploit opportunities—of our rapidly urbanizing society. On many counts, though, the ultimate outcomes have been different than anticipated. We no longer have malnutrition; but instead of greater health and longevity, we now have more chronic diseases and escalating health costs. Although the modernizing food system aimed to address food safety and waste problems, we've nevertheless ended up with widespread contamination and damaging environmental pollution. Though we bet on using cheap fossil fuels to make the food system efficient in the twentieth century, we are beginning to realize that securing petroleum will carry greater risks and costs in the future. Here, early in the twenty-first century, it has become clear that we must now cope with a whole new set of challenges.

No one has articulated the vital connections between food and other major issues facing America today better than journalist Michael Pollan. In a seminal article published in the *New York Times* in October 2008, "An Open Letter to the Next Farmer in Chief," Pollan advised the still unknown president-elect that to address our nation's three most pressing matters—energy independence, climate change, and health care—we need to fundamentally change how we grow, process, and eat food in America.[4]

Pollan's argument is persuasive. Indeed, with American soldiers' lives at risk in a protracted war in the Middle East, the connection between oil supply and national security has never been clearer. Since the 1970s, scholars have warned that our nation's petroleum-based food system consumed ten times more energy than it produced, but the consequences of this energy imbalance were largely ignored with cheap oil in secure, plentiful supply. Only in recent years, with high fuel costs, war, and more widespread talk of peaking oil production, have the limits of this unsustainable equation and the vulnerability of our food system come into sharper focus. Shifting agriculture away from its dependence on fossil fuels will be key to avoiding more wars in the coming century.

It would also help to mitigate climate change, arguably the globe's most urgent problem. With ice sheets near the poles rapidly eroding, scientists agree that atmospheric changes are happening more quickly than predicted even just a few years ago.[5] According to recent estimates, in industrialized nations, food systems are responsible for 29 percent of greenhouse gas emissions.[6] The most significant emissions come from petroleum—used for everything from the production of synthetic nitrogen fertilizers and pesticides to the fueling of tractors, trucks, and planes carrying food as freight. Even our drives to the supermarket and our humming refrigerators contribute in sizable ways.[7] Another major source is methane gas generated in the guts of livestock. In the United States, methane belched by animals—trivial though it may sound—actually accounts for 24 percent of agriculture's greenhouse gas emissions. This is troubling because methane is twenty times more efficient than carbon in trapping the sun's heat.[8]

Reducing all these food-system-generated greenhouse gases is critical because climate change will challenge food production as never before. In some regions of the United States, water for farming will become even scarcer than it is today. For example, over the next several decades, snowpack in the Sierra Nevada and flows in the Colorado River, both major water supplies for California farms that provide much of our nation's fruits and vegetables, are predicted to decline substantially.[9] Beyond scarce water, erratic weather and worsening pest problems will make farming more difficult.[10] Additional carbon in the atmosphere will alter how plants absorb nutrients, possibly boosting production in the short run but depleting soils in the longer term.[11] Researchers at the University of California predict that many farmers may need to shift to new and more varied crops.[12] With the prospect of uncertain climate, having more diversified farms in different regions could be an important strategy for increasing our food system's resilience.

Beyond energy independence and climate concerns, recent national debates about spiraling health costs have made the connection between public health and food more compelling than ever. Since 1980, adult obesity rates have doubled from 15 to 30 percent, while childhood obesity rates have more than tripled. With rising obesity has come increased incidence of chronic, debilitating, and deadly diseases, including heart disease, type-2 diabetes, cancer, and stroke. According to the Trust for America's Health, more than a quarter of health care costs are now related to obesity.[13] And children today are likely to be the first generation of Americans that will not outlive their parents.[14]

Although we've long tended to regard being overweight as a personal matter, the abrupt shift on a population-wide scale—many have called it an "epidemic of obesity"—indicates larger forces at play. One prime cause behind this rise in overweight is that our food system has been subsidized to make the least healthy foods most affordable and accessible. Agricultural policies heavily favor the overproduction of commodity crops, giving farmers incentives to grow corn and soybeans that become ingredients in nearly all processed foods. Thus cheap beverages and junk foods packed with corn syrup—a substance high in calories but low in nutritional value—have become pervasive in Americans' diets. According to New York University nutrition and food studies professor Marion Nestle, in the last ten years, the price of fruits and vegetables has increased between 40 and 50 percent while the price of junk food has declined about the same amount.[15] Though many shoppers may be economizing at supermarkets and fast food outlets, they pay with their health; and we are all paying more in the long term through taxes and skyrocketing insurance premiums. A recent article in the health policy journal *Health Affairs* estimated the annual cost of obesity in America to be a budget-breaking $1,250 per household.[16]

To recognize that all these problems—oil scarcity, climate change, and declining public health—are intimately connected to our food system can be constructive, but it can also be overwhelming. And so the critical question for many of us remains, How do we address these concerns in our own daily lives? This is the question I found weighing most heavily on peoples' minds as I traveled around discussing *Kitchen Literacy*. As one keen reader framed the matter, "Is taking personal responsibility enough, or do we need major policy reform?" Clearly, it's not an either-or matter. There is no doubt that the personal choice of what we cook and eat every day—multiplied by millions of us—drives the food economy. Yet it would be naïve to think we could "shop" our way out of such complicated problems. Consumer choices and policy reforms can only work hand in hand. We need to take actions in our kitchens and communities, and we also need to press for changes in agriculture and food safety policies that can push our food system to produce healthier fare in a more sustainable manner. That's why learning the stories of our foods—on many levels—remains as important as ever.

Consider once again the problem of obesity. Taking personal responsibility for one's own health by exercising and by eating less junk food and more fresh vegetables is the optimal response. But given widespread confusion about what's best to eat, many individuals lack the knowledge to choose and cook healthy foods. Moreover with the prevalence of cheap junk foods, many people, especially those on tight budgets, have little choice. As a result, we've ended up with a health divide that mirrors disparities in wealth between richer and poorer Americans.[17] For these reasons, thoughtful policy reforms could encourage better health and lower health costs across the board. For example, if good health were truly the goal, wouldn't it make more sense to give farmers incentives to produce more fresh fruits and vegetables rather than more corn and soybeans? This approach was supported by the American Medical Association, a group that weighed in on agricultural policy for the first time in 2007. Recognizing important connections between food production and public health, the physicians went on to pass a "sustainable food" resolution in 2009.[18]

Climate change is another problem that can be addressed only with a

mix of personal actions and broad policy reforms. Consider the stagger-
ing enteric emissions generated by livestock. Recently, leading food
writer Mark Bittman of the *New York Times* suggested a relatively easy
way for individuals to make a difference: eat less meat.[19] Researchers have
calculated that if Americans were to reduce meat consumption by only
20 percent it would be comparable to everyone switching from a standard sedan to an ultra-efficient hybrid car.[20] Thus, if American families
substituted just one non-meat meal per week, it could make a sizable
dent in greenhouse gas emissions. But this is not enough. With trillions
of methane-producing farm animals worldwide, there needs to be an
"upstream" policy response, too. This might entail investing in research
about how farm animals' diets affect their digestion and about convert-
ing methane from manure into useful energy sources. In both these
cases, pressing for policy change requires a measure of civic responsibility, which means political responsibility: voting for candidates who are
willing to work for meaningful reform.

   Already we've seen the potential for personal and political responsibility to work in tandem. Consumers' rising demand for local and
organic foods has helped not only to kindle a revival of small farms but
also to transform food culture in a powerful way. Just in the past two
years, the Farm Bill of 2008, a piece of legislation historically lorded over
by powerful senators from Corn Belt states and agribusiness lobbyists,
came under unprecedented public scrutiny. There were dozens of articles about the farm bill in food magazines and in newspapers not only in
farm states but in East and West Coast cities. The food magazine *Saveur*
called 2008 the year "the farm bill became sexy."[21] With broadening
awareness that the legislation would govern not only farms but also the
foods that show up on America's dinner plates, more citizens and citizens' groups lobbied Congress for reforms. Although massive subsidies
for commodity crops remained untouched, the farm bill included many
steps forward, such as new support for small farms, for young farmers,
for farmers' markets, and for assisting farmers with transition to organic
production.[22] While critics have called these programs "crumbs" or
"mere fleas on the elephant in the room," from a historic perspective we
can see that the discourse unmistakably shifted in important ways.[23]

With increased attention from consumers and public health advocates, there will likely be more meaningful reform the next time the farm bill is reauthorized.

The dual approaches of policy reform and personal responsibility are showing promise on more local levels as well. In Portland, Oregon, a city that considers itself a leader in sustainability, Multnomah County officials have started an initiative to increase the amount of food grown locally over the next fifteen years and to make it more accessible to people in lower income brackets. Already, the county has started a farm on unused land that has provided several area food pantries with fresh produce. The initiative will also encourage a broadscale, grow-your-own movement in backyard gardens, school yards, community parks, and vacant lots.[24] By creating public programs and policies that encourage local food production, county leaders hope to tackle issues of hunger and public health while reducing energy use and greenhouse gas emissions. Similar initiatives have started in Atlanta and Minneapolis and are budding out elsewhere, too.[25]

Such efforts to rebuild local food systems tap into a deep well of America's heritage—the agrarian ideal and the related notion of self-sufficiency. But they also kindle modern dreams of a more healthful and sustainable food system. These ideals and dreams capture the imagination of people everywhere on the political spectrum. I encountered this firsthand as I talked about *Kitchen Literacy* on talk-radio venues as divergent as Fox affiliates (conservative), the *Thom Hartmann Show* (liberal), public radio, Christian stations, and *Martha Stewart*. It made me realize that the project of building local food systems has tremendous potential for rebuilding the very fabric of society in this age of political polarization. Those from both the political left and the right recognize the value of supporting small farms, reviving rural economies, and providing wholesome foods to more people. I encountered this mix of attitudes not only on the radio waves in cities but also in rural areas where I had the opportunity to speak, often in conjunction with local food events. Individuals of all sorts are drawn to the elemental promise of knowing the real stories of their food.

I've certainly found this to be the case in my own small town. In addition to our new CSA, there have been other hopeful happenings in the past few years. A retired gardener started a new demonstration garden to show more people how to grow vegetables. The farm and garden help to supply a local food bank with fresh produce. Local fishermen are now selling lingcod and halibut in town and at a farmers' market in a nearby city. A new Web site is in the works to help consumers find local food producers. A new elementary school program teaches where foods come from and will turn soil for a children's garden next spring.

With all these efforts, big and small, a wholesome revolution is now under way. Not only are more people seeking to know the stories of their foods, but they are also taking actions to fundamentally change those stories in new and promising ways. When I first started writing *Kitchen Literacy* ten years ago, I didn't imagine this possibility, but now I can. Perhaps someday, it will once again become customary and normal for Americans to know about the foods they eat. I hope that, with deepening knowledge, more people will be inspired by the possibilities of health, good taste, and the promise of creating a better world for all.

NOTES

Introduction: *Missing Stories*

1. Peter Farb and George Armelagos, *Consuming Passions: The Anthropology of Eating* (New York: Washington Square Press, 1980), 124. Lévi-Strauss was comparing the foodways of different cultural groups. Whether foodways are culturally or materially based was heatedly debated in the 1970s by anthropologists Marvin Harris and Mary Douglas. For further discussion about what light history sheds on this dispute, see Harvey Levenstein, *Revolution at the Table: The Transformation of the American Diet* (New York: Oxford University Press, 1988), 173–174.

2. Margaret Cussler and Mary L. de Give, *'Twixt the Cup and the Lip: Psychological and Socio-Cultural Factors Affecting Food Habits* (New York: Twayne, 1952), 110–111, 159.

3. John L. Shover, *First Majority, Last Minority: The Transforming of Rural Life in America* (DeKalb: Northern Illinois University Press, 1980), 6–7. In 1948, the largest 10 percent of farms were responsible for 10 percent of total farm output; this increased to 48 percent in 1964. The trend of consolidation picked up further steam in the 1960s, when the total number of farms decreased, but larger farms with higher incomes increased by 50 percent.

4. Michael Pollan, *The Omnivore's Dilemma: A Natural History of Four Meals* (New York: Penguin, 2006), 10.

Chapter 1. *A Meal by Martha*

1. Martha Ballard's Diary Online (MBDO), Aug. 15, 1790. MBDO is available through an educational Web site hosted by the George Mason University Center for History and New Media: www.dohistory.org/diary/index.html. I conducted most of my research with this source during January and February 2005. By some quirk of the Web site, this particular entry can be accessed by searching for "bakt lamb" but not by searching for "Aug. 15, 1790."

2. Laura Thatcher Ulrich, *A Midwife's Tale: The Life of Martha Ballard, Based on Her Diary, 1785–1812* (New York: Knopf, 1990; 2d ed., Vintage Books, 1991). Martha Ballard's "diary" is actually a collection of small hand-sewn booklets that her great-great granddaughter had bound in 1930 into two volumes, which are housed at the Maine State Library.

3. Ibid., 18–19.

4. MBDO, 1790, passim. These include days when Martha hoed, spread ashes, set plants, sowed seeds, weeded, hilled cabbages, and harvested.

5. MBDO, Aug. 11, 1790; June 17, 1790; June 15, 1790; Apr. 30, 1793; July 9, 1795; May 22, 1790; June 13, 1786. For more about general layout of colonial New England gardens, see Rudy J. Favretti, *Early New England Gardens, 1620–1840* (Sturbridge, MA: Old Sturbridge Village, 1966), 5, 10.

6. U.S. Census Bureau, "United States: Urban and Rural, 1790–1990," table 4 in *1990 Census of Population and Housing,* http://www.census.gov/population/censusdata/table-4.pdf.

7. David M. Tucker, *Kitchen Gardening in America: A History* (Ames: Iowa State University Press, 1993), 32. Tucker refers to gardens out of town and bases his size estimate on travelers' accounts; Carolyn Merchant, *Ecological Revolutions: Nature, Gender, and Science in New England* (Chapel Hill: University of North Carolina Press, 1989), 182. Merchant bases her estimate on an analysis of production and consumption; Sara F. McMahon, "A Comfortable Subsistence: The Changing Composition of Diet in Rural New England, 1620–1840," *William and Mary Quarterly* 42 (Jan. 1985): 39. Based on her study of wills and probate records, McMahon found that widows were allotted up to a quarter of an acre for gardening.

8. MBDO, May 12, 1797; Aug. 23, 1791; Aug. 29, 1791. Many of the details in this paragraph represent a composite drawn from several sources, including Favretti and Merchant (see note 7).

9. MBDO, Aug. 3, 1790.

10. Ulrich, *Midwife's Tale,* 84–86; James A. Henretta, "Families and Farms: Mentalité in Pre-Industrial America," *William and Mary Quarterly* 35 (1978): 19; Richard L. Bushman, "Family Security in the Transition from Farm to City, 1750–1850," *Journal of Family History* (Fall 1981): 241.

11. MBDO, May 30, 1791; June 1, 1791; Ulrich, *Midwife's Tale,* 129. Over time, families slowly accumulated livestock; the Ballards started a flock of sheep the following year when they moved to a farm north of Augusta.

12. MBDO, June 24, 1804; Apr. 13, 1805; June 25, 1803; May 30, 1807.

13. MBDO, July 31, 1810; Ulrich, *Midwife's Tale,* 335. Also, on Aug. 22, 1794, after the family moved from Bowman's Brook to a nearby farm, Martha wrote about " 2 Bushels of wheat of our own raising. it made Beautifull flower."

14. MBDO, Apr. 12, 1790 (wooden trough); Ulrich, *Midwife's Tale,* 85 (oven in Martha's chimney).

15. MBDO, Mar. 8, 1792.

16. William P. Hedden, *How Great Cities Are Fed* (Boston: D.C. Heath, 1929), 20. Hedden's is the earliest usage of the term "foodshed" that I found.

17. Merchant, *Ecological Revolutions,* 182–183. Merchant's detailed estimates

for colonial farm sizes include woodlots, which not only supplied wood but were rotated with pastures and field crops on a fifteen-year cycle.

18. Merchant, *Ecological Revolutions*, 179–180.

19. Washington Irving, "The Legend of Sleepy Hollow" [1820], quoted in John L. Hess and Karen Hess, *The Taste of America*, 3d ed. (New York: Viking, 1977; reprint, Columbia: University of South Carolina Press, 1989), 32–33.

20. Of seventy different foods mentioned in Martha's diary, fifty-four were from her gardens and farm, or the local area. One food she frequently traded for or purchased was salted cod, which presumably came from the coast off Maine or Boston. The only ingredients of more-distant provenance that Martha used routinely were sugar, chocolate, molasses, rice, raisins, salt, pepper, ginger, cinnamon, and the beverages coffee and tea. A few exotic items were used only rarely; for example, she noted only one orange, three lemons, and a bag of tamarinds over the course of twenty-seven years. Many of these special items were recorded in her diary in a year-end list that detailed accounting with storekeepers. See for example, MBDO, Dec. 31, 1795. The seventy local foods do not include numerous herbs that Martha grew primarily for medicinal purposes, such as anise, coriander, sage, and mustard, nor the many varieties of vegetables she grew, including blue potatoes, blue corn, and crambury beans, nor foods prepared from other ingredients, such as rice pudding and sausage. Nor did I include spirits such as cider, beer, and rum, some of which were homemade from local ingredients, others of which were purchased. As Rolla Tryon explained in his classic study, in 1805 it still cost 50 cents to haul 100 pounds 20 miles; so few products justified the cost of transport. Rolla Milton Tryon, *Household Manufacture in the United States, 1640–1860* (Chicago, 1917), 105.

21. Barbara Wheaton, "The Cooks of Concord," *Journal of Gastronomy* (Fall 1984): 8. In a system of cooking based on local ingredients, class differences were expressed by more or less abundance. In colonial New England communities, no one had all that much more livestock than anyone else. In the South, class and race played larger roles in determining what a person might eat, though the nature of the land still set the spread. Particular ecologies gave rise to particular regional cuisines based on a set of ingredients available to local cooks. For descriptions of these regional cuisines, see Evan Jones, *American Food: The Gastronomic Story* (New York: Vintage Books, 1981), 1–32; Raymond Sokolov, *Fading Feast: A Compendium of Disappearing American Regional Foods* (New York: Farrar, Straus, Giroux, 1981). For an excellent description of how a contemporary meal was cooked, see Ruth Schwartz Cowan, *More Work for Mother: The Ironies of*

Household Technology from the Open Hearth to the Microwave (New York: Basic Books, 1983), 22–24. For a wonderful and more detailed account of New England cookery, see also Keith Stavely and Kathleen Fitzgerald, *America's Founding Food: The Story of New England Cooking* (Chapel Hill: University of North Carolina Press, 2003).

22. Wes Jackson, "Farming in Nature's Image: Natural Systems Agriculture," in *The Fatal Harvest Reader: The Tragedy of Industrial Agriculture,* ed. Andrew Kimbrell (Washington, DC: Island Press, 2002), 65–70; Daniel J. Hillel, *Out of the Earth: Civilization and the Life of the Soil* (New York: The Free Press, 1991), 47–51.

23. Richard W. Judd, *Common Lands, Common People: The Origins of Conservation in Northern New England* (Cambridge, MA: Harvard University Press, 1997), 59; Merchant, *Ecological Revolutions,* 128–133. For more on the modern gardener's relationship with nature, see also Michael Pollan, *Second Nature: A Gardener's Education* (New York: Delta, 1991).

24. MBDO, passim. Shelling bean varieties included Poland (July 11, 1800), scarlit (Sept. 17, 1804), and crambury (May 16, 1797).

25. MBDO, June 13, 1786.

26. MBDO, Nov. 1, 1790; June 25, 1791.

27. MBDO, May 7, 1786; Dec. 26, 1800.

28. MBDO, May 22, 1809 (quince); May 9, 1806 (plums); June 17, 1807 (apples); Apr. 28, 1794 (currants); Aug. 19, 1803 (gooseberries); July 27, 1810 (cherries); May 1, 1810 (rhubarb); fruit tarts were baked on many days, including July 10, 1801, May 23, 1804.

29. Ulrich, *Midwife's Tale,* 353–364; MBDO, passim.

30. Tucker, *Kitchen Gardening,* 39–40; MBDO, July 28, 1791; May 2, 1794; Apr. 30, 1791; Oct. 28, 1790.

31. MBDO, May 6, 1799; Sept. 1, 1790; Sept. 8, 1790; Sept. 14, 1790. Martha gathered and saved most of her seeds, a practice that served to select plants best suited to conditions in local gardens. Occasionally, Martha bought seeds (May 26, 1790), which she saved in subsequent years (Aug. 20, 1791). Not until the early nineteenth century did commercial seed businesses begin to take over this traditional task from gardeners. See Tucker, *Kitchen Gardening,* 72–85; Earl W. Hayter, *The Troubled Farmer: Rural Adjustment to Industrialism, 1850–1900* (Dekalb: Northern Illinois University Press, 1968), 181–182.

32. George Lyman Kittredge, *The Old Farmer and His Almanack: Being Some Observation on Life and Manners in New England a Hundred Years Ago* (Cambridge, MA: Harvard University Press, 1924), 306–309; Robb Sagendorph, *America and Her Almanacs: Wit, Wisdom, and Weather* (Dublin,

NH: Yankee Inc., 1970), 126; Merchant, *Ecological Revolutions,* 141; Hayter, *Troubled Farmer,* 6–8; Tucker, *Kitchen Gardening,* 41.

33. Gerald Carson, *The Old Country Store* (New York: Oxford University Press, 1954), 230; Merchant, *Ecological Revolutions,* 117; MBDO, 1785–1811. For the years 1785–1811, Martha usually sowed her first seeds in the third week of April, though, in some years, late frosts delayed planting.

34. Rodney C. Loehr, "Farmers' Diaries: Their Interest and Value as Historical Sources," *Agricultural History* 12, no. 4 (Oct. 1938): 314; MBDO, passim; Anne Sinkler Whaley LeClercq, *An Antebellum Plantation Household Including the South Carolina Low Country Receipts and Remedies of Emily Wharton Sinkler* (Columbia: University of South Carolina Press, 1996), 8.

35. Seeing farms and nature in providential terms: Judd, *Common Lands,* 59; Influence of astrology: Merchant, *Ecologial Revolutions,* 116, and Sagendorph, *America,* 152–153. Almanac editors, who tended to be more highbrow and erudite than their readers, wanted to drop astrology, but because the section was so popular, they feared losing sales.

36. MBDO, Aug. 6, 1792; July 26, 1788; Ulrich, *Midwife's Tale,* 50, 296.

37. MBDO, July 7, 1795; May 6, 1805. In addition to using animal manures, Martha followed the long-standing practice of using human manure to enrich her garden soils. (MBDO, May 15, 1806: "Clear. I have Sett my Sage roots and Done other matters in my gardin, brot manure from behind ye out hous.") Tucker, *Kitchen Gardening,* 101; Ulrich, *Midwife's Tale,* 247. According to Ulrich, using "night soil" to fertilize vegetable gardens may have been common in eighteenth-century Maine, but it also served to complete another, hidden garden cycle. Although it was not understood at the time, the intestinal parasite *Ascaris lumbricoide* was routinely transmitted through fecal matter when insufficiently composted human waste was used to fertilize vegetable gardens. In her diary, Martha sometimes noted that suffering patients and family members "pukt up long worms" after she prescribed emetic rhubarb and senna (May 21, 1802; Aug. 3, 1802; Ulrich, *Midwife's Tale,* 246–247). According to Ulrich, adult *Ascaris* worms are the "diameter of a lead pencil" and could reach 14 inches in length. Although preindustrial families perceived themselves to be embedded in the larger cycles of the natural world that provided their sustenance, they didn't grasp how their guts were also part of farm ecology. According to Tucker, use of night soil fell out of favor by the 1840s.

38. MBDO, May 5, 1792 (beans and beets); May 16, 1794 (cabbage and turnips); May 28, 1795 (beans again).

39. MBDO, June 26, 1795. In the summer of 1790, Martha weeded on at least thirteen days.

40. MBDO, Aug. 1, 1795; July 2, 1790.

41. Merchant, *Ecological Revolutions*, 164. Horace Greeley, who grew up on a Vermont farm, recalled that one of his boyhood jobs was to work ahead of his father "as he hoed his corn, dig open the hills, and kill the wire-worms and grubs." Nearly a century later in 1888, on the prairies, one Kansas mother similarly noted her children working in cornfields day after day. Elliott West, *Growing Up with the Country: Childhood on the Far Western Frontier* (Albuquerque: University of New Mexico Press, 1989), 8.

42. Tucker, *Kitchen Gardening*, 93; Kittredge, *Old Farmer*, 189–190.

43. MBDO, May 28, 1794; June 19, 1799; June 25, 1807; July 1, 1807; June 25, 1808; June 13, 1809; June 16, 1810.

44. MBDO, June 25, 1808.

45. Amelia Simmons, *The First American Cookbook: A Facsimile of "American Cookery," 1796* (New York: Dover Publications, 1984), 45.

46. Judd, *Common Lands*, x; *American Farmer* 1, no. 1 (Apr. 2, 1819): 2. One farmer explained, as a matter of course, that his turnip plantings yielded twenty-two pounds of seed, "besides what the little birds took as their share for having kept down the caterpillars." J. Hector St. John de Crèvecoeur, *Letters from an American Farmer: An 18th-Century Thoreau Writes of the New World* [1782] (New York: Dutton, 1957), 22. Crèvecoeur had observed that kingbirds ate his beloved bees, but they also chased pesky corn-eating crows from his fields. Birds also woke family members with their songs and signaled planting times with their arrival.

47. *Old Farmer's Almanac* [1813], quoted in Kittredge, *Old Farmer*, 119.

48. St. John de Crèvecoeur, *Letters*, 22.

49. Consider the welcome flush of early greens Martha served on May 19, 1796, when she wrote "had a fine mess of greens today from my cabbage stumps." The story of this spring meal can be traced back to the previous fall when Martha tucked the cabbages in the cellar, and then to the day in early May when she noted replanting the stumps (MBDO, Nov. 11, 1795).

50. MBDO, May 26, 1792.

51. MBDO, Apr. 28, 1792; May 4, 1792; May 6, 1792; June 2, 1792.

52. MBDO, Oct. 21, 1792; Dec. 18, 1792.

53. MBDO, Sept. 24, 1786.

54. MBDO, May 31, 1796; passim; McMahon, "Comfortable Subsistence," 38. Cows were mentioned at least eighty times in Martha's diary. On Feb. 13, 1810, her diary entry reveals a sense of desperation: "Clear. I have washt, done hous wk and knit. mr Petengail took [ ] our Cow for Taxes. what we are to do God only knows."

55. MBDO, Apr. 17, 1786; Dec. 14, 1800.

56. MBDO, July 12, 1788; Nov. 26, 1795.

57. MBDO, Apr. 12, 1802; May 11, 1800; May 5, 1808.

58. MBDO, Apr. 12, 1802; May 19, 1800.

59. MBDO, Mar. 17, 1797. That neighbors sometimes dropped off their own cows for Martha to tend suggests that she is always keeping watch on and milking her own cows though she rarely mentions this in her diary.

60. McMahon, "Comfortable Subsistence," 38; MBDO, Jan. 11, 1790; Nov. 5, 1800. Martha not only churned but also bought and received butter in exchange for her midwifery work. An analysis of how she obtained her butter suggests that she did more churning as she became older and perhaps had more time and received less butter as income. Total sums of the butter amounts she mentioned in her diary from 1785 through 1811 suggest that she bought about 122 pounds, churned about 98 pounds, and received about 90 pounds.

61. MBDO, June 4, 1796; July 27, 1785; Ulrich, *Midwife's Tale*, 222–223.

62. MBDO, Jan. 9, 1798.

63. Lafayette Mendel, *Changes in the Food Supply and Their Relation to Nutrition* (New Haven: Yale University Press, 1916), 49–50.

64. MBDO, June 5, 1805; Oct. 26, 1804.

65. Susan Strasser, *Waste and Want: A Social History of Trash* (New York: Metropolitan, 1999), 29.

66. MBDO, Nov. 26, 1795.

67. Ulrich, *Midwife's Tale*, 82. According to Ulrich, thirty-nine young women worked in Martha's household at various times between 1785 and 1800. In rural households, housewives faced with enormous productive workloads depended heavily on extra help from daughters, cousins, and neighbors' daughters, who took apprentice-like work stints to assist with young children and housework.

68. MBDO, Oct. 20, 1803.

69. Merchant, *Ecological Revolutions*, 44, 58. Merchant makes a fascinating comparative exploration of the consciousness of both Native Americans and early colonists in New England, showing how Euro-Americans privileged the visual as their source of knowledge while Native Americans relied on all senses and a participatory mimetic awareness.

70. Merchant, *Ecological Revolutions*, 185–190; Charles Fischman, "The Maine of Martha Ballard: A Self-Guided Tour," pamphlet (Portland: The Maine Humanities Council, n.d.), 3, http://www.dohistory.org/martha/MB_WalkingTour.pdf.

Chapter 2. *To Market, to Market*

1. Amelia Simmons, *The First American Cookbook: A Facsimile of "American Cookery,"* 1796 (New York: Dover Publications, 1984), 1, 28, 34. See also Karen Hess's suggestion that Simmons's cuisine may be of Dutch influence, in her introduction to Amelia Simmons, *American Cookery; or, The Art of Dressing Viands, Fish, Poultry, and Vegetables . . .* , a facsimile of the 2d ed. printed in Albany, NY, 1796 (Bedford, MA: Applewood Books, 1996), xi.

2. Simmons, *First American Cookbook,* 40, 44.

3. Ibid., 45.

4. Ibid.

5. Ibid., 31. This type of "under the cow" syllabub recipe can be found in cookbooks stretching back to Shakespeare's day and may reflect the accretive and at times nostalgic nature of cookbooks. Simmons also included syllabub recipes that did not rely on the heat of a cow's body for those cooks without cows of their own.

6. Sidney W. Mintz, *Sweetness and Power: The Place of Sugar in Modern History* (New York: Penguin, 1985), 79–80. The spice trade had enabled the English to use small amounts of distant flavorings such as cinnamon, nutmeg, mace, ginger, and pepper in cooking since AD 1100.

7. Mintz, *Sweetness and Power,* 64–65. The expansion of slavery and sugar production in the colonial tropics lowered the price of sugar and made it more widely available in eighteenth-century America.

8. George Lyman Kittredge, *The Old Farmer and His Almanack: Being Some Observation on Life and Manners in New England a Hundred Years Ago* (Cambridge, MA: Harvard University Press, 1924), 127.

9. Ibid., 121–122; in the 1807 *Almanac,* Thomas explained: "there is a great satisfaction derived from living as much as possible upon the produce of one's own farm; where no poor slave has toiled in sorrow and pain; where no scoundrel has lorded over your fields; but where honest industry walks peaceful amidst the smiling fruits of his labour." Philadelphia's Dr. Benjamin Rush was another advocate of maple sugaring as a means of protesting slavery.

10. Even abolitionist Lydia Child recommended using Havana sugar. Mrs. Lydia Child, *The American Frugal Housewife, Dedicated to Those Who Are Not Ashamed of Economy,* 12th ed. (Boston: Carter, Hendee and Co., 1832), 20.

11. Simmons, *First American Cookbook,* 18, 46.

12. Alice Kessler-Harris, *Out to Work: A History of Wage-Earning Women in the United States* (New York: Oxford University Press, 1982), 6–7; Daniel E.

Sutherland, *Americans and Their Servants: Domestic Service in the U.S. from 1800 to 1920* (Baton Rouge: Louisiana State University Press, 1981), 46.

13. Simmons, *First American Cookbook*, 3.

14. Simmons, *American Cookery*, 6. In fact, this was a matter with which Amelia did not "consider any way connected" with her own branch of expertise, cookery. In the house where Amelia worked, a male servant may have done the marketing. According to historian Daniel Sutherland, male servants in the most affluent homes were often given this role. See Sutherland, *Americans and Their Servants*, 93.

15. Simmons, *American Cookery*, 5–6. Simmons identified the "transcriber" as either "ignorant" or "evil-intentioned," but the gender of the transcriber remains unknowable.

16. Ibid.

17. Ibid.

18. U.S. Census Bureau, "United States: Urban and Rural, 1790–1990," table 4 in *1990 Census of Population and Housing*, http://www.census.gov/population/censusdata/table-4.pdf (in the 1820 census, "urban" denotes towns with populations over 2,500).

19. Simmons, *First American Cookbook*, 5–17. In archaic usage, "catering" meant buying provisions.

20. Ibid., 7.

21. Mary Randolph, *The Virginia House-wife* [1824] (Columbia: University of South Carolina Press, 1984), 37.

22. Simmons, *First American Cookbook*, 6. In addition to knowing where a fish came from, some shoppers paid attention to lunar phase because the moon was said to affect not only planting and farm chores but food spoilage as well. A salmon tasted best when it was kept for several days out of water, we're told, but only if it could be kept from the heat and the "injurious effect" of the moon.

23. Ibid., 14. The cabbages of Simmons's day were likely "smellier" than modern cabbages, which have been bred to reduce their cooking odors. The transcriber describes particular garden conditions for five different types of cabbages: Low Dutch, Early Yorkshire, Green Savoy, Yellow Savoy, and Red. Note also, the notion that "cabbages require[d] new ground" was based on the assumption that new ground was readily available, or had been available when the anonymous transcriber devised her thoughts about cabbage quality. Such "new grounds" would have persisted only where farmers routinely rotated and fallowed their fields.

24. Ibid., 15.

25. Ibid., 5.

26. Ibid., 8.

27. Ibid., 6–7, 9. The transcriber also mentioned "deceits" used with old cheeses.

28. Ibid., 8. In choosing fowl, close visual inspection of the anus (vent) revealed whether a bird was fresh-killed ("tight vent") or stale ("loose open vent").

29. Ibid., 7–8. Ultimately the transcriber admonished cooks: "if deceits are used, your smell must approve or denounce them [fish]."

30. Ibid., 5.

31. Lydia Maria Child, *The American Frugal Housewife*, with an introduction by Jan Longone (Mineola, NY: Dover Publications, 1999), 53. Child similarly advised pressing upon a bird's breastbone. If it gave easily, the bird was young and succulent, but if it was stiff, the bird was old and tough. Child, in true frugal style, gave recipes for birds both young and old.

32. Simmons, *First American Cookbook*, 9; Child, *American Frugal Housewife*, 14–15. The transcriber, who seemed most concerned with flavor, recommended obtaining butter in May. Child, who seemed most concerned with spending the least money, recommended obtaining butter in September.

33. Sarah Josepha Hale, *Early American Cookery: "The Good Housekeeper," 1841* (Mineola, NY: Dover, 1996), 42.

34. Child, *American Frugal Housewife*, 61.

35. Stephen Nissenbaum, *Sex, Diet, and Debility in Jacksonian America: Sylvester Graham and Health Reform* (Westport, CT: Greenwood Press, 1980), 5; Ruth Schwartz Cowan, *More Work for Mother* (New York: Basic Books, 1983), 47.

36. Eric Bunger, "Dairying and Urban Development in New York State, 1850–1900," *Agricultural History* 29, no. 4 (Oct. 1955): 170. Owing to its highly perishable nature, milk consumed in cities had customarily been produced right in the city. As New York and other large cities had grown and swallowed up their meadows and pastures, milk was produced in distillery dairies—squalid stables where cows fed on mashed grain residue from the whiskey stills. This "swill milk" was unclean, foul tasting, nutrient poor, and often dangerous, especially to the health of infants. In response to demand for cleaner, purer milk, generated largely by citizen activists and philanthropists, by 1843, the Erie Railroad was hauling more than three million quarts from Orange County into New York City. Farmers milked cows in the morning and poured the milk into cans, cooling it by stirring with an ice-filled metal tube. The milk was then brought by wagon to the railroad for its roughly sixty-mile, four-and-one-half-hour journey to market, where it was again cooled by ice wand until it was sold.

37. This transition happened at different times in different places. For example

in the Boston suburb Brookline, farmers started to shift from growing largely for themselves to growing food for Boston in the late 1700s. By 1845, vegetables, fruit, and hay for the urban market accounted for 78 percent of the town's agricultural production. Ronald Dale Karr, "The Transformation of Agriculture in Brookline, 1770–1885," *Historical Journal of Massachusetts* 15 (Jan. 1987): 33–39.

38. George Rogers Taylor, *The Transportation Revolution, 1815–1860* (New York: Rinehart & Co., 1951), 79; Louis M. Hacker et al., *The U.S.: A Graphic History* (New York: Modern Age Books, 1937), 44; James L. McCorkle, Jr. "Moving Perishables to Market: Southern Railroads and the Nineteenth Century Origins of Southern Truck Farming," *Agricultural History* 66, no.1 (Winter 1992): 42–62; L. D. H. Weld, *The Marketing of Farm Products* (New York: Macmillan, 1916), 226–227; John L. White, *The Great Yellow Fleet: A History of American Railroad Refrigerator Cars* (San Marino, CA: Gold West Books, 1986), 13–15.

39. "Abattoirs: History of New-York Slaughter-Houses, Interesting and Curious Data," *New York Times*, April 1, 1866. De Voe became an apprentice in 1827.

40. Thomas F. De Voe, *The Market Assistant: containing a brief description of every article of human food sold in the public markets of the cities of New York, Boston, Philadelphia, and Brooklyn; including the various domestic and wild animals, poultry, game, fish, vegetables, fruits, with many curious incidents and anecdotes* (New York: Orange Judd, 1866), 225.

41. Ibid., 211.

42. Ibid., 201.

43. Ibid., 155, 288–300. Throughout the fish section, De Voe makes repeated reference to DeKay's *New York Fauna*.

44. Ibid., 145–180.

45. Ibid., 26.

46. Ibid., 85.

47. Ibid., 179, 118. According to De Voe, Charlevoix had claimed two eaglets he'd eaten "made very good food." Audubon had described mule deer meat as "tender and good flavored."

48. Ibid., 405.

49. U.S. Census Bureau, "United States: Urban and Rural, 1790–1990," table 4; Campbell Gibson, "Population of the 100 Largest Cities and Other Urban Places in the United States: 1790 to 1990," Population Division Working Paper no. 27 (Washington, DC: U.S. Census Bureau, June 1998), table 5, http://www.census.gov/population/www/documentation/twps-0027.html.

50. U.S. Census Bureau, "United States: Urban and Rural, 1790–1990," table 4.

51. Kessler-Harris, *Out to Work,* 121.

52. De Voe, *Market Assistant,* 21; Faye Dudden, *Serving Women: Domestic Service in 19th-century America* (Middletown, CT: Wesleyan University Press, 1983), 136. According to Dudden, there is other evidence to suggest the ragged chronological shifts from husbands to homemakers to servants doing the shopping in affluent families. Inveterate traveler Frances Trollope described the scene in early nineteenth-century Cincinnati: "It is the custom for the gentleman to go to market . . . the smartest men in the place, and those of the 'highest standing' do not scruple to leave their beds with the sun, six days in the week, and, prepared with a mighty basket, to sally forth in search of meat, butter, eggs, and vegetables." By the mid-1900s, men began to reject their "marketing" role as too closely related to female work of preparing food and started to foist it back onto women. One gent complained that husbands had quite enough to do "without the additional burden of what properly belongs to their wives. Going to market, dealing with the grocer."

53. Gerda Lerner, "The Lady and the Mill Girl: Changes in the Status of Women in the Age of Jackson," in *Our American Sisters: Women in American Life and Thought,* ed. Jean E. Friedman, William G. Shade, and Mary Jane Capozzoli (New York: D. C. Heath, 1987), 131–134.

54. Kessler-Harris, *Out to Work,* 49; Dudden, *Serving Women,* 54, 155. Note at the time, the term "housekeeper" referred to the mistress who managed the whole household, as in *Good Housekeeping* magazine, not to the hired maid. I have used the term "homemaker" as much as possible in order to avoid confusion that might come from mixing up the contemporary Victorian meaning with the modern meaning of "housekeeper."

55. Sutherland, *Americans and Their Servants,* 46; Dudden, *Serving Women,* 66.

56. Joseph P. Ferrie, *Yankeys Now: Immigrants in the Antebellum U.S., 1840 to 1860* (New York: Oxford University Press, 1999), 35; John Blum et al., ed., *The National Experience: A History of the United States* (San Diego: Harcourt Brace, 1989), 283.

57. Kessler-Harris, *Out to Work,* 69–70. Many black women sought domestic work at midcentury, but their numbers would increase after emancipation.

58. Helen C. Callahan, "Upstairs Downstairs in Chicago, 1870–1907: The Glessner Household," *Chicago History* 6 (1977–1978): 195–209; Lerner, "Lady and Mill Girl," 132.

59. Dudden, *Serving Women,* 66

60. Ibid.

61. Hale, *Early American Cookery,* 133.

62. Child, *American Frugal Housewife*, 91–98.

63. Ibid., 92. Child lamented young women's indolence.

64. Dudden, *Serving Women*, 172–173.

65. Catherine Beecher and Harriet Beecher Stowe, *The American Woman's Home; or, Principles of Domestic Service* (New York: J. B. Ford, 1869), 436. They continued, "Nothing so thoroughly ensures the intelligent obedience of orders, as evidence that the person ordering knows exactly what is wanted." Catherine Beecher was one of the most influential domestic feminist writers of the nineteenth century. Her sister Harriet Beecher Stowe was, of course, better known for her abolitionist novel *Uncle Tom's Cabin*.

66. Janice Williams Rutherford, *Selling Mrs. Consumer: Christine Frederick and the Rise of Household Efficiency* (Athens: University of Georgia Press, 2003), 9. This woman was the grandmother of Christine Frederick, a home efficiency expert who we'll read about in chapter 6.

67. Catherine Beecher, *Miss Beecher's Domestic Receipt-Book*, 5th ed. (New York: Harper and Bros., 1870), 230, quoted in Dudden, *Serving Women*, 174.

68. Sutherland, *Americans and Their Servants*, 30–32, 114; Dudden, *Serving Women*, 119, 132. Even foods ordered and delivered by clerks were usually ushered in through back doors and then stored in the cellar, effectively cloaking the physical needs to the family in Victorian decorum. In the most affluent households, the mistress rarely even saw the food arrive. Only after it was cooked, and thereby refined, was food carried upstairs or hauled via dumbwaiter to a higher-level dining room where it was eaten.

69. Cowan, *More Work for Mother*, 120, for the number of women working as domestics.

70. Susan J. Kleinberg, "Technology and Women's Work: The Lives of Working Class Women in Pittsburgh, 1870–1900," *Labor History* 17 (Winter 1976): 62–63.

71. "The Food Question," *Good Housekeeping*, Aug. 6, 1887, 171; Kleinberg, "Technology," 69–70.

72. Harvey Levenstein, *Revolution at the Table: The Transformation of the American Diet* (New York: Oxford University Press, 1988), 23–26; Cowan, *More Work for Mother*, 80, 162–165. As Cowan has pointed out, "the other half" comprised more than half of the population at this time, but it is difficult to make generalizations about their diets and food preferences. Some were skilled wageworkers; others were unskilled. Some were immigrants from foreign nations facing language barriers and prejudices; some were from rural areas. Some immigrants cherished their traditional foodways; others had less strong desires to maintain these customs. See Cowan and Levenstein for good descriptions of working-class diets.

73. Cowan, *More Work for Mother*, 99, 122.

74. Eunice Bullard Beecher, *Motherly Talks with Young Housekeepers* (New York: J. B. Ford, 1873), 91, and Eunice Bullard Beecher, *All Around the House; or, How to Make Homes Happy* (New York: D. Appleton & Co., 1885), 89, quoted in Dudden, *Serving Women*, 136–137.

75. Maria Parloa, "The Household Market Basket," *Good Housekeeping*, Jan. 1893, 2.

76. Ibid.

77. Ibid.

78. Ibid., July 1893, 1.

79. Ibid., Jan. 1893, 2.

80. Mrs. Benson's column in *Good Housekeeping* ran from 1886 to 1887; Maria Parloa's popular "Household Market Basket" column in *Good Housekeeping* ran in 1893.

81. Maria Parloa, *Choice Receipts and Specimen Pages from Miss Parloa's New Cook-Book and Marketing Guide* (New York: Orange Judd Co., 1881), National Museum of American History, Warshaw Collection, Cookbooks, Box 1. In addition, America's homemakers had the responsibility to know what constituted quality and value at the market in order to uphold the morality of market men and commercial enterprise in general. By many accounts, a shopper who permitted herself to be duped by a deceitful vendor was considered the provocateur of such immoral behavior.

Chapter 3. *Mystifying the Mundane*

1. Mrs. F. A. Benson, "Table Supplies and Economies: What to Buy, When to Buy and How to Buy Wisely and Well," *Good Housekeeping*, July 9, 1887, 128. As just one example of many, Mrs. Benson specified that butter tasted best in July when "cows were not yet troubled by flies."

2. Maria Parloa, "The Household Market Basket," *Good Housekeeping*, Jan. 1893, 2.

3. "All Kinds of Food," *Good Housekeeping*, Feb. 6, 1886, 216; Mrs. F. A. Benson "Seasonable Table Supplies," *Good Housekeeping*, Feb. 20, 1886, 248.

4. Mrs. F. A. Benson, "Table Supplies and Economies," *Good Housekeeping*, May 14, 1887, 32.

5. Ibid., July 9, 1887, 128.

6. Ibid., May 14, 1887, 32.

7. Ibid., Aug. 7, 1886, 180.

8. Newton Norton, "A Cholera Food: A Plea for Well-Matured Fruit," *Good Housekeeping*, April 1893, 169. At the time, many believed that unripe fruit might be a cause of cholera.

9. Mrs. F. A. Benson, "Seasonable Table Supplies," *Good Housekeeping*, March

20, 1886, 304. Mrs. Benson scornfully warned against March strawberries that had arrived from Florida "not in satisfactory condition being only half ripe."

10. Maria Parloa, "Gastronomic Thoughts and Suggestions," *Good Housekeeping,* Jan. 23, 1886, 173.

11. Mrs. F. A. Benson, "Table Supplies and Economies," *Good Housekeeping,* May 28, 1887, 56.

12. Thomas F. De Voe, *The Market Assistant: containing a brief description of every article of human food sold in the public markets of the cities of New York, Boston, Philadelphia, and Brooklyn; including the various domestic and wild animals, poultry, game, fish, vegetables, fruits, with many curious incidents and anecdotes* (New York: Orange Judd, 1866), 110–111. According to De Voe, on Feb. 1, 1823, the *Commercial Advertiser* had announced that two wagons from Sullivan County arrived at the Fulton Market filled with hares, partridges, venison, and even a panther to sell.

13. De Voe, *Market Assistant,* 160–161.

14. Ibid., 200–201; Mrs. F. A. Benson, "Seasonable Table Supplies," *Good Housekeeping,* Feb. 20, 1886, 248; May 1, 1886, 388; March 20, 1886, 304.

15. De Voe, *Market Assistant,* 149, 152, 159. "Partridges" (actually ruffed grouse; we have no true partridges in the United States) were to be avoided after heavy snowstorms, when they were often forced to eat the leaves of green laurel, which, according to De Voe, contained a poison that could kill a heedless eater.

16. Ibid., 161.

17. Mrs. F. A. Benson, "Seasonable Table Supplies," *Good Housekeeping,* Sept. 4, 1886, 228. Benson wrote, "Game hooks are growing fantastic with the long needle-bills and slender claws of snipe."

18. Gary Kulik, "Dams, Fish and Farmers: Defense of Public Rights in Eighteenth Century Rhode Island," in *The Countryside in the Age of Capitalist Transformation: Essays in the Social History of Rural America,* ed. Stephen Hahn and Jonathan Prude (Chapel Hill: University of North Carolina Press, 1985), 25–50. Many other fish species and eels were also affected by river-blocking dams; only in the past twenty years have some of these runs been restored.

19. Tim Palmer, *Endangered Rivers and the Conservation Movement* (Berkeley: University of California Press, 1986), 16. With factories, the larger mainstem rivers were dammed. In 1789, Hadley Falls Dam blocked three hundred miles of fish habitat on the Connecticut River, and in 1838, Edwards Dam blocked Martha Ballard's Kennebec near Augusta.

20. De Voe, *Market Assistant,* 241.

21. Louis S. Warren, *The Hunter's Game: Poachers and Conservationists in Twentieth Century America* (New Haven: Yale University Press, 1997), 48–51.

22. Maria Parloa, "Gastronomic Thoughts and Suggestions," *Good Housekeeping,* Feb. 20, 1886, 236. Parloa suggested specific substitutions of one type of game for another, such as stall-fed pigeons for wild, and ptarmigan from Canada for grouse. Even recently, shopper's mentality impelled Idaho's Rep. Helen Chenoweth in 1996 to block endangered species protection for wild salmon runs in her state. She could not understand how a fish found canned on supermarket shelves could possibly be endangered.

23. Mrs. Sarah T. Rorer, *Philadelphia Cookbook* (Philadelphia: Arnold & Co., 1886), 210–211. In several of Mrs. Benson's 1886 market reports, wild pigeon were still available for $2.50 per dozen compared with $3 per dozen for stall-fed birds.

24. De Voe, *Market Assistant,* 174–175. According to De Voe, the *Boston Weekly Post-boy* of May 2, 1771, reported, "The great numbers of pigeons that have been brought to our market with in the fortnight past has greatly reduced the prices of all kinds of provisions. It is said that nearly fifty thousand were sold in one day."

25. Maria Elisa Rundell, *American Domestic Cookery* (New York: Evert Duyckinck, 1823), 156, quoted in Jennifer Price, *Flight Maps: Adventures with Nature in Modern America* (New York: Basic Books, 1999), 10.

26. De Voe, *Market Assistant,* 174.

27. Price, *Flight Maps,* 4.

28. Ibid., 5.

29. Ibid., 36.

30. Ibid., 40, 46. I am indebted to Price's fine analysis for this section on passenger pigeons. Price explains that the upper-crust diners who ate the last wild pigeons were unaware of the connection between their own eating and the pigeon's ultimate collapse. In fact, many had the gall to blame market hunters—who had killed the same birds they feasted on—for the pigeons' demise.

31. Mrs. J. Chadwick, *Home Cookery* [1853], cited in Joseph Conlin, "Consider the Oyster," *American Heritage* 31, no. 2 (Feb./Mar. 1980): 70. Most of an oyster's weight is in its shell, so obtaining six pounds of meat requires quite a number of oysters.

32. Conlin, "Consider the Oyster," 64; Evan Jones, *American Food: The Gastronomic Story* (New York: Vintage Books, 1981), 129–130. Conlin called the nineteenth "the oyster century."

33. "Oyster Trade of Virginia," *Debow's Review* 24, no. 3 (March 1858): 259;

"Protecting Oyster Beds," *New York Times,* Sept. 3, 1886, 8; "Spoiling the Oyster Beds," *New York Times,* June 20, 1886, 10.

34. "Oyster Protector Appointed," *New York Times,* Feb. 18, 1886, 2.

35. "Oyster Beds in Sound—Injury by Garbage from Street-Cleaning Department Dumps," *New York Times,* Sept. 3, 1886, 4.

36. "Oyster Protector Appointed," "Protecting Oyster Beds," "Spoiling the Oyster Beds." Such acids killed off oysters and fish at a concentration of 1 part sludge acid to 1,000 parts water. See also Mark Kurlansky, *The Big Oyster: History on the Half Shell* (New York: Ballantine, 2006), 259–262.

37. "Our Tables Will Suffer: Terrapin and Canvas-back Surely Disappearing," *New York Times,* 15 Feb. 1891, 19. "Blue Point" eventually came to refer to any oyster taken on the south shore of Long Island. Kurlansky, *The Big Oyster,* 133–134.

38. "Our Tables Will Suffer."

39. Ibid.

40. Walter Minot, "The Game Food of America," *International Review* 9 (1880): 136–142; Henry T. Finck, *Food and Flavor: A Gastronomic Guide to Health and Good Living* (New York: The Century Co., 1913), 478.

41. Benson, "Seasonable Table Supplies," Sept. 4, 1886, 228; Benson, "Table Supplies and Economies," May 28, 887, 56.

42. "Game Bill Passes Senate; Prohibits Sale of Many Species, but Allows Breeding on Farms," *New York Times,* May 26, 1911, 8; "Scarcity Forces America to Protect Its Game," *New York Times,* Sept. 3, 1911, Sm-7.

43. Mrs. Henry Ward [Eunice] Beecher, *The Home: How to Make it and Keep it* (Minneapolis: Buckeye Publishers, 1885), 381–383; Mrs. Sarah T. Rorer, *Philadelphia Cookbook* (Philadelphia: Arnold & Co., 1886), 198, 207.

44. De Voe, *Market Assistant,* 65.

45. Ibid., 49–50.

46. "The Market Systems of the Country, Their Usages and Abuses," in *Report of the Commissioner of Agriculture for the Year 1870* (Washington, DC: GPO, 1871), 250–251.

47. Ibid., 251.

48. "How New York is Fed," *Scribner's Monthly* (Oct. 1877), reprinted in *The Journal of Gastronomy* 4 (Spring 1988): 73. This article explained that by 1877 cattle were rested and watered twice en route from Chicago but still called the manner of their transportation "inhuman to the extreme." Texas cattle were also subject to tick infestations as they were driven north.

49. "The Market Systems of the Country, Their Usages and Abuses," 253–254.

50. Hosia R. Diner, *Hungering for America: Italian, Irish, and Jewish Foodways*

in the Age of Migration (Cambridge, MA: Harvard University Press, 2001), 12–13.

51. William Cronon, *Nature's Metropolis: Chicago and the Great West* (New York: W.W. Norton, 1991), 236. I am indebted to Cronon's analysis of how the Chicago packing industry fundamentally changed the nature of how meat was raised and sold.

52. Ibid., 228–234.

53. Ibid., 235, 239. At first, the most direct rail lines, which profited from the ponderous livestock freight, were not interested in hauling less weight in the more expensive, time-consuming, and labor-intensive ice cars. Swift took his business to the underdog Grand Trunk, a railroad that swung far north on its path east. Eventually, other railroads acceded to haul refrigerator cars packed with meat.

54. Louis F. Swift, *The Yankee of the Yards: The Geography of Gustavus Franklin Swift* (Chicago: A.W. Shaw & Co., 1927), 207. For most, the very "idea of eating meat a week or more after it had been killed," Swift's son later wrote, "met with a nasty-nice horror"; quoted in Cronon, *Nature's Metropolis*, 235. Maria Parloa also referred to prejudice against dressed beef when it was first sent east; see Parloa, "The Household Market Basket," *Good Housekeeping*, Oct. 1893, 151–152.

55. Swift, *Yankee of the Yards*, 70.

56. Cronon, *Nature's Metropolis*, 241–242; David C. Smith and Anne E. Bridges, "The Brighton Market: Feeding Nineteenth Century Boston," *Agricultural History* 56 (Jan. 1982): 13.

57. Cronon, *Nature's Metropolis*, 237.

58. Ibid., 243.

59. "Hog Killing at the Chicago Stock Yards," *Scientific American*, Nov. 7, 1891, 291.

60. Upton Sinclair, *The Jungle* [1905], 12th ed. (New York: Signet Classics, 1960), 39–40.

61. Ibid., 40; Cronon, *Nature's Metropolis*, 208. English visitor and writer Rudyard Kipling (*From Sea to Sea: Letters of Travel*, 1899) was also disturbed by the bold indifference of his fellow visitors and worried what effect such mass killing might have on the souls of human eaters. He regarded their mien as evidence of a disturbing American brutality and ferocity.

62. Parloa, "The Household Market Basket," Oct. 1893, 151–152.

63. Ibid.

64. "Beef Is Always in Season," in *Swift & Company Year Book* (1924), 26–27, Smithsonian Institution, National Museum of American History, Archives Center, Warshaw Collection of Business Americana, Meat, Box 4.

Chapter 4. *Denaturing the Senses*

1. Mrs. F. A. Benson, "Table Supplies and Economies," *Good Housekeeping,* Aug. 6, 1887, 176.

2. Ibid., July 9, 1887, 128.

3. Ibid., May 28, 1887, 56.

4. Ad for Imperium Granum, *Ladies' Home Journal,* Jan. 1892, 13.

5. *A Compendium of the Ninth Census* (Washington, DC: GPO, 1872), 800–809, cited in Mark William Wilde, "Industrialization of Food Processing in the United States, 1860–1960" (Ph.D. diss., University of Delaware, 1988), 22; Edward F. Keuchel, "Master of the Art of Canning: Baltimore, 1860–1900," *Maryland Historical Magazine* 67, no. 4 (Winter 1972): 355.

6. Wilde, "Industrialization of Food Processing," 33, 48; James Harvey Young, *Pure Food: Securing the Federal Food and Drug Act of 1906* (Princeton: Princeton University Press, 1989), 108–109.

7. L. I. Wiegel, "Quality," in *The Burt Olney Canning Company* (Oneida, NY: Ryan & Burkhart, ca. 1911), n.p. Bitting Collection, Library of Congress.

8. Arvil W. Bitting and Katherine G. Bitting, *Canning and How to Use Canned Foods* (Washington, DC: National Canners Association, 1916), 9, quoted in Wilde, "Industrialization of Food Processing," 46.

9. Christine Terhune Herrick, "What I Have Learned about Canned Foods: The Whole Story of a Vanished Prejudice," *Women's Home Companion,* Feb. 1914, 20.

10. Laurence A. Johnson, *Over the Counter and on the Shelf* (Rutland, VT: Tuttle Co., 1961), 87.

11. Wilde, "Industrialization of Food Processing," 41–42; James Harvey Young, "Botulism and the Ripe Olive Scare of 1919–1920," *Bulletin of the History of Medicine* 50 (1976): 372–391.

12. *The Grocer's Review* 21, no. 1 (Mar. 1912): 14.

13. J. F. J. Sykes, "Tinned Foods," *Good Housekeeping,* Oct. 1897, 178; Sarah T. Rorer, "For Those Who Live Out of Cans," *Ladies' Home Journal,* Jan. 1909, 42.

14. Perry Duis, *Challenging Chicago: Coping with Everyday Life, 1837–1920* (Urbana: University of Illinois Press, 1998), 118.

15. Alex J. Wedderburn, *A Popular Treatise on the Extent and Character of Food Adulterations,* Bulletin no. 25, U.S. Dept. of Agriculture, Division of Chemistry (Washington, DC: GPO, 1890), 7; Henry T. Finck, *Food and Flavor: A Gastronomic Guide to Health and Good Living* (New York: The Century Co., 1913), 17. See also *New York Times* online archive: a search for "adulterat* food" yielded over 600 stories for the period 1850–1900.

16. Young, *Pure Food*, 110; "Canned Foods," *Public Opinion in a Comprehensive Summary of Press throughout the World on All Important Current Topics*, Sept. 23, 1893, 578; "Is Canned Food Poisonous? *New York Times*, Apr. 10, 1884, 5; Keuchel, "Master of the Art of Canning," 360.

17. Florence Corbett, *Canned Foods: Fruits and Vegetables* (New York: Teacher's College, Columbia University, 1913), 10, quoted in Wilde, "Industrialization of Food Processing," 45.

18. Olive Lyle, "Cottonseed Oil in the Kitchen," *Good Housekeeping*, June 26, 1886, 100. Lyle called the new lards and lard and vegetable shortenings "manufactured mysteries."

19. Harvey W. Wiley, *Foods and Their Adulteration: Origin, Manufacture and Composition of Food Products, Description of Common Adulterations, Food Standards and National Food Laws and Regulations* (Philadelphia: P. Blakiston's Sons, 1907), 228, 370.

20. Ellen Richards, *Food Materials and their Adulteration* [1885], quoted in Susan Strasser, *Satisfaction Guaranteed: The Making of the American Mass Market* (New York: Pantheon, 1989; reprint, Washington, DC: Smithsonian Institution Press, 1995), 255; Sarah T. Rorer, *Canning and Preserving* (Philadelphia: Arnold and Co., 1887), preface, quoted in Wilde, "Industrialization of Food Processing," 56.

21. "Guard Against Adulteration" Good Housekeeping, Sept. 18, 1886, 250.

22. Lyle, "Cottonseed Oil," 100.

23. Herrick, "What I Have Learned," 20.

24. "Adulteration of Foods: Abstinence from Many 'Prepared' Foods a Safe Rule to Follow," *Good Housekeeping*, Sept. 1893, n.p.

25. Johnson, *Over the Counter and on the Shelf*, 87.

26. Strasser, *Satisfaction Guaranteed*, 39–41.

27. "Brookside Sugar Corn," can label, Smithsonian Institution, National Museum of American History (NMAH), Archives Center, Warshaw Collection of Business Americana (Warshaw), Food, Box 22, corn, n.d. (ca. 1880s).

28. *American Grocer*, New York, Mar. 7, 1874, clipping, NMAH, Warshaw, Food, Folder 14.

29. William Longyear, "Contemporary Labels," *Modern Packaging*, Dec. 1947, 118–120.

30. "Try Our New Package," trade card, NMAH, Warshaw, Meat, Box 4, Swift Co., n.d. (ca. 1880s).

31. Robert Jay, *The Trade Card in Nineteenth Century America* (Columbia: University of Missouri Press, 1987), 3; "Teacher — What is the most important production of the U.S.?" trade card, NMAH, Warshaw, Meat, Box 4, Swift Co., n.d. (ca. 1880s).

32. "Corn Makes Me King," trade card, NMAH, Warshaw, Meat, Box 4, N. K. Fairbanks, n.d. (ca. 1880s).

33. "Boston Codfish Balls," trade card, NMAH, Warshaw, Meat, Box 3, Henry Mayo & Co., n.d. (ca. 1870s).

34. William Cronon, *Nature's Metropolis: Chicago and the Great West* (New York: W.W. Norton, 1991), 116–118.

35. "The Choicest Foods," trade cards, NMAH, Warshaw, Cereal, Box 1, American Breakfast Cereal, 1880.

36. "Health, Wealth, and a Good Breakfast," ad, NMAH, Warshaw, Cereal, Box 1, Folder 1, American Cereal Company (Quaker Oats), 1896; Box 2, Folder 10, American Cereal Company, 1895.

37. "Oleomargarine—How It Is Made," *Scientific American*, April 24, 1880, 258–259; Young, *Pure Food*, 71–73.

38. Earl Hayter, *The Troubled Farmer: Rural Adjustment to Industrialism, 1850–1900* (DeKalb: Northern Illinois University Press, 1968), 63.

39. J. H. van Stuyvenberg, ed. *Margarine: An Economic, Social and Scientific History, 1869–1969* (University of Toronto Press, 1969), 261; "Bread and ____," pamphlet, NMAH, Product Cookbooks Collection, Box 4, Folder 7, Swift Co., 1916.

40. Hayter, *The Troubled Farmer*, 67.

41. Ibid., 72; Young, *Pure Food*, 73.

42. Young, *Pure Food*, 83.

43. Ibid., 87; Hayter, *The Troubled Farmer*, 61.

44. "Artificial Butter and Butter Swindles," *Scientific American*, July 15, 1893, 34; Hayter, *The Troubled Farmer*, 69.

45. "Artificial Butter and Butter Swindles," 34.

46. Young, *Pure Food*, 73; James Harvey Young, "'This Greasy Counterfeit,' Butter versus Oleomargarine in the United States Congress, 1886," *Bulletin of the History of Medicine* 53, no. 3 (1979): 392–414; Hayter, *The Troubled Farmer*, 81.

47. Tamara K. Hareven and Randolph Langenbach, *Amoskeag: Life and Work in an American Factory-City* (New York: Pantheon Books, 1978), 53. This response was slightly later than the period I am discussing (1902). Ads would continue to refer to homemakers' unfair "prejudice" against margarine for decades.

48. Dana Frank, "Housewives, Socialists, and the Politics of Food: The 1917 New York Cost-of-Living Protests," *Feminist Studies* 11, no. 2 (Summer 1985), 262.

49. Wedderburn, *A Popular Treatise*, 27.

50. Rep. Richard Lee Beale (VA), *Congressional Record*, 46th Congress, 1st session (March 23, 1879), 1552, quoted in Young, *Pure Food*, 48.

51. Rep. Robert La Follette (WI), *Congressional Record,* 49th Congress, 1st session, Appendix, 223–226, cited in Young, "This Greasy Counterfeit," 398.

52. Rep. Lewis Beach (NY), *Congressional Record,* 49th Congress, 1st session, 4910, quoted in Young, *Pure Food,* 84.

53. Young, "This Greasy Counterfeit," 392.

54. Young, *Pure Food,* 72.

55. Rep. Ferris Jacobs (NY), Hearings before the Committee on Ways and Means in Relation to House Bill 142, Apr. 25 [and May 9], 1882, 47th Congress, 1st session, 1882, quoted in Young, *Pure Food,* 75.

56. Sen. John Franklin Miller (CA), *Congressional Record,* 49th Congress, 1st session, 7078, quoted in Young, *Pure Food,* 75.

57. Young, "This Greasy Counterfeit," 407–408.

58. "Food Fairs," *New England Kitchen Magazine,* Oct. 1894, 43, quoted in Laura Shapiro, *Perfection Salad: Women and Cooking at the Turn of the Century* (New York: Henry Holt, 1986), 197. The full quote is, "The practices which have savored of dishonesty on the part of some dealers have had their origin through the ignorance of the consumer." Again, this quote pins moral responsibility to shoppers.

59. George K. Holmes, "Consumers' Fancies," in *Yearbook of Agriculture* (U.S. Department of Agriculture, 1904), 433.

60. "The Pure Food Problem," *Journal of Public Health* 3, no. 4 (Feb. 1906): 1.

61. Wiley, *Foods and Their Adulteration,* 185.

62. Young, *Pure Food,* 100–106; Donna J. Wood, "The Strategic Use of Public Policy: Business Support for the 1906 Food and Drug Act," *Business History Review* 59, no. 3 (1985): 408; Wedderburn, *A Popular Treatise,* 14.

63. Wedderburn, *A Popular Treatise,* 9.

64. Ibid., 16, 21, 29.

65. Wiley, *Foods and Their Adulteration,* 371.

66. Ibid., 370–371.

67. Ibid., 372.

68. Ibid.

69. "The Pure Food Problem," 1.

70. Harvey Wiley, "Food Reconstruction," *Good Housekeeping,* Feb. 1919, quoted in Harvey Levenstein, *Revolution at the Table: The Transformation of the American Diet* (New York: Oxford University Press, 1988), 251, note 48.

71. Wiley, *Foods and Their Adulteration,* 374.

Chapter 5. *A New Longing for Nature*

1. Maud Howe Elliot, "Country Maids and City Wives," *Ladies' Home Journal,* February 1892, 7.

2. T. J. Jackson Lears, "From Salvation to Self-Realization: Advertising and the Therapeutic Roots of the Consumer Culture," in *The Culture of Consumption: Critical Essays in American History, 1880–1980*, ed. Richard Wightman Fox and T. J. Jackson Lears (New York: Pantheon, 1983), 6–7. Lears has called these "feelings of unreality." Nervous breakdowns were frequently diagnosed as neurasthenia. According to Dr. George Beard, this "epidemic of advanced civilization" was caused by the nerve-wracking stresses of modern life, which taxed the body's nerve force too heavily. The recommended treatment was a break from the urban bustle. George Beard, *American Nervousness: Its Causes and Consequences* (New York, 1881), quoted in James C. Whorton, *Crusaders for Fitness: The History of American Health Reformers* (Princeton, NJ: Princeton University Press, 1982), 148–150.

3. Peter J. Schmitt, *Back to Nature: The Arcadian Myth in Urban America* (New York: Oxford University Press, 1969), viii.

4. Ibid., xvii–xxi.

5. Lois Whitney, *Primitivism and the Idea of Progress in English Popular Literature of the Eighteenth Century* (Baltimore: Johns Hopkins Press, 1934), 137.

6. Carolyn Merchant, *Ecological Revolutions: Nature, Gender, and Science in New England* (Chapel Hill: University of North Carolina Press, 1989), 114–115.

7. Carl Anthony, "Ecopsychology and the Deconstruction of Whiteness," in *Ecopsychology: Restoring the Earth, Healing the Mind*, ed. Theodore Roszak, Mary E. Gomes, and Allen D. Kanner (San Francisco: Sierra Club Books, 1995), 27.

8. Catherine Beecher, *A Treatise on Domestic Economy* (New York: Marsh Capen Lyon and Webb, 1841), 40, quoted in Laura Shapiro, *Perfection Salad: Women and Cooking at the Turn of the Century* (New York: Henry Holt and Company, 1986), 29.

9. David M. Katzman, *Seven Days a Week: Women and Domestic Service in Industrializing America* (New York: Oxford University Press, 1978), 44, 59, 128; Lucy Maynard Salmon, *Domestic Service* (New York: Macmillan, 1897; reprint, New York: Arno Press, 1972), 69–70.

10. Norbert Elias, *The Civilizing Process: Sociogenetic and Psychogenic Investigations*, trans. Edmund Jephcott, rev. ed. (Malden, MA: Blackwell, 2000), 429–430.

11. Mary Douglas, *Purity and Danger: An Analysis of the Concepts of Pollution and Taboo* (London: Routledge & Kegan Paul, 1966), 2–3.

12. R. A. McCance and E. M. Widdowson, *Breads White and Brown: Their Place in Thought and Social History* (London: Pitman Medical Publishing Co.

Ltd., 1956), 46–47. This book is primarily about England but includes information about the U.S. wheat industry because England imported a great deal of U.S. wheat; Ida M. Tarbell, *The Nationalizing of Business, 1878–1898* (New York: Macmillan Co. 1936; reprint, 1946), 128–129; Ruth Schwartz Cowan, *More Work for Mother: The Ironies of Household Technology from the Open Hearth to the Microwave* (New York: Basic Books, 1983), 51.

13. Mary J. Lincoln, *The Boston Cook Book,* rev. (Boston: Little, Brown, 1900), 458, quoted in Harvey Levenstein, *Revolution at the Table: The Transformation of the American Diet* (New York: Oxford, 1988), 32–33.

14. Sarah Josepha Hale, *Early American Cookery: "The Good Housekeeper,"* 1841 (Mineola, NY: Dover, 1996), 21; Sarah Josepha Hale, *Manners; or, Happy Homes and Good Society All the Year Round* (Boston: J. E. Tilton & Co. 1868), 27; Isabella Beeton, *Beeton's Book of Household Management* (1861), 39, cited in Michael Symons, *A History of Cooks and Cooking* (Urbana: University of Illinois Press, 2000), 206. This concept of cooking as civilizing force may be traced back at least to Brillat-Savarin, who wrote, "Cooking is also of all the arts the one which has done the most to advance our civilization, for the needs of the kitchen were what first taught us to use fire, and it is by fire that man has tamed Nature itself." Brillat-Savarin, *Meditation* 27 (1971): 279, quoted in Symons, 207. See also later examples of this motif in Shapiro, *Perfection Salad,* 90, 95.

15. Catherine Beecher, *The New Housekeeper's Manual* (New York: J. B. Ford & Company, 1873), 170.

16. Modern anthropologists have recently given credence to this civilizing story, linking the development of cooking to the evolution of humans' large brains and small teeth. See Natalie Angier, "Cooking and How it Slew the Beast Within," *New York Times,* May 28, 2002, F1–10, which refers to the work of Harvard anthropologist Dr. Richard W. Wrangham.

17. Hector St. John de Crèvecoeur, *Letters from an American Farmer* (New York: Dutton, 1957), 215–216; Merchant, *Ecological Revolutions,* 64–65.

18. Mrs. E. A. Howland, *The New England Economical Housekeeper* (Montpelier, VT: E. P. Walton and Sons, 1845), 13, quoted in Eleanor T. Fordyce, "Cookbooks of the 1800s," in *Dining in America, 1850–1900,* ed. Kathryn Grover (Amherst: University of Massachusetts Press, and Rochester, NY: Margaret Woodbury Strong Museum, 1987), 99.

19. *What to Eat for Breakfast* [1882], quoted in Levenstein, *Revolution at the Table,* 21.

20. "How New York is Fed," *Scribner's Monthly* (Oct. 1877), reprinted in *The Journal of Gastronomy* 4 (Spring 1988): 73.

21. Sylvester Graham, *Lectures on the Science of Human Life,* 2 vols. (Boston,

1839), 311–312, quoted in Richard Osborn Cummings, *The American and His Food: A History of Food Habits in the United States* (Chicago: University of Chicago Press, 1940), 45; Stephen Nissenbaum, *Sex, Diet, and Debility in Jacksonian America: Sylvester Graham and Health Reform* (Westport, CT: Greenwood Press, 1980), 6–9.

22. Whorton, *Crusaders for Fitness*, 44–57.

23. Maria Parloa, "Gastronomic Thoughts and Suggestions," *Good Housekeeping*, June 27, 1885, 14; Aug. 21, 1886, 194.

24. Newton Norton, "A Cholera Food: A Plea for Well-Matured Fruit," *Good Housekeeping*, April 1893, 169.

25. Sarah T. Rorer, "Mrs. Rorer's Cooking Lesson: Eighth Lesson, Making Bread and Rolls," *Ladies' Home Journal*, Sept. 1897, 25; Maria Parloa, "The Household Market Basket: A Practical Family Provider, Chap. VI," *Good Housekeeping*, June 1893, 231; William G. Panschar, *Baking in America*, vol. 1 (Evanston, IL: Northwestern University Press, 1956), 47.

26. Loren H. B. Knox, "Our Lost Individuality," *Atlantic Monthly*, Dec. 1909, 818–824.

27. Lears, "From Salvation to Self-Realization," 7–10.

28. Bill McKibben, *Maybe One* (New York: Simon & Schuster, 1998), 19–29. McKibben refers to Dorothy Ross's biography, *G. Stanley Hall: The Psychologist as Prophet* (Chicago: University of Chicago Press, 1972).

29. David B. Danbom, *The Resisted Revolution: Urban America and the Industrialization of Agriculture, 1900–1930* (Ames: Iowa State University Press, 1979), 23–28.

30. Granville Stanley Hall, "The Contents of Children's Minds Entering School," *Pedagogical Seminary* 1 (1891): 146–150, 155–156; Schmitt, *Back to Nature*, 77–78.

31. Alice R. Northrup, "Flower Shows in City Schools," *Nature Study Review* 1 (May 1905): 106, quoted in Schmitt, *Back to Nature*, 94.

32. Clifton Hodge, *Nature Study and Life* (Boston: Ginn & Co. 1902), 132, 10, quoted in Schmitt, *Back to Nature*, 91.

33. Hodge, *Nature Study and Life*, vii.

34. M. H. Carter, *Nature Study with Common Things* (New York: American Book Co., 1904), 8–9, passim; Horace H. Cummings, *Nature Study, By Grades* (New York: American Book Co. 1908); Lida B. McMurry, *Nature Study Lessons for Primary Grades* (New York: Macmillan Co., 1905); Liberty Hyde Bailey, *The Nature Study Idea* (New York: Doubleday, Page, 1903), 14.

35. Frederick L. Holtz, *Nature-Study: A Manual for Teachers and Students* (New York: Charles Scribner's Sons, 1908), 259.

36. Liberty Hyde Bailey, "What is Nature Study?" Cornell Nature-Study

Leaflets Series, State of New York, Dept. of Agriculture (Albany: J. B. Lyon Co. 1904), leaflet 1, 16.

37. Bailey, *Nature Study Idea*, 11–12; Anna Botsford Comstock, *Handbook of Nature-Study* (Ithaca, NY: Comstock Publishing Co. 1911; 6th ed., 1916), 21.

38. Comstock, *Handbook of Nature-Study*, 21.

39. Chris Sellars, "The Post-Agricultural Nature of Levittown," Paper presented at annual meeting of the American Society for Environmental History, Tucson, AZ, April 1999.

40. Donna R. Gabbacia, *We Are What We Eat: Ethnic Food and the Making of Americans* (Cambridge: Harvard University Press, 1998), 36.

41. Hosia R. Diner, *Hungering for America: Italian, Irish, and Jewish Foodways in the Age of Migration* (Cambridge: Harvard University Press, 2001), 56–63.

42. John M. Blum et al., eds. *The National Experience: A History of the United States* (San Diego: Harcourt Brace, 1989), 439, 497.

43. Diner, *Hungering for America*, 2, 56; Antonio Stella, *Some Aspects of Italian Immigration to the U. S.* (New York: Knickerbocker Press, 1924; reprint, New York: Arno, 1975), 11.

44. Diner, *Hungering for America*, 62–63.

45. Gabbaccia, *We Are What We Eat*, 51–55.

46. Louis S. Warren, *The Hunter's Game: Poachers and Conservationists in Twentieth Century America* (New Haven: Yale University Press, 1997), 27. Warren describes the escalation of this contentious issue in Hillsville, PA.

47. Ibid., 25–26; Ann Vileisis, *Discovering the Unknown Landscape: A History of America's Wetlands* (Washington, DC: Island Press, 1997), 151–156.

48. Richard W. Judd, *Common Lands, Common People: The Origins of Conservation in Northern New England* (Cambridge: Harvard University Press, 1997), 79–85.

49. Hale, *"The Good Housekeeper,"* 53.

50. Thomas F. De Voe, *The Market Assistant: containing a brief description of every article of human food sold in the public markets of the cities of New York, Boston, Philadelphia, and Brooklyn; including the various domestic and wild animals, poultry, game, fish, vegetables, fruits, with many curious incidents and anecdotes* (New York: Orange Judd, 1866), 146.

51. Ibid., 175.

52. John F. Lacey, quoted in Warren, *The Hunter's Game*, 25. Lacey is best known for introducing the Lacey Act in 1900, the first federal law to prohibit interstate traffic in birds and wildlife and to encourage states to adopt model conservation laws. Vileisis, *Discovering the Unknown Landscape*, 151–156. For earlier instances of this tension in Europe, see Keith Thomas,

Man and the Natural World: Changing Attitudes in England, 1500–1800
(Allen Lane, 1983; reprint, Oxford University Press, 1996), 116–117.

53. William Hornaday, quoted in Warren, *The Hunter's Game*, 26.

54. John Reiger, *American Sportsmen and the Origins of Conservation*, 2d ed.
(Norman: University of Oklahoma Press, 1986), 37–38, 60–61, passim.

55. Whorton, *Crusaders for Fitness*, 5–7.

56. John Armstrong, *The Art of Preserving Health* (Kennebunk, ME, 1804), 33,
quoted in Whorton, *Crusaders for Fitness*, 16.

57. James Johnson, *The Influence of Civic Life, Sedentary Habits, and Intellectual Refinement, on Human Health and Happiness; Including An Estimate of the Balance of Enjoyment and Suffering in the Different Gradations Of Society*, 2d American ed. (Philadelphia: Matthew Carey & Son, Thomas Dobson & Moses Thomas, 1820), 20–21.

58. Eugene N. Anderson, Jr., "Why Is Humoural Medicine So Popular?" *Social Science and Medicine* 25 (1987): 331; Eugene N. Anderson, *Ecologies of the Heart: Emotion, Belief and the Environment* (New York: Oxford University Press, 1996), 37.

59. Hale, "*The Good Housekeeper*," 14–15. Hale was apparently influenced by Sylvester Graham's view of natural foods, but she strongly disagreed with his vegetarianism.

60. Ibid., 16.

61. Mrs. D. A. [Mary J.] Lincoln, *Boston Cooking School Cook Book: A Reprint of the 1884 Classic* (Mineola, NY: Dover Publications, 1996), 467. In her 1884 *Boston Cooking School Cookbook*, Mrs. Lincoln similarly explains, "Nature has given us an unerring guide to a proper choice of diet. An unperverted appetite is the voice of the physical system making known its needs, and it may always be trusted to indicate the food necessary to the preservation of health. But as the voice of nature is often unheeded, it is necessary to exercise intelligence in selecting our food and adapting it to the circumstances of life. By a proper choice we can often counteract the effects of a violation of nature's laws."

62. "Food and the Human Body," *Good Housekeeping*, June 1896, 252.

63. Maria Parloa, "The Household Market Basket: A Practical Family Provider, Chap. II," *Good Housekeeping*, Feb. 1893, 48; Sarah T. Rorer, "A June Dinner," *Good Housekeeping*, June 1914, 854–855.

64. Emma Seifrit Weigley, *Sarah Tyson Rorer: The Nation's Instructress in Dietetics and Cooking* (Philadelphia: American Philosophical Society, 1977), 103. According to Weigley, while Mrs. Rorer taught cooking at the Chautaqua at Mount Gretna, she enrolled in a literature class and studied

Thoreau and Emerson. These studies may very well have influenced her thinking about nature as an ideal.

65. Sarah T. Rorer, "What Nature Really Intended Us to Eat," *Ladies' Home Journal*, Sept. 1908, 40.

66. Shapiro, *Perfection Salad*, 72.

67. Rorer, "What Nature Really Intended Us to Eat," 40.

68. Charles G. Stockton, quoted in Ellen H. Richards, *The Cost of Food: A Study in Dietaries* (New York: John Wiley & Sons, 1901), 5.

69. Richards, *The Cost of Food*, 5.

70. Rorer, "What Nature Really Intended Us to Eat," 40; Sarah T. Rorer, "Markets, Supplies, and Measures," *Ladies' Home Journal*, April 1897, 28; Sarah T. Rorer, "For Those Who Live Out of Tin Cans," *Ladies' Home Journal*, January 1909, 42. In winter, she also recommended avoiding tomatoes, which were becoming readily available year-round in cans, because they were "not a winter vegetable in cold climates," and "one's blood does not need thinning in the winter."

71. "Food and the Human Body," *Good Housekeeping*, May 1896, 217.

72. Rorer, "What Nature Really Intended Us to Eat," 40.

73. Mrs. Arthur Stanley, "Health in Summer," *Good Housekeeping*, May 1897, 190–191.

74. Daniel Pope, *The Making of Modern Advertising* (New York: Basic Books, 1983), 25–27.

75. James D. Norris, *Advertising and the Transformation of American Society, 1865–1920* (Westport, CT: Greenwood Press, 1990), 36.

76. Robert Atwan, Donald McQuade, and John W. Wright, *Edsels, Luckies and Frigidaires: Advertising the American Way* (New York: Dell, 1979), 188.

77. Pope, *The Making of Modern Advertising*, 4–5, 34, 77, 94.

78. Phillip Nelson, "Advertising as Information," *Journal of Political Economy* 82 (July–Aug. 1974): 752.

79. Susan Strasser, *Satisfaction Guaranteed: The Making of the American Mass Market* (Washington, DC: Smithsonian Institution Press, 1995), 51.

80. Norris, *Advertising*, 44; Walter Dill Scott, *The Theory of Advertising* (Boston: Small, Maynard and Co., 1903), passim.

81. Walter Dill Scott, *The Psychology of Advertising in Theory and Practice* (reprint, Boston: Small, Maynard and Co., 1921), 346.

82. Scott, *Psychology of Advertising*, 335–339.

83. Ibid., 107; trade cards, Smithsonian Institution, National Museum of American History (NMAH), Archives Center, Warshaw Collection of Business Americana, Cereal, Box 2, Folder 10, 1894, 1895, American Cereal

Company (Quaker Oats); "Household Insects," *Good Housekeeping*, Jan. 1897, 19.

84. Scott, *Psychology of Advertising*, 335–339.

85. Ibid., 348–349.

86. Strasser, *Satisfaction Guaranteed*, 146–149; Roland Marchand, *Advertising the American Dream: Making Way for Modernity, 1920–1940* (Berkeley: University of California Press, 1985), xix.

87. I analyzed food ads in four issues (one for each season) per year of the *Ladies' Home Journal* from 1892 to 1912 and found the natural pitch used in 9 percent of food ads in 1897, 13 percent in 1907, and 11 percent in 1909. The popularity of the natural pitch was likely piqued by rising interest in "pure food" related to the Pure Food and Drug Act of 1906. During the same period, references to purity and pure foods appeared in 14 percent of food ads in 1897, 45 percent in 1907 (right after passage of the act), and 22 percent in 1912. By 1913, an article in the advertising trade journal *Printers' Ink* described "the present creed of the average conscientious parent that a child must have the benefit of a maximum amount of fresh air and outdoor life." "Influence of Children upon sales," *Printers' Ink*, Jan. 23, 1913, 33.

88. "Keep in Step with Nature," ad, *Ladies' Home Journal*, April 1907, 65; Egg-O-See ad, *Ladies' Home Journal*, July 1907, 33.

89. Cereal ads, NMAH, N.W. Ayer Advertising Agency Collection, Box 7, Folder 2, Pettijohn's Flaked Breakfast Food, 1902.

90. "For Indoor People," ad, NMAH, Ayer, Box 7, Folder 2, Pettijohn's Flaked Breakfast Food, 1902; Scott, *Psychology of Advertising*, 340, 345; Mark Casson, "Brands, Economic Ideology, and Consumer Society," in *Adding Value: Brands and Marketing in Food and Drink*, ed. Geoffrey Jones and Nicholas J. Morgan (London: Routledge, 1994), 53. Pettijohn's remained a popular cereal until bought out by competitor Quaker Oats.

91. Beecher, *The New Housekeeper's Manual*, 123.

92. Strasser, *Satisfaction Guaranteed*, 132. "The Vital Question" cookbook was published in sixteen editions of 250,000 each.

93. H. D. Perky, "The Vital Question," promotional booklet (ca. 1897), NMAH, Warshaw, Cereal, Box 1, Natural Food Co.

94. "The Shredded Wheat Method of Newspaper Advertising," *Printers' Ink*, Nov. 24, 1909, 28–29. The company publicist described Shredded Wheat ads as "plain talk style . . . with nothing freakish or sensational . . . and no crazy pictures that have no relation to the product."

95. Lears, "From Salvation to Self-Realization," 23. Another similar ad proclaimed, "It is now known that the chief cause of sickness and disease is the

use of unnatural foods.""Satisfies Sense and Senses," ad, NMAH, Ayer, Box 11, Folder 1 (1902).

96. "To Hold the Mirror up to Nature," ad, NMAH, Ayer, Box 11, Folder 1 (1902).

97. "The Wonders of Niagara: Scenic and Industrial," factory tour booklet, NMAH, Warshaw, Cereal Box 2, Folder 2, n.d.

98. "Flips and Flings from a Cynic," *Printers' Ink,* Oct. 27, 1909, 50.

99. Strasser, *Satisfaction Guaranteed,* 113. The two million biscuits figure is for the year 1907.

100. The natural pitch packed such potency that food companies used it to promote other types of products, too. For example, an ad for Van Camp's canned pork and beans gloated that its rich nutty flavor was "compounded by old Mother Nature herself in her happiest mood." *Ladies' Home Journal,* Jan. 1907, 48. An ad for Wedgwood Butter claimed that "Nature's Best makes this *Best* Butter," NMAH, Ayer, Box 28, Folder 1, 1912.

101. "The Rival of the Bee," ad, NMAH, Ayer, Box 30, Folder 2, 1903, Karo Corn Syrup.

102. "MAN CANNOT IMPROVE NATURE," ad, NMAH, Ayer, Box 11, Folder 1, 1902.

103. Macaroni ad, NMAH, Ayer, Box 35, Folder 2, United States Macaroni, Nov. 17, 1908; "Desserts of the World" (New York: Genesee Pure Food Co., 1909), promotional booklet, NMAH, Warshaw, Food, Genesee Pure Food.

104. Cracker ad, Ayers, Box 152, Folder 2, 1902, National Biscuit Company (Nabisco). The custom of eating oysters during the "R" months likely arose because the mollusks tend to be less savory during the summer spawning season. See Mark Kurlansky, *The Big Oyster: History on the Half Shell* (New York: Ballantine Books, 2006), 79.

105. Canned vegetable ad, NMAH, Ayer, Box 49, Folder 1, 1911, The Morey Mercantile, Co.

106. Egg ad, NMAH, Ayer, Box 27, Folder 1, 1908, Dillon & Douglas.

107. Canned fish ad, NMAH, Ayer, Box 39, Folder 1, 1911, Crown Sea Foods.

108. Henri Lefebvre, *Everyday Life in the Modern World* (New York, 1971), 110–123, cited in Lears, "From Salvation to Self-Realization," 21.

109. Several ads promoted these new meanings; for example, an ad for powdered milk claimed it to be "fresh—as the icy springs of the Catskills." Powdered milk ad, NMAH, Ayer, Box 44, Folder 1, Meridale Farms, 1921. In addition, it is interesting to note that in 1907, Harvey Wiley indicated that most "fresh" beef served in the United States was an average of one month old. Harvey Wiley, *Foods and Their Adulteration* (Philadelphia: P. Blakiston's Sons, 1907), 35.

110. Marc Linder and Lawrence S. Zacharias, *Of Cabbages and Kings County: Agriculture and the Formation of Modern Brooklyn* (Iowa City: University of Iowa Press, 1999), 1–15.

Chapter 6. *Rise of the Modern Food Sensibility*

1. "Experiments in Food Preservatives Conducted by the Department of Agriculture," *Scientific American*, May 2, 1903, 336–337.

2. James Harvey Young, *Pure Food: Securing the Federal Food and Drug Act of 1906* (Princeton, NJ: Princeton University Press, 1989), 112.

3. Harvey Wiley, quoted in Henry T. Finck, *Food and Flavor: A Gastronomic Guide to Health and Good Living* (New York: The Century Co., 1913), 31.

4. Young, *Pure Food*, 135–139. For more on Wiley's life, see Oscar E. Anderson, *The Health of a Nation* (Chicago: University of Chicago Press, 1958).

5. James Harvey Young, "The Science and Morals of Metabolism: Catsup and Benzoate of Soda," *Journal of the History of Medicine* 23 (Jan. 1968): 97; Donna J. Wood, "The Strategic Use of Public Policy: Business Support for the 1906 Food and Drug Act," *Business History Review* 59, no. 3 (1985): 407; Wallace F. Janssen, "The Squad That Ate Poison," *FDA Consumer* 15 (Dec. 1981–Jan. 1982): 6–11.

6. Young, "Morals," 89–90.

7. Ibid., 90; Young, *Pure Food*, 151–157; "Dangers Attending So-Called Food Preservatives," *Scientific American*, Sept. 24, 1898, 194. According to the *Scientific American* article, boracic acid is another name for salicylic acid and borax is sodium biborate.

8. R. James Kane, "Populism, Progressivism and Pure Food," *Agricultural History* 38 (1964): 163.

9. Oscar E. Anderson, Jr., "The Pure-Food Issue: A Republican Dilemma, 1906–1912," *American Historical Review* 61, no. 3 (1956): 550–573.

10. Young, *Pure Food*, 151–173.

11. Clayton A. Coppin and Jack High, *The Politics of Purity: Harvey Washington Wiley and the Origins of the Federal Food Policy* (Ann Arbor: University of Michigan Press, 1999), 65.

12. Wood, "Strategic Use of Public Policy," 417–420.

13. Ibid., 403; James Harvey Young, "The Pig That Fell into the Privy: Upton Sinclair's *The Jungle* and the Meat Inspection Amendments of 1906," *Bulletin of the History of Medicine* 59, no. 4 (1985): 480. The laws were passed on June 30, 1906.

14. I analyzed ads for content in four issues of *Ladies' Home Journal*, one per season in 1896 and in 1907. "The New Food Labels: What Do They Mean?"

Good Housekeeping, Oct. 1907, 423–433; "Progress Toward Pure Food," *Good Housekeeping,* April 1907, 438–439.

15. Mark William Wilde, "Industrialization of Food Processing in the United States, 1860–1960" (Ph.D. diss., University of Delaware, 1988), 53; Young, "Morals," 91. For more on Henry J. Heinz, see Robert C. Alberts, "The Good Provider," *American Heritage* 23, no. 2 (1972): 26–47, or Alberts's book by the same title, *The Good Provider: H. J. Heinz and His 57 Varieties* (Boston: Houghton Mifflin, 1973). The proprietary secret that enabled Heinz to bottle ketchup without preservatives was to boost the acidity slightly.

16. "A Health Warning to You," ad, National Museum of American History (NMAH), N.W. Ayer Collection, Box 247, Folder 1, 1909; "Truth about Chemical Preservatives," ad, Ayer, Box 246, Folder 1, 1908. The reports were penned by Wiley and then accidentally released prematurely, much to the consternation of President Roosevelt.

17. "Good Ketchup Needs No Drugs," ad, NMAH, Ayer, Box 247, Folder 1, 1909.

18. "What Benzoate of Soda is!" ad, NMAH, Ayer, Box 247, Folder 1, 1909.

19. Ketchup labels, NMAH, Warshaw, Food, Box 22, Ketchup, Folder 2; Coppin and High, *Politics of Purity,* 122. Before consolidation in the food industry, there were literally dozens of local or regional brands of ketchup; a 1912 study found 142 brands!

20. Young, *Pure Food,* 213.

21. House Committee on Interstate and Foreign Commerce, Pure Food Hearings, Feb. 13–27, 1906, 259, cited in Young, "Morals," 92.

22. Ibid., 92.

23. Young, *Pure Food,* 213.

24. Ibid., 216.

25. The widespread adoption of preservative use sidelined other strategies for coping with food spoilage, such as systematic elevation of hygiene standards in the chain of production, which was more costly.

26. Wood, "Strategic Use of Public Policy," 430–432; Coppin and High, *Politics of Purity,* 104. Wiley believed that large-scale food manufacturers, such as Heinz, could more safely supply growing urban markets than could smaller, less sophisticated companies.

27. Perry Duis, *Challenging Chicago: Coping with Everyday Life, 1837–1920* (Urbana: University of Illinois Press, 1998), 118.

28. Artemas Ward, "Package Advertising," *Fame* [1900], reprinted in *Printers' Ink,* Aug. 15, 1910, 30, quoted in Susan Strasser, *Satisfaction Guaranteed: The Making of the American Mass Market* (New York: Pantheon, 1989; reprint, Washington, DC: Smithsonian Institution Press, 1995), 29.

29. Mira Wilkins, "When and Why Brand Names in Food and Drink?" in *Adding Value: Brands and Marketing in Food and Drink,* ed. Geoffrey Jones and Nicholas J. Morgan (London: Routledge, 1994), 15–20.

30. Christine Terhune Herrick, "What I Have Learned about Canned Foods: The Whole Story of a Vanished Prejudice" *Women's Home Companion,* Feb. 1914, 20.

31. Edward Atkinson, *The Science of Nutrition* (Boston: Damrell and Upham, 1896), 35, quoted in Laura Shapiro, *Perfection Salad: Women and Cooking at the Turn of the Century* (New York: Henry Holt, 1986), 150. Note Atkinson's insinuation that poor food handlers are animal-like in their mien; the prevalent narrative of civilization and savagery ordered the thinking of many middle- and upper-class Americans in the late nineteenth century.

32. Nancy Tomes, *The Gospel of Germs: Men, Women, and the Microbe in American Life* (Cambridge: Harvard University Press, 1998), 101–102; Miriam Birdseye, "An Abuse in the Distribution of Food Stuffs," *Journal of Home Economics* 1, no. 3 (June 1909): 267–268.

33. Heinz ad, *Town and Country,* Jan. 14, 1911, 33; Alberts, "The Good Provider," 36–39. H. J. Heinz was known as the "prince of paternalism," because in addition to manicures, he gave his workers free medical and dental care, a gym, a swimming pool, a roof garden, a library, and free lectures and classes in topics such as cooking, sewing, and drawing.

34. Armour's ad, *Ladies' Home Journal,* April 1907, n.p.

35. Ads among many that use the "no hands" pitch include Royal Egg Macaroni —"made by American machinery" and "untouched by hand"—*Ladies' Home Journal,* Sept. 1892, n.p., and Hawaiian pineapple—"No human hand touches the fruit in peeling or packing"—*Ladies' Home Journal,* Feb. 1909, n.p.

36. The words "always uniform" in ad for Imperium Granum, *Ladies' Home Journal,* Jan. 1892, 13, and "sterilized" in ad for Highland Evaporated Cream, *Ladies' Home Journal,* May 1892, n.p.

37. Tomes, *Gospel of Germs,* 153.

38. "News of the Food Supply," *Good Housekeeping,* Nov. 1911, 688.

39. Christine Frederick, *Selling Mrs. Consumer* (New York: The Business Bourse, 1929), 332.

40. Strasser, *Satisfaction Guaranteed,* 52. Ninety percent of Chicago grocers interviewed said that more than three-quarters of their customers asked for baked beans by brand name.

41. The word "ignorant" was frequently used to describe homemakers and their lacking skill. See Shapiro, *Perfection Salad,* 35, 40, 50.

42. Shapiro, *Perfection Salad,* 40, 169–170. As Richards saw it, the majority of

materials women used in their day-to-day lives, including foods, were increasingly supplied by industry, but women remained woefully "ignorant of the principles" of science that guided industry. It was this disjuncture she aspired to remedy. Feminist writer Charlotte Perkins Gilman had a similar vision, writing that there was "nothing special or private about preparing food . . . if we are willing to receive our water from a pipe — why not food?" Quoted in Susan Strasser, *Never Done: A History of American Housework* (New York: Pantheon, 1982), 221–222.

43. Ellen Richards, "Housekeeping in the Twentieth Century," *American Kitchen Magazine,* March 1900, 203–207, quoted in Shapiro, *Perfection Salad,* 169–170.

44. Ibid.

45. Shapiro, *Perfection Salad,* 176–177.

46. Glenna Matthews, *Just a Housewife: The Rise and Fall of Domesticity in America* (New York: Oxford University Press, 1987), 148. By 1900, there were thirty Home Economics departments, chiefly associated with land grant colleges. For this section, I am indebted to the work of four outstanding historians and writers — Susan Strasser, Ruth Ann Cowan, Glenna Matthews, and Laura Shapiro — each of whom have offered insightful interpretations of the Home Economics movement at the turn of the twentieth century.

47. Gabriella Turnaturi, "Between Public and Private: The Birth of the Professional Housewife and Female Consumer," in *Women and the State,* ed. Anne Showstack Sassoon (London: Hutchinson, 1987), 273; Shapiro, *Perfection Salad,* 115–116; Strasser, *Never Done,* 213–223.

48. *New England Kitchen Magazine,* 1896, quoted in Shapiro, *Perfection Salad,* 42. At the time, electricity was just beginning to enter households, and dishwashing machines were still operated by a hand crank.

49. Tomes, *Gospel of Germs,* 147–148; Harvey Levenstein, *Revolution at the Table: The Transformation of the American Diet* (New York: Oxford University Press), 72–85; Shapiro, *Perfection Salad,* 202, 209–213.

50. Levenstein, *Revolution at the Table,* 46. Discoveries about the nutritional constituents of foods were first popularized in the United States by Wilbur O. Atwater in a series of articles in *Century* magazine in 1887.

51. Shapiro, *Perfection Salad,* 76.

52. A 1918 ad for Quaker Oatmeal perpetuated this rudimentary understanding of food values, suggesting that for $1, one could buy 19,440 calories in oats but only 2,500 calories in beef. Conflating calories with food value, that ad claimed that oatmeal had "twice the nutrition of beef per pound, and six times that of chicken." *Saturday Evening Post,* Apr. 13, 1918, 68. Also, when the United States entered World War I, government programs designed to

assure orderly distribution of foods on the home front promoted these concepts broadly.

53. Levenstein, *Revolution at the Table*, 22–23, 147–160, 166. One 1928 cookbook explained, "The word 'calorie' is as familiar as the word 'food' and is heard in conversation at the luncheon table."

54. John Kendrick Bangs, "Keep Your Own Machinery Fit," quoted in Jessie W. Harris and Elisabeth Lacey Speer, *Everyday Foods*, Riverside Home Economics Series (Boston: Houghton Mifflin Co., 1933), 227–228. In this Home-Ec textbook, the language came from a poem by popular turn-of-the century humorist John Kendrick Bangs, humor editor at three *Harper's Magazines* between 1889 and 1901, who poked fun at people lavishing attention on their cars but paying little heed to their health. This textbook explained that "the body is often likened to a car," as if the metaphor were already in common usage.

55. Wood, "Strategic Use of Public Policy," 415. According to Donna Wood, many business leaders had recognized cheap and plentiful food for workers as a critical input of their industrial productivity. Wood links development of Frederick Taylor's scientific management with the budding systems concept of the human body as a machine. Scientists also used the body-as-engine metaphor to conceptualize nutrition. See Lafayette Mendel, *Changes in the Food Supply and their Relation to Nutrition* (New Haven: Yale University Press, 1916), 49–50.

56. A participant at the Fourth Lake Placid Conference on Home Economics, 1904, quoted in Matthews, *Just a Housewife*, 151.

57. Matthews, *Just a Housewife*, 155–156; Shapiro, *Perfection Salad*, 90, 168–175.

58. Shapiro, *Perfection Salad*, 73, 128, 137; Matthews, *Just a Housewife*, 146.

59. Matthews, *Just a Housewife*, 150–151. Matthews aptly places this trend in the context of a growing culture of professionalism. Domestic scientists sought to emulate and gain the prestige of existing male professionals and to do so they had to distance themselves from lowly amateur housewives. Although their goals of easing women's work burdens were laudable, Matthews elucidates how the home economists regrettably followed the same methods of scientific management used by industry to advance its aims. Like factory managers who had found it necessary to destroy workers' faith in their own judgment in order to gain complete control over their efforts, home economists similarly denigrated the traditional knowledge, competence, and abilities of homemakers in order to establish the authority of their own profession.

60. Mary Lincoln, "Cheese: From Cottage to Cave, Concluded," *American Kitchen Magazine*, Mar. 1902, 211. The active promotion of the value of

uniformity continued through several decades. A 1929 magazine article had this to say: "Uniformity—this is the passion of the food manufacturer of today. When he talks about it, there is a light in his eyes. Every package, every can, every jar of a product, he will tell you, must be the same as every other in flavor and quality. And the only way to secure this uniformity, we know, is by rigid scientific control." Gove Hambridge, "The New Era in Foods," *Ladies' Home Journal,* May 1929, 26–27, 156, 158, 159.

61. Levenstein, *Revolution at the Table,* 156–158.
62. Herrick, "What I Have Learned about Canned Foods," 20. Christine T. Herrick was author of *The New Idea Home and Cookbook* (1900) and with her mother, well-known domestic expert Marion Harland, she also had co-authored *The Consolidated Library of Modern Cooking and Household Recipes* (1904–1905), a comprehensive series of cookbooks.
63. Ibid.
64. Ibid.
65. Ibid.
66. Ibid.
67. Christine Ellis, interview referring to how things were in 1914, in *Rank and File,* ed. Staughton Lynd and Mary Lynd (Boston: Beacon Press, 1973), 15, quoted in Levenstein, *Revolution at the Table,* 107.
68. Martha Bensley Bruère, "Scientific Marketing," *Good Housekeeping,* Sept. 1913, 384.
69. Ibid. By "wholesale" she means simply buying all one's foods.
70. Ruth Ann Cowan, "The 'Industrial Revolution' in the Home: Household Technology and Social Change in the 20th Century," *Technology and Culture* 17 (Jan. 1976): 14.
71. Levenstein, *Revolution at the Table,* 156–157; 198–199.
72. John B. Leeds, "The Household Budget: With a Special Inquiry into the Amount and Value of Household Work" (Ph.D. diss., Columbia University, 1917), cited in Ruth Schwartz Cowan, *More Work for Mother: The Ironies of Household Technology from the Open Hearth to the Microwave* (New York: Basic Books, 1983), 245; JoAnn Vanek, "Time Spent in Housework," *Scientific American,* Nov. 1974, reprinted in *A Heritage of Her Own,* ed. Nancy F. Cott and Elizabeth H. Pleck (New York: Touchstone, 1979), 500–502. Vanek's study indicates that in the 1920s, women not employed outside the home (a large majority) spent an average of fifty-two hours per week on housework, approximately twenty-five hours of which was food prep and cleanup. Shopping took an additional two hours. Remarkably, Vanek determined that women not employed outside the home in 1965 spent roughly the same number of hours on housework.
73. Levenstein, *Revolution at the Table,* 71.

74. Harvey W. Wiley, "False 'Ads' and Lying Labels," *Good Housekeeping,* Sept. 1913, 387.

75. Isaac E. Lambert, *The Public Accepts: Stories behind Famous Trade-marks, Names and Slogans* [1941] (reprint, New York, Arno Press, 1976), 128. See also John D. Weaver, *Carnation: The First 75 Years, 1899–1974* (Los Angeles: Carnation Company, 1974).

76. Strasser, *Satisfaction Guaranteed,* 126.

77. Wiley, "False 'Ads,'" 387.

78. Ibid., 392.

79. Ibid.

80. Ibid., 393; T. J. Jackson Lears, "From Salvation to Self-Realization," in *The Culture of Consumption: Critical Essays in American History, 1880–1980,* ed. T. J. Jackson Lears and Richard Wightman Fox (New York: Pantheon, 1983), 20. The issue of truth in advertising was vigorously debated in the advertising industry. Ironically, one adman suggested the term "mother earth" to signify clear copy based on facts of a product and "blue sky," to signify ads that used "fluff" copy and had nothing to do with the actual product. Humphrey Bourne, "'Mother Earth' vs. 'Blue Sky' Copy," *Printers' Ink,* Oct. 24, 1912, 17.

81. Susan D. Jones, *Valuing Animals: Veterinarians and Their Patients in Modern America* (Baltimore: Johns Hopkins University Press, 2003), 68–73.

82. Christopher P. Wilson, "The Rhetoric of Consumption: Mass-Market Magazines and the Demise of the Gentle Reader, 1880–1920," in Lears and Fox, *Culture of Consumption,* 44. Wilson argues that the format of magazines, with their ads, promotional articles, one-to-one columns, and personal stories helped to foster a new realm of unreality. As *Good Housekeeping* began to confer its seal of approval to advertisers, Wiley's columns, despite their skepticism, nevertheless gave his tacit imprimatur to all sorts of prepared foods that he'd probably have preferred not to promote. By 1931, advertising psychologist Henry Link reported that only 4 to 5 percent of the public believed certain advertising assertions and that even the most credible assertions convinced only 37 percent of those surveyed. Roland Marchand, *Advertising the American Dream: Making Way for Modernity, 1920–1940* (Berkeley: University of California Press, 1985), 314.

83. The issues raised by Harvey Wiley's 1914 exposé about Carnation have striking similarities with the recent lawsuit brought against the California Milk Advisory Board for fictive TV ads extolling the health and well-being of California cows. See "PETA takes on California's 'Happy Cow' Ads," *Washington Times,* Jan. 6, 2000.

84. Daniel Pope, *The Making of Modern Advertising* (New York: Basic Books,

1983), 22–29; Theodore MacManus, *The Sword Arm of Business* (New York, 1927), quoted in Marchand, *Advertising the American Dream*, 6. In April 1926, the *Ladies' Home Journal* reached a record 270 pages, 162 of which were ads.

85. *Printers' Ink*, Dec. 13, 1917, 148, quoted in Marchand, *Advertising the American Dream*, 6. It is important to note that scholars who study advertising have long debated whether ads actually influence people to buy particular products or if consumers are too sophisticated to fall for their pitches. Whatever the case may be, marketing research has made it abundantly clear that ads can successfully establish the criteria by which people think about products. Most prosaically, ads could make a food's spout-top package or extra bacon in beans seem important. More broadly, food ads in the 1920s promoted the desirability of the modern and so boosted the appeal of manufactured food products. Marchand, *Advertising the American Dream*, xx; Pope, *Making of Modern Advertising*, 54; Richard Elliott and Mark Ritson, "Post-structuralism and the Dialectics of Advertising," in *Consumer Research, Postcards from the Edge*, ed. Stephen Brown and Darach Turley (London: Routledge, 1997), 196–200. Elliott and Ritson describe several ideological strategies of advertising that function to change society, including legitimization, universalization, naturalization, and enlightened false consciousness.

86. Harvey Wiley, "Food Reconstruction," *Good Housekeeping*, Feb. 1919, quoted in Levenstein, *Revolution at the Table*, 159; Amy Bentley, *Eating for Victory: Food Rationing and the Politics of Domesticity* (Urbana: University of Illinois Press, 1998), 124. The wartime gardens of World War I became known as "victory gardens" when the war was won; the term "victory gardening" would be further popularized during World War II.

87. Levenstein, *Revolution at the Table*, 137–146; Bentley, *Eating for Victory*, 20–21; Laura Shenone, *A Thousand Years over a Hot Stove* (New York: W.W. Norton, 2003), 277–280; Dana Frank, "Housewives, Socialists, and the Politics of Food: The 1917 New York Cost-of-Living Protests," *Feminist Studies* 11, no. 2 (Summer 1985): 252–255; Frank A. Pearson and Don Paarlberg, *Food* (New York: Knopf, 1944), 154.

88. Wilde, "Industrialization of Food Processing," 57–58. By the 1920s, the canned foods trade industry was already beginning to lament the plebian stigma increasingly attached to their products.

89. "When the telephone was first introduced," ad, NMAH, Ayer, Box 47, Folder 1, Purity Margarine, 1917; baked bean ad from *Ladies' Home Journal*, March 1910, reproduced in James D. Norris, *Advertising and the Trans-*

formation of American Society, 1865–1920 (Westport, CT: Greenwood Press, 1990), 112.

90. *Woman's Home Companion,* March 1914, 33.

91. Ad for Van Camp's Pork and Beans, *Saturday Evening Post,* Nov. 6, 1920, 43; The ad urged readers to "learn what modern science" had added to this dish and further swathed its copy in the lingo of science by suggesting that their zesty sauce "savors every atom." Some capable traditional cooks had kept the herb savory growing in their gardens; savory acted as a carminative, preventing flatulence. See also, Van Camp's ad, *Ladies' Home Journal,* Dec. 1917, 60.

92. Marchand, *Advertising the American Dream,* 351–352.

93. Ibid., 233. Marchand discusses how frequent iteration of certain themes in advertising gave certain patterns of thinking a sense of inevitability and reality that ultimately established the very ideological framework by which matters were considered.

94. Ibid., 351–352.

95. Ibid.

96. Robert S. Lynd and Helen M. Lynd, *Middletown: A Study in Contemporary American Culture* (New York, 1929), 156, cited in Wilde, "Industrialization of Food Processing," 57–58. In their famous 1925 study of Muncie, Indiana, the Lynds found homemakers reluctant to feed their families food from cans; in fact, a local women's club was debating the issue "Shall a Conscientious Housewife Used Canned Foods?"

97. Gove Hambidge, "The Grocery Revolution," *Ladies' Home Journal,* Nov. 1928, 99, quoted in Levenstein, *Revolution at the Table,* 163.

98. Marchand, *Advertising the American Dream,* 11–12. Admen would later explain their change in strategy as a shift from a "factory viewpoint" to concern with "the mental processes of the consumer." According to Marchand, this change reflected admen's awareness that consumers were beginning to become cynical—and while they embraced the benefits of new products, they resented certain indignities of the mass society.

99. Cream of Wheat ad, *Ladies' Home Journal,* Sept. 1929, second cover, cited in Marchand, *Advertising the American Dream,* 217.

100. *Printers' Ink,* Jan. 1, 1925, 58, quoted in Marchand, *Advertising the American Dream,* 24.

101. T. J. Jackson Lears, *Fables of Abundance: A Cultural History of Advertising in America* (New York: Basic Books, 1994), 171. Lears found this trend in the majority of ads for all products in the 1920s, indicating what he has described as "an almost panicky reassertion of culture over nature—an

anxious impulse to extirpate all signs of biological life from one's immediate environment."

102. Marchand, *Advertising the American Dream,* 223–226. For a slightly later period, Marchand describes one natural pitch (ca. 1930), which he calls the "Parable of Civilization Redeemed." Ads using this pitch taught consumers that the advance of civilization never need exact any real costs because modern products could always solve any problems that might arise.

103. William Braznell, *California's Finest: The History of the Del Monte Corporation and the Del Monte Brand* (San Francisco: Del Monte Corporation, 1982), 45–48. Braznell explains that the ad campaign started in the *Saturday Evening Post* on April 21, 1917.

104. Robert Atwan, Donald McQuade, John W. Wright, *Edsels, Luckies, and Frigidaires: Advertising the American Way* (New York: Dell, 1979), 199.

105. Ibid. The metaphysical tones were echoed by other ads that depicted troops of pixies whimsically making oatmeal, cornflakes, and other products, shrouding the process of factory production in a sort of magic. Armour cereal ad, *Ladies' Home Journal,* July 1919. Strasser makes a similar point about the pixie genre in *Satisfaction Guaranteed,* 116.

106. Del Monte ad, *Ladies' Home Journal,* March 1919, 60.

107. Steven Stoll, *The Fruits of Natural Advantage: Making the Industrial Countryside in California* (Berkeley: University of California Press, 1998), 95–99, 119–123; Douglas Cazaux Sackman, "'By Their Fruits Ye Shall Know Them,' Nature Cross Culture Hybridization and the California Citrus Industry, 1839–1939," *California History* 75, no. 1 (Spring 1995): 86–91.

108. Marchand, *Advertising the American Dream,* 340; Stuart Ewen, *Captains of Consciousness: Advertising and the Social Roots of the Consumer Culture* (New York: McGraw-Hill, 1976), 105, 199.

109. Olga Samaroff, "My Experiences in My Kitchen," *Ladies' Home Journal,* April 1919, 138.

110. "What could you do with a hog?"—an ad for Swift & Company ham—similarly underscores the idea of not knowing about food as a virtue. In the ad, a well-heeled man in a suit scratches his head while looking down at a hog. Depicted in Harry Tipper and George French, *Advertising Campaigns* (New York: D. Van Nostrand, 1923), 59.

Chapter 7. *The Covenant of Ignorance*

1. For a virtual tour of a reconstructed version of the first Piggly Wiggly market, see http://www.memphismuseums.org/piggly%20wiggly.htm [accessed Jan. 27, 2007]. For photographic images of early Piggly Wiggly

stores, see also the Library of Congress online Prints and Photograph collection, Lot 9998, at http://www.loc.gov/rr/print/catalog.html.

2. Richard S. Tedlow, *New and Improved: The Story of Mass Marketing in America* (New York: Basic Books, 1990; reprint, Boston: Harvard Business School Press, 1996), 194–195.

3. Ibid., 190–194, 209–210; Lizabeth Cohen, *Making a New Deal; Industrial Workers in Chicago, 1919–1939* (Cambridge: Cambridge University Press, 1990), 106–107. Cohen points out that chain stores generally avoided working-class neighborhoods where allegiances to local stores, often based on ethnic ties and credit, were strong. Chain stores proved so successful that they incurred intense opposition from the independent grocers and their neighborhood supporters, spurring passage in 1936 of the Robertson-Patman Act, which prohibited chains from engaging in anticompetitive price discrimination.

4. J. Tevere MacFayden, "The Rise of the Supermarket," *American Heritage* 36, no. 6 (1985): 25; Will Soper, "Supermarkets," *American History Illustrated*, March 1983, 44, cited in Tedlow, *New and Improved*, 231.

5. Christine Frederick, *Selling Mrs. Consumer* (New York: The Business Bourse, 1929), 24.

6. "Armed with New Knowledge," ad for Piggly Wiggly Stores, *Good Housekeeping*, Sept. 1928, 179.

7. "Is She a Better Business Man Than Her Husband?" ad for Piggly Wiggly Stores, *Good Housekeeping*, April 1928, 185.

8. Kim Humphrey, *Shelf Life: Supermarkets and the Changing Cultures of Consumption* (Cambridge: Cambridge University Press, 1998), 33.

9. Janice Williams Rutherford, *Selling Mrs. Consumer: Christine Frederick and the Rise of Household Efficiency* (Athens: University of Georgia Press, 2003), 20, 43–47.

10. Frederick, *Selling Mrs. Consumer*, 2–3.

11. Ibid., 4–5.

12. Ibid., 14.

13. Rutherford, *Selling*, 148. Rutherford unravels many of Frederick's contradictory beliefs. She testified in favor of legislation to prevent price-cutting, but she generally abhorred political action if it ran counter to her business-oriented views: "The consumer's real hope is not political agitation *but cooperation and consultation with manufacturers, plus the use of the purchasing vote*, instead of the political ballot" (Frederick's italics).

14. Ibid., 152.

15. Frederick, *Selling Mrs. Consumer*, 329.

16. Ibid., 22.

17. Ibid., 323.

18. Ibid., 321.

19. Ibid., 320.

20. Ibid., 22, 331.

21. Ibid., 334.

22. Ibid., 334, 336.

23. Ibid., 334.

24. Tedlow, *New and Improved*, 183.

25. Ibid., 238.

26. M. M. Zimmerman, *Super Market: Spectacular Exponent of Mass Distribution* (New York: Super Market Publishing Co., 1937), 73.

27. Ibid., 6–7, 52–53, 73; Randolph McAusland, *Supermarkets: 50 Years of Progress* (Washington, DC: Food Marketing Institute, 1980), 5; MacFayden, "The Rise of the Supermarket," 27–28; Tedlow, *New and Improved*, 230.

28. MacFayden, "The Rise of the Supermarket," 29.

29. Humphrey, *Shelf Life*, 33.

30. Steven Stoll, *The Fruits of Natural Advantage: Making the Industrial Countryside in California* (Berkeley: University of California Press, 1998), 97–98. Pests had also become a problem in the orchard districts of Michigan in the 1870s. Margaret Beattie Bogue, "The Lake and the Fruit: The Making of Three Farm Type Areas," *Agricultural History* 59 (Oct. 1985): 502–503.

31. *American Agriculturist* 37 (1978): 315, quoted in James C. Whorton, *Before Silent Spring: Pesticides and Public Health in Pre-DDT America* (Princeton: Princeton University Press, 1974), 30; James C. Whorton, "Insecticide Spray Residues and Public Health, 1865–1938," *Bulletin of the History of Medicine* 45, no. 3 (1971): 222–223.

32. Whorton, *Before Silent Spring*, 126. In his excellent book, Whorton provides a thorough, balanced, and insightful analysis of lead-arsenate issues, describing the nuanced motives and constraints of fruit growers, agency personnel, and consumers.

33. Stoll, *Fruits of Natural Advantage*, 117–118; Whorton, "Insecticide Spray Residues," 224.

34. Whorton, *Before Silent Spring*, 120.

35. Whorton, *Before Silent Spring*, 40–67; Whorton, "Insecticide Spray Residues," 226.

36. Whorton, *Before Silent Spring*, 95–96; Whorton, "Insecticide Spray Residues," 233.

37. Whorton, "Insecticide Spray Residues," 234.

38. Whorton, *Before Silent Spring,* 126; Whorton, "Insecticide Spray Residues," 234. In his article, Whorton suggests that fruit growers' representatives denied that residues were a hazard but agreed to try to reduce them if the bureau promised not to publicize the problem.

39. Stoll, *Fruits of Natural Advantage,* 119; Whorton, *Before Silent Spring,* 166. Further, western growers perceived the bureau's efforts to restrict their pesticide use as government interference in their business and a favoring of eastern city dwellers, an antagonism kindled by broader cultural dynamics between east and west, urban and rural.

40. Whorton, *Before Silent Spring,* 127.

41. Ibid., 128.

42. Whorton, *Before Silent Spring,* 133–137; Whorton, "Insecticide Spray Residues," 236.

43. Whorton, *Before Silent Spring,* 178; Whorton, "Insecticide Spray Residues," 234. According to Whorton, files of the Bureau of Chemistry from the 1920s contain "extensive documentation to support the charge that officials of [this] important public health agency continually subordinated public welfare to agricultural convenience."

44. Whorton, *Before Silent Spring,* 181; Whorton, "Insecticide Spray Residues," 240; Thomas R. Dunlap, *DDT: Scientists, Citizens, and Public Policy* (Princeton: Princeton University Press, 1981), 49.

45. C. N. Meyer, Binford Throne, Florence Gustafson, and Jerome Kingsbury, "Significance and Danger of Spray Residue," *Industrial and Engineering Chemistry* 25 (June 1933): 624, quoted in Stoll, *Fruits of Natural Advantage,* 120.

46. A. F. Kraetzer, *Journal of the American Medical Association* 94, no. 2 (1930): 1036, quoted in Whorton, *Before Silent Spring,* 177–180. Lead and arsenic were also prevalent in smelter fumes, auto exhaust, and coal smoke in American cities and in daily household items, including playing cards, flypaper, cooking utensils, and house paints. Distribution of lead and arsenic had become so common in urban environments that scientists determined that all members of industrialized populations carried some traces of these substances in their bodies.

47. A. B. Cannon, *New York State Journal of Medicine* 35 (1936): 36, 233, quoted in Whorton, *Before Silent Spring,* 180; Suzanne Rebecca White, "Chemistry and Controversy: Regulating the Use of Chemicals in Foods, 1883 to 1959" (Ph.D. diss., Emory University, 1994), 191. Cannon was likely referring to Fowler's solution, a potassium arsenite liquid used in medicine to treat skin and blood disorders.

48. Whorton, *Before Silent Spring*, 185

49. Frederick J. Schlink and Stuart Chase, *Your Money's Worth* (New York, 1927), 256, 264, quoted in Whorton, *Before Silent Spring*, 187.

50. Whorton, *Before Silent Spring*, 188; R. Joyce and F. J. Schlink, "Fruits and Vegetables—How to Eat Them without Being Poisoned," *Consumers' Research Bulletin*, Nov. 1934, 17–19.

51. Frederick J. Schlink, *Eat, Drink, and Be Wary* (Washington, NJ: Consumers' Research, 1935), 262.

52. Arthur Kallet and Frederick J. Schlink, *100,000,000 Guinea Pigs: Dangers in Everyday Foods, Drugs, and Cosmetics* (New York: Grosset and Dunlap, 1933), 291. The book was reprinted thirty times by 1935.

53. Ibid., 6.

54. Ibid., 302–303.

55. Ibid., 52.

56. Whorton, *Before Silent Spring*, 191. Other muckraking books in a group that has come to be called "guinea-pig" literature include Ruth de Forest Lamb's *American Chamber of Horrors: The Truth About Food and Drugs* (1936); Schlink's *Eat, Drink, and Be Wary* (1935); Kallett's *Counterfeit—Not Your Money but What it Buys* (1935); and Rachel Lynn Palmer's *40,000,000 Guinea Pig Children* (1937).

57. Whorton, *Before Silent Spring*, 237; White, "Chemistry and Controversy," 197.

58. Whorton, *Before Silent Spring*, 251.

59. Ibid., 249.

60. "Startling" and "somewhat alarming" are descriptions given by U.S. Army researcher James Simmons, quoted in Edmund Russell, "The Strange Career of DDT: Experts, Federal Capacity, and Environmentalism in World War II," *Technology and Culture* 40 (Oct. 1999): 775–776, 780–781; McKay McKinnon, Jr., "Industrial and Legal Viewpoints: Application of the Federal Food, Drug, and Cosmetic Act to Food War Materials Bearing Chemical Residues," *Food Technology* 4 (Jan. 1950): 27–28. "Startling" and "somewhat alarming" effects on lab animals included convulsions, paralysis, and organ damage when DDT was ingested or applied to skin over the long term; effects were less when exposure was through inhalation.

61. *Reader's Digest*, Nov. 1945, 84, quoted in Whorton, *Before Silent Spring*, 248; editorial, *Chicago Tribune*, reprinted in *Sanitary Chemicals*, April 1944, 135, quoted in Russell, "Strange Career of DDT," 783.

62. California Dept. of Agriculture, *26th Annual Report* 34, no. 4 (1945): 260. Within only a few months, four hundred products containing DDT were registered with the California Dept. of Agriculture.

63. Edmund Russell, *War and Nature: Fighting Humans and Insects with Chemicals from World War I to Silent Spring* (Cambridge: Cambridge University Press, 2001), 168; Whorton, *Before Silent Spring*, 249.

64. Russell, *War and Nature*, 168–170.

65. Louis C. Barail, "Bacteriology of Food Package Materials," *Modern Packaging*, Nov. 1947, 149–151.

66. Edmund Russell, "'Speaking of Annihilation': Mobilizing for War against Human and Insect Enemies, 1914–1945," *The Journal of American History* 82 (March 1996): 1505–1520; Russell, "Strange Career of DDT," 795. According to Russell, the National Association of Insecticide and Disinfectant Manufacturers noted, "BUGS! Bugs! Bugs! All through the war, bugs and how to kill them received a billion dollars worth of publicity, — every dollar of it a mighty sales asset to the insecticide industry"; Mark L. Winston, *Nature Wars: People vs. Pests* (Cambridge, MA: Harvard University Press, 1997), 170. Winston also suggests other pop-cultural influences, including the 1958 movie *The Fly*, that spread the new bug phobia.

67. John H. Perkins, "Insects, Food, and Hunger: The Paradox of Plenty for U.S. Entomology, 1920–1970," *Environmental Review* 7, no. 1 (1983): 78.

68. Christopher J. Bosso, *Pesticides and Politics: The Life Cycle of a Public Issue* (Pittsburgh: University of Pittsburgh Press, 1987), 63.

69. California Dept. of Agriculture, *31st Annual Report* 39, no. 4 (1950): 316–318.

70. California Dept. of Agriculture, *33d Annual Report* 41, no. 4 (1952): 228–233, 346.

71. Dunlap, *DDT*, 64.

72. Ibid., 65; California Dept. of Agriculture, *California Department of Agriculture Bulletin* 38, no. 2 (1949): 303.

73. Dunlap, *DDT*, 65–66.

74. Russell, "Speaking of Annihilation," 1526; Dunlap, *DDT*, 63.

75. Whorton, *Before Silent Spring*, 250.

76. Linda J. Lear, "Bombshell in Beltsville: The USDA and the Challenge of 'Silent Spring,'" *Agricultural History* 66, no. 2 (Spring 1992): 152; Dunlap, *DDT*, 48.

77. Pete Daniel, *Lost Revolutions: The South in the 1950s* (Chapel Hill: University of North Carolina Press, 2000), 71–74.

78. Joshua Blu Buhs, "Dead Cows on a Georgia Field: Mapping the Cultural Landscape of the Post–World War II American Pesticide Controversies," *Environmental History* 7, no. 1 (Jan. 2002): 99–101; Daniel, *Lost Revolutions*, 68–69.

79. Daniel, *Lost Revolutions*, 71.

80. Paul B. Dunbar, "The FDA Looks at Insecticides," *Food Drug Cosmetic*

Quarterly 4 (June 1949): 234–239, quoted in Russell, *War and Nature,* 175; Testimony of Paul Dunbar, House Select Committee to Investigate the Use of Chemicals in Food Products, *Chemicals in Food Products,* 81st Congress, 2d session, 236, quoted in Dunlap, *DDT,* 67.

81. Wilbur A. Gould et al., "Flavor Evaluations of Canned Fruits and Vegetables Treated with Newer Organic Insecticides," *Food Technology* 5 (Apr. 1951): 129, 133; R. W. Olsen et al., "Examination of Citrus Juices Processed from Parathion-Sprayed Fruit," *Food Technology* 6 (Sept. 1952): 350–351.

82. Dunlap, *DDT,* 66–68.

83. Ibid., 69.

84. Ibid., 74–75; Bosso, *Pesticides and Politics,* 76–77.

85. Bosso, *Pesticides and Politics,* 78. By shifting the burden of proving safety to manufacturers and giving the FDA a new regulatory role to set tolerance levels for pesticide residues on foods, the new law fundamentally changed the paradigm of pesticide regulation.

86. Dunlap, *DDT,* 71–75; USDA, *Pesticide Review 1966,* 3, cited in Perkins, "Insects, Food, and Hunger," 93, note 44; Ralph G. Martin, "How Much Poison Are We Eating?" *Harper's,* April 1955, 63; J. Brooks Flippen, "Pests, Pollution, and Politics: The Nixon Administration's Pesticide Policy," *Agricultural History* 71, no. 4 (Fall 1997): 442. According to Perkins, pesticide production figures for years before 1963 are sparse. By 1980, pesticide use would rise to over 1.5 billion pounds per year. Bosso, *Pesticides and Politics,* 237.

87. Ralph B. March, "Laboratory and Field Studies of DDT Resistant Houseflies in Southern California," *California Dept. of Agriculture Bulletin* 38, no. 2 (1949): 93–100; Russell, *Nature and War,* 197–201.

88. "German Insecticide Effective Against Aphids," *Chemical and Engineering News,* July 25, 1946, 1954, quoted in Russell, *War and Nature,* 173. Organophosphate pesticides were derived from research of German scientists on poison nerve gases, some of which had been used in concentration camps during World War II. See Russell, *War and Nature,* 87, 199.

89. Dunlap, *DDT,* 254.

90. Paul A. Clifford, "Pesticide Residues in Fresh Milk Survey of 1955–1956," Dec. 1956, no. 709, Agricultural Research Service, Record Group 310, National Archives, quoted in Daniel, *Lost Revolutions,* 71–72.

91. Daniel, *Lost Revolutions,* 74–75; John Wargo, *Our Children's Toxic Legacy: How Science and Law Fail to Protect Us from Pesticides* (New Haven: Yale University Press), 168.

92. Dunlap, *DDT,* 18; Daniel, *Lost Revolutions,* 74–75. Daniel quotes internal

memos from Don Paarlberg, White House liaison for USDA affairs, about elevated residues in meats and potential public relations problems.

93. William Boyd, "Making Meat: Science, Technology, and American Poultry Production," *Technology and Culture* 42, no. 4 (2001): 639–643, 646–648; Susan Jones, *Valuing Animals: Veterinarians and Their Patients in Modern America* (Baltimore: Johns Hopkins, 2003), 101–114.

94. Harvey Levenstein, *Paradox of Plenty: A Social History of Eating in Modern America* (New York: Oxford University Press, 1993), 85.

95. Ibid., 80–81.

96. "Off the Editor's Chest," *Consumer Reports*, Jan. 1945, 2, 26; Levenstein, *Paradox of Plenty*, 80, 83. Rationed amounts were not particularly lean (2.5 pounds of meat and a half pound of sugar per person per week), but the sight of empty supermarket shelves caused by erratic supplies put people on edge and spurred hoarding.

97. Amy Bentley, *Eating for Victory: Food Rationing and the Politics of Domesticity* (Urbana: University of Illinois Press, 1998), 32–33.

98. Bentley, *Eating for Victory*, 32; "War and Advertising," *Consumer Reports*, Oct. 1948, 47.

99. Laura Shapiro, *Something from the Oven: Reinventing Dinner in 1950s America* (New York: Viking, 2004), 184, 11–12.

100. One General Mills ad during the war promised: "Soon our research staffs will help turn out many new products, new foods for a better world." *Saturday Evening Post*, Jan. 15, 1944, n.p.

101. J. R. Hildebrand, "Revolution in Eating," *National Geographic*, Mar. 15, 1942, 273.

102. George Poindexter, "Tomorrow's Foods," *Saturday Evening Post*, Feb. 12, 1944, 17.

103. White, "Chemistry and Controversy," 219.

104. George P. Larrick, "Pure Food and Progress," *Food Technology*, Oct. 1956, 456.

105. Karal Ann Marling, *As Seen on TV: The Visual Culture of Everyday Life in the 1950s* (Cambridge, MA: Harvard University Press, 1994), 226.

106. Esther Lloyd-Jones, "Progress Report of Pertinent Research," in *Potentialities of Women in the Middle Years*, ed. Irma Gross (East Lansing: Michigan State University Press, 1956), 23, cited in Shapiro, *Something from the Oven*, 134.

107. Shapiro, *Something from the Oven*, 19.

108. Jane Holt, "New Food Products," *New York Times Magazine*, Oct. 21, 1945, 30.

109. David S. Burt, "Men, Meat and the Tin Can," *The National Provisioner*, May

22, 1948, 1, reprint, Smithsonian Institution, National Museum of American History, Archives Center, Warshaw Collection of Business Americana, Meat, Box 6.

110. "America's amazing new EASY FOODS," *Look,* Jan. 6, 1959, 16–17; Burt, "Men, Meat and the Tin Can," 3; "Revolution in the Kitchen," *U.S. News and World Report,* Feb. 15, 1957, 60. Historians Ruth Schwartz Cowan and Joann Vanek have persuasively shown that as housework standards became more elaborate and as demands for a second income grew, modern women have, in fact, ended up working just as much as their forebears, taking on paid jobs outside the home plus more "housework" in new arenas, such as shopping. See Ruth Schwartz Cowan, *More Work for Mother* (New York: Basic Books, 1983), and Joann Vanek, "Time Spent in Housework," *Scientific American* (1974), 116–121, reprinted in *A Heritage of Her Own: Toward a New Social History of American Women,* ed. Nancy Cott and Elizabeth H. Pleck (New York: Touchstone, 1979), 500–501.

111. Shapiro, *Something from the Oven,* 43. A 1952 *Business Week* article touted the food industry's version of their success with the new foods: "When the food manufacturers moved into the kitchen, the housewife was waiting with outstretched arms." For this section, I am indebted to Shapiro's excellent research on this period.

112. Ibid., 44.

113. Ibid., 45.

114. Ibid., 46; Harry H. Harp and Denis F. Dunham, "Convenience Foods in the Grocery Basket," *U.S. Dept. of Agriculture Marketing Bulletin* 22 (Sept. 1962): 2. Convenience foods were expensive if a homemaker's time wasn't taken into account, and after decades of habitual frugality, most women were in a habit of not valuing their time.

115. Shapiro, *Something from the Oven,* 47–48.

116. Ibid., 52–53; "Should the Homemaker Use Ready-made Mixes," *Journal of Home Economics* 42 (June 1950).

117. Shapiro, *Something from the Oven,* 54.

118. Mrs. Raymond W. Gregory, "The Consumer's Reaction toward the Food Industry and Its Products," *Food Technology* 6 (Feb. 1952): 66; Shapiro, *Something from the Oven,* 80.

119. Marling, *As Seen on TV,* 227–230; "The Pleasures of Convenience Foods," *Ladies' Home Journal,* Nov. 1963, 133.

120. Jane Nickerson, "Staff of Life, Ready Mixed," *New York Times Magazine,* Jan. 8, 1950, 32–33.

121. "For Novice Cooks," *Good Housekeeping,* May 1950, 282–283.

122. Poppy Cannon, *The Can-Opener Cook Book* (New York: Thomas Y.

Crowell, 1951) [2d ed. 1953], quoted in John L. Hess and Karen Hess, *The Taste of America,* 3d edition (Columbia: University of South Carolina Press), 154–155; see also the insightful chapter about Poppy Cannon in Laura Shapiro's *Something from the Oven,* 87–127.

123. Hess and Hess, *The Taste of America,* 154; Shapiro, *Something from the Oven,* 27–28, 65–66.

124. Poppy Cannon, *The Bride's Cookbook* (New York: Henry Holt, 1954), quoted in Shapiro, *Something from the Oven,* 127.

125. "Just Heat and Serve," *Time,* Dec. 7, 1959, 93.

126. "The Pleasures of Convenience Foods," 133.

127. "Revolution in the Kitchen," 60.

128. Ernest Dichter, *Handbook of Consumer Motivations: The Psychology of the World of Objects* (New York: McGraw-Hill, 1964), 44.

129. Ibid., 44, 420–421. Other evidence of this industry attitude: When asked about the driving force behind the "revolution in the kitchen," Campbell's Soup executive William B. Murphy attributed it primarily to "aggressive action" by the food industry (quoted in "Revolution in the Kitchen," 56). General Foods top executive Charles Mortimer countered the popular saying that the food industry provided what women demanded: "I think it's a lot of malarkey that women demand things. To say that women demanded better soluble coffee, for instance, is crazy. We gave them one and said, 'Come and get it.' You don't miss what you don't know" (quoted in "Just Heat and Serve," 96).

130. Franklin C. Bing, "Chemicals Introduced in the Processing of Foods, *American Journal of Public Health* 40 (Feb. 1950): 164.

131. Vance Packard, *The Hidden Persuaders* (New York: David McKay, 1957), 78; Marling, *As Seen on TV,* 226: Shapiro, *Something from the Oven,* 68–84.

132. Marling, *As Seen on TV,* 227.

133. Packard, *Hidden Persuaders,* 78.

134. "The History of Mixes: Ten Year Success Story," *Practical Home Economics,* Sept. 1958, 76. Though marketers generally give Dichter the credit for boosting sales, fresh eggs may well have made the cakes taste better, too.

135. Marling, *As Seen on TV,* 227.

136. White, "Chemistry and Controversy," 220.

137. Shapiro, *Something from the Oven,* xxv.

138. Packard, *Hidden Persuaders,* 67.

139. McAusland, *Supermarkets,* 53.

140. "Breakfast Cereal," *Consumer Reports,* May 1961, 238. In 1960, $60 million was spent on advertising breakfast cereals—two-thirds of this was for TV ads.

141. "Get 'Em Young," *Modern Packaging*, Nov. 1953, 91.

142. "Breakfast Cereal," 238.

143. "Breakfast Cereal," 238; Lincoln Diamant, *Television's Classic Commercials: The Golden Years, 1948–1958* (New York: Hastings House, 1971), 278. By 1970, the total would more than double.

144. "Use Today's Foods in Today's Lessons," *What's New in Home Economics*, March 1960, 21.

145. "Food Is a New Product Business," *Business Week*, Jan. 31, 1959, 34; White, "Chemistry and Controversy," 216. White puts the value at $63.4 billion in 1950 and $82.1 billion in 1960.

146. Shapiro, *Something from the Oven*, 21.

147. "Better Days for Housewives as Food Industry Changes" *U.S. News and World Report*, Mar. 22, 1965, 119; Marling, *As Seen on TV*, 226. By 1965, an estimated 25.5 million woman were in the workforce — just over one-third.

148. "Just Heat and Serve," 93.

149. George P. Larrick, "Pure Food and Progress," *Food Technology*, Oct. 1956, 456.

150. Bing, "Chemicals," 161; White, "Chemistry and Controversy," 229.

151. G. W. Newell et al., "Role of 'Agenized' Flour in the Production of Running Fits," *Journal of the American Medical Association* (Nov. 22, 1947), cited in Harold Aaron, "Is White Bread Slow Poison?" *Consumer Reports*, Feb. 1948, 78; White, "Chemistry and Controversy," 234.

152. Aaron, "White Bread," 77–78; "Your Bread: How Safe Is It?" *Consumer Reports*, Oct. 1949, 460–461. In the wake of the Agene studies, the American Medical Association and the National Research Council had called for the "rigorous exclusion, so far as possible, of additions to bread and other foodstuffs of ingredients of non-biological origins which have not been fully demonstrated to be wholesome and non-toxic."

153. Ruth E. Brecher, "The Chemicals We Eat," *The Nation*, June 23, 1951, 585.

154. James O. Clarke, director of the FDA's Division of Program Research, quoted in Harold Aaron, "Chemicals in Food," *Consumer Reports*, July 1951, 327.

155. Testimony of Henry H. Favor, *Chemicals in Food Products*, (Dec. 14, 1950), 777.

156. Aaron, "Chemicals in Food," 326; "Your Bread," 460–461; Bing, "Chemicals," 161, 164. According to testimony, the amount of nutritive oils and fats used in bread and rolls had dropped from 4 percent to 1.5–2.0 percent with the use of the new emulsifiers.

157. Testimony of Dr. Faith Fenton, *Chemicals in Food Products* (Dec. 13, 1950), 738.

158. White, "Chemistry and Controversy," 226.

159. Ibid., 321.

160. Testimony of Mrs. Leslie B. Wright, *Chemicals in Food Products* (Dec. 14, 1950), 775.

161. Testimony of Mrs. Harvey Wiley (Anna Kelton Wiley), *Chemicals in Food Products* (Dec. 15, 1950), 831.

162. Testimony of Henry H. Favor, *Chemicals in Food Products*, 777; Alan I. Marcus, *Cancer from Beef: DES, Federal Food Regulation and Consumer Confidence* (Baltimore: Johns Hopkins University Press, 1994), 32–34.

163. C. N. Frey, "Chemicals in Foods," *Science* 120 (Sept. 9, 1954): 7A, cited in Marcus, *Cancer from Beef*, 32–34.

164. A. A. Schaal, "Industrial and Legal Viewpoints: Chemical Agents and Residues in Foods: From the Viewpoint of the Consumer," *Food Technology* 4 (Nov. 1950): 460. See also Levenstein, *Paradox of Plenty*, 111, for several other examples of industry leaders describing the ignorance of housewives.

165. Martin, "How Much Poison Are We Eating?" 64, 66. Aside from Martin's article in *Harper's*, Brecher's article in *The Nation*, and a few *New York Times* articles, there was little coverage of the Delaney Hearings in the press, and none in women's magazines. *Consumer Reports* provided extensive coverage of the issue to its subscribers.

166. Levenstein, *Paradox of Plenty*, 113, 133; "Chemicals in Foods: Official Indifference," *Consumer Reports*, Feb. 1952, 107.

167. "Some Principles for a Bill to Safeguard Consumers," *Consumer Reports*, Feb. 1958, 106; *Federal Register* 19 (Mar. 5, 1954), 1239, cited in Donna Vogt, "Food Additive Regulation: A Chronology," Congressional Research Service, 1995, 13, http://NCSEonline.org/nle/crsreports/pesticides/pest-5.cfm [accessed Jan. 28, 2006].

168. "Chemicals in Our Food Supply," *Consumer Reports*, Sept. 1956, 456; "Of Cranberries, Chickens, Lipsticks and Black Jelly Beans," *Consumer Reports*, Feb. 1960, 97; "Coloring of Oranges: A Chronology," *Consumer Reports*, Aug. 1959, 444; Vogt, "Food Additive Regulation," 14. In another incident, children were made sick by an unusually high concentration of orange coloring in Halloween candy "corns."

169. "Food and Cancer," *Scientific American*, Oct. 1956, 68–71.

170. "New Hope for Food Additives Law," *Journal of Agricultural and Food Chemistry* 6 (1958): 563, quoted in Marcus, *Cancer from Beef*, 42.

171. "Congress Must Act on Food Additives," *Ladies' Home Journal*, Feb. 1958, n.p.

172. White, "Chemistry and Controversy," 340. The new law codified a shift in FDA philosophy that had occurred over several decades, reflecting changes

in postwar scientific understanding: in the past, the agency had generally disapproved the addition of *any* known poisons, but now it accepted small doses scientifically determined not to be harmful.

173. Wargo, *Our Children's Toxic Legacy,* 76.

174. Warren J. Belasco, *Appetite for Change: How the Counterculture Took On the Food Industry, 1966–1988* (New York: Pantheon, 1989), 136; "A Nutritionist Looks at Food and the Marketplace: Interview with Joan Dye Gussow," *FDA Consumer,* Feb. 1977, 13.

175. An Act to Protect the Public Health by Amending the Federal Food, Drug, and Cosmetic Act to Prohibit the Use in Food of Additives Which Have Not Been Adequately Tested to Establish Their Safety" (P.L. 85-929) *U.S. Statutes* 71 (1958): 1784–89, quoted in Marcus, *Cancer from Beef,* 43.

176. White, "Chemistry and Controversy," 340–345. White contends that the Delaney Clause, which has subsequently been criticized as antiscientific and technologically stifling, is often misunderstood. She writes that it is important to remember the Delaney Clause was "a statement of public policy, not a scientific statement," and that it reflected the experience and concerns of many scientists during the period in which it was enacted.

177. Levenstein, *Paradox of Plenty,* 134; Winston, *Nature Wars,* 159; "Poisons in Your Food," *Consumer Bulletin,* May 1960, 13.

178. Marcus, *Cancer from Beef,* 54–55, 99. DES was also taken as an anti-miscarriage drug by pregnant women in the '50s and '60s, and would in the 1970s be linked to a rare vaginal cancer in young daughters. In addition, DES came into widespread use as a growth hormone added to cattle feed; this use would not be restricted until 1979.

179. "Row Over Pure Food," *U.S. World and News Report,* Dec. 28, 1959, 34.

180. White, "Chemistry and Controversy," 393.

181. Linda Lear, *Rachel Carson: Witness for Nature* (New York: Henry Holt, 1997), 153, 374; "The Facts about Fall-Out Scares," *U.S. World and News Report,* June 29, 1959, 44–45.

182. Marcus, *Cancer From Beef,* 64.

183. G. E. Quinby et al., "DDT Storage in the United States Population," *Journal of the American Medical Association* 191 (1965): 109, cited in Mary L. Schafer, "Pesticides in Blood," *Residue Reviews* 24 (1968): 20.

184. Sandra Steingraber, *Living Downstream: A Scientist's Personal Investigation of Cancer and the Environment* (New York: Random House, 1997; reprint, Vintage Books, 1998), 169. The FDA reported that average DDT intake between 1965 and 1970 was twenty-three times higher than it was in 1982.

185. U.S. Centers for Disease Control and Prevention, *Second National Report*

on Human Exposure to Environmental Chemicals (Jan. 2003), cited in *Chemical Trespass: Pesticides in our Bodies and Corporate Accountability* (San Francisco: Pesticide Action Network: 2004), 7.

Chapter 8. *Kitchen Countertrends*

1. "Good News, Naugatuck: Tuesday's the Day!" ad supplement, *Naugatuck Daily News,* 11 Oct. 1971.
2. Philip Wylie, "Science Has Spoiled My Supper," *The Atlantic,* Apr. 1954, 45.
3. Laura Shapiro, *Something from the Oven: Reinventing Dinner in 1950s America* (New York: Viking, 2004), 26.
4. Thomas Whiteside, "Tomatoes," *The New Yorker,* Jan. 24, 1977, 59.
5. "U.S. Grows Educated Palate," *Business Week,* Jan. 31, 1959, 28–30.
6. Julia Child, Louisette Bertholle, and Simone Beck, *Mastering the Art of French Cooking* (New York: Knopf, 1961); Joan Reardon, *M.F.K. Fisher, Julia Child, and Alice Waters: Celebrating the Pleasures of the Table* (New York: Harmony Books, 1994), 153; Shapiro, *Something from the Oven,* 213–230; John L. Hess and Karen Hess, *The Taste of America* (New York: Grossman/ Viking, 1977; reprint, Columbia: University of South Carolina Press, 1989), 173–191.
7. Of course, the well-known *Joy of Cooking* was also highly influential in this regard. For an insightful history of this popular cookbook, see Anne Mendelson, *Stand Facing the Stove: The Story of the Women Who Gave America the* Joy of Cooking® (New York: Scribner, 1996).
8. Reardon, *Fisher, Child, and Waters,* 81; Hess and Hess, *Taste of America* 62–63, 152–172; Craig Claiborne, ed. *The New York Times Cookbook* (New York: Harper & Row, 1961), 246–247, 262. Many who promoted the refined flavors of gourmet foods found themselves taking shortcuts offered by convenience products. Craig Claiborne, who reigned for twenty years as taste arbiter at the *New York Times* food department, included ingredients such as pre-made stuffing mix, canned tuna, and Kitchen Bouquet (liquid flavoring) in several of his recipes, and he often commended convenience versions of "gourmet" fare, such as frozen beef Bourguignon dinners.
9. Ernest Dichter, *Handbook of Consumer Motivations: The Psychology of the World of Objects* (New York: McGraw-Hill, 1964), 44–51.
10. Ibid., 44–51.
11. Warren J. Belasco, *Appetite for Change: How the Counterculture Took On the Food Industry, 1966–1988* (New York: Pantheon, 1989), 41. Much of this section is based on Belasco's perceptive interpretations of this fascinating chapter of food history.

12. Gene Marine and Judith Van Allen, *Food Pollution: The Violation of Our Inner Ecology* (New York: Holt, Rinehart, 1972), cited in Belasco, *Appetite for Change,* 87.

13. "Fish Deaths Laid to Endrin by U.S.; Pesticide Is Cited in Official Health Agency Findings," *New York Times,* June 27, 1964, 9; "U.S. Curbs the Use of 2 Insecticides; Discovers Illegal Residues of Aldrin and Dieldrin," *New York Times,* Feb. 5, 1966, 4; "Wood, Field, and Stream: DDT Residue Picked Up in Sea Food Is Leading to Decline of Fish and Birds," *New York Times,* March 12, 1968, 53; John C. Devlin, "A Scientist Fears DDT Will Wipe Out the Bald Eagle," *New York Times,* April 28, 1969, 43; David R. Zimmerman, "Last Hope for the Ospreys of Long Island Sound," *New York Times Magazine,* Dec. 12, 1971, 38; John Wargo, *Our Children's Toxic Legacy: How Science and Law Fail to Protect Us from Pesticides* (New Haven: Yale University Press, 1996), 101, 141.

14. Randal S. Beeman and James A. Pritchard, *A Green and Permanent Land: Ecology and Agriculture in the Twentieth Century* (Lawrence: University of Kansas Press, 2001), 24–34.

15. Julie Guthman, *Agrarian Dreams: The Paradox of Organic Farming in California* (Berkeley: University of California Press, 2004), 4; Beeman and Pritchard, *Green and Permanent Land,* 45–49

16. Guthman, *Agrarian Dreams,* 112–113. See Beeman and Pritchard for more on the philosophical guidance offered by the writings of an earlier generation of radical back-to-the-landers: Louis Bromfield, Ralph Borsodi, and Scott and Helen Nearing.

17. Belasco, *Appetite for Change,* 76; Guthman, *Agrarian Dreams,* 5–6.

18. Belasco, *Appetite for Change,* 83.

19. Ibid., 142.

20. James S. Turner, *The Chemical Feast: Ralph Nader's Study Group Report on the Food and Drug Administration* (New York: Grossman, 1970; reprint, Penguin, 1976).

21. Belasco, *Appetite for Change,* 116, 146.

22. Ibid., 173. As another example of how TV could generate concern, in 1969, Walter Cronkite announced on the CBS nightly news: "The American consumer is surrounded by an arsenal of products which can kill or maim him. That's the gist of a confidential report prepared by seven members of the FDA."

23. Belasco, *Appetite for Change,* 140.

24. Ibid., 141.

25. "Arsenic Residues Found in Poultry," *New York Times,* Jan. 7, 1971, 29; "More Illegal Drug Residues Found in Meat and Poultry," *New York Times,* Aug. 12,

1973, 59; William Robbins, "Meat-Poultry Plant Check Finds 38 Dirty, Many Problems," *New York Times,* June 18, 1973, 66; Richard D. Lyons, "A G.A.O. Statement on Poultry Plants Cites Uncleanliness," *New York Times,* Nov. 17, 1971, 20; Seth S. King, "Illegal Residues Found in 14 Percent of Meat and Poultry," *New York Times,* April 22, 1979, 23.

26. Belasco, *Appetite for Change,* 141.
27. Tom R. Watkins, "The New Consumer and the Notion of Minimally Processed Food," in *Alterations in Food Production,* ed. Dietrich Knorr and Tom R. Watkins (New York: Van Nostrand Reinhold, 1984), 154–155; G. Burton Brown et al., "Additives and Processing: What the U.S. Consumer Knows, Thinks — and Practices When it Comes to Nutrition," *Food Product Development,* May 1978, 35; "Survey Shows Consumers Emphasize Quality," *Food Product Development,* Apr. 1978, 90.
28. John S. Steinhart and Carol E. Steinhart, "Energy Use in the U.S. Food System," *Science* 184, no. 4134 (April 19, 1974): 313.
29. F. J. Francis, "Public Information: Science and Ethics," *Food Technology* 35, no. 3 (1981): 11, cited in Dietrich Knorr, "Quality of Natural/Organic/Health Foods," in Knorr and Watkins, *Alterations in Food Production,* 177.
30. "What We Do to Our Internal Environment Shouldn't Happen To The Hudson River," ad reproduced in Robert Atwan, Donald McQuade, and John W. Wright, *Edsels, Luckies, and Frigidaires: Advertising the American Way* (New York: Dell, 1979), 215. In contrast, Dannon promoted its own product as "the natural yogurt, no artificial anything."
31. Knorr, "Quality of Natural," 175–177.
32. Belasco, *Appetite for Change,* 115–116.
33. Ibid., 117. Belasco offers the humorous punch line, "These were questions for policymakers, not dictionaries."
34. Ibid.
35. Ibid., 115.
36. Ibid., 117.
37. Ibid., 129.
38. Adam C. Smith, "The Power of the Dollar: Consumer Activism in the 20th Century: From the National Consumers' League to the Student Antisweatshop Movement" (senior thesis, Georgetown University, Mar. 2002), 17–33, http://www.georgetown.edu/departments/justice_peace/resources/theses/theses2002/smith_adam.pdf [accessed Sept. 27, 2006]
39. Ibid., 119–122.
40. Ibid., 121; John H. Perkins, "Insects, Food, and Hunger: The Paradox of Plenty for U.S. Entomology, 1920–1970," *Environmental Review* 7, no. 1 (1983): 84–90.

41. Belasco, *Appetite for Change*, 119; Guthman, *Agrarian Dreams*, 110.

42. Belasco, *Appetite for Change*, 185–186.

43. N. J. Leinen, "Survey Reports Significant Jump in 'Natural is Better' Consumer Attitude," *Food Processing* 39 (1978): 28, cited in Knorr, "Quality of Natural," 177.

44. A. O. Sulzberger, Jr., "Strict Rules Urged for Food Ads," *New York Times*, Nov. 28, 1978, D1; Karen Dewitt, "How F.T.C. has Defined 'Natural' for Food Ads," *New York Times*, Oct. 15, 1980, C-10.

45. G. Burton Brown et al., "Additives and Processing," 35–36.

46. Dept. of Health, Education, and Welfare (21 CFR Ch.1), Dept. of Agriculture (7 CFR, Ch. XXVIII), and Federal Trade Commission (16 CFR Ch. 1), "Food Labeling: Tentative Position of Agencies, Advanced Notice of Proposed Rulemaking," *Federal Register* 44, no. 247 (Dec. 21, 1979): 76012–76013; Federal Trade Commission (16 CFR Part 437), "Food Advertising: Request for Comments and Proposals for Voluntary or Regulatory Action," *Federal Register* 45, no. 69 (Apr. 8, 1980): 23706; Dewitt, "How F.T.C.," C-10; Kate Clancy, "The Federal Trade Commission Rulemaking on the Term 'Natural'" in Advertising," in Knorr and Watkins, *Alterations in Food Production*, 208–210; Belasco, *Appetite for Change*, 192.

47. "It's Natural, It's Organic, or Is It?" *Consumer Reports*, July 1980, 410–415, quoted in Belasco, *Appetite for Change*, 185–186.

48. Kate Clancy and Frederick Kirschenmann, "Keeping It 'Organic': Making Sense Out of the Processing of Organic Food," June 4, 1999, http://www.biotechinfo.net/keeping_organic.html [accessed Dec. 15, 2006].

49. Belasco, *Appetite for Change*, 212.

50. "Natural—From Our Laboratory," *Nutrition Action*, Sept. 1984, 6, quoted in Belasco, *Appetite for Change*, 222.

51. Jane Brody, "Concern for Rain Forest Has Begun to Blossom," *New York Times*, Oct. 13, 1987.

52. "McDonald's Hamburger Sales," interview with McDonald's Walt Riker by John Ruch, Oct. 4, 2001, http://archives.stupidquestion.net/sq10401.html [accessed Jan. 15, 2007].

53. Brody, "Concern."

54. Nicola Graydon, "Rainforest Action Network: The Inspiring Group Bringing Corporate America to Its Senses," *The Ecologist* 36, no.1 (Feb.–Mar., 2006), http://ran.org/media_center/news_article/?uid=1849 [accessed Dec. 15, 2006].

55. Pete Singer and Jim Mason, *The Way We Eat and Why Our Food Choices Matter* (Emmaus, PA: Rodale Press, 2006), 233–234. While ethicist Singer acknowledges the impact of the burger boycotts, he contends that although

fast-food hamburgers may not be derived from cattle raised on pastures that were Amazonian rain forest, other beef is, and so are soybeans that are grown on cutover rain forest for export as animal feed. In effect, he cynically argues, the market simply rearranged itself, ultimately defeating this attempt at ethical eating.

56. "Tuna Importers Told to Cut Dolphin Deaths," *New York Times*, March 18, 1988. This incident is reminiscent of cultural differences between Italian American songbird hunters and American conservationists, revealing the complications inherent in trading arrangements with countries with different cultural values about conservation.

57. Anthony Ramirez, "'Epic Debate' Led to Heinz Tuna Plan," *New York Times*, April 16, 1990, 1. Star-Kist is now owned by Del Monte.

58. Trish Hall, "How Youths Rallied to Dolphins' Cause," *New York Times*, April 18, 1990, 1.

59. Kim Foltz, "Advertising Agency with a Cause," *New York Times*, May 21, 1990, D-14.

60. Ramirez, "'Epic Debate,'" 1.

61. Monroe Friedman, *Consumer Boycotts: Effecting Change through the Marketplace and the Media* (New York: Routledge, 1999), 194–195; Ramirez, "'Epic Debate,'" 1.

62. Reardon, *Fisher, Child, and Waters*, 232. For this section on Alice Waters's life and influence, I am indebted to Joan Reardon's biography.

63. Ibid., 210–214.

64. Ibid., 218–219.

65. Ibid., 253.

66. Ibid., 266.

67. Guthman, *Agrarian Dreams*, 16.

68. Belasco, *Appetite for Change*, 90.

69. Belasco used the term "hip enterprise," 94–95.

70. Guthman, *Agrarian Dreams*, 25.

71. Ibid., 29; Samual Fromartz, *Organic, Inc.: Natural Foods and How They Grew* (New York: Harcourt, 2006), 108–144; Michael Pollan, *The Omnivore's Dilemma* (New York: Penguin, 2006), 164. Earthbound Farms, after several mergers, is now known as Natural Selection Foods, a company implicated in the 2006 spinach contamination scare.

72. Fromartz, *Organic, Inc.*, xvii.

73. Belasco, *Appetite for Change*, 176.

74. Ibid., 225–228.

75. Wargo, *Our Children's Toxic Legacy*, 116–117; 266; Guthman, *Agrarian Dreams*, 25.

76. National Academy of Science (NAS), *Regulating Pesticides in Foods: The Delaney Paradox* (Washington, DC: NAS Press, 1987) and NAS, *Pesticides in the Diets of Infants and Children* (Washington, DC: NAS Press, 1993), cited in Wargo, *Our Children's Toxic Legacy,* 10–13; Fromartz, *Organic, Inc.,* 3.

77. R. Wiles et al., *Herbicides in Drinking Water* (Washington, DC: Environmental Working Group and Physicians for Social Responsibility, 1995), cited in Wargo, *Our Children's Toxic Legacy,* 12.

78. U.S. General Accounting Office, *Farmworkers Health and Well-Being At Risk,* GAO/HRD-92-46 (Washington, DC: GAO, 1992), 12–13.

79. P. K. Mills and S. Kwong, "Cancer Incidence in the United Farm Workers of America (UFW) 1987–1997," *American Journal of Industrial Medicine* 40 (2001): 596–603; P. K. Mills, "Correlation Analysis of Pesticide Use Data and Cancer Incidence Rates in California Counties," *Archives of Environmental Health* 53 (1998): 410–413, cited in *Chemical Trespass: Pesticides in Our Bodies and Corporate Accountability* (San Francisco: Pesticide Action Network, 2004), 17; S. H. Zahm and A. Blair, "Cancer among Migrant and Seasonal Farmworkers: An Epidemiological Review and Research Agenda," *American Journal of Industrial Medicine* 24 (1993): 753–766, cited in Margaret Reeves et al., *Fields of Poison: California Farmworkers and Pesticides* (San Francisco: Pesticide Action Network, 1999), 19.

80. D. A. Schwartz et al., "Parental Occupation and Birth Outcome in an Agricultural Community," *Scandinavian Journal of Work, Environmental and Health* 12 (1986): 51–54, cited in Reeves et al., *Fields of Poison,* 19.

81. Wargo, *Our Children's Toxic Legacy,* 182–183, 261; Sandra Steingraber, *Living Downstream: A Scientist's Personal Investigation of Cancer and the Environment* (New York: Random House, 1997; reprint, Vintage Books, 1998), 110–114; Reeves et al., *Fields of Poison,* 19; U.S. House of Representatives, *Health Effects of Estrogenic Pesticides: Hearings before the Subcommittee on Health and the Environment,* 103rd Congress, 1st session, Oct. 21, 1993; "Reproductive Health Hazards in the Workplace: Policy Options for California," *California Policy Seminar Brief,* Feb. 1992, 2, http://www.ucop.edu/cprc/rephlthhzd.pdf [accessed Dec. 12, 2007].

82. Fromartz, *Organic, Inc.,* 225.

83. E. Melanie DuPuis, "Not In My Body: BGH and the Rise of Organic Milk," *Agriculture and Human Values* 17, no. 3 (Sept. 2000): 285–286.

84. Marian Burros, "Developing A Taste For Organic Milk," *New York Times,* Oct. 30, 1996; Kate Murphy, "Business; More Buyers Asking: Got Milk Without Chemicals?" *New York Times,* Aug. 1, 1999. RBGH is also known as rBST, recombinant bovine somatotropin hormone, and by its trade name Posilac.

85. Guthman, *Agrarian Dreams*, 27.

86. Belinda Martineau, *First Fruit: The Creation of the Flavr Savr™ Tomato and the Birth of Biotech Food* (New York: McGraw-Hill, 2001), 233, 236. Another gene (ominously dubbed "terminator") proposed for use in a range of crops would prevent engineered plants from producing viable seeds (to protect patented changes in germ plasm) so farmers could not save seed and would have to purchase it each year from seed companies, leading critics to charge it could gravely affect small-scale farmers in developing countries.

87. Ibid., 85, 145, 186; John Seabrook, "Tremors in the Hothouse," *The New Yorker*, July 19, 1993, 37; "Roundup Unready," editorial, *New York Times*, Feb. 19, 2003, A-24.

88. David Barboza, "Modified Foods Put Companies in a Quandary," *New York Times*, June 4, 2000, 1; David Barboza, "As Biotech Crops Multiply, Consumers Get Little Choice," *New York Times*, June 10, 2001, 1; Martineau, *First Fruit*, 229; Andrew Pollack, "Labeling Genetically Altered Food is a Thorny Issue," *New York Times*, Sept. 28, 2000.

89. In 2006, Whole Foods Market had 180 stores in the United States, http://www.wholefoodsmarket.com/stores/list_allstores.html [accessed Dec. 15, 2006].

90. Nicols Fox, *Spoiled: The Dangerous Truth about a Food Chain Gone Haywire* (New York: Basic Books, 1997), 291–331.

91. Singer and Mason, *The Way We Eat*, 62; Fox, *Spoiled*, 330; Eric Schlosser, *Fast Food Nation: The Dark Side of the All-American Meal* (Boston: Houghton Mifflin, 2001), 202; Michael Pollan, "Cattle Futures?" *New York Times Magazine*, Jan. 11, 2004.

92. "National News Briefs: 12th Death Is Linked to Tainted Meat at Plant," *New York Times*, Jan. 27, 1999; Elizabeth Becker, "Consumer Groups Accuse U.S. of Negligence on Food Safety, Leading to Meat Recalls," *New York Times*, Oct. 15, 2002.

93. Sarah Kershaw, "Mad Cow Disease in the United States: Farmer; Second Farm is Quarantined and Cattlemen Are Worried," *New York Times*, Dec. 27, 2003; Eric Schlosser, "The Cow Jumped Over the USDA," *New York Times*, Jan. 2, 2004.

94. Fromartz, *Organic, Inc.*, 5.

95. Carolyn Johnson, *Raising a Stink: The Struggle Over Factory Hog Farms in Nebraska* (Lincoln; University of Nebraska Press, 2003), 125–134. Epidemiological studies show increased incidents of respiratory illness for people who live near giant hog farms, but scientific evidence about cause and effect remains inconclusive.

96. Ibid., 117–124; Elizabeth Becker, "Feedlot Perils Outpace Regulation, Sierra Club Says," *New York Times*, Aug. 13, 2002; Robert F. Kennedy, Jr. and Eric Schaeffer, "An Ill Wind from Factory Farms," *New York Times*, Sept. 20, 2003; Robert F. Kennedy, Jr. "Good Food versus Green Eggs and Ham," *Waterkeeper Magazine*, Spring 2006, 4–5.

97. Schlosser, *Fast Food Nation*.

98. Erin Speiser Ihde, "Milking the Organic Market," http://www.brand-channel.com/print_page.asp?ar_id=133&section=main [accessed Sept. 30, 2006].

99. Fromartz, *Organic, Inc.*, 230.

100. "Organic Valley Introduces Truly Organic Soymilk," press release, June 25, 2004, http://organicvalley.coop/newsroom/article.html?cat=1&id=57 [accessed Dec. 2006].

101. "Find your farmer," at www.organicvalley.coop/products_recipes/soy.htm [accessed Dec. 13, 2006].

102. Pollan, *Omnivore's Dilemma*, 137.

103. Fromartz, *Organic, Inc.*, 241.

104. Ibid., 230–233. For a useful scorecard on organic milk dairies, see www.cornucopia.org.

105. Guthman, *Agrarian Dreams*, 113; Fromartz, *Organic, Inc.*, 196–197.

106. Guthman, *Agrarian Dreams*, 113. California had passed an earlier Organic Food Act in 1979, which was amended in 1982, but the state declined to enforce it, which led to fraudulent sales of organic foods.

107. Guthman, *Agrarian Dreams*, 115–116.

108. Fromartz, *Organic, Inc.*, 198–199.

109. Ibid., 137; Pollan, *Omnivore's Dilemma*, 138.

110. U.S. Dept. of Agriculture, Economic Research Service, "Table 3 — Certified Organic and Total U.S. Acreage, Selected Crops and Livestock, 1995–2005," http://www.ers.usda.gov/Data/Organic [accessed Jan. 3, 2007].

111. Pollan, *Omnivore's Dilemma*, 168; Organic Trade Association, 2006 Manufacturers' Survey, http://www.ota.com/pics/documents/short%20overview%20MMS.pdf [accessed Jan. 3, 2007].

112. Guthman, *Agrarian Dreams*, 178–179; Melanie Warner, "What is Organic? Powerful Players Want a Say," *New York Times*, Nov. 1, 2005. Guthman argues that high rents in California, based on extremely high yields and other historic factors, exert a sharp cost-cutting influence on organic farms, pressing them to become more and more like the farms they initially sought to distinguish themselves from.

113. Fromartz, *Organic, Inc.*, 240.

114. Ibid., 250.

115. Ibid., 253–256.

Epilogue: *Returning Stories to the Modern Kitchen*

1. Marian Burros, "In Oregon, Thinking Local," *New York Times,* Jan. 4, 2005, Food Section, 1.

2. For an ethicist's take on how to make decisions about food, see Peter Singer and Jim Mason, *The Way We Eat and Why Our Food Choices Matter* (Emmaus, PA: Rodale, 2006).

3. Samual Fromartz, *Organic, Inc.: Natural Foods and How They Grew* (New York: Harcourt, 2006), 2–4.

4. U.S. EPA, "2000–2001 Pesticide Market Estimates: Usage," World and U.S. Pesticide Amount Used, http://www.epa.gov/oppbead1/pestsales/01pestsales/usage2001.html [accessed Dec. 16. 2006].

5. Amanda Paulson, "As 'Organic' Goes Mainstream, Will Standards Suffer?" *Christian Science Monitor,* May 17, 2006, http://www.csmonitor.com/2006/0517/p13s01-lifo.htm [accessed Dec. 9, 2006].

6. "Farmers Market Growth, 1994–2006," http://www.ams.usda.gov/farmersmarkets/FarmersMarketGrowth.htm [accessed Jan. 3, 2007].

7. Michael Ableman, *Fields of Plenty: A Farmer's Journey in Search of Real Food and the People Who Grow It* (San Francisco: Chronicle Books, 2005), 69.

8. See Web site for the Home Grown Wisconsin cooperative CSA, http://www.homegrownwisconsin.com/csa.htm [accessed Jan. 30, 2007].

Afterword: *Toward a New Kitchen Literacy*

1. U.S. Dept. of Agriculture, Agricultural Census of 2007, "Organic Production Survey," www.agcensus.usda.gov/ [Accessed Nov. 6, 2009]; U.S. Dept. of Agriculture, Agricultural Marketing Service, "Number of Farmers Markets Continues to Rise in U.S." New Release, AMS 173-0, www.ams.usda.gov/AMSv1.0/ams.fetchTemplateData.do?template=Template U&navID=&page=Newsroom&resultType=Details&dDocName=STEL PRDC5072471&dID=100574&wf=false&description=Number+of+Farmers+Markets+Continues+to+Rise+in+U.S.+&topNav=Newsroom &leftNav=&righ [Accessed Oct. 12, 2009].

2. National Gardening Association, "The Impact of Home and Community Gardening in America," (2009) survey results summary, www.gardenresearch.com/index.php?q=show&id=3126 [Accessed Nov. 8, 2009]. According to NGA, this is seven million more households; the 2009 increase followed a 10 percent increase in 2008.

3. "Oxford Word Of The Year: Locavore," OUP blog: Oxford University Press, Nov. 12, 2007, http://blog.oup.com/2007/11/locavore/ [Accessed Nov. 9, 2009]; "Locavore Is a New Word in Webster's Dictionary," *Huffington Post,* July 9, 2009, www.huffingtonpost.com/2009/07/09/locavore-is-a-new-word-in_n_228485.html [Accessed Nov. 9, 2009].

4. Michael Pollan, "The Food Issue: An Open Letter to the Next Farmer In Chief," *New York Times,* Oct. 9, 2008, www.nytimes.com/ 2008/10/ 12/magazine/12policy-t.html?scp=2&sq=farmer+in+chief&st=nyt [Accessed Nov. 5, 2009].

5. Paul Eccleston, "Climate change is 'faster and more extreme' than feared," *The Daily Telegraph,* Oct. 19, 2008, www.telegraph.co.uk/news/world news/3226747/Climate-change-is-faster-and-more-extreme-than-feared .html [Accessed Nov. 9, 2009]; "Seas will rise faster than predicted, say scientists," *The London Times,* Dec. 17, 2008, www.timesonline.co.uk/tol/ news/environment/article5355574.ece [Accessed Nov. 9, 2009].

6. Sonja Brodt, Gail Feenstra, Thomas Tomich, "White Paper—The Low-Carbon Diet Initiative: Reducing Energy Use and Greenhouse Gas Emissions in the Food System from a Life Cycle Assessment Perspective," University of California-Davis Agricultural Sustainability Institute, Sept. 2008, http://asi.ucdavis.edu/Research/Energy_Food_System _Symposium/White_Paper_on_Energy_Use.pdf [Accessed Nov. 9, 2009].

7. Janet Byron, "'Low-carbon diet' research looks at total energy usage of foods," *California Agriculture* 63(2): 55, http://ucanr.org/repository/ CAO/landingpage.cfm?article=ca.v063n02p55&fulltext=yes [Accessed Nov. 8, 2009].

8. U.S. Environmental Protection Agency, "Agriculture," Inventory of U.S. Greenhouse Gas Emissions and Sinks: 1990–2007 (April 2009), www .epa.gov/climatechange/emissions/usinventoryreport.html [Accessed Nov. 9, 2009]; Elizabeth Rosenthal, "As More Eat Meat, A Bid to Cut Emissions," *New York Times,* Dec. 3, 2008, www.nytimes.com/2008/12/ 04/science/earth/04meat.html?scp=1&sq=As+More+Eat+Meat%2C+a+ bid+to+&st=nyt [Accessed Nov. 9, 2009].

9. Amy L. Luers, Daniel R. Cayan, Michael Hanemann, Bart Croes, and Guido France, "Our Changing Climate: Assessing the Risks to California," California Climate Change Center (2006): 15, http://meteora.ucsd.edu/ cap/pdffiles/CA_climate_Scenarios.pdf [Accessed Nov. 8 2009].

10. John T. Trumble and Casey D. Butler, "Climate change will exacerbate California's insect pest problems_," *California Agriculture* 63(2): 73–78, http://ucanr.org/repository/CAO/landingpage.cfm?article=ca.v063n02p 73&fulltext=yes [Accessed Nov. 8, 2009].

11. Arnold J. Bloom, "As carbon dioxide rises, food quality will decline without careful nitrogen management_," *California Agriculture* 63(2): 67–72, http:// ucanr.org/repository/CAO/landingpage.cfm?article=ca.v063n02p67& fulltext=yes [Accessed Nov. 8, 2009].

12. Robin Meadows, "UC scientists help California prepare for climate change," *California Agriculture* 63(2): 56–58, http://ucce.ucdavis.edu/files/repositoryfiles/ca6302p56-65644.pdf [Accessed Nov. 8, 2009].

13. The Trust for America's Health and the Robert Wood Johnson Foundation, "*F as in Fat: How Obesity Policies Are Failing in America 2009,*" http://healthyamericans.org/obesity/ [Accessed Nov. 6, 2009].

14. Majid Ezzati, Ari B. Friendman, Sandeep C. Kulkarni, and Christopher J. L. Murray, "The Reversal of Fortunes: Trends in County Mortality and Cross-County Mortality Disparities in the United States," (2009) *PLoS Medicine* 5(4): e66, www.plosmedicine.org/article/info:doi/10.1371/journal.pmed.0050066 [Accessed Nov. 16, 2009].

15. Nikole Hannah-Jones, "Multnomah County Begins David and Goliath Food Fight," *Oregonian,* Oct. 18, 2009, www.oregonlive.com/portland/index.ssf/2009/10/county_begins_david-and-goliath.html [Accessed Nov. 6, 2009].

16. Eric A. Finkelstein, Justin G. Trogdon, Joel W. Cohen, and William Dietz, "Annual Medical Spending Attributable to Obesity: Payer- and Service-Specific Estimates," *Health Affairs* 28(5): w822–w831 (Published online July 27, 2009), cited in David Leonhardt, "Fat Tax," *New York Times,* Aug. 12, 2009, www.nytimes.com/2009/08/16/magazine/16FOB-wwln-t.html?scp=2&sq=David+Leonhardt+obesity&st=nyt [Accessed Nov. 6, 2009].

17. Robert Pear, "Gap in Life Expectancy Widens for the Nation," *New York Times,* March 23, 2008, www.nytimes.com/2008/03/23/us/23health.html [Accessed Nov. 18, 2009]; Nicholas Bakalar, "More Americans on the Road to Obesity," *New York Times,* Aug. 10, 2009, www.nytimes.com/2009/08/11/health/11stat.html?_r=1&ref=science [Accessed Nov. 18, 2009]; Daniel Engber, "Does poverty make people obese, or is it the other way around?" *Slate Magazine,* Sept. 28, 2009, www.slate.com/id/2229523/pagenum/all/[Accessed Nov. 18, 2009].

18. American Medical Association, Report of the Council on Science and Public Health, Resolution 405 (a-08), "Sustainable Food," CSAPH Report 8-A-09 [www.ama-assn.org/ama1/pub/upload/mm/475/refcomd.pdf [Accessed Nov. 13, 2009]; "American Medical Association Passes Resolution Supporting Sustainable Food System," Reuters News Service, June 17, 2009 (published online), www.reuters.com/article/pressRelease/idUS205658+17-Jun-2009+PRN20090617 [Accessed Nov. 13, 2009].

19. Mark Bittman, "Rethinking the Meat-Guzzler," *New York Times,* Jan. 27, 2008, www.nytimes.com/2008/01/27/weekinreview/27bittman.html?scp=1&sq=Bittman%20meat%20guzzler&st=cse [Accessed Nov. 9, 2009]; Mark Bittman, "What's wrong with what we eat," (Dec. 2007) TED lecture,

www.ted.com/talks/mark_bittman_on_what_s_wrong_with_what_we_
eat.html [Accessed Nov. 17, 2009].

20. Gidon Eshel and Pamela A. Martin, "Diet, Energy, and Global Warming,"
Earth Interactions 10(9): 1.

21. Michael Pollan, "Weed It and Reap," *New York Times,* Nov. 4, 2007, www
.nytimes.com/2007/11/04/opinion/04pollan.html?pagewanted=2&_r=1&
adxnnl=1&adxnnlx=1258669059-4Q4ajdyKERCoH1citxH67Q [Accessed
Nov. 15, 2009]; "Alicia Silverstone makes house calls," *USA Today,* Nov. 5,
2007, www.usatoday.com/life/people/2007-11-05-silverstone_N.htm [Ac-
cessed Nov. 15, 2009]; "The 2008 Saveur List," *Saveur* (Jan. 2008), www
.saveur.com/article/back-issue/The-2008-SAVEUR-100 [Accessed Nov. 15,
2009]; Brian DeVore, "Why the Farm Bill Matters," *Edible Twin Cities,* Fall
2006, www.edibletwincities.com/content/index.php/fall-2006/why-the-
farm-bill-matters.htm [Accessed Nov. 15, 2009].

22. David M. Herszenhorn, "Reaching Well Beyond the Farm," *New York
Times,* May 20, 2008; National Sustainable Agriculture Coalition, Grassroots Guide to the 2008 Farm Bill, http://sustainableagriculture.net/
publications/grassrootsguide/organic-production/ [Accessed Nov. 9,
2009].

23. Pollan, "Weed It and Reap."

24. Nikole Hannah-Jones, "Multnomah County Begins David and Goliath
Food Fight."

25. Atlanta Local Food Initiative, "The Plan for Atlanta's Sustainable Food
Future," (Summer 2008), www.atlantalocalfood.org/plan.htm [Accessed
Nov. 12, 2009]; City of Minneapolis, Homegrown Minneapolis initiative,
www.ci.mpls.mn.us/dhfs/homegrown-home.asp [Accessed Nov. 12,
2009].

ILLUSTRATION CREDITS

1.1. "Milking," woodcut from *The Progress of the Dairy: Descriptive of the Making of Butter and Cheese for the Information of Youth* (1819), 7, Sinclair Hamilton Collection, Graphic Arts Collection, Department of Rare Books and Special Collections, Princeton University Library.

2.1. "Maid having spilled tray of food," stereograph (ca. 1899–1907). Courtesy of the Library of Congress, LC-USZ62-61419.

3.1. "Shopping for Game at Washington Market," engraving from George Augustus Sala, *America Revisited*, 3d ed., vol. 1 (London, 1883), 98.

3.2. "Henry Broll & Son, butcher, Stall 27," photograph from booklet, Lexington Market (ca. 1910), 18, Meat, Box 5, Warshaw Collection of Business Americana, Archives Center, National Museum of American History, Behring Center, Smithsonian Institution.

3.3. "Diagram of Beef," from Catherine Beecher and Harriet Beecher Stowe, *The American Woman's Home; or, Principles of Domestic Service*, 2d ed. (New York: J. B. Ford, 1873), 437. Author's collection.

3.4. "Beef Is Always in Season," in *Swift & Company Year Book* (1924), 27, Meat, Box 4, Warshaw Collection of Business Americana, Archives Center, National Museum of American History, Behring Center, Smithsonian Institution.

4.1. "Brookside Sugar Corn," can label (n.d., ca. 1880s), in Food, Box 22, corn, Warshaw Collection of Business Americana, Archives Center, National Museum of American History, Behring Center, Smithsonian Institution.

4.2. "Corn Makes Me King," trade card (n.d., ca. 1880s), Meat, Box 4, N. K. Fairbanks, Warshaw Collection of Business Americana, Archives Center, National Museum of American History, Behring Center, Smithsonian Institution.

4.3. "The choicest foods in the world," trade card (1883), Cereal, Box 1, American Breakfast Cereals, Warshaw Collection of Business Americana, Archives Center, National Museum of American History, Behring Center, Smithsonian Institution.

4.4. "'Swift's Premium' Oleomargarine," image from booklet, "Bread and _____," inside cover, Box 4, Folder 7, Product Cookbooks Collection, Archives Center, National Museum of American History, Behring Center, Smithsonian Institution.

5.1. "New York School Children Marking Garden," photograph (ca. 1907). Courtesy of the Library of Congress, LC-DIG-ggbain-03334.

5.2. "To Hold the Mirror up to Nature," Shredded Wheat ad (1902), Box 11, Folder 1, N. W. Ayer Advertising Agency Records, Archives Center, National Museum of American History, Behring Center, Smithsonian Institution.

6.1. "Harvey Washington Wiley," portrait. Courtesy of the Food and Drug Administration, History Office.

6.2. "Home Economics Class," photograph, Washington, D.C. (ca. 1899). Courtesy of the Library of Congress, LC-USZ62-45083.

6.3. "From Contented Cows," Carnation ad (ca. 1919), Milk, Box 1, Warshaw Collection of Business Americana, Archives Center, National Museum of American History, Behring Center, Smithsonian Institution.

6.4. "The Modern Genie of the Can," Del Monte ad (ca. 1919). Author's collection.

7.1. "Shopping at Piggly Wiggly," photograph (ca. 1918). Courtesy of the Library of Congress, LC-USZ62-25657.

7.2. "Armed with New Knowledge," ad for Piggly Wiggly stores, *Good Housekeeping*, Sept. 1928, 179.

7.3. "Christine Frederick, portrait" (ca. 1912–1914). The Schlesinger Library, Radcliffe Institute, Harvard University.

8.1. "Bad choices at the Supermarket" (ca. 1986). Courtesy of artist Tom Meyer.

E.1. "Shopping at Farmer's Market in Santa Cruz, CA" (2001), photo by Tim Palmer. Author's collection.

E.2. "Industrial strawberry fields near Watsonville, CA" (1999), photo by Tim Palmer. Author's collection.

E.3. "Organic farm on Vashon Island, WA" (1998), photo by Tim Palmer. Author's collection.

ACKNOWLEDGMENTS

In the long journey of writing this book, many friends contributed help and encouragement. At the very top of the list is my dear husband, Tim Palmer, an accomplished writer and photographer who has been ever-generous in his support and love—critical ingredients that helped me to persist in bringing this difficult project to its culmination. Tim's dedication, joie de vivre, and boundless energy are a tremendous inspiration to me.

A particularly helpful and generous group of friends commented on drafts of my manuscript: Vicki Graham, Nathaniel Hart, Marcel LaFollette, Jeffrey Stine, Florence Williams, Jane Riley, and Cyane Gresham. Many of them also sent newspaper articles, shared ideas, and otherwise aided in pushing my work along.

A short-term fellowship at the National Museum of American History enabled me to delve into the Smithsonian Institution's rich archival materials and to mingle with a stellar set of scholars. In particular, Pete Daniel shared his outstanding research about profligate pesticide spraying in the South, and G. Terry Sharer was generous in sharing his files about the development of food technology. Tom McCarthy, a fellow fellow, shared his insights about consumerism. When it came time to pull together this book's illustrations, Kay Peterson was extremely helpful.

At Mesa Refuge in Point Reyes, California, I enjoyed several weeks of writers' fellowship and solitude that enabled me to tackle a challenging part of this book —all the time nourished by an extraordinary setting where people are striving to rebuild their local food system. There, too, I had the good fortune to meet organic farmer, activist, writer, and photographer Michael Ableman, who inspired me with his vision—and passion—for supplying cities with more delicious, healthy, and sustainable foods.

In the first years of this project, Tim and I lived mostly as nomads, traveling in our van as we pursued our research, but often settling into digs for the shortest days of winter. Pat Compton and the late Jim Compton generously offered us their beach house in Santa Cruz as a place to work during this time. Georgia Stigall and Bill Prince gave me a terrific camp spot to work while Tim was away one month, and Anne Kelleher and Joaquin Feliciano offered friendship and hospitality when I was doing research at the University of California–Davis, as did Mike and Eryn Branch at the University of Nevada–Reno. Tim's brother Jim Palmer and his wife, Lois, provided logistical help when I was in Washington, D.C. Tim's sister Becky Schmitz and her husband, Steve, welcomed us at their home in Charlottesville. In particular, Becky helped me to gain access to some crucial materials in deep storage at the University of Virginia Library.

A number of friends have given timely encouragement and unflagging support over the course of many years: Vibeke Wilberg, Tiffany Cunningham, Jamie Williams, Beth Jacobi, Julie Holding, Betsy Mendelsohn, Cindy Ott, Jenny Price, E. Sandy Powell, and Jenny Schmitz. Thanks also to all my neighbors and friends in Port Orford for their day-to-day encouragement, especially Molly Cooley, Cathy Boden, John Shipp, Jim Rogers, Dana Amarisa, Linda Tarr, Foncy Prescott, Bonnie Allen, Michael McDonough, and Evan Kramer. Thanks also to local organic farmers Abby Bradbury and Betsy Harrison for helping to keep us well-nourished with their outstanding produce.

At Island Press, thanks to Chuck Savitt for his vision and commitment to publishing books that help us all to better understand today's environmental challenges; editor Jonathan Cobb helped me to refine this book's prose and pace, and always kept me laughing. I greatly appreciate his care for language, ideas, and all that goes into making a book. (Thanks also to Jonathan's wife, Susanna, for her input.) Thanks to Barbara Dean, editor of my first book, for her continuing enthusiasm for my work; to Emily Davis for sharing her thoughts and helping with countless details; to Jessica Heise for overseeing this book's production; and to copyeditor Darlene Bledsoe for her sharp eye and helpful insights. My agent, Victoria Shoemaker, helped to keep the project moving forward at a critical time with her enthusiasm and book-publishing savvy.

An interpretive, narrative work of this sort would be impossible without the research and writing of other scholars and authors whose books and articles I've learned from and drawn upon. Many of these people are colleagues in the field of environmental history. Foremost is Bill Cronon, my college mentor, whose brilliance in exploring connections between people and the environment has long inspired me. Others in the field whose work has influenced and informed my own include Carolyn Merchant, Richard Judd, Jennifer Price, Louis Warren, Ed Russell, John Perkins, Thomas Dunlap, Donald Worster, Joel Tarr, Linda Nash, Susan Jones, Steven Stoll, Douglas Cazaux Sackman, Maril Hazlett, Linda Lear, Brian Donahue, and James Pritchard.

Other authors and scholars whose works have informed *Kitchen Literacy* include Michael Pollan, Harvey Levenstein, Warren Belasco, Susan Strasser, Laura Shapiro, James Harvey Young, James Whorton, Laura Thatcher Ulrich, Ruth Schwartz Cowan, T. J. Jackson Lears, Roland Marchand, Angus Wright, Marion Nestle, Sandra Steingraber, Gerry Mander, Theodore Roszak, John Wargo, Bill McKibben, Wendell Berry, and Gary Nabhan. I highly recommend these excellent writers to anyone who is curious to learn more.

Deep thanks to David R. Lewis and to many other professors and earlier teachers, whose curiosity and intellect fostered my own. Thanks also to Maureen Hinkle, whose work as an agriculture policy specialist for the National Audubon Society first inspired me to consider the close interrelationship between agriculture and the environment.

Finally, endless thanks to my family: first for the extraordinary love, wisdom, and support of my mother, Janet Taylor, and my stepfather, Marc Taylor, and also for the abiding love and support of Regina Still, Peter and Lucienne Vileisis, and Birute Vileisis.

INDEX

ABOUT THE AUTHOR

ANN VILEISIS is an independent scholar and author. Her first book, *Discovering the Unknown Landscape: A History of America's Wetlands,* won both the prestigious Herbert Feis Award from the American Historical Association for the best book written by an independent or public historian, and the George Perkins Marsh Prize from the American Society for Environmental History for the best environmental history book. She studied history and environmental studies at Yale University and received a master's degree from Utah State University.

An avid gardener and cook, she now resides on the Oregon coast where she is actively engaged in local issues of environment and agriculture. This is her second book.

Photo by Tim Palmer, 2009

About Island Press

Since 1984, the nonprofit Island Press has been stimulating, shaping, and communicating the ideas that are essential for solving environmental problems worldwide. With more than 800 titles in print and some 40 new releases each year, we are the nation's leading publisher on environmental issues. We identify innovative thinkers and emerging trends in the environmental field. We work with world-renowned experts and authors to develop cross-disciplinary solutions to environmental challenges.

Island Press designs and implements coordinated book publication campaigns in order to communicate our critical messages in print, in person, and online using the latest technologies, programs, and the media. Our goal: to reach targeted audiences—scientists, policymakers, environmental advocates, the media, and concerned citizens—who can and will take action to protect the plants and animals that enrich our world, the ecosystems we need to survive, the water we drink, and the air we breathe.

Island Press gratefully acknowledges the support of its work by the Agua Fund, Inc., The Margaret A. Cargill Foundation, Betsy and Jesse Fink Foundation, The William and Flora Hewlett Foundation, The Kresge Foundation, The Forrest and Frances Lattner Foundation, The Andrew W. Mellon Foundation, The Curtis and Edith Munson Foundation, The Overbrook Foundation, The David and Lucile Packard Foundation, The Summit Foundation, Trust for Architectural Easements, The Winslow Foundation, and other generous donors.

The opinions expressed in this book are those of the author(s) and do not necessarily reflect the views of our donors.